HILL

Published by Green Feather Books 2018

ISBN 978-0-9574777-3-5

Green Feather Books
The Studio
The Nelson Arms
Main Street
Middleton
Matlock
DE4 4LU

# Introduction

**HILL** is the story of one Derbyshire Hill, told in photography, sculpture, poetry, film and song. The story is in four parts:

**On** the Hill tells of the farming families who earn their living rearing sheep and cattle on the hill, a working life that is set by the seasonal changes to the landscape around them.

**Under** the Hill focusses on the Hill's network of disused mines, and on its quarries - still an important part of the local economy.

**Shelter** of the Hill tells of the various communities around the Hill and of the events and ordinary moments that aren't really ordinary at all. Kate has used some of her earlier work in this chapter as well as recent images to tell a human story of continuity and change on the Hill.

**Above** the Hill explores the marks and features of the hill from above ground, and tells of the importance of the Hill to the people who live there.

# Thanks

Kate, Lucy and Sally would like to thank all the people of the Hill and the communities around it that gave this project it's life and story. HILL would not have happened without all your support in a hundred different ways!

Thanks to the Lomas Family of Griffe Walk Farm for their kindness and support. Ian Lomas who's patience and solid support for HILL from the beginning idea to the end Exhibition has been steadfast. He only slightly widened his eyes when we asked if Sally could measure one of his cows for her sculpture!
Another massive, rock solid thankyou to all the people at Longcliffe quarry. They were always up for a poet to press the explosive button for inspiration or supplying the raw materials for the Hill cow. Jon Murgatroyd had patience by the digger bucketfull with Kate on her photographic visits to the Quarry.
Thanks also to Andy Littler and Mr Shields of Longcliffe Quarries for their support in all things HILL.

Thanks to Wirksworth Mines Research Group and the Goodluck Mine Preservation Club - the Miner-explorers of Golconda and Good Luck mine, for sharing such amazing otherworld places with us.

Thanks to Emma Allsop for braving Kate's camera on stormy days and to Nick Wilson for his amazing creative metal work for the HILL Exhibition, artisan made after a hard day of work in the quarry.

Glennie, Brian and Jack Kindred-Boothby for all their elemental creative energy and great accommodation for Sally on her visits. Sky high thanks to Nick Fischer for the great double act with Kate on the aerial pictures for HILL, his skill as a pilot and patience with Kate's sense of direction has been priceless! Julia Hadfield for her beautiful earth panels for the Exhibition and Pam Smedley for her great but seemingly never ending framing task. James at 'Sixprint' in Cornwall, ever patient to get things right for Kate. Colin, Oli and David at Petts Stonemasons in Middleton for their work on the Wordstones and for giving Kate some great very last minute photographic gold! Ruth and Neil Brown for stabling our

Thought Sheep, Jim and Margaret Wain for all their kindness. Jane the Landlady of the Nelson Pub in Middleton for all her hospitality and support and Steve Pepper for his kindness and cake.

Thanks also to the various people who helped in other ways, especially Mark Gwynne-Jones, all the Middleton walkers, Middleton Mountain Bike Group, John Doxey, Ruth Woolsey, Jim Gilmour, Christine Smith, Andy Martin, Kevin Repton and Leah Skellern-Brown.

Kate would also like to thank her ever patient partner Karim for putting up with her pursuit of the HILL story through thick and thin and Gabriel her young Son for running up and down those slopes of life with such energy and enthusiasm! Kate would also like to thank Lucy, Sally, Gavin and Carol for taking HILL from the idea, when Karim's car engine blew up and Kate had to walk and cycle everywhere, then you all took the project creatively upwards and onwards with all the people of this place who have given HILL it's solid foundations, thank you!

**Hook by Nick Wilson**

littoral arts trust

Supported using public funding by

ARTS COUNCIL
ENGLAND

Kate at work, surrounded by sheep. Photo by Ian Lomas.

# About the artists

### Kate Bellis

Since being an award winner of the Observer Young Photojournalist of the Year Competition in 1992, Kate has travelled the world exploring the extraordinary along with the very 'ordinary' lives of people through the lens of her Leica camera.

Kate is fascinated by people's relationship with the land around them and her work often documents a way of life that it under threat, creating an important visual record of a culture that may disappear within a generation.

Kate's previous books include 'On The Edge' (2001) and 'Gathering' (2005). Her images have been published in many national and international newspapers and magazines, including the Guardian, The Times and the American Photo Review.

### Gavin Repton

Gavin specialises in creative video making. Recent projects include National Trust Kedleston Hall Restoration Project, and 2 short films, *The Lost Pubs of Wirksworth* and *When T'owd Man Faced T'Kaiser.*

### Lucy Peacock

Lucy performs poetry regularly in Derbyshire and is currently studying for a PhD in literary linguistics at Nottingham University. Her short story collection, Some *Very Short Stories about Love* was published in 2012, and a collection of her other poems is due to be published in 2018. She lives on the hill.

### Carol Fieldhouse

Carol is a songwriter and performer whose music is described as English Art Folk. Her debut album Linen will soon be followed by Continuum – an album exploring motherhood through song as part of her recent MA in Songwriting and Performance. Carol performs regularly and has written and performed original songs for Graham Sellors' theatre play, *Gorsey Bank to Gommecourt* and will write and arrange songs for his new play in 2019.

### Sally Matthews

Sally's drawings and sculpture are made in praise of animals and her art is deeply rooted in a sense of place, creating her animal forms with materials and in locations that are integral to the meaning of the work. Over the past thirty years she has created an impressive range of work sited across the UK and elsewhere, including Grizedale Forest , Poland, Norway and Canada.

**Kate rolling fleeces**

# About the Hill

The hill of the project title is the South East corner of the White Peak limestone plateau, the area shaded in blue ("Derbyshire Limestone") in the map below from 1820 ("A New Geological Map of England and Wales by W. Smith, Engineer" ©NERC 1820)

It isn't a famous hill, and the part of it we've chosen to explore is just outside the boundaries of the Peak District National Park. The High Peak Trail, Carsington Water and the Wirksworth Arts Festival bring tourists, but not in large numbers. It's a Derbyshire hill, full of meadows and quarries and the spoil heaps of old mine shafts from nobody knows when.

The limestone bedrock means that the ancient woodland that covers the steepest slopes is mainly hazel and blackthorn, while the rest is mostly farmland or cut away by quarries. There are factories too, built to process the spoils of the mines and quarries. Stone from the quarries is still processed here, though the minerals are imported now. They stand alone in the landscape of windswept fields and stone walls like great monuments of steel and concrete from another place.

Limestone from the Hill has been used all over the UK. The famous Hopton-Wood Stone from Middleton Mine has been used for buildings around the country including the Houses of Parliament, and was carved into thousands of headstones for the First World War graves in Europe. The mine lies empty now, but its enormous tunnels - 30m high in places - permeate the hill. "That hill is on legs," as former Middleton Mine worker John Doxey puts it.

## Community

There is an obvious sense of community in the area, and it's regularly on display at events such as the carnival and the well dressings in Wirksworth, and at the annual "clypping" ceremony at St Mary's Church, in which parishioners join hands around the church as if they are embracing it.

Some Wirksworth families have lived and worked here for generations, though newcomers are usually made to feel welcome. It's easy to feel a connection to the surrounding landscape, wherever you come from.

Many of the locals are still employed in quarrying and related industries, while others commute to nearby cities. It's not as well-heeled an area as some of the Peak District towns to the North , but people are proud of this place, and it shows.

## History

There is evidence of lead mining in the area from Roman times, and the sides of the hill are pocked with steel cages which cap the entrances of old lead mines. Lead mining was still the main industry when Daniel Defoe visited in the 1720s.

Of Wirksworth, he wrote, "The inhabitants are a rude boorish kind of people, but they are a bold, daring, and even desperate kind of fellows in their search into the bowels of the earth"

Defoe also wrote specifically about our Hill:

> A little on the other side of Wirksworth, begins a long plain called Brassington Moor, which reaches full twelve miles in length another way, (viz.) from Brassington to Buxton. At the beginning of it on this side from Wirksworth, it is not quite so much. The Peak people, who are mighty fond of having strangers shewed every thing they can, and of calling everything a wonder, told us here of another high mountain, where a giant was buried, and which they called the Giant's Tomb.

The Wirksworth people are still fond of having strangers (and local artists) shewed everything they can, and for this we are very grateful.

## Researching the Project

HILL began as a project in March 2016, and over the following two years, we helped with lambing and shearing sheep, explored mines, visited quarries, and talked to people as much as we could. We descended a 300m shaft on a bit of rope in order to explore Golconda Mine, walked into the bowels of the earth at Good Luck Mine, watched explosions at Longcliffe Quarry, chanted at the winter solstice at the cave at Harborough Rocks and measured cows.
It's been wonderful.

**Sally with a cow**

**Lucy, pressing the detonation button at longcliffe Quarry.**

On

# Winter

The wind makes mountains
of soft, white snow,
and throws ice, like darts,
in your eyes as it blows.
It freezes the air
as the cold increases,
and ceaselessly goes
through coats and fleeces.

Ian Lomas Herding Sheep, Back of Harboro' Rocks, Brassington Moor, 11th December, 2017.

# Lambs

In the barn,
in straw stained with afterbirth,
the ewes gather
as they wait
for the forces inside them
to bring new life.

A ewe walks in circles as she labours. In her movements there's fear. And
there's fear too in the cries of the ewes that labour beside her.

It's been too long.

She tries to run as they pull her to the ground, but they hold her firmly as
Ian pulls the lamb from her body. She is released.

**Right: Ian and Zoe, Lambing a Ewe, Griffe Walk Farm, 1st May 2016.**

Seconds into the World, Steam Rises from a New Born Lamb, 6.24am, 3rd May, 2017.

Griffewalk at lambing time is a magical place....

Watching my brother go about his work, quietly,
methodically, like his father before him.

The lambing shed is a place of reverence.

Checking, watching, waiting and scanning the panting,
steaming bellies of the pregnant ewes.

The shed has a smell of home:
Oily fleeces, sheep nuts, bedding and fresh hay.

Cold long nights followed by the uplifting and optimistic
day break.

Sunlight that finds its way through the gaps and cracks
in the barn,
Re-energising and spotlighting the stars of the show.

The arrival of new life –
But also the stark realisation that even after a long well
managed pregnancy and labour, it can result in dead
lambs for no rhyme or reason.

Carol Lomas

**Twins Newly Born, in Minutes the Ewe Begins to
Clean and Talk to her Lambs, 6.26am, 3rd May, 2017.**

These are the moments when
life is most fragile.
When a swing by the legs,
or a helping breath
can be the difference
between spluttering life
and death.

With quiet precision,
Ian cuts the skin from
a stillborn lamb.
So now wearing that skin,
a motherless lamb
can feed from

the lambless ewe.

**Left: Ian Swinging a Lamb to
Release Fluid from it's Lungs,
Watched by his Nephew, Josh,
24th April 2016.**

**Ian Lomas Skinning a Stillborn Lamb
to put the Hide on an Orphan, Griffe
Walk Farm, 16th April, 2016.**

Ian Fits a Dead Lambs Hide on an Orphan to 'Mother Up' with the Dead Lambs Ewe, 25th April 2017.

Ian with John Bowler, Griffe Walk Dairy, after Lambing all Night and Milking the Herd, Two Weeks into Night Lambings, 25th April, 2017.

# Stillborn

Sometimes
nothing
can revive
that tiny thing
that seemed alive.

**New Mother Trying to Revive her Dead Lamb, 6.39am, 11th May, 2017.**

# Psychobilly Shepherd

Ian Lomas was a Psychobilly* Rocker in his young wild days. From the Mosh pit to the slurry pit at Griffe Walk is quite a journey I think as I watch him skilfully, carefully switch a triplet lamb onto a ewe that has given birth but has nothing to show for it. This has to be done the instant the newborn drops, aquatic wet, bloodied and steaming onto the straw. Its birth Mother is busy talking and licking her other two lambs. He picks the slippery, stretched streak of new life up and drops it in a hush and rush of afterbirth and steam, oozing, wriggling behind it's new foster ewe. She turns and looks, a moment's hesitation, then she greets her new lamb with a nuzzle, then a lick and she starts to talk in short quick breaths and rhythms to this, her lamb. Where else could it have come from, so wet and new? Neither birth Mother or foster Mother seem to notice the switch as Ian watches quietly, to make sure all goes well and as it should.

A few mornings later I am back in the lambing shed, Ian is milking and I keep an eye while he is busy, But when I arrive there is a still born lamb. I go over quickly, trying not to disrupt the sleeping, waiting ewes. The lamb is still warm so I check its airway, rub it down with straw and swing it, nothing, the lambs Mother watches. Frustrated that life is not coming back this time, I stop my efforts after a while. But the watching ewe does not. I fall away, backing off in my failure. She comes forward to her dead lamb and begins to paw it where it's lungs could wheeze and splutter it back to life. She's not giving up, I photograph her quietly as she nuzzles, licks and paws at her lamb. Her eyes hold something that's hard to watch, but I am very lucky to witness. Still she will not give up, this is her first lamb, her only lamb, until that Psychobilly Shepherd finishes his milking shift and can again trick nature. Skinning her dead lamb and putting it's lifeless coat on a new body that is warm, pulsing and hungry, blaating for life and that ewes milk. 'The Clubfoot', London's rocking heartbeat in the 80's, never saw these things that happen on this Hill, these heartbeats that stop and sometimes start again.

Kate Bellis,
May 17th 2017.

**Afterthought....**
I didn't know until later, discussed over a cup of tea in the farm kitchen, that Ian lambed this ewe before I arrived that morning, he left the lamb alive to start milking the herd. Half an hour later he checks on the ewes and the lamb is dead. He's cross with himself for that, for not staying an extra five minutes when the dairy herd demanded milking. As he eats his breakfast he checks on Twitter, the frustrations and thoughts of other shepherds on other Hills.

*Psychobilly, Music that blends Punk Rock and Rockabilly.

Derek Lomas, Ian's Uncle, Taking Ewes and Lambs to Pasture Under the Turbines, 18th May, 2017.

# Fields

When the lambs
are licked clean,
they follow the ewes
to the fields,
where the dew
reflects the rising sun
and dances under footsteps.
And when the mist fades,
they'll be there on the hillside
in their plastic coats,
under the turbines,
by the rocks.

**Derek Turning Ewes and Lambs
Out to Pasture for the First Time,
18th May, 2017.**

Early Morning Light, Ewe
and Her New Born Lamb,
6.20am, 25th April 2017.

# Light

Well here it is, I'm being laughed at again, which I deserve. There's amusement because I never quite make dawn which is at 5.30 am at this time of the year. My old car usually finds its way to Griffe Walk around 6 am. There's a good reason for my timing, the light that hits this grey block shed at around 6.30 am, in the cold early morning, is a gift. Ian's been up every night for two weeks and John Bowler, who helps with the milking, has been here since the shrinking blackness of predawn. It's hard for them to get excited about what I'm seeing, but I almost hold my breath, just in case it drifts into black again like the dust that's tumbled in that light now.

They go to let the cows out and check the other lambing shed, I'm left to keep an eye in here. Sally is with me, HILL's sculptor, she sits on the water trough and watches the light too, I can here her pencil move on paper. There's a ewe lambing and she's chosen her spot, pawing the ground, right in this biblical slant of light. She is doing her job so well, she doesn't need me to interfere. The first lamb slithers into existence, out of its mother and twists of steam climb from its warm, new body. She is up then talking to her lamb, licking the mucus from its nose, the first communication is something special. Again she gets down and on with the job of creation and her next lamb. The light stays with us all the time, pulling the steam upwards in coils as the second lamb is born easily in front of me. I help clear the mucus from this ones nose as its mother is busy licking and talking to her first. Then, with fingers sticky with after-birth, I photograph, quietly stealing those images out of the light. During the night lambings, in the drowsy, dark shed,
Ian knows when a ewe has lambed because he can hear
this 'talking' between the ewe and her newborn.

Kate Bellis, May 2017

John Bowler Milking the Griffe Walk Herd, 5.23am, 17th July, 2017.

Eve, Ian's Daughter, with Shep the Work Dog, 21st April, 2017.

Gathering the Sheep for Shearing, 5.03am, 17th July, 2017.

Shearing Time, Griffe Walk Farm,
17th July, 2017.

Left and right: Shearing the Tups,
Griffe Walk Farm, 17th July, 2017.

Ian Gathering Sheep in the Snow, Duke, his Favourite Dog, Holding the Sheep for Ian, Back of Harboro' Rocks, 11th December, 2017.

Left: After Shearing Four Hundred Sheep, taking a Breather, 17th July, 2017.

Duke bringing the Sheep to Ian, 11th December, 2017.

WHAT THIS HILL MEANS TO ME:

EVERYTHING.

LIFE, FAMILY, HOME, WORK,

FUN, HAPPINESS, SADNESS

AND HARDSHIPS.
BUT I WOULDN'T CHANGE

IT FOR ANYTHING!

Ian P hands.

Duke with Ian, 10th
December, 2017.

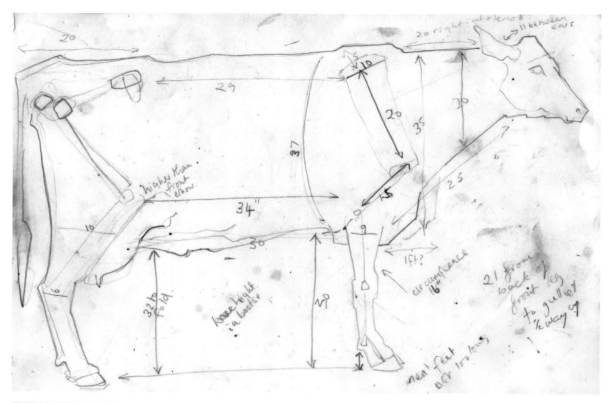

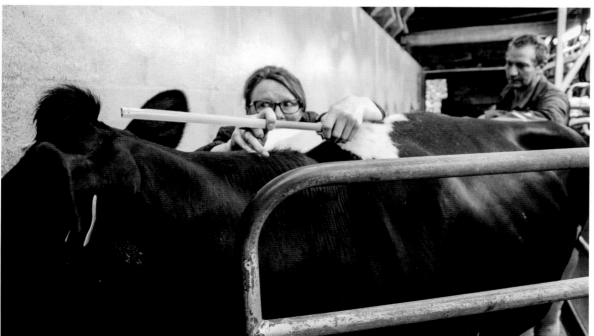

slightly longer hair

narrow behind

up the back is
strongest line

nose is as wide
as between eyes

Friesian Cow from limestone and coal dust

# Rocks

At Harborough, the rocks escape to the surface,
their ancient, pocked faces looking up at the sun.
Red-hatted children line up to climb them,
while walkers scramble up the hillside through the mud.

Eons before,
the rocks unformed,
and re-formed,
atom by atom,
creating great caverns
far beneath

their feet.

# Under

# Descent into Golconda Mine

October 2nd 2016, 10.40am

I am spinning slowly on my thread of survival. Harnessed to a rope, I am descending 360 feet away from the iris of light above my head and down under the Hill into Golconda.

On the surface, shivering with cold, or something else, I'd photographed the mine research team disappear into this impossible man hole, a vertical door to a strange world I had no real knowledge of. I was in full denial that I was going through that breath stealing door too. I just kept on photographing on the surface of the Hill, in the light, it's what I do. There was only myself, the winch operator, and Andrew our expert guide, left on the surface. Lucy, Hill's poet, has gone down ahead, smiling through gritted teeth.

Now I am very alive, as I drop into the darkness and begin to spin slowly. My adrenalin has told me to breathe and has woken me from my denial daze and my mind watches, oh so very carefully, my descent with a survivors alertness. My head torch lights the chisel marks of the miners who dug this impossible hole. How? When? I wonder and spin slowly. There are rough candle niches in the walls that would have given a little light on their descent to this other world, old and rotten bits of wooden ladder, a platform and a tunnel leading away into that deep darkness. I move my head to see these clues of human industry and I spin again because of this small movement, my body bangs into the stone walls that hold these secrets. I am not cold now and I spin and drop and look and smell. It smells very old, primeval, metallic wet in my dry mouth.

I hear voices below me now and the shaft opens out into a larger chamber. My feet touch the rickety platform, 360 feet under the Hill - but still 60 feet from the bottom. I am to learn that this was the easy bit.

Kate Bellis

**Lucy Peacock, about to descend the 110m shaft.**

**Golconda is the deepest mine on the Hill. It is likely to be the mine mentioned by Defoe, which the miners told him was 75 fathoms deep. The level we explored is not the deepest.**

**Originally a lead mine, it was mainly mined for barytes from the late 19th century. It contains many natural caverns, including the enormous Great Shack, where the picture on the next page was taken. It was closed in 1953.**

# Mine

A Sunday in Autumn.

Before the sun has reached the top of the shaft,
the miner-explorers line up
to be
winched
slowly
down
to where
the water
runs over
the rocks
at the sides
and where
crystals
glisten.

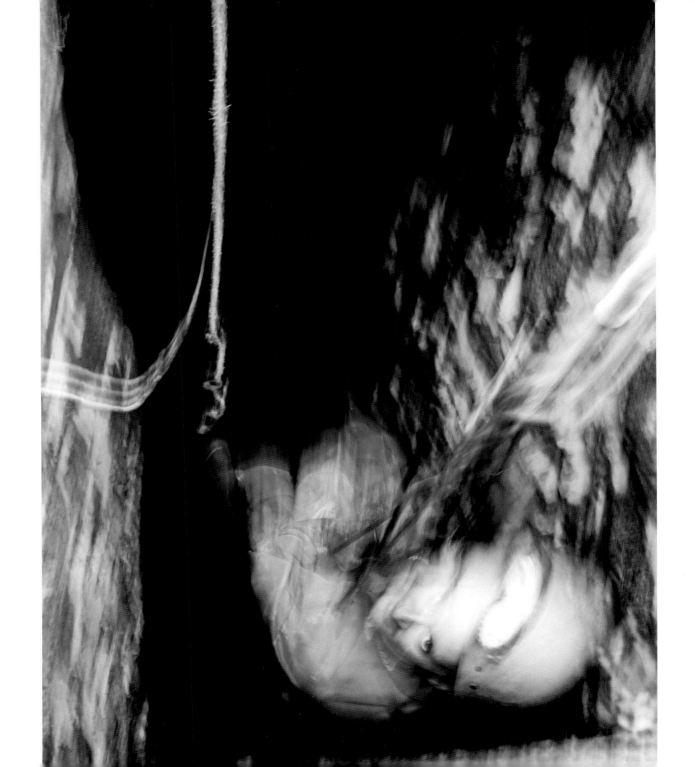

**Mine Explorer at the Entrance of Golconda Mine,
360 ft Descent on a winch Rope, Brassington
Moor, October 2nd, 2016.**

We mapped this mine, from Great Shack to the Forest.
But it changes.
The rocks fill the spaces
and the spaces collide,
uncovering
the secrets
of the hill.

This is where the roof came down. Can you see the cracks? And in weeks
or months, or years from now, the roof up there will be the floor.
It's quiet down here. And when you turn off your light, there's a darkness
that's darker
than
anything
up there.

**Right: Mine Researcher Andrew Quigley, Golconda Mine,
Great Shack, Natural Cavern, October 2nd, 2016.**

## T'Owd Man

He's there, t'owd man,
in the pick marks on the walls,
in the tools and the trolleys,
and the perfectly balanced
deads overhead.

He's in the coffin levels,
and the sound of the water
that drips through the shafts
to the soughs, and out
to the river.

This is his place, his museum.
And there's no
velvet rope.

**"T'owd man" (or the old man) is the name given by Derbyshire miners to the miners who worked in the past. It is also the name given to the famous stone carving (above) in St Mary's Church, Wirksworth.**

Wirksworth Mine Research Group ( L-R: Steve Dalgleish, Scott Humphries, Andrew Quigley, John Hardwick) in the Rising Sun Pub, Middleton, after Exploring Golgonda Mine, October 2nd, 2016.

Nicki Taylor ,Directing Cleaning of the Face, Dene Quarry, Cromford Hill, 2003.

Right: Engineer Fixing the Conveyor, Longcliffe Limestone Quarry, Brassington Moor, March 23rd, 2017.

Kevin Beacham, Face Excavator
Driver, Longcliffe Quarry,
March 23rd, 2017.

Quarrying is a traditional
industry in this Area of
Derbyshire and has provided
Jobs for Local people for
many generations.

K Beacham.

CAME HERE IN NOVEMBER WAS ONLY
GOING TO STAY UNTILL AFTER
CHRISTMAS. BUT 20 PLUS YEARS
I AM STILL HERE THINK THAT
TELLS A STORY ABOUT THE
PLACE

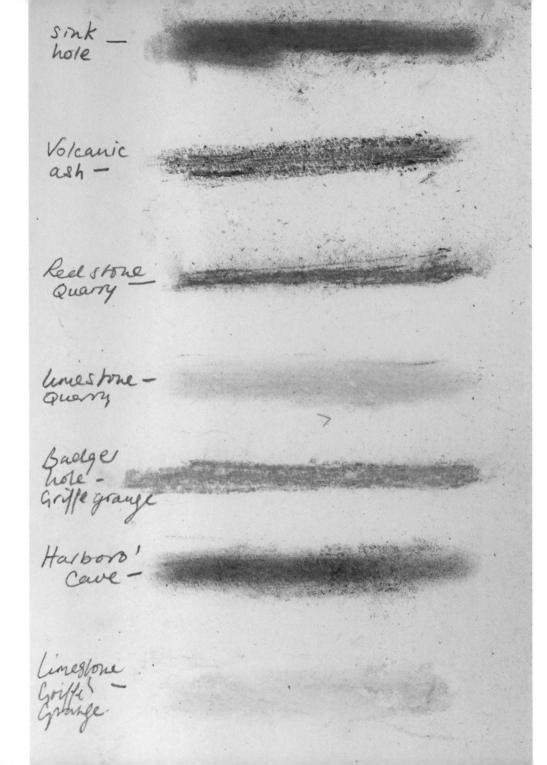

sink
hole —

Volcanic
ash —

Redstone
Quarry —

Limestone —
Quarry

Badger
hole —
Griffe grange

Harboro'
Cave —

Limestone
Griffe —
Grange.

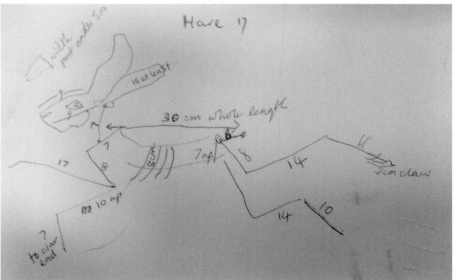

Hare 17

30 cm whole length

Hare - earth pigments.

# Quarry

The quarry,
that place of fire and dust,
where rocks are blasted,
cut and crushed.

Where the sides
rise high above, a vast
cathedral inverted,
formed by blast after blast.

When the holes are drilled and loaded,
and the plastic coil unwound,
the siren wails.

A spark,
a crack,
a roaring sound,
and the rocks slump
to uncover
new inscriptions
in the great
cathedral
walls.

Blasting Limestone, Longcliffe Quarry, March 23rd, 2017.

# Quarry

Longcliffe March 2017

I'm crouched under the belly of this Beast, like a cowardly knight, waiting for it to wake up and devour me whole. But this Leviathan slumbers on, only the skill of the engineering team will wake it up, the conveyer belt had busted that morning, just before my first visit to Longcliffe Quarry.

I am kneeling in the limestone dust under the conveyer, it's so fine, like volcanic ash. Around me are half a dozen quarry workers, they've been sent to shovel out this stone powder while the beast slumbers. One, troglodyte like, is kneeling in the semi dark, it's awkward to shovel like that I think, but he gives me time and talks to me and laughs a bit. This technical malfunction is good for me, I can get up close and get some good working shots.

I climb now upwards along the metal spine and into the belly, following my guide, who works with the blasting team. This is where the conveyer is being fixed, the engineer works quickly, they're losing time and money. Sparks fly out, new rivets glow like polished gems in this dark centre. It's a strange environment, metallic and alien to me, I photograph quickly and get my shot, the engineer shrouded in his protective gear, doesn't hear me leave as metal grinds on metal. Light floods his workplace briefly as I step out from the dark.

This is a fragmented landscape, stripped bare to its ancient layers. My eyes time travel down through this Hill, the siren calls out, then a rumble, deep and primitive echoes through my chest. The layers fold and crumble in front of me, dust rolls like waves from the blast and the Hill gives us it's limestone treasure for toothpaste and a thousand other things we want and need.

Kate Bellis

**Cleaning under the conveyor**

**Right: After Blast Landscape, Longcliffe Quarry, March 23rd, 2017.**

Longcliffe Tea Break, (Left to Right) Sarah-Jane Owen, Julie Carey, Sarah Williams, Karen Holmes. December 5th, 2017.

Longcliffe Workers in the Canteen, (Left to Right) Paul Hadfield, Martin Hollindale, Mark Spencer, Andre Needham. December 5th, 2017

Glynis Spencer, The Weighbridge, Longcliffe Quarry, December 5th, 2017.

Left: Longcliffe Workers on a Quarry Dumper, (Top) Jon Murgatroyd, Andre Needham, (Bottom)
Kevin Beacham, Martyn Hollinsdale, Mark Stinson, Colin Roper, Mark Spencer.  December 5th, 2017.

Longcliffe Limestone Quarry, Brassington Moor, December 18th, 2017.

Jon Murgatroyd Checking the Conveyor, Longcliffe Quarry, December 5th, 2017.

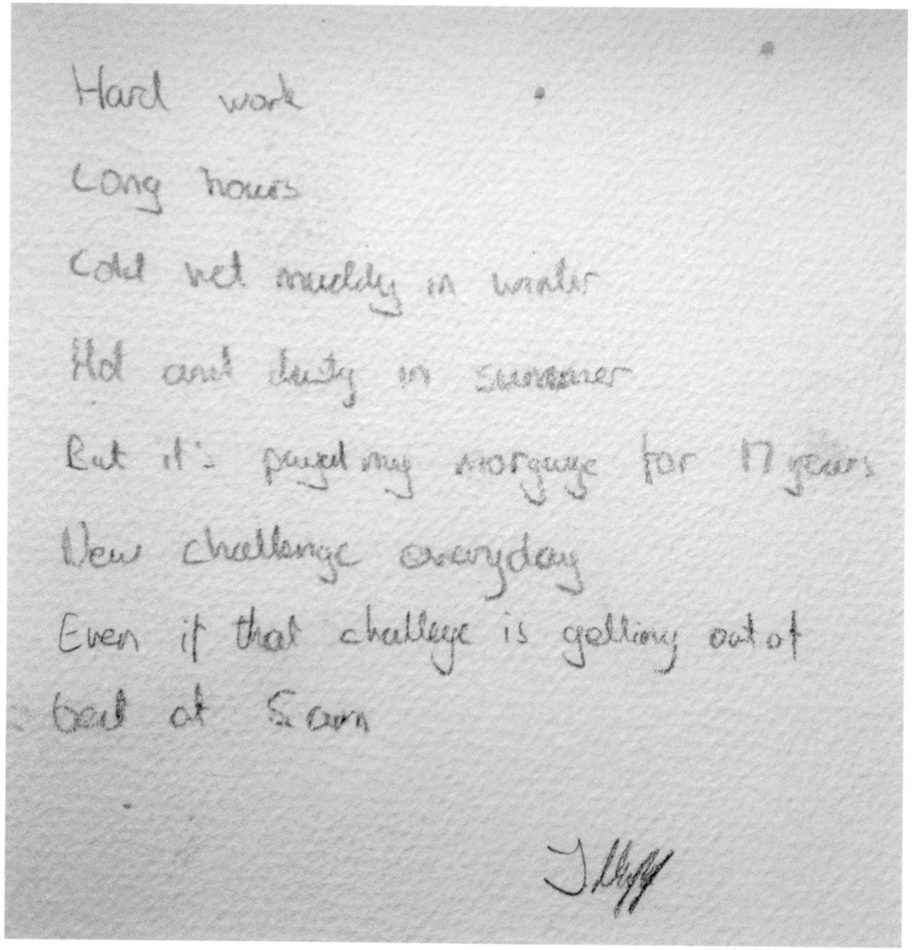

Hard work

Long hours

Cold wet muddy in winter

Hot and dusty in summer

But it's payed my morgage for 17 years

New challenge everyday

Even if that challege is getting out of

bed at 5 am

Jon Murgatroyd

# Shelter

## Trains

Trains ran along here,
loaded with stone -
heavy with pieces
of the heart of the hill.
But those mighty machines
were not mighty enough
for this hill.
They had to be pulled
on ropes and pulleys
powered
by engines
even mightier.

## Walkers

The railway line carries people now.
Cyclists
and joggers
and walkers
with dogs.

And after they've gone,
at night,
by torchlight
through the darkness,
through fog, through snow,
through driving hail,
we'll still walk these paths
each week, without fail.

When we're old, we'll bring ladders, so we can still climb the fences, and
we won't have to crawl through the gaps. But we'll still be here, slip-
sliding in the mud in the darkness in winter, and watching the wildlife as it
changes through the year.

And we won't
take the short cuts.

## Cyclists

Downhill.
Fast round the Dene,
or down the wooded slopes
where it's too extreme
for some of them.
Or sliding on the corners
of the forbidden track -
a free ride through the bracken,
but one you'll have to pay back,
on those
long
hard
climbs
back up

to the top.

## Snow

When the hill is white,
and the biting wind
has blown away.
When the shining tracks
of sledging races
cover the field by the lane.
Families
with scarlet faces
make their way
along untrodden paths
across the moor -
paths which seem much longer
than they ever were

before.

Mary Wain, Beeches Farm, Ible, February 20th 2001.

This place
belongs
to none of them,
but they belong
to it.

Emma Allsop, Next generation of Farming
women at Beeches Farm, Mary Wain's Old
Home in Ible, Sheltering from an Autumn
storm. October 10th, 2017.

**Emma feeding her Pigs,
October 10th, 2017**

Doing what my ansestors did.
farming is in the blood....

No matter the Weather!!

Emma Allsop.

After a long day it
looks like it could be
a long night

Nick Wilson

Nick Wilson, Emma's partner, Waiting
for his Sow to Farrow, after a day's work
in the Quarry, September 8th, 2017.

'Rocky' Spencer with his Son Will and their Goats
Bill and Ben, Middleton, 29th November 2015.

# The Pub

On a dark night
you can look through the windows
and you'll see a pub
that's alive.

Where friendships are made
and feuds begun,
dominoes played,
and arguments won.

And where you can revel
in the conversation,
whatever your level
of inebriation.

And sometimes,
beneath the paintings
and Jane's golden statues,
you'll hear singing.

Jane, Landlady of The Nelson Arms,
with her Neighbour Walt, Middleton,
December 11th, 2015.

Teenagers Going Conkering, Brassington Village, October, 2001.

Children Playing in the Fire Engine Water, Middleton school Fair, 10th July 2015.

# Middleton Mine

Middleton Mine was created in 1959, when it had become uneconomic to continue to extract the high quality limestone by quarrying. It has an entrance at Middleton, and further entrances at Hopton Quarry, on the other side of the moor. It has over 30 miles of tunnels.

The indentation you can see in the foreground of the photo on the right was caused by the collapse of some of the tunnels in the 1980s. No-one was injured.

The following is an extract from an interview with Middleton resident John Doxey, about his work in the mine.

> "There'd be two of us on the drill rig, and we'd usually drill three holes - a threble. They'd set the holes for the explosions, and then set all three off together. It made a good heap of stone, which would be taken to the crusher. Afterwards, they loaded it onto the trains that would come up two or three times a day from Bolehill. The trains would take the stone down to the yard near Cromford cemetery [now Steeple Grange Light Railway], and then down to Cromford bottom, and away they went.
>
> There were many different roads in the mine. There might have been five or six different headings with all those threbles in. Then we'd do the same further on, but we'd leave a piece about 25 yards square, and that took the weight of the roof.
>
> There were two levels - there was a top level, which was taken out first. Then there's a level underneath, which you used to get to by turning right at the top of the hill as you went in. Then eventually afterwards we started taking the middle bit out as well, so instead of two 30ft high tunnels, it'd be 100ft high in places. That hill - it's standing on legs."

**Fixing Caterpillar Tracks, Slinter Mining, Cromford Hill, January 26th 2017.**

Sheep Trails Form an "Eye" around the Hill Collapse on Middleton Moor, Middleton Village Behind. November 13th, 2017.

Steve Pepper making Eccles Cakes, Middleton, February 16th 2018.

"Jesus said,
Man shall not live by bread alone"

This community is like a big family,
we all have a place in each others'
lives.
A hug shows love one for
another and makes a person
feel special.

Right: Hug for Steve Pepper, Middleton
Baker, at his 'Pie Van' Queue, Nelson
Pub Carpark, July 4th 2014.

Bill with his Christmas Brussels from his Allotment,
Middleton. December 16th, 2016.

Portrait of Vaila with Tulips,
Hopton, March 1st, 2017.

IF I COULD HAVE
ALL THE MONEY
IN THE WORLD OR
GO ANYWHERE IN
THE WORLD I WOULD
CHOOSE MY BELOVED
HILLS OVER WIRKSWORTH
WITH MY DOGS
P Spencer.

Phill Spencer with his Dog Clyde, Washgreen,
Wirksworth. August 17th, 2015.

Phill Spencer with his Dogs Bonnie and Clyde, Wirksworth in the Valley, December 18th, 2017.

Children Playing on the Steps of St Mary's Church During the Clypping Service.  September 12th, 2010.

# Clypping

A circle of arms
around the churchyard,
each body connected
in one embrace.

This place
belongs
to none of them,
but they belong
to it.

**Clypping Ceremony, St Mary's Church, Wirksworth.**

**Street Wedding, Wirksworth . May 10th, 2015.**

Last working Days of Bolehill Chapel, Children with Cakes.  March 23rd, 2010.

Left: Remembrance Sunday Ceremony, Bolehill
War Memorial.  November 12th, 2017.


Portrait of Dorothy, Remembrance Sunday, Bolehill War Memorial.

Jim Wain, Mary Wain's Nephew, with the Bull, Little Broadgate Farm.  September 20th, 2017.

Margaret Wain Looking at her Back Door Garden, Little Broadgate Farm.  September 8th, 2017.

Arthur Wheeldon Listening to Radio Derby,  Moor Cottage Farm, Wirksworth Moor, 2001.

Peter Melbourne, Arthur Wheeldon's Nephew, Yearly Tradition of Laying Christmas
Wreaths on Arthur's and Family and Friends Graves.  December 2015.

Joe, Emma Allsop's Nephew, with his
Favorite Boudica Pig. March 7th, 2017.

Colin Julian with his Apprentice Son Oli, 10th and 11th Generation Stone Masons, Middleton. February 16th 2018.

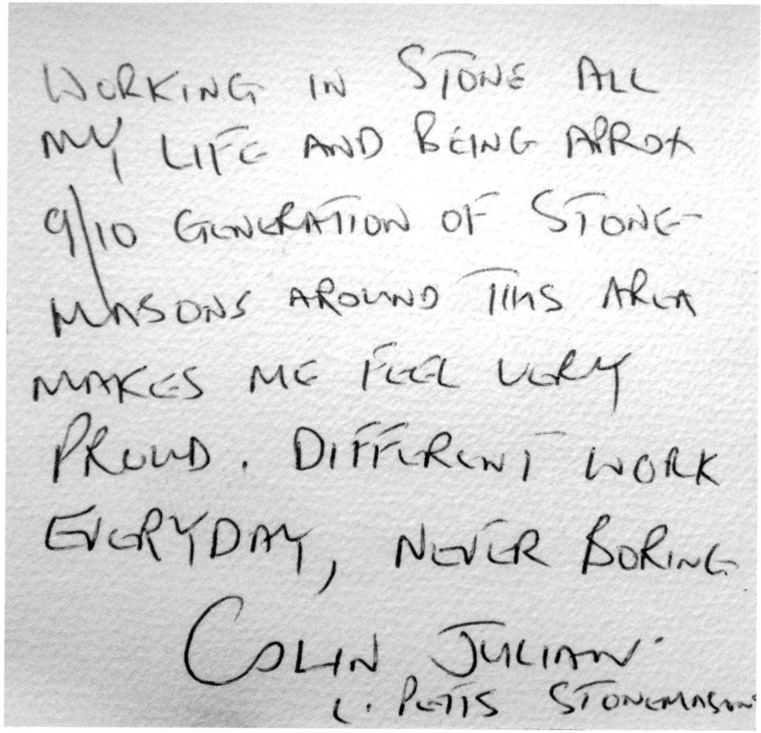

WORKING IN STONE ALL
MY LIFE AND BEING APPROX
9/10 GENERATION OF STONE-
MASONS AROUND THIS AREA
MAKES ME FEEL VERY
PROUD. DIFFERENT WORK
EVERYDAY, NEVER BORING.

COLIN JULIAN
(. PETIS STONEMASON)

# Above

Harboro' Rocks, Cave and Well, Brassington Moor.  October 16th, 2017.

# Trespass

I should not know
that the grass that grows
on the other side of the barbed wire fence
really is more green.

And I should not have been
to the top of the steepest field
by climbing through brambles
on hands and knees.

And I should not have seen
the place, where in between
the rocks grow orchids, like a forest
of tiny, curling trees.

These are my trespasses.
Forgive me.

After School, Via Gellia Woods, Griffe Grange.
April 20th, 2016.

Dawn Blessing at the Well, Harboro' Rocks, for Winter Soltice, December, 2016.

Chanting to the Ancestors, Harboro Cave, for Winter Soltice, December, 2016.

Harboro' Rocks, Autumn Morning in the mist, October 16th, 2017.

# Hill

I will walk this hill, to the very top of the moor,
to where the giant wings of the turbines soar
and rise up to greet you.

I'll clamber down its steeply wooded sides,
while balancing carefully and wondering at the way the light
scatters as it hits the ground.

I'll stand on the ledges of the quarries so I can see
the lines that time has carved in the walls beneath
and below them, the abyss.

I'll place my footsteps where millions of feet have gone before,
and I will walk this hill until I walk no more.

Dawn Sun Rising behind the
Turbines, Brassington Moor.
May 2nd 2017.

'Thought Sheep', Ewe Waiting to Lamb, Early Morning Light, Griffe Walk Farm. April 23rd, 2017.

Right: Setting Sun Behind the Bull on Middleton Moor. November 5th, 2017.

'Griffe Walk Wolf', Duke, Ian Lomas's Favorite Work Dog, Holding the Sheep. December 10th, 2017.

Duke Gathering Carsington Pastures, taking Ewe's for Scanning, February 8th, 2018.

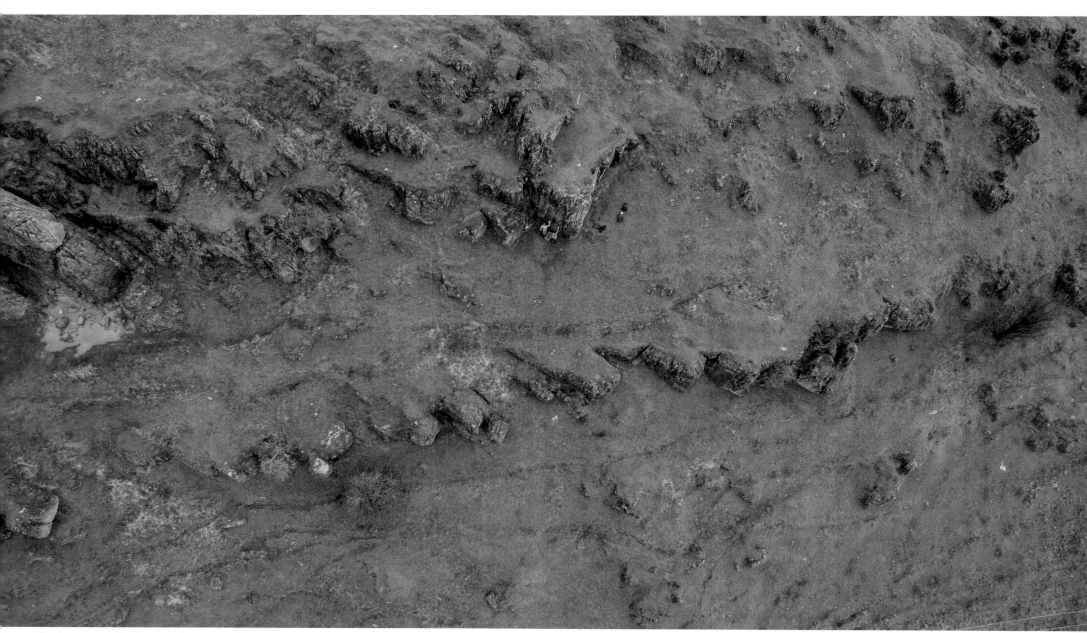

Climbers touch the Rocks at Harboro'.  October 16th, 2017.

Middleton Postman Steve Repton Running his Dog on Middleton Moor after his Rounds.  November 8th, 2017.

# Harboro' Rocks

**Stone and Bone**

25 November 2016.

Stone and Bone were always here, on this Hill.
A child buried with love long ago.
The urn and contents now removed
To some museum store.

I watch my son teasing his shadow on the back wall of Harboro' Cave. He twists and dances with it, balancing on one leg on the eon smooth boulders that crouch down on the cave floor. Arms up, he does 'bunny ears'; leg up arm thrust out, then there is a Dragon of sorts.

I close my eyes against the sword of Autumn light that slants so strongly into the cave at this time of year. When I do, I can still see my Son, shadow dancing at the back of my iris, my brain and eye echoing this intensity of light and dark. I open my eyes again and there he is, skipping between two worlds.

I photograph him with a ghost dog barking at his feet, but this is a light trick, it is a strange shadow cast by one of the boulders he hops on and off. I capture this image in this World, as this boy of mine plays with a shadow dog from another place and time of his imaginings.

Kate Bellis.

**Boys in the Druid's Chair at Harboro Rocks**

**The Druid's chair in 1976, before it was vandalised. Photo: C Smith**

Shadow Dancing, Harboro' Cave. November 25th, 2016.

Once, there were sharks here.
Now their bones are encased
in the limestone remains
of all the creatures that swam
in that ancient sea.

Oli Julian Portrait, 11th generation
Derbyshire Stone Mason, Middleton,
February 16th 2018.

# Thoughts on the HILL

As part of our research for HILL, we asked various members of the community to contribute their thoughts and photos. Here is a selection of them.

"Living here is great because you can look up at the stars and you can hear the quiet."

"Just seeing the world laid out beneath you - it's like owning the planet."

"I stand on the moor and I breathe in the air, and I feel content."

"I like the moor. I like the top of the moor. I like the dip from the mine collapse - I just like going across there and looking. Everywhere's below you. It's fantastic."

"There was a lot of dust years ago, but it were Middleton's bread and butter, years ago wasn't it? It isn't now and I suppose it's quite picturesque I talk to visitors and they say oh what a beautiful village! And it is, it is."

"Running off the week's stresses and strains. Finding oneself on the moor unable to continue because your throat is closing up as past painful memories engulf. Stopping near that wonderful wraggly lone tree with the sheep wool attached to it. Breathing. Stopping. Acknowledging the feelings and letting them pass. Look up at the deep blue sky on this gorgeous April afternoon. Silence. A bumblebee drone and the distant whirl of the turbines giving a sense of hope for the future. Look over to black rocks. Time to move on." Ruth Woolsey

"Flying kites on a windy day and running up to the very top and then rolling down the hill."

"We're halfway up the hill, on the edge of the mine so we were right on the edge of the mine and overlooking it. So we're in the shadow of the hill, the shade of the hill, overlooking a great big abyss of the mine. So it's quite...it's a little bit spooky."

**The Thought Sheep at Celebrate Middleton, July 2017**

"We bought a house before we saw inside the house. We bought it because we liked the hill. We walked up onto the moor - and it was snowy - and it was beautiful, and we didn't care what the house was like, we were just going to live here. That's what we think about the hill."

"I've been coming here for years and years and I'm an old man of sixty and it's been my friend for life."

"It's really down to the fresh air and when you're on the top, no matter where you look, the view's always different from day to day with different clouds"

"I walk out my door and you just look up, and you see the most amazing stars which, you know, living in Northampton, you don't get that because you've got all the smog and everything. You don't see stars....and the fresh air, you know, the air is lovely. You can tell, when you breathe in, the air is clearer. It's just nice."

Sheep coming over Harboro Rocks for a feed, by Ian Lomas, Shepherd, Griffe Walk Farm.

Above and Right: the Thought Sheep on Middleton Moor with members of the local community.
Aerial photo: Jim Gilmour

Left: more images from Celebrate Middleton, July 2017

# Teacher Compa

**MyMaths**

for Key Stage 3

3A

Powered by **MyMaths**.co.uk

**OXFORD**

UNIVERSITY PRESS

Great Clarendon Street, Oxford, OX2 6DP, United Kingdom

Oxford University Press is a department of the University of Oxford.
It furthers the University's objective of excellence in research, scholarship,
and education by publishing worldwide. Oxford is a registered trade mark of
Oxford University Press in the UK and in certain other countries.

British Library Cataloguing in Publication Data
Data available

9780198304685

10 9 8 7 6 5 4 3 2 1

Paper used in the production of this book is a natural, recyclable product made
from wood grown in sustainable forests. The manufacturing process conforms
to the environmental regulations of the country of origin.

Printed in Great Britain by Bell and Bain Ltd., Glasgow


**Acknowledgements**

The editors would like to thank Mike Heylings, Katie Wood and Ian Bettison
for their excellent work on this book.

**Number**

**1** **Whole numbers and decimals**

Introduction .................................................2

**1a** Powers of 10 .........................................4

**1b** Rounding .............................................6

**1c** Order of operations.............................8

**1d** Multiples, factors, divisibility and
prime numbers....................................10

**1e** Prime factors, the HCF and the LCM........12

**1f** Ordering decimals..............................14

MySummary/MyReview .....................16

MyPractice ..........................................18

**Geometry**

**2** **Measures and area**

Introduction ...............................................20

**2a** Metric measures .................................22

**2b** Imperial measures ..............................24

**2c** Area ....................................................26

**2d** Area of a triangle ...............................28

**2e** Area of a parallelogram .....................30

**2f** Circumference of a circle....................32

MySummary/MyReview .....................34

MyPractice ..........................................36

**Algebra**

**3** **Expressions and formulae**

Introduction ...............................................38

**3a** Simplifying expressions .....................40

**3b** Using brackets ...................................42

**3c** Formulae............................................44

**3d** Making expressions ...........................46

MySummary/MyReview .....................48

MyPractice ..........................................50

**CS1** Why do bikes have gears? ................52

**Number**

**4** **Fractions, decimals and percentages**

Introduction ...............................................54

**4a** Adding and subtracting fractions 1 ............56

**4b** Adding and subtracting fractions 2 ............58

**4c** Fraction of a quantity .........................60

**4d** Multiplying and dividing fractions..............62

**4e** Fractions and decimals ......................64

**4f** Percentage of a quantity ...................66

**4g** Percentage problems..........................68

**4h** Financial maths 1: Percentage change .....70

MySummary/MyReview .....................72

MyPractice ..........................................74

MyAssessment 1 .....................................76

**Geometry**

**5** **Angles and 2D shapes**

Introduction ...............................................78

**5a** Angles and lines.................................80

**5b** Angles in a triangle ...........................82

**5c** Properties of triangles .......................84

**5d** Angles in a quadrilateral ...................86

**5e** Properties of quadrilaterals ...............88

MySummary/MyReview .....................90

MyPractice ..........................................92

**Algebra**

**6** **Graphs**

Introduction ...............................................94

**6a** Horizontal and vertical lines .....................96

**6b** Tables of values.................................98

**6c** Drawing straight-line graphs ................. 100

**6d** Problem solving using
straight line graphs........................... 102

**6e** Straight line rules ............................. 104

**6f** Interpreting real-life graphs................... 106

**6g** Time-series graphs ........................... 108

MySummary/MyReview ................... 110

MyPractice ........................................ 112

**CS2** Jewellery business................................ 114

**Number**

**7** **Calculations**

Introduction ............................................. 116

**7a** Addition and subtraction ........................ 118

**7b** Mental × and ÷ ................................. 120

**7c** Written multiplication........................ 122

**7d** Written division................................ 124

**7e** Estimating and approximating................ 126

**7f** Using a calculator ............................ 128

MySummary/MyReview ................... 130

MyPractice ........................................ 132

**Statistics**

**8** **Statistics**

Introduction ............................................. 134

**8a** Designing a survey ........................... 136

**8b** Collecting data ................................. 138

**8c** Frequency tables .............................. 140

**8d** Bar charts......................................... 142

**8e** Pie charts.......................................... 144

**8f** Calculating averages ........................ 146

**8g** Scatter graphs.................................. 148

**8h** Stem-and-leaf diagrams.................... 150

**8i** Frequency diagrams ......................... 152

**8j** Writing a statistical report................. 154

MySummary/MyReview ................... 156

MyPractice ........................................ 158

MyAssessment 2.................................... 160

**Geometry**

| | | |
|---|---|---|
| **9** | **Transformations and symmetry** | |
| | Introduction | 162 |
| 9a | Reflection and rotation symmetry | 164 |
| 9b | Reflection | 166 |
| 9c | Translation | 168 |
| 9d | Rotation | 170 |
| 9e | Enlargement | 172 |
| 9f | Enlargement through a centre | 174 |
| 9g | Scale drawings | 176 |
| | MySummary/MyReview | 178 |
| | MyPractice | 180 |
| CS3 | Climate change | 182 |

**Algebra**

| | | |
|---|---|---|
| **10** | **Equations** | |
| | Introduction | 184 |
| 10a | Equality and inequality | 186 |
| 10b | Solving equations | 188 |
| 10c | Balancing equations 1 | 190 |
| 10d | Balancing equations 2 | 192 |
| 10e | Writing equations | 194 |
| | MySummary/MyReview | 196 |
| | MyPractice | 198 |

**Number**

| | | |
|---|---|---|
| **11** | **Powers and roots** | |
| | Introduction | 200 |
| 11a | Square numbers and square roots | 202 |
| 11b | Using square numbers and square roots | 204 |
| 11c | Indices | 206 |
| 11d | Standard form | 208 |
| | MySummary/MyReview | 210 |
| | MyPractice | 212 |

**Geometry**

| | | |
|---|---|---|
| **12** | **Constructions** | |
| | Introduction | 214 |
| 12a | Using a protractor | 216 |
| 12b | Perpendicular lines | 218 |
| 12c | Perpendicular bisectors | 220 |
| 12d | Angle bisectors | 222 |
| 12e | Constructing triangles | 224 |
| 12f | Bearings | 226 |
| | MySummary/MyReview | 228 |
| | MyPractice | 230 |
| CS4 | Garden design | 232 |
| | MyAssessment 3 | 234 |

| | | |
|---|---|---|
| | Homework book answers | on CD-ROM |
| | Practice book answers | on CD-ROM |
| | Scheme of Work | on CD-ROM |

| | | |
|---|---|---|
| | Answers | 324 |
| | Index | 330 |

**Algebra**

| | | |
|---|---|---|
| **13** | **Sequences** | |
| | Introduction | 236 |
| 13a | Term-to-term rules | 238 |
| 13b | Position-to-term rules | 240 |
| 13c | The $n$th term formula | 242 |
| 13d | Recursive sequences | 244 |
| | MySummary/MyReview | 246 |
| | MyPractice | 248 |

**Geometry**

| | | |
|---|---|---|
| **14** | **3D shapes** | |
| | Introduction | 250 |
| 14a | Three dimensional shapes | 252 |
| 14b | Nets | 254 |
| 14c | Plans and elevations | 256 |
| 14d | Volume of a cuboid | 258 |
| 14e | Shapes made from cuboids | 260 |
| 14f | Surface area of a cuboid | 262 |
| | MySummary/MyReview | 264 |
| | MyPractice | 266 |
| CS5 | Golden rectangle | 268 |

**Ratio**

| | | |
|---|---|---|
| **15** | **Ratio and proportion** | |
| | Introduction | 270 |
| 15a | Ratio | 272 |
| 15b | Dividing in a given ratio | 274 |
| 15c | Ratio and proportion | 276 |
| 15d | Percentages and proportion | 278 |
| 15e | Proportional reasoning | 280 |
| 15f | Financial maths 2: Living on a budget | 282 |
| | MySummary/MyReview | 284 |
| | MyPractice | 286 |

**Statistics**

| | | |
|---|---|---|
| **16** | **Probability** | |
| | Introduction | 288 |
| 16a | Probability | 290 |
| 16b | Mutually exclusive events | 292 |
| 16c | Theoretical probability | 294 |
| 16d | Counting outcomes | 296 |
| 16e | Two events | 298 |
| 16f | Probability experiments | 300 |
| 16g | Venn diagrams | 302 |
| | MySummary/MyReview | 304 |
| | MyPractice | 306 |
| CS6 | Crime scene investigation | 308 |
| | MyAssessment 4 | 310 |

**Functional**

| | | |
|---|---|---|
| **17** | **Everyday maths** | |
| | Introduction | 312 |
| 17a | The AfriLinks project | 314 |
| 17b | Building the schoolhouse | 316 |
| 17c | Raising the roof and laying the path | 318 |
| 17d | The basketball court | 320 |
| 17e | The school garden | 322 |

This Teacher Companion is part of the MyMaths for Key Stage 3 series which has been specially written for the new National Curriculum for Key Stage 3 Mathematics in England. It accompanies Student Book **3A** and is designed to help you have the greatest impact on the learning experience of lower ability students towards the end of their Key Stage 3 studies.

The author team collectively bring a wealth of classroom experience to the Teacher Companion making it easy for you to plan and deliver lessons with confidence.

The structure of this book closely follows the content of the student book so that it is easy to find the information and resources you need. These include for each

**Lesson**: objectives; a list of resources – including MyMaths 4-digit codes; a starter, teaching notes, plenary and alternative approach; simplification and extension ideas; an exercise commentary and full answers; the key ideas and checkpoint questions to test them; and a summary of the key literacy issues.

**Chapter**: National Curriculum objectives; any assumed prior knowledge; notes supporting the Student Book introduction and starter problem; the associated MyMaths and InvisiPen resources – including those offering extra support to weaker students; questions to test understanding; and how the material is developed and used.

The accompanying CD-ROM makes all the lesson plans available as Word files, so that you can customize them to suit your students' needs. Also on the CD are full sets of answers for Homework Book **3A**.

## The integrated solution

This teacher guide is part of a set of resources designed to support you and your students with a fully integrated package of resources.

**MyMaths**
Direct links to the ever popular site's lessons and auto-marked homeworks.

**Online Student Book**
Digital versions of the student books for home and classroom use.

**Online Testbank**
A complete suite of assessment tests: Good to Go, formative (including feedback), auto-marked and print based.

**InvisiPen solutions**
Student friendly videos explaining just what is needed to solve a sample problem.

**Homework Book**
Handy, pocket-sized books, tailored to the content of each student book lesson.

**Workbook**
Accessible, write in books designed to support weaker students making the transition from KS2 to KS3.

**Student Book**
The three books in a phase are organized to cover topics in the same order but at three ability levels.

## Learning outcomes

**N2** Order positive and negative integers, decimals and fractions; use the number line as a model for ordering of the real numbers; use the symbols $=, \neq, <, >, \leq, \geq$ (L5)

**N3** Use the concepts and vocabulary of prime numbers, factors (or divisors), multiples, common factors, common multiples, highest common factor, lowest common multiple, prime factorisation, including using product notation and the unique factorisation property (L5)

**N4** Use the 4 operations, including formal written methods, applied to integers, decimals, proper and improper fractions, and mixed numbers, all both positive and negative (L5)

**N13** Round numbers and measures to an appropriate degree of accuracy [for example, to a number of decimal places or significant figures] (L5)

**N14** Use approximation through rounding to estimate answers and calculate possible resulting errors expressed using inequality notation $a < x \leq b$ (L5)

## Introduction

The chapter starts by looking at multiplying and dividing by powers of ten. The next section covers rounding to the nearest 10, 100, 100 or a number of decimal places. A section on correctly applying the order of operations precedes a section on factors, multiples and primes. Prime factorisation, HCF and LCM are then covered before the final section on ordering decimals.

The introduction discusses the need for accuracy in certain jobs. It discusses the accuracy required from navigators and engineers to successfully land the Mars Exploration Rover in the right place when the spacecraft had travelled such a long distance but also the need for accuracy in jobs such as doctors and nurses who administer drugs and other treatments. Getting the dosage of powerful drugs wrong, even by a few milligrams could have catastrophic effects on the health of the patient.

It is supposed that if the designers of the channel tunnel had been out by as much as half a millimetre in their plans, then the two halves of tunnel would have missed meeting up in the middle when they were dug from opposite sides of the English Channel!

## Prior knowledge

Students should already know how to…

- Complete simple arithmetic sums
- Work with square numbers

## Starter problem

The starter problem considers the cost of keeping a pet. It might be nice at the start to do a quick survey of the pets that the students in the class have and then get them to estimate the likely cost of the various types. It might be expected that the smaller the pet is, the cheaper it is to keep but when you take into account the cost of things like cages and fish tanks for the smallest of pets this might not be quite so clear cut.

Students could be given a specific pet to investigate (or pick one of their own) and produce a short report (following some research time) on how much it would cost to keep that particular animal.

A time frame should also be considered – are we talking about keeping them for week, a year, or through their lifetime?

## Resources

**MyMaths**

| | | | | | |
|---|---|---|---|---|---|
| Rounding to 10, 100 | 1003 | Rounding decimals | 1004 | Multiplying by 10 and 100 | 1027 |
| Factors and primes | 1032 | LCM | 1034 | Multiples | 1035 |
| HCF | 1044 | Ordering decimals | 1072 | Order of operations | 1167 |
| Dividing by 10 and 100 | 1392 | | | | |

**Online assessment**

| | |
|---|---|
| Chapter test | 3A–1 |
| Formative test | 3A–1 |
| Summative test | 3A–1 |

**InvisiPen solutions**

| | | | |
|---|---|---|---|
| Place value | 111 | Rounding | 112 |
| Multiply and divide by powers of 10 | | | 114 |
| Order of operations | 124 | Multiples and factors | 171 |
| HCF and LCM | 172 | Primes and prime factors | 173 |

## Topic scheme

Teaching time = 6 lessons/2 weeks

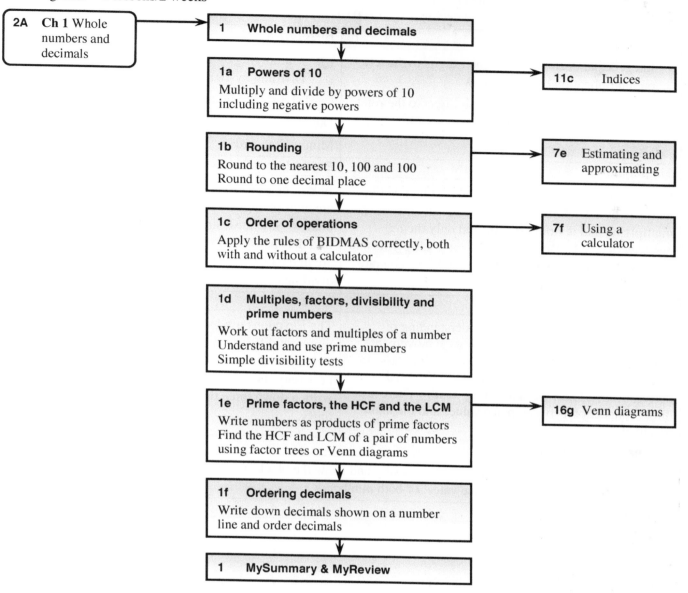

**2A  Ch 1** Whole numbers and decimals

**1  Whole numbers and decimals**

**1a  Powers of 10**
Multiply and divide by powers of 10 including negative powers

**11c  Indices**

**1b  Rounding**
Round to the nearest 10, 100 and 100
Round to one decimal place

**7e  Estimating and approximating**

**1c  Order of operations**
Apply the rules of BIDMAS correctly, both with and without a calculator

**7f  Using a calculator**

**1d  Multiples, factors, divisibility and prime numbers**
Work out factors and multiples of a number
Understand and use prime numbers
Simple divisibility tests

**1e  Prime factors, the HCF and the LCM**
Write numbers as products of prime factors
Find the HCF and LCM of a pair of numbers using factor trees or Venn diagrams

**16g  Venn diagrams**

**1f  Ordering decimals**
Write down decimals shown on a number line and order decimals

**1  MySummary & MyReview**

## Differentiation

| **Student book 3A**  2 – 19 |
| --- |
| Multiply and divide by powers of 10
Round integers and decimals to the nearest 1, 10, 100, 1000 and a given number of decimal places
Order of operations
Factors, multiples and primes including prime factors, HCF and LCM
Order decimals |

| **Student book 3B**  2 – 15 |
| --- |
| Multiply and divide by powers of 10
Round numbers to a given place, including decimal places and significant figures
Work with factors and multiples, LCM, HCF and prime factors
Estimate the answer to calculations by rounding |

| **Student book 3C**  2 – 15 |
| --- |
| Round numbers to a given number of significant figures
Work out and calculate with upper and lower bounds
Use numbers written in index form |

## Objectives

(L5)
(L6)

- Multiply and divide integers and decimals by 10, 100, and explain the effect.
- Multiply and divide integers and decimals by 0.1, 0.01.

| Key ideas | Resources |
|---|---|
| 1  Integers and decimals move their digits to the left on multiplication by 10 and 100. <br><br> 2  Integers and decimals move their digits to the right on division by 10 and 100. | Multiplying by 10 and 100                  (1027) <br> Dividing by 10 and 100                        (1392) <br> Card showing columns for place values <br> Dienes apparatus <br> Mini whiteboards |

| Simplification | Extension |
|---|---|
| Concentrate only on multiplying and dividing whole numbers by 10 before moving on to consider multiplying and dividing by 100 and only then consider decimals. Do not worry about multiplying and dividing by 0.1 and 0.01  Students should concentrate on questions **1** to **4** in the exercise. | Ask students to complete similar examples where they are multiplying and dividing by 1000 or 0.001. Ask them to generate a simple rule which can be used to find the answer, irrespective of how many zeros there are in the number which they are multiplying or dividing by. |

| Literacy | Links |
|---|---|
| This exercise is based on a firm understanding of 'place value' and knowing that, for each movement leftwards from column to column, a digit increases in value tenfold, and vice versa. The word 'decimal' derives from a Latin word meaning 'tenth'. There is a direct connection between place values and the name 'decimal'. | The Egyptians used seven different symbols to represent different powers of ten. To write a number, each symbol was written down as many times as was necessary. For example, the symbol for ten would be written down three times to represent the number thirty. |

## Alternative approach

Use Dienes apparatus to represent, say 23, visually and show the blocks which are ten times bigger. Use column headings H, T, U to show the 'place vales' of both numbers.

## Checkpoint

Complete these calculations.

| | | |
|---|---|---|
| a | $13 \times 0.1$ | (1.3) |
| b | $77 \times 0.001$ | (0.077) |
| c | $145.1 \div 0.01$ | (14 510) |
| d | $58.9 \times ? = 0.0589$ | (0.001) |

## Starter – Order!

Write the following list of fractions on the board.

$\frac{1}{2}, \frac{3}{8}, \frac{1}{3}, \frac{7}{10}, \frac{2}{5}, \frac{3}{4}, \frac{3}{10}, \frac{3}{5}$

Ask students to put them in order from the lowest value to the highest value.

$[\frac{3}{10}, \frac{1}{3}, \frac{3}{8}, \frac{2}{5}, \frac{1}{2}, \frac{3}{5}, \frac{7}{10}, \frac{3}{4}]$

Can be differentiated by the choice of fractions.

## Teaching notes

Explain to students that they are going to do arithmetic without a calculator. Explain that they are going to be multiplying and dividing by 10, 100, 0.1 and 0.01.

Starting with an initial problem, say $34 \times 10$, ask students what '10 lots of 34' is. Repeat the exercise with an example multiplying by 100 and also give examples where the students are multiplying a decimal number by 10 and 100. Mini whiteboards can be used here to get quick responses to questions. Where the initial number is an integer (not a decimal), explain why it is like adding one or two zeros to the number; while, for decimals, it is like 'moving the decimal point' one or two places. Students can complete questions 1 to 4 from the exercise at this point. Let students use cards with columns for place value if they need more visual support.

Explain that multiplying by 0.1 is like dividing by 10 and that multiplying by 0.01 is like dividing by 100. Give students examples and allow them time to practise this.

Explain that if multiplying by 0.1 is like dividing by 10, then the inverse is that dividing by 0.1 is like multiplying by 10. Give the same explanation for dividing by 0.01. Students should then complete the exercise to practise this skill.

## Plenary

A quick-fire quiz using mini whiteboards can be used to assess the progress made in the lesson. True/False or multiple-choice questions can also be used in this context.

## Exercise commentary

**Questions 1** to **4** – Routine practice; students should be guided through them accordingly.

**Questions 5** and **6** – These questions require students to work with multiplying and dividing by decimals and they may need support for the first few examples.

**Question 7** – This is working backwards and students should be encouraged to look for patterns arising from questions **5** and **6**.

**Questions 8** and **9** – Two contextualised questions which require students to divide or multiply by powers of 10. Further problems of this type could be given to the students if time permits.

## Answers

**1**

| 40 | 90 | 180 | 370 |
|------|------|------|------|
| 640 | 800 | 2560 | 4570 |
| 1010 | 65 | 48 | 112 |
| 5 | 6.5 | 0.7 | 0.63 |
| 10.5 | 0.09 | 203 | 700.7 |

**2**

| 4 | 7 | 12 | 25 |
|------|------|------|------|
| 62 | 41 | 4.5 | 3.2 |
| 5.1 | 12.5 | 20.7 | 64.8 |
| 0.7 | 0.48 | 0.14 | 0.062 |
| 0.03 | 0.0403 | 0.007 | 2.005 |

**3**

| 500 | 800 | 2300 | 1400 |
|------|------|------|------|
| 2400 | 6200 | 670 | 190 |
| 2340 | 371 | 648 | 906 |
| 2456 | 761.7 | 1358.2 | 1200.3 |
| 211200 | 67 | 10010 | 3008 |

**4**

| 4 | 6 | 8 | 26 |
|------|------|------|------|
| 18 | 87 | 5.5 | 4.7 |
| 6.15 | 9.04 | 28.5 | 60.57 |
| 0.62 | 0.57 | 0.239 | 0.2001 |
| 0.003 | 0.0046 | 0.0701 | 0.7008 |

**5** a $7 \times 0.1 = 0.7$    b $6 \div 0.1 = 60$

c $9 \times 0.1 = 0.9$    d $4 \times 0.1 = 0.4$

e $12 \div 0.1 = 120$    f $16 \times 0.1 = 1.6$

**6** a $5 \div 0.01 = 500$    b $5 \times 0.01 = 0.05$

c $8 \div 0.01 = 800$    d $7 \times 0.01 = 0.07$

e $25 \times 0.01 = 0.25$    f $19 \div 0.01 = 1900$

**7** a $8 \times 0.1 = 0.8$    b $8 \times 0.01 = 0.08$

c $6 \div 0.01 = 600$    d $5 \div 0.1 = 50$

e $9 \times 0.1 = 0.9$    f $7 \div 0.01 = 700$

g $12 \times 0.1 = 1.2$    h h $15 \div 0.1 = 150$

i $18 \div 0.01 = 1800$    j $24 \times 0.1 = 2.4$

k $26 \times 0.01 = 0.26$    l $40 \div 0.1 = 400$

**8** £25.90

**9** £427

## Objectives

- Round positive numbers to any given power of 10.  (L4)
- Round decimals to the nearest whole number or to one decimal place.  (L5)

| Key ideas | Resources |
|---|---|
| 1  Rounding gives a 'ball-park' figure when the headline is more important than the detail. <br> 2  Always round up from the midpoint. | Rounding to 10, 100  (1003) <br> Rounding decimals  (1004) <br> Mini whiteboards <br> Number lines |

| Simplification | Extension |
|---|---|
| Give the students examples of integers which are close to either end of the number line and avoid the issue of rounding from the midpoint until later on. Keep the numbers small and allow them plenty of time to practise numerous examples before moving on. <br><br> Move to decimals only when rounding integers is secure. | Introduce the notions of decimal places and significant figures to the students and demonstrate how these rounding methods work. Ask the students to explain the similarities and the differences between the two methods. |

| Literacy | Links |
|---|---|
| 'Rounding' is used generally as 'making something complete or whole' like a rounded personality and a rounded education. So, in mathematics, 'rounding' can be thought of as removing the 'bits' of a number to give a more overall size. | The time taken for the Earth to make one complete revolution around the sun is about 365.2422 days. To reduce the error in rounding the year to 365 days, the Gregorian calendar adds an extra day every four years (except for those years divisible by 100 but NOT by 400) to keep the calendar aligned with the seasons. Even with the addition of leap years, the Gregorian calendar is still inaccurate by 1 day in every 3236 years. There is more information about the Gregorian calendar at http://jonathan.rawle.org/hyperpedia/calendar.php |

## Alternative approach

Write the number with its column headings and place a card over the parts that are to be rounded. For example, when rounding 1357 to the nearest 100, write Th H T U above 1357 and cover the T and U columns with the card. Under the card will only be zeros, but the part removed (the 57) is more than halfway to 400 and so makes the 3 hundred into a 4 hundred.

## Checkpoint

Round the number 17 827.608 to the nearest

| | | |
|---|---|---|
| a | 100 | (17 800) |
| b | 10 | (17 830) |
| c | 1 d.p. | (17 827.6) |
| d | 2 d.p. | (17 827.61) |
| e | 10 000 | (20 000) |

**Starter** – The question is…

Challenge students to find as many different questions as they can in three minutes with an answer of 0.2.

Can be differentiated by the choice of answer.

## Teaching notes

Explain to the students why rounding numbers is a useful skill. Explain that it makes the numbers easier to deal with in communicating ideas and in calculations where the exact answer is less important than a 'ball-park' figure.

Explain, using a prepared number line if necessary, that numbers are rounded either up or down, depending where they lie on the number line and the level of accuracy required.

Explain that numbers which lie at the midpoint of the interval are always rounded up. Give students examples of numbers rounded to the nearest 10, 100 or 1000. Mini whiteboards can be used for students' responses to make this exercise quicker.

Give examples of decimals which need to be rounded to one decimal place and explain that the principle is the same. Give examples, including numbers which lie at the midpoint of an interval.

Students can then practise rounding using questions from the exercise.

## Plenary

Mini whiteboards can be used to answer questions in a quick-fire quiz or true/false questions can be used to assess student progress. Prepared multiple-choice questions could also be used in this context.

## Exercise commentary

**Questions 1** to **2** – These questions are routine practice. Students should be told to take care with rounding numbers ending in 5 and to work from a number line if necessary.

**Question 3** – This question applies the process of rounding to a practical example. Ask students why they think it would be useful to round these values.

**Questions 4** and **5** – Remind students to take care, as before, when rounding numbers ending in 5.

**Questions 6** and **7** – Point out that 'the nearest 10p' is actually the first decimal place. Alternatively, have students work only in pence rather than pounds.

## Answers

| | | | | | | | | |
|---|---|---|---|---|---|---|---|---|
| 1 | a | 30 | b | 30 | c | 80 | d | 40 |
| | e | 100 | f | 100 | g | 220 | h | 310 |
| | i | 1690 | j | 1560 | k | 20 | l | 200 |
| 2 | a | 200 | b | 400 | c | 0 | d | 100 |
| | e | 300 | f | 400 | g | 700 | h | 3500 |
| | i | 1200 | j | 2900 | k | 300 | l | 200 |

3
| | | | |
|---|---|---|---|
| Bideford | 15000 | Keswick | 5000 |
| Brecon | 8000 | Ludlow | 11000 |
| Ely | 15000 | Redruth | 12000 |
| Filey | 7000 | Shanklin | 8000 |
| Heysham | 4000 | Tetbury | 5000 |

Heysham, Keswick, Tetbury, Filey, Brecon, Shanklin, Ludlow, Redruth, Bideford, Ely

| | | | | | | | | |
|---|---|---|---|---|---|---|---|---|
| 4 | a | 3 | b | 0 | c | 14 | d | 4 |
| | e | 1 | f | 22 | g | 28 | h | 40 |
| | i | 100 | j | 50 | k | 1 | l | 10 |
| 5 | a | 0.3 | b | 0.2 | c | 4.3 | d | 8.7 |
| | e | 8.1 | f | 2.4 | g | 0.2 | h | 1.5 |
| | i | 0.6 | j | 1.0 | k | 10.0 | l | 0.1 |
| 6 | a | £2·40 | b | £5·50 | c | £3·20 | d | £11·80 |
| | e | 60p | f | £4·00 | g | £1·00 | h | 50p |
| | i | £5·00 | j | £1·00 | | | | |

7 Original price = £34.86
New price = £35.00
The customer will spend more now the prices have been rounded.

## Objectives

- Use the order of operations, including brackets, with more complex calculations. (L5)

| Key ideas | Resources |
|---|---|
| 1 The order of operations in a calculation matters.<br>2 The mnemonic BIDMAS provides a reminder of the correct order. | Order of operations (1167)<br>Calculators which do and don't apply BIDMAS.<br>Mini whiteboards<br>Dictionaries |

| Simplification | Extension |
|---|---|
| Initially, provide examples which require BIDMAS but which have only two distinct operations; for example, $3 + 4 \times 2$. Later, introduce brackets; for example, compare $3 + 4 \times 2$ and $(3 + 4) \times 2$. | Ask students, in pairs, to write their own calculations which involve indices and brackets. Having worked out the answer themselves, they challenge their partner to find the answer. They discuss to reach agreement on disputed answers. |

| Literacy | Links |
|---|---|
| Language has its grammar which provides rules and order to sentences. Mathematics has its rules and order which have to be followed in calculations. If the rules and order in language or mathematics are not obeyed, then there is only nonsense! | Bring in dictionaries for the class to use. 'Indices' is the plural of the word 'index' which can have several different meanings. Ask the class to find the meanings and to decide in which area of the curriculum each meaning would be most relevant. |

### Alternative approach

Have at least two different calculators with different logics, some obeying BIDMAS and some not. Find the answers to simple calculations such as $3 + 4 \times 2$ and explore why answers differ. Have students find which answer their own calculators give. Build up the complexity of the calculations, have students discover the hierarchy of operations and have them invent the mnemonic 'BIDMAS' themselves.

### Checkpoint

What is the correct answer to this calculation? (**b** is correct)

$13 - 3 \times 4 + 15 \div 5$

a  11
b  4
c  16
d  43

**Starter** – Powers of ten

Write 10.3 on the board. Ask students to multiply the number, in turn, by 100, 10 and 0.1. Repeat using different starting numbers. Students respond on mini whiteboards. Extend using division.

## Teaching notes

Ask students to complete some simple one operation quick-fire questions as a warm-up, using mini whiteboards for quick feedback.

Give an example of a calculation which has two operations, say $3 + 4 \times 2$ and ask students to work out the answer. Expect most students to incorrectly work it out to be 14. Check answers using calculators which give answers of 14 and 11. Explain at this stage that the order in which we do the operations is important and that multiplication should come before addition, giving the correct answer 11.

Work through the order of operations with students using BIDMAS and ask them to write down the correct sequence themselves. Work towards giving students more complicated examples involving multiple operations, such as $3 \times (4 + 2) \div 3^2$ [Answer 2]. Show students how to set out a problem of this type correctly and apply the correct order of operations. Give students further examples where necessary and then ask them to practise applying the principles of BIDMAS themselves.

## Plenary

Allow students to refer to BIDMAS as they undertake a quick-fire quiz using mini whiteboards or a multiple choice quiz. True/False questions or bingo can also be used. Then remove any visual aid showing BIDMAS.

## Exercise commentary

A written visual reminder of what BIDMAS means is useful for the whole class. After some time, remove it.

**Question 1** – This question is suitable for whole-class discussion.

**Question 2** – The questions here get more complex. Students may need more guidance from part **j** onwards.

**Question 3** – Emphasise putting the sum into calculators exactly as written including the brackets. Some cheaper calculators may have no brackets.

**Question 4** – Students should do these calculations step-by-step (and set out working as in the worked examples on the previous page) using the correct order of operations.

**Question 5** – This question is suitable for whole-class discussion.

**Question 6** – Some students may find it a help to have the numbers in the squares written on cards, so they can rearrange them more easily.

**Question 7** – Students should be encouraged to experiment with different operations and may like to use a calculator to make checking quicker.

---

## Answers

1 Jack is right because multiplication is completed before subtraction.

| 2 | a | -1 | b | 8 | c | 17 | d | 7 |
|---|---|-----|---|----|---|----|---|---|
| | e | 8 | f | 15 | g | 10 | h | 7 |
| | i | 14 | j | 32 | k | 90 | l | 8 |
| | m | 15 | n | 9 | o | 66 | p | 5 |
| | q | 22 | r | 50 | | | | |

| 3 | a | 525 | b | 178 | c | 396 | d | 16 |
|---|---|-----|---|-----|---|-----|---|----|
| | e | 102 | f | 276 | | | | |

| 4 | a | 14 | b | 13 | c | 19 | d | 27 |
|---|---|----|---|----|---|----|---|----|
| | e | 22 | f | 21 | | | | |

5 c gives a different answer, because the part of the calculation in the brackets must be completed first, giving $100 \div 2 = 50$, rather than $10 \div 5 = 2$, which a and b give.

6   a   $8 \times 2 + 4 = 20$
    b   $5 \times (2^2 + 3) = 35$
    c   $4 \times 2 + 3^2 = 17$
    d   $10 \div 5 + 2^2 = 6$
    e   $8 + 3 \times 2 - 1 = 13$
    f   $4^2 \div 2 - 4 + 2 = 6$

7   a   $8 \div 2 + 5 = 9$     b   $8 + 2 \times 5 = 18$
    c   $8 - 2 + 5 = 11$     d   $8 - 2 \times 5 = -2$
    e   $4 - 4 \times 4 = -12$     f   $4 + 4 - 4 = 4$

| Objectives | |
|---|---|
| • Recognise and use multiples, factors, prime numbers and tests of divisibility. | (L5) |

| Key ideas | Resources | |
|---|---|---|
| 1 Multiples of a number are found in its times table.<br>2 Factors are numbers which divide exactly into another number.<br>3 A prime number has only two factors. | Factors and primes<br>Multiples<br>10 by 10 or 12 by 12 multiplication grids<br>Mini whiteboards | (1032)<br>(1035) |

| Simplification | Extension |
|---|---|
| Have students make a table with three columns labelled *Number, Multiples* and *Factors*. Give a number from the 'times tables', such as 8. Write it in the first column, use the 'times table' for 8 to write multiples in the second column, and then use factor pairs to list factors for the third column. | Ask the students to write down the factors of larger numbers; for example, 64 or 80. Ask them to find a way of systematically determining the factors to ensure that they have found all of them. Listing factor pairs in order is usually the best way. |

| Literacy | Links |
|---|---|
| Multiples and factors are often confused. There are clues in the words that explain their meaning and serve as an aid to memory.<br><br>'Multiples' can come from 'Multiplication tables' – they are the answers when reciting a table.<br><br>'Factors' (like 'factories') are where large numbers are made from small numbers; for example 2 × 6 make 12, so 2 and 6 are factors of 12. | Students will be familiar with divisibility tests for all the numbers 2 through 9, except for 7. There is a neat divisibility test, and though it relies on a knowledge of the modulus of a number, the method itself may inspire students to try to work out why it might work. See:<br><br>http://www.aaamath.com/div66_x7.htm |

**Alternative approach**

Use a 10 by 10 or a 12 by 12 multiplication grid (showing all the times tables from 1 to 10 or 12). Ask students to find all the answers for, say, the 6 times table – these are the first 10 or 12 multiples of 6. Ask students to find all the pairs of numbers that give the same answer, say 12 – these are the factor pairs of 12. Use a table with three columns labeled *Number, Multiples* and *Factors* to list the factors and multiples for given numbers up to 10 or 12. Ask how to find factors and multiples for numbers over 12.

**Checkpoint**

Which number is divisible by all of the numbers 2, 3, 4, 5, 6 and 7?    (**c** is correct)

a  300
b  360
c  420
d  540

**Starter** – Codewords

Write a coded message on the board, for example, ITEEOEOKOIHSHRHMWRTNGT.

Students decode it by writing the second half of the message under the first half (11 × 2 array) and then read pairs of letters downwards, working across to the right. [Answer: Is there homework tonight.]

Another possible message is:

IOEAHMTCLVMTEAIS        [I love mathematics]

## Teaching notes

Explain to students that a multiple is a number that appears in a times table and give examples. Explain that we can list multiples by writing out the numbers in a times table. Mini whiteboards can be used for quick responses to requests for multiples.

Explain to students that a factor is a number which divides exactly *into* another number, so, for example 6 is a factor of 12. Explain that all factors of a number can be listed as 'factor pairs' (such as 1 × 6, 2 × 3 for the factor pairs of 6) or as a list 1, 2, 3, 6 which can be found from factor pairs.

Students should then practise writing factor pairs and lists of factors.

Explain that a prime number has only two factors, 1 and itself and identify prime numbers from the list of their factors.

Discuss and practise the five divisibility tests given in the students' book. Check divisions using a calculator.

## Plenary

Students use their mini whiteboards to give the factors of a number, the first few multiples of a number and the prime numbers below, say, 10. They say whether a given number is divisibly by 2, 3, 4, 5 or 10.

## Exercise commentary

**Questions 1** to **4** – These questions ensure that students are secure with the key words 'multiple' and 'factor'.

**Questions 5** and **6** – These questions check students' ability to use the divisibility tests.

**Question 7** – This question is suitable for class discussion.

**Questions 8** and **9** – Recap on the meanings of 'factor', 'multiple' and 'prime'.

**Question 10a** – Refer students to their 'times tables'.

**Question 10b** – Students don't need to divide 500 by 3 to answer this question.

## Answers

1  a  3, 6, 9, 12, 15, 18        b  7, 14, 21, 28, 35, 42
   c  10, 20, 30, 40, 50, 60
2  a  1, 2, 5, 10        b  1, 2, 4, 8, 16
   c  1, 5, 7, 35        d  1, 2, 3, 4, 6, 9, 12, 18, 36
   e  1, 2, 3, 4, 6, 8, 12, 16, 24, 48
   f  1, 2, 4, 5, 10, 20, 25, 50, 100
3  No
4  No
5  a  Yes        b  No        c  No        d  Yes
   e  Yes        f  No
6  a (1005) , c (2005) , e (4035) , f (1 000 005)
7  a  2 + 5 + 0 = 7.  7 is not divisible by 3, so 250 is not divisible by 3.
   b  A and C are true.
8  a  1, 2, 3, 6, 9, 18.  18 is not prime.
   b  1, 19.  19 is prime
   c  1, 3, 9, 27.  27 is not prime.
   d  1, 3, 5, 15, 67, 201, 335, 1005.  1005 is not prime.
   e  1, 2, 4, 23, 46, 92.  92 is not prime.
   f  1, 3, 17, 51.  51 is not prime.
   g  1, 31.  31 is prime.
   h  1, 2, 3, 6, 7, 14, 21, 42.  42 is not prime.
   i  1, 41.  41 is prime.
9  a  7, 35        b  6, 8        c  7, 17
10 a  i  30        ii  60        iii  70
   b  i  No. 500 is not divisible by 3.
      ii  You would need 1 more soldier.

## Objectives

- Use multiples, factors, highest common factors, lowest common multiples and primes. (L5)
- Find the prime factor decomposition of a number. (L5)

| Key ideas | Resources |
|---|---|
| 1  A prime number has only the number 1 and itself as factors. Any other number can be written as the product of its prime factors.<br>2  Two numbers will have factors and multiples in common. | ⊕ Factors and primes (1032)<br>    LCM (1034)<br>    HCF (1044)<br>Counters and calculators<br>100 squares<br>10 by 10 or 12 by 12 multiplication grids<br>Mini whiteboards |

| Simplification | Extension |
|---|---|
| Use multiplication times tables as the introduction to multiples of numbers up to 10 or 12.<br><br>Use multiplication tables in reverse to find factor pairs but make sure students know this will not find the larger factors of numbers.<br><br>Use lists of the multiples or factors of numbers to find the lowest common multiple and the highest common factor. Do not rush into prime factorisation too early and do not use indices to express the product of the prime factors. | Students explore further divisibility tests using research on the Internet. Ask them to use these tests to find whether certain numbers are divisible by, for example, 6, 9 or 25. |

| Literacy | Links |
|---|---|
| Two new diagrams are used in this lesson: the factor tree and the Venn diagram. Like real trees, the prime factor tree can grow in different ways depending on how the tree 'sprouts' when new branches are formed. The eventual 'fruits' on a full-grown tree (that is, the prime factors) are the same, no matter how the tree has grown. | Encrypting credit card information relies on the difficulty of finding the prime factors of large numbers. Encryption companies have to keep up with new methods for factorising numbers and until 2007, the company RSA offered prizes worth thousands of pounds to anyone who managed to find the two prime factors of certain given numbers. Some of the numbers have never been factorised. |

## Alternative approach

Counters can be used to find the smaller prime numbers. Give pairs of students a pile of counters. They take two, three, four, five, … counters, in turn, and arrange them into as many rectangular arrays as possible. They note the size of the arrays. For example, four counters give $1 \times 4$, $2 \times 2$, $4 \times 1$, which gives the list of all factors of 4 as 1, 2, 4. However, five counters give only $1 \times 5$, so 5 is a prime number.

A method for finding prime numbers up to 100 is to use 'The Sieve of Eratosthenes'. Take a 100 square and cross out the number 1. Shake the sieve and all multiples of 2 (but not 2 itself) fall out, so cross them off. Take the least surviving number, 3. Shake the sieve so all multiples of 3 (but not 3 itself) fall out; cross them off. Take the least surviving number, 5, and repeat. Continue until no other numbers fall out. The survivors are the primes.

## Checkpoint

Use a Venn diagram to find the HCF and LCM of the numbers 1260 and 2310.    (HCF = 210, LCM = 13 860)

**Starter** – What is my number?

Students respond on their mini whiteboards. They will need time for questions of this type; for example,

My number is a multiple of 6. It has a factor of 4. It is less than 20. [12]

My number is a multiple of 3. It is also a multiple of 2. It is less than 10. [6]

My number is a factor of 36. It does not have a factor of 2. It is greater than 5. [9]

## Teaching notes

Remind students that a prime number is a number which has only two factors: one and the number itself. Emphasise that 1 is *not* a prime number since it has only one factor. Ask students to write down a list of the prime numbers which are less than 20 (that is: 2, 3, 5, 7, 11, 13, 17, 19) and agree them. Explain that we begin to tell if a number is prime by dividing it by, say, 2, 3, 5, and 10. Remind them of the divisibility tests from the previous lesson. Use mini whiteboards to recap the divisibility tests.

Explain how a factor tree can be used to 'decompose' (or break down) numbers which are not prime into their 'prime factors'. Show how to express the number as a product of its prime factors using indices.

The HCF and LCM of two numbers can be found by:

• *either* writing a list of all the factors of each number and comparing the lists;
• *or* constructing a factor tree and, from it, a Venn diagram of the prime factors.

## Plenary

Summarise the major learning objectives by asking quick-fire questions with students responding on mini whiteboards; for example, "Is 8 a factor of 32?", "Is 8 a multiple of 2?", "Is 8 a prime number?", "What is the lowest prime number greater than 8?", "What are the first three multiples of 8?", "What are the factors of 8?", "What is the highest common factor of 8 and 10?".

## Exercise commentary

**Question 1** – The method is to use factor trees. Students should know that it doesn't matter how the trees 'grow', the final result is the same.

**Questions 2** and **3** – These questions are suitable for whole-class discussion. Students can either use lists of factors and multiples, or find the prime factors using factor trees.

**Questions 4** and **5** – Students could use lists of factors and multiples but should be encouraged to use prime factors and Venn diagrams.

**Question 6** – The multiples of 30, 40 and 50 give the times at which the guards report to the control centre. These three lists allow the common times to be selected.

**Question 7** – This question is suitable for whole-class discussion.

---

## Answers

**1**
a $2 \times 2 \times 2 \times 3 = 24$    b $3 \times 3 \times 5 = 45$
c $2 \times 2 \times 3 \times 3 = 36$    d $2 \times 2 \times 2 \times 2 \times 5 = 80$
e $2 \times 5 \times 5 = 50$    f $2 \times 2 \times 3 \times 5 = 60$
g $2 \times 2 \times 5 \times 5 = 100$    h $2 \times 2 \times 2 \times 3 \times 3 = 72$
i $2 \times 5 \times 5 \times 5 = 250$

**2** Zach is right because the HCF is the product of the shared prime factors, so the HCF of 75 and 250 is $5 \times 5 = 25$.

**3** Jack is right because the LCM is the product of the shared and not shared prime factors. So the LCM is $2 \times 2 \times 3 \times 3 = 36$.

**4**
a $2 \times 2 \times 3 = 12$    b $2 \times 2 \times 3 \times 3 = 36$
c $2 \times 2 \times 2 \times 7 = 56$    d $3 \times 3 \times 5 = 45$

**5**
a $2 \times 2 \times 3 \times 3 \times 5 = 180$    b $2 \times 2 \times 3 \times 5 \times 7 = 420$

**6** 600 minutes = 10 hours

**7** Check Venn diagrams
The products are the same

## Objectives

- Use place value to place decimals, write decimals and order decimals (L5)
- Estimate decimals from number lines (L5)

| Key ideas | Resources |
|---|---|
| 1 Find decimals on number lines | ⊞ Ordering decimals (1072) |
| 2 Write decimals using place value considerations | |
| 3 Order lists of decimals | |
| 4 Compare decimals using inequality signs | |
| 5 Estimate decimals from number lines | |

| Simplification | Extension |
|---|---|
| When comparing and/or ordering decimals, concentrate on decimals to one decimal place and ensure students understand the value represented by this decimal place. When ordering decimals of this type, the magnitude of the tenths digit should tell them where the number lies relative to the others in the list. | Students can be given lists of decimals to more than two decimal places and/or lists that are closer together in value such as 0.11, 0.101, 0.1, 0.111, 0.011, 0.001. Working through the lesson independently without guidance will also encourage more careful thought and stretch more able students. |

| Literacy | Links |
|---|---|
| Place value<br>Inequality | Question **6** highlights an area where ordering and comparing decimals is an important skill. Not being able to order the times of runners crossing the line in a race would mean that the finishing order could not be determined. In the 100 m final, working to hundredths of a second is vital. Is it so vital for longer distance races? Students could investigate recorded results for other Olympic events and look at the degrees of accuracy that are used.<br><br>http://www.olympic.org/olympic-results/london-2012/athletics |

## Alternative approach

Students could be given decimal numbers on cards and asked to work in pairs to discuss the size of the numbers and order them. Having cards means that they can swap them around as often as necessary to get the correct order and it encourages communication between the students.

## Checkpoint

Order the following decimals, smallest to largest:

0.6, 0.64, 0.54, 0.06, 0.61, 0.56                    (0.06, 0.54, 0.56, 0.6, 0.61, 0.64)

**Starter** – Decimal mental addition

Give a starting number to the students, for example 2. Ask them to successively add on five decimals given to one decimal place, in their heads (or using mini-whiteboards if necessary). What is the final number? An example: What is $2 + 0.1 + 0.3 + 0.6 + 1.2 + 1.4$? (5.6)

**Teaching notes**

The first student task is to read from a one decimal place scale and this can be worked through as a class, perhaps using a projected example. When the students are then asked to write down decimals using the place value, ensure sufficient examples are provided to model the structure of the place value system.

The second key task is to order decimals as a list and then using inequality symbols. Useful class discussion could be about the nature of the inequality signs, the comparison of the digits in various places and the use of 'stacking' decimals in a table such as that in question **3**.

The final task is to estimate the position of a decimal on a number line. Refer back to the examples and/or question **1** to encourage students to 'see' how far the number lies along the number line.

**Plenary**

Give students a new list of decimals (to one and two decimal places) and ask them to order them. They can use mini-whiteboards here and it should be quick to check the learning from observing their answers.

**Exercise commentary**

**Question 1**– Students read from the scale and record the decimal numbers. All numbers are to one decimal place.

**Questions 2** and **3** – Students are given place value considerations to first write decimals and then order a list of decimals.

**Question 4** – Ensure students are familiar with the inequality notation. None of the pairs should be particularly hard to decide the order.

**Question 5** – Here a ruler might be useful to measure the line and then approximate how far the arrows lie along the interval.

**Question 6** – An application of decimal ordering which can be extended (see **Extension**).

**Question 7** – An open-ended investigation that can generate good class discussion and encourage students to think more deeply about what decimals actually are.

---

**Answers**

**1**  **A** 2.2  **B** 2.7  **C** 2.9  **D** 3.6
   **E** 1.9  **F** 3.2

**2**  **a** 1.3  **b** 6.8  **c** 7.1  **d** 0.9
   **e** 13.6  **f** 25.5

**3**  0.9, 5.2, 6.1, 8.3, 9.0, 10.0, 12.3

**4**  **a** >  **b** <  **c** <  **d** >
   **e** >  **f** >  **g** <  **h** <
   **i** >  **j** >  **k** <  **l** <

**5**  **a** A = 1.7, B = 2.8  **b** A = 2.8, B = 0.6
   **c** A = 0.6, B = 0.8

**6**  9.63, 9.75, 9.79, 9.8, 9.88, 9.94, 9.98, 11.99

**7**  **a, b** Any decimal between 0.9 and 1
   **c** Infinite

| Key outcomes | Quick check |
|---|---|
| Multiply and divide by powers of 10. L6 | Work out<br>**a** $340 \times 0.1$ (34)      **b** $0.762 \times 100$ (76.2)      **c** $451 \div 0.1$ (4510) |
| Round whole numbers and decimals. L5 | Round to the given degree of accuracy<br>**a** 367.2 nearest 10 (370) **b** 0.1256 one d.p. (0.1) **c** 7.58 whole number (8) |
| Work out calculations using BIDMAS. L5 | Work out<br>**a** $3 \times 4 + 7 \times 8$ (68)      **b**      $(2 + 3)^2 - 4 \times 5$ (1) |
| Identify multiples, factors and prime numbers. L5 | **a** Write down the first four multiples of 7 (7, 14, 21, 28)<br>**b** Write down the factors of 16 (1, 2, 4, 8, 16) |
| Use product of prime factors to find HCF and LCM. L5 | **a** Work out the HCF of 16 and 28 (4)<br>**b** Work out the LCM of 25 and 40 (200) |
| Order decimals. L5 | Write these decimals in order, smallest to largest:<br>0.11, 0.101, 0.1, 0.111, 1.01 (0.1, 0.101, 0.11, 0.111, 1.01) |

## ⊕ MyMaths extra support

| Lesson/online homework | | | Description |
|---|---|---|---|
| Negative numbers 1 | 1069 | L3 | Extending beyond zero when counting in steps. Understanding and ordering negative numbers. Calculating temperature differences across 0 degrees. |
| Negative numbers 2 | 1068 | L5 | Negative sums in the context of temperature |
| Decimal place value | 1076 | L4 | Use hundred grids to compare the sizes of decimals |

# My Review

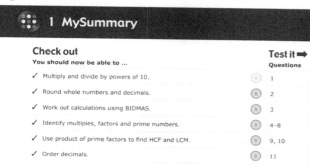

## 1 MySummary

### Check out
**You should now be able to ...**

**Test it ➡**
Questions

✓ Multiply and divide by powers of 10.  •1

✓ Round whole numbers and decimals.  •2

✓ Work out calculations using BIDMAS.  •3

✓ Identify multiples, factors and prime numbers.  •4-8

✓ Use product of prime factors to find HCF and LCM.  •9, 10

✓ Order decimals.  •11

| Language | Meaning | Example |
|---|---|---|
| Rounding | Writing a number with fewer non-zero digits. It makes numbers easier to work with. | 123 ≈ 120 to the nearest 10<br>6.75 ≈ 6.8 to one decimal place |
| BIDMAS | BIDMAS helps you to remember the order of operations: brackets, indices, division, multiplication, addition and subtraction. | $(4 \times 3 - 2)^2 + 3 = 103$<br>$4 \times 3 - 2^2 + 3 = 11$ |
| Factor | A number which divides exactly into another number. | 1, 3, 9 and 27 are all factors of 27.<br>$27 = 1 \times 27 = 3 \times 9$ |
| Highest common factor (HCF) | The highest number that is a factor of two or more numbers. | The HCF of 24 and 36 is 12. |
| Lowest common multiple (LCM) | The smallest number that is a multiple of two or more numbers. | The LCM of 24 and 36 is 72. |
| Multiple | A multiple of a number is a number in its times table. | 12 and 18 are multiples of 6.<br>$12 = 2 \times 6$, $18 = 3 \times 6$ |
| Prime | A prime number has two factors. | 2, 3, 5, 7, 11 ... are prime.<br>1 is *not* a prime number |

16  **Number**  Whole numbers and decimals

## 1 MyReview

1 Calculate
a  78 ÷ 10  b  325 ÷ 100
c  9 × 0.1  d  6 × 0.01
e  0.7 ÷ 0.01  f  170 × 0.01
g  35 ÷ 0.1  h  0.92 × 0.1

2 Round 6096.5
a  to the nearest whole number
b  to the nearest 10
c  to the nearest 100
d  to the nearest 1000

3 Calculate these using the correct order of operations.
a  $23 + 5 \times 2$
b  $24 - 8 \div 4$
c  $(25 + 7) \times 3$
d  $65 - 3 \times (4 + 1)$
e  $2 \times 4^2 + 3 \div 3$
f  $\dfrac{(2 + 1)^2}{15 - 4 \times 6}$

4 Which of the following numbers are factors of 8?
1  2  3  8  12  16  24

5 Which of the following numbers are multiples of 8?
1  2  3  8  12  16  24

6 Use divisibility tests to answer these questions and explain your answer.
a  Is 3 a factor of 564?
b  Is 610 a multiple of 4?
c  Is 103 a prime number?
d  Is 6745 divisible by 5?

7 Write each of these numbers as a product of its prime factors.
a  42  b  175

8 Which of the following numbers are prime numbers?
1  3  6  7  9

9 Find the highest common factor of each pair of numbers.
a  18 and 45  b  96 and 180

10 Find the lowest common multiple of each pair of numbers.
a  11 and 8  b  28 and 70

11 Put these decimals in order from smallest to largest.
a  3.5  3.2  3.0  4
b  0.1  0.01  0.12  0.21
c  9.8  9.08  8.99  9.91
d  0.8  0.78  0.09  0.81

### What next?

| Score | |
|---|---|
| 0 – 4 | Your knowledge of this topic is still developing. To improve look at Formative test: 3A-1; MyMaths: 1003, 1004, 1027, 1032, 1034, 1035, 1044, 1072, 1167 and 1392 |
| 5 – 9 | You are gaining a secure knowledge of this topic. To improve look at InvisiPen: 111, 112, 114, 124, 171, 172 and 173 |
| 10 – 11 | You have mastered this topic. Well done, you are ready to progress! |

● **MyMaths**.co.uk

17

## Question commentary

**Question 1** – Students can think of multiplying by a negative power of 10 as dividing by the positive power.

**Question 2** – Remind students the rule for rounding fives.

**Question 3** – Parts **d**, **e** and **f** are likely to cause the most issues here. Encourage students to show stages of working.

**Questions 4 to 10** – Students may need reminding of the key definitions and divisibility tests. When working out prime factors, encourage the use of factor trees and then Venn diagrams for finding HCFs and LCMs.

**Question 11** – Students may find a number line helpful to visualize the placement of the decimals.

## Answers

1  a  7.8  b  3.25  c  0.9  d  0.06
   e  7  f  1.7  g  350  h  0.092

2  a  6097  b  6100  c  6100  d  6000

3  a  33  b  22  c  96  d  50
   e  33  f  -1

4  1, 2, 8

5  8, 16, 24

6  a  3 is a factor of 564 because 5 + 6 + 4 = 15, which is divisible by 3, so 564 is divisible by 3.
   b  610 is not a multiple of 4 because 610 ÷ 2 = 305, which is odd.
   c  103 is only divisible by 1 and 103, so 103 is prime.
   d  6745 ends in 5 so it is divisible by 5.

7  a  $2 \times 3 \times 7$  b  $5 \times 5 \times 7$

8  3, 7

9  a  9  b  12

10 a  88  b  140

11 a  3.0, 3.2, 3.5, 4
   b  0.01, 0.1, 0.12, 0.21
   c  8.99, 9.08, 9.8, 9.91
   d  0.09, 0.78, 0.8, 0.81

# 1 MyPractice

**1a**

**1** Find the answer to each of these multiplication problems.
- **a** $3.2 \times 100$
- **b** $4.63 \times 10$
- **c** $0.72 \times 1000$
- **d** $0.092 \times 10$
- **e** $37.6 \times 100$
- **f** $4.9 \times 1000$
- **g** $0.3 \times 10$
- **h** $0.476 \times 100$
- **i** $32.7 \times 1000$

**2** Find the answer to each of these division problems.
- **a** $21 \div 10$
- **b** $3.7 \div 10$
- **c** $6.21 \div 10$
- **d** $37 \div 100$
- **e** $2.9 \div 100$
- **f** $4.7 \div 1000$
- **g** $6.92 \div 10$
- **h** $63.7 \div 100$
- **i** $47.9 \div 1000$

**1b**

**3** Round each of these numbers to the nearest whole number.
- **a** 2.8
- **b** 7.4
- **c** 11.9
- **d** 15.5
- **e** 29.4
- **f** 0.3

**4** Round each number to the nearest 10.
- **a** 23
- **b** 35
- **c** 46
- **d** 98
- **e** 104
- **f** 225

**5** Round each number to the nearest 100.
- **a** 55
- **b** 236
- **c** 250
- **d** 43
- **e** 661
- **f** 919

**1c**

**6** Calculate these, remembering the BIDMAS rule.
- **a** $3 \times 3 + 4 =$
- **b** $12 - 8 \div 2 =$
- **c** $3 + 3 \times 4 =$
- **d** $3 \times 4 + 9 \div 3 =$
- **e** $25 - 5 \times 5 + 2 =$
- **f** $5 + 3^2 \times 2 =$
- **g** $(4 + 9) - 6 \div 3^2 =$
- **h** $4^2 + (6 - 2) \times 5 =$
- **i** $8 + (8 - 3) + (6 + 2) \times 2 =$
- **j** $20 \div 2^2 + (12 - 7) - 3^2 =$

**1d**

**7** List the first six multiples of 7.

**8** Jane says that 6 is a factor of 84.

Anita says that 6 is a factor of 84, because 7 is a factor of 84.

Who is correct?

Explain your answer.

---

**1d**

**9 a** Test these numbers to see if they are divisible by 3.
- **i** 21
- **ii** 28
- **iii** 32
- **iv** 84
- **v** 96
- **vi** 1011

**b** Which of the numbers in part **a** are divisible by 2?

**10** Use divisibility tests to say whether or not these numbers are prime.
- **a** 2
- **b** 18
- **c** 29
- **d** 81
- **e** 87
- **f** 58
- **g** 51
- **h** 41
- **i** 43
- **j** 20970

**1e**

**11** Copy and complete these diagrams and then write each number as a product of its prime factors.

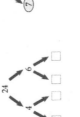

**12 a** Copy and complete these diagrams.

**b** Find the HCF of 24 and 56.

**1f**

**13** Put these numbers in order, starting with the smallest.

1.32, 13.2, 0.13, 0.2, 2.1, 0.5, 3, 0.001.

🔴 **MyMaths**.co.uk

## Question commentary

**Questions 1** and **2** – Remind students to move the digits of the number left or right the appropriate number of places.

**Question 3** to **5** – Students may need reminding of the rule for rounding fives.

**Question 6** – Encourage students to show their working out, step-by-step, in order to get the correct answers.

**Questions 7** to **10** – Check that students understand the terminology used. Question **8** is particularly good for class discussion.

**Questions 11** and **12** – The framework for these questions is already in place through the copy and complete structure. A Venn diagram could be used for question **12b**.

**Question 13** – A number line could be used to help students visualise the placement of the numbers.

## Answers

**1**  a  320   b  46.3   c  720   d  0.92
   e  3760   f  4900   g  3   h  47.6
   i  32700

**2**  a  2.1   b  0.37   c  0.621   d  0.37
   e  0.029   f  0.0047   g  0.692   h  0.637
   i  0.0479

**3**  a  3   b  7   c  12   d  16
   e  29   f  0

**4**  a  20   b  40   c  50   d  100
   e  100   f  230

**5**  a  100   b  200   c  300   d  0
   e  700   f  900

**6**  a  13   b  8   c  15   d  15
   e  2   f  23   g  16   h  36
   i  29   j  20

**7**  7, 14, 21, 28, 35, 42

**8**  6 and 7 are both factors of 84, so Jane is correct. Anita is correct that 7 is a factor of 84, but she is wrong saying that for this reason 6 is not a factor.

**9**  a  21, 84, 96, 1011 are all divisible by 3 because the sum of each of their digits is a multiple of 3. 28 and 32 are not multiples of 3.
   b  28, 32, 82, 96 are divisible by 2.

**10**  a  Prime   b  Not prime
    c  Prime   d  Not prime
    e  Not prime   f  Not prime
    g  Not prime   h  Prime
    i  Prime   j  Not prime

**11**  a  $42 = 7 \times 3 \times 2$   b  $36 = 2 \times 2 \times 3 \times 3$
    c  $58 = 2 \times 29$   d  $125 = 5 \times 5 \times 5$

**12**  a  Check students diagrams
    b  8

**13**  0.001, 0.13, 0.2, 0.5, 1.32, 2.1, 3, 13.2

## Learning outcomes

**G1** Derive and apply formulae to calculate and solve problems involving: perimeter and area of triangles, parallelograms, trapezia, volume of cuboids (including cubes) and other prisms (including cylinders) (L5/6)

**G2** Calculate and solve problems involving: perimeters of 2D shapes (including circles), areas of circles and composite shapes (L6)

**N12** Use standard units of mass, length, time, money and other measures, including with decimal quantities (L5)

## Introduction

The chapter starts by looking at converting between metric units of length, capacity and mass before covering similar content involving imperial units. Areas of rectangles, triangles and parallelograms including compound shapes are covered before the final section on the circumference of a circle.

The introduction discusses Usain Bolt and his world record 100 metre time. It compares his time to that of some of the fastest land animals and points out that his average (or even top) speed is nothing compared to these creatures. It is interesting to note that his 200 metre world record was completed at almost the same average speed (10.42 m/s as opposed to 10.44 m/s). Michael Johnson's 400 metre world record of 43.18 seconds implies an average speed of 9.26 m/s which over a much longer distance is still pretty fast!

Students could be invited to work out the average speed of some other athletic world records. A table of these records can be found at:

http://www.iaaf.org/records/by-category/world-records

## Prior knowledge

Students should already know how to…

- Calculate the perimeter and area of simple 2D shapes
- Understand basic units of measure

## Starter problem

The starter problem requires students to maximise the area enclosed by a shape of perimeter 60 metres. They will almost certainly begin by setting up some simple rectangles such as the one hinted at in the example.

A 10 metre by 20 metre rectangle encloses an area of $200 \text{ m}^2$. They should be able to work out fairly quickly that the maximum area possible with a rectangle is actually when it is a square of side 15 metres.

$15 \times 15 = 225 \text{ m}^2$.

Beyond the scope of this problem, the area can be further increased by increasing the number of sides of the regular polygon while retaining the 60 metre perimeter. In fact, the limiting area (hence the overall maximum possible) is achievable as the number of sides approaches infinity (i.e. when it is a circle). This maximum area is equal to $286.4788976… \text{ m}^2$.

## Resources

### MyMaths

| | | | | | |
|---|---|---|---|---|---|
| Metric conversion | 1061 | Area of rectangles | 1084 | Circumference of a circle | 1088 |
| Converting measures | 1091 | Area of a parallelogram | 1108 | Area of a triangle | 1129 |

### Online assessment

| | |
|---|---|
| Chapter test | 3A–2 |
| Formative test | 3A–2 |
| Summative test | 3A–2 |

### InvisiPen solutions

| | | | |
|---|---|---|---|
| Area of shapes made from rectangles | | | 313 |
| Area of a triangle | 314 | Area of a parallelogram | 315 |
| Metric measures | 332 | | |
| Metric and imperial measures | | | 333 |
| Circumference of a circle | 351 | | |

# Topic scheme

Teaching time = 6 lessons/2 weeks

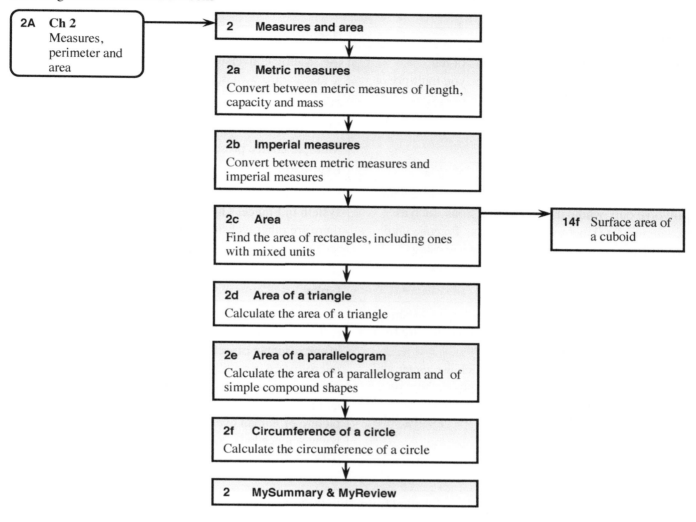

**2A   Ch 2**
Measures, perimeter and area

**2      Measures and area**

**2a    Metric measures**
Convert between metric measures of length, capacity and mass

**2b    Imperial measures**
Convert between metric measures and imperial measures

**2c    Area**
Find the area of rectangles, including ones with mixed units

**14f   Surface area of a cuboid**

**2d    Area of a triangle**
Calculate the area of a triangle

**2e    Area of a parallelogram**
Calculate the area of a parallelogram and of simple compound shapes

**2f    Circumference of a circle**
Calculate the circumference of a circle

**2      MySummary & MyReview**

# Differentiation

| Student book 3A        20 – 37 | Student book 3B        16 – 33 | Student book 3C        16 – 29 |
|---|---|---|
| Convert between metric and metric and imperial units<br>Calculate the areas of simple 2D shapes including triangles and parallelograms<br>Find the circumference of a circle | Covert between metric units and between metric and imperial units<br>Calculate the area of 2D shapes including compound shapes<br>Find the circumference and area of a circle<br>Work with compound measures | Convert between units of measure<br>Understand dimension<br>Calculate lengths and areas of 2D shapes<br>Work with compound measures |

## Objectives

- Convert one metric unit to another.

(L5)

## Key ideas

1 Metric units are based on powers of ten.
2 To convert between metric units, you multiply or divide by 10, 100 or 1000.

## Resources

⊞ Metric conversion     (1061)

A place value grid from Th (1000) to th ($\frac{1}{1000}$)

Objects to estimate mass and capacity

Mini whiteboards

Multiple choice presentation

## Simplification

Restrict examples in the first instance to those which involve only whole number conversions, such as changing 3000 metres to kilometres. Practise until confident before moving to conversions using decimals, such as 300 metres to kilometres.

## Extension

Use the Internet to research the creation of the metric system in France. This website gives very full details; there are other websites too.

http://en.wikipedia.org/wiki/History_of_the_metric_system

## Literacy

The word *metre* comes from a Greek word meaning 'measure'. The prefixes 'milli-' and 'centi-' are from Latin; the prefix 'kilo-' is from Greek.

Beware the American spellings which use *meter* and *liter*. In British English, a 'meter' is a machine for measuring quantities of something, such as a gas meter. British English does not use the spelling 'liter'.

## Links

Scientists use a unit called a 'micrometre' (sometimes called a 'micron') to measure the thickness or diameter of microscopic objects. There are one thousand micrometres in a millimetre and the abbreviation for a micrometre is μm. Human hair is about 100 μm wide and red blood cells are 7 μm in diameter. There is a picture of human eye tissue in clusters of 50–200 μm at www.sciencedaily.com/releases/2007/06/070624121236.htm

## Alternative approach

Use a grid of place values with headings labelled from Th (1000) to th ($\frac{1}{1000}$). Discuss how the grid can be used to change from one metric unit to another.

Measure the heights of students in centimetres and use the grid to write the heights in millimetres and in metres.

## Checkpoint

1 How many millimetres are there in 2.7 km?     (270 000)
2 How many kg are there in 225 g?     (0.225)

## Starter – Estimate

Students estimate in centimetres the lengths, widths and heights of objects in the room and then convert the measurements into millimetres and into metres.

Repeat with the masses of objects in kilograms and the capacity of containers in litres. Convert to grams and millilitres.

## Teaching notes

Students suggest units of measurement of length, mass and capacity. Form two lists, metric units and imperial units, and explain the difference between them. Explain that it is often necessary to convert between units of measure, both within each list and between imperial and metric.

With the whole class, solve simple problems in context, such as "You start to bake with a full bag of flour weighing 2 kg. You use 450 grams. How much do you have left (in grams and in kilograms)?" [Answer: 1550 grams; 1.55 kg]

## Plenary

Students can use mini whiteboards for a quick-fire quiz with the whole class.

Start with multiple-choice questions and then ask students to find the answer to questions. For example, "Is 2.3 metres equal to 23 cm, 230 cm or 0.23 cm?"; "I run 600 metres. What is this in kilometres?"; "You drink 200 ml from a 2-litre bottle. How much is left?"

## Exercise commentary

**Question 1** – Make sure that students are multiplying or dividing by 10, 100 or 1000 appropriately.

**Question 2** – Routine conversions but in an applied situation. Ensure students multiply rather than divide by 100.

**Question 3** – This question is suitable for class discussion and further examples could be given, or asked for from the students.

**Question 4** – It is debatable whether it is easier to work in kilograms or grams. Discuss both ways with students.

**Question 5** – This is a two-stage problem, requiring multiplication and subtraction. The subtraction is best done by adding on to reach the required total.

**Question 6** – This is a challenging question. Finding the total volume of the drinks is the key to the problem. A calculator may be needed.

## Answers

| | | | | | | | | |
|---|---|---|---|---|---|---|---|---|
| 1 | a | 650 cm | b | 150 cl | c | 45 mm | d | 2300 mm |
| | e | 190 ml | f | 2.4 kg | g | 4.5 tonnes | h | 958 ml |
| | i | 100 g | | | | | | |

| | | | | | | | | |
|---|---|---|---|---|---|---|---|---|
| 2 | a | 150 cm | b | 450 cm | c | 50 cm | d | 750 cm |
| | e | 125 cm | f | 75 cm | | | | |

| | | | | | | |
|---|---|---|---|---|---|---|
| 3 | a | 100 g | b | 33 cl | c | 600 km |

4   20 packs

5   100 metres

6   2.1 bottles

## Objectives

- Know rough metric equivalents of imperial measures in common use. (L5)

| Key ideas | Resources |
|---|---|
| 1 There are imperial units for length, mass (weight) and capacity.<br>2 The conversions between imperial and metric units are not exact. | ⊞ Converting measures    (1091)<br>Mini whiteboards |

| Simplification | Extension |
|---|---|
| There are two situations to practise:<br><br>- converting between imperial units;<br>- converting between metric and imperial units.<br><br>Initially, convert between imperial units, such as inches to feet and ounces to pounds.<br><br>Later, convert between metric and imperial units. Note that 5 miles is approximately 8 km; in the student book this is given as 1 mile ≈ 1.6 km. Initially, approximate 1 litre to 2 pints for mental calculations, but use 1 litre to 1.75 pints with a calculator. | Ask students to draw up a more detailed conversion chart to include imperial measures such as furlong and hundredweight. They could invent situations where these conversions are needed.<br><br>Ask students to research different imperial measures, for example: an acre, a rod, a perch, a firkin. Get them to look into the origin of these types of measure and suggest why some of them are still in use today while others are 'forgotten'. They could also look at old paper sizes and wine bottle sizes. |

| Literacy | Links |
|---|---|
| The word 'pound' is used for money and an imperial measure of mass. The word has travelled around much of western Europe over the years, originally coming from a Latin word meaning 'weight'. A pound by weight of silver gave rise to the use of 'pound' as a unit of money.<br><br>The symbols £ and lb are both from the Latin word 'libra' meaning 'pound'. | In 1983, an Air Canada Boeing 767 ran out of fuel in mid-flight due to confusion between metric and imperial units. The amount of fuel needed for the flight had been calculated manually and, although 22 300 kilograms of fuel was required, only 22 300 pounds (approximately 10 115 kilograms) was put in the fuel tanks. The pilot had to glide the plane to land at an abandoned airbase. The news report about the incident, which came to be known as the Gimli Glider, can be found at www.cbc.ca/archives (search for 'Gimli Glider'). |

## Alternative approach

For conversion between metric and imperial units, draw a line with imperial units marked on one side and metric units on the other. As a simple example, use a ruler with centimetres on one edge and inches on the other edge. Draw a line 10 inches long, marking each inch. Then, use the centimetre scale on the other edge to mark the other side of the line at centimetre intervals. Similar lines can be drawn for pints to litres and pounds to kilograms.

## Checkpoint

Using the conversion approximation 1 inch = 2.5 cm, what is the difference between 55.25 cm and 19.5 inches?

(6.5 cm)

## Starter – Metric match

Ask students to find equivalent pairs in the following.

300 m,    120 cl,   0.45 t,    3000 mm,    4.5 kg,
3 m,      120 ml,   0.3 km,    12 cl,      450 kg,
1.2 litres,   4500 g

[Answers: 300 m = 0.3 km; 120 cl = 1.2 litres;
0.45 t = 450 kg; 3000 mm = 3 m; 4.5 kg = 4500 g;
120 ml = 12 cl]

Extend by including extra quantities as red herrings and ask students to make matches for them.

## Teaching notes

Explain some of the background history of imperial units of measure. Explain the importance of 'standard' units of measure.

Ask if they know other non-metric units, such as 'furlong' and 'dram'. Ask students to give examples of where imperial measures are still used today and of imperial equivalents that they know. Ensure students have a full list of metric–imperial conversions. Explain that there are various approximate equivalents for converting between metric and imperial units.

Students use this list to answer simple questions, such as "How many pints in 2 litres?", displaying their answers on mini whiteboards.

## Plenary

Have a quick-fire quiz including true/false, multiple-choice and open questions which students answer on their mini whiteboards. Discuss answers where necessary.

## Exercise commentary

**Questions 1 to 3** – Students should refer to the table of conversions.

**Question 4** – Students should find and convert the total of the masses in ounces first before adding on the mass in pounds at the end.

**Questions 5 and 6** – These questions test students' skill with approximate conversions between imperial and metric units. Students should refer to the list of approximate conversions.

## Answers

1  a   15 feet           b   72 inches
   c   48 ounces         d   48 pints
   e   70 pounds         f   36 inches

2  6 tiles

3  40 bottles

4  5 pounds

5  a   10 inches         b   3 kilograms
   c   4 feet            d   100 g
   e   6 litres          f   3 stone
   g   6 kilometres      h   4 gallons

6  Accept reasonable approximations
   4 pounds ≈ 2 kilograms
   5 pints ≈ 2.5 litres
   3.5 yards ≈ 3.5 metres
   6 inches ≈ 15 centimetres
   10 ounces ≈ 300 grams

## Objectives

- Know and use the formula for the area of a rectangle. (L5)

(L5)

| Key ideas | Resources |
|---|---|
| 1  Area is a measure of space inside any 2D flat shape.<br>2  Area is measured in square units using $^2$.<br>3  The area of a rectangle is found by multiplying its length by its width. | ⊞  Area of rectangles (1084)<br>Plastic sheets with a centimetre-squared grid<br>Centimetre-squared paper<br>Mini whiteboards |

| Simplification | Extension |
|---|---|
| Provide students with rectangles drawn on square grids for them to count the squares in the rectangle. Later, apply the formula. | Students find the area of shapes which are made from two rectangles (such as an L-shape) or include a rectangular hole inside the rectangle. |

| Literacy | Links |
|---|---|
| The word 'area' comes from a Latin word meaning 'level ground'. The level ground need not be rectangular. It is important that students do not associate area only with rectangles and the formula 'length × width'. | There is a table listing countries of the World by area at<br>http://en.wikipedia.org/wiki/List_of_countries_and_outlying_territories_by_area<br>Ask "Which is the smallest country in the World?" [Vatican City] "Which is the largest?" [Russia] "Which country is larger, France or Spain?" [France] |

### Alternative approach

Develop students' concept of area of irregular shapes with curved sides (leading to areas in context, such as maps of countries). Use a centimetre-squared grid on a plastic sheet to count squares, applying the rule to squares at the edge of 'count if more than half in; don't count if less than half in'. Use the plastic sheet with irregular shapes with straight sides.

Ask students which shape would be the easiest for counting squares. Decide on the rectangle; count the squares in one row; count the number of rows. Ask how these numbers can give the area quickly and decide on multiplication. This development leads to the formula being derived from a visual approach. Stress that this particular formula only works for rectangles.

### Checkpoint

Find the area of a rectangle that measures 35.5 mm by 7.6 cm (26.98 cm$^2$)

How many squares of side 3 cm will fit into a rectangle that measures 0.9 m by 0.54 m ? (540)

## Starter – True or false?

Give statements and ask students if they are true or false. For example:

| | |
|---|---|
| 4 inches $\approx$ 10 cm | (True) |
| 5 km is more than 5 miles | (False) |
| $\frac{1}{2}$ gallon $\approx$ 4.5 litres | |
| (False: 1 gallon $\approx$ 4.5 litres) | |
| 10 lb $\approx$ 5 kg | (True) |

## Teaching notes

Explain that area is measured in square units and these are often written using $^2$.

Students draw various rectangles on centimetre-squared paper and count the squares that they enclose. Explain that, for rectangles, area is found by multiplying the length of the rectangle by the width. Stress that this method will not work for other shapes. Give students further examples of rectangles drawn without a grid, or simply described, and ask them to apply to formula to calculate the areas. Give examples set in context. Mini whiteboards can be used for quick response.

## Plenary

Give a variety of questions, without and with context, to find areas of rectangles. Use multiple-choice and open questions. Students answer on mini whiteboards.

## Exercise commentary

**Question 1** – In parts **a** and **b**, students can count all the squares: count the squares in one row and the number of rows and then multiply, or simply multiply length by width.

**Question 2** – Students will need to use the formula.

**Question 3** – This question involves decimals. You may wish students to use calculators.

**Question 4** – Students must convert the lengths to the same unit and then be careful to give the correct unit with the answer.

**Question 5** – This is a significantly harder question than earlier ones. Students should convert the 1.2 metres to centimetres and see how many rectangles will fit into one row and how many rows there will be.

---

## Answers

1  a  21 cm$^2$   b  20 cm$^2$   c  35 cm$^2$   d  70 cm$^2$
   e  49 cm$^2$

2  a  66 cm$^2$   b  45 cm$^2$   c  15 m$^2$   d  230 m$^2$

3  a  24.07 cm$^2$         b  19.5 cm$^2$

4  a  99 cm$^2$           b  15 cm$^2$

5  1440

## Objectives

- Deduce and use the formula for the area of a triangle. (L6)

| Key ideas | Resources |
|---|---|
| 1 All triangles can be enclosed by a rectangle such that the area of the triangle is half the area of the rectangle.<br>2 The area of a triangle is a half of the base multiplied by the perpendicular height. | ⊕ Area of a triangle (1129)<br>Card and scissors<br>Centimetre-squared paper<br>Mini whiteboards |

| Simplification | Extension |
|---|---|
| Use examples where the base and one of the sides are perpendicular (that is, a right-angled triangle) in order to make the 'perpendicular height' explicitly clear in the diagrams.<br>When the students move on to use the formula, they could write their values for $b$ and $h$ before substituting them into the formula. | Students find the area of compound shapes made of triangles and rectangles. They explain the steps that they use to find their answers. |

| Literacy | Links |
|---|---|
| Links with algebra can be made when using the formula to calculate area.<br>Have students write the formula in symbols, substitute values for $b$ and $h$ and show their working thereafter. Units need only be shown at the very end in the answer.<br>For example, for a triangle with a base of 6 cm and a height of 4 cm, the layout is:<br><br>Area of triangle $= \frac{1}{2} \times b \times h$<br>$\qquad = \frac{1}{2} \times 6 \times 4$<br>$\qquad = \frac{1}{2} \times 24$<br>$\qquad = 12 \text{ cm}^2$ | The area containing the Parliamentary Buildings in Canberra, Australia is known as the Parliamentary Triangle. Canberra is the capital of Australia and was planned by American architect Walter Burley Griffin after winning a competition in 1911. He designed the Parliamentary Triangle in the shape of an equilateral triangle with Parliament House (representing the government) at one vertex, the Defence Headquarters (representing the military) at the second and City Hill (representing the civilian part of Canberra) at the third. There is more information about the Parliamentary triangle at www.library.act.gov.au/reflectionscd/REFLECT/actv/t d3/td3.htm<br>and at<br>http://en.wikipedia.org/wiki/Parliamentary_Triangle,_ Canberra |

## Alternative approach

Use visual approaches to establish the formula for the area of a triangle.

Take any rectangle, cut it along a diagonal, place one piece on the other, show that both pieces are halves and hence find the area of either right-angled triangle from the area of the rectangle by measuring sides (using a calculator for large numbers if necessary).

Take two congruent, non-right-angled triangles. Place one triangle enclosed within a rectangle. Cut the other triangle into two pieces (they are not likely to be halves) along its perpendicular bisector. Fit these two pieces into the empty spaces of the enclosing rectangle. Explain why the area of either triangle is half the area of the enclosing rectangle. So the formula for the area of a triangle applies whether it is right-angled or not.

## Checkpoint

Find the area of a triangle with base 6cm and height 12cm. ($36\text{cm}^2$)

Find the area of a triangle with base 2.8cm and height 2cm. ($2.8\text{cm}^2$)

**Starter** – Puzzling areas

A square has a side of 6 cm.
Find two different rectangles, each having half the area of the square. [1 × 18, 2 × 9]
Find two different rectangles, each having one-third the area of the square. [3 × 4, 2 × 6 or 1 × 12]
Find two different rectangles, each having one-quarter the area of the square. [1 × 9, 0.5 × 18]

## Teaching notes

Students draw various triangles with the base always horizontal on centimetre-squared paper. They count squares to find the areas of their triangles – it is highly likely that the answers will not be exact. They draw an enclosing rectangle, discover what fraction every triangle is of the enclosing rectangle, and so arrive at the accurate areas of their triangles. Lead the students to a formal statement of the formula for the area of a triangle. Emphasise that they can:

• either find the area of the enclosing rectangle first and then halve it;

• or they can halve the base length of the triangle and then multiply by the perpendicular height.

Students can practise applying this formula with further examples as a whole class using mini whiteboards.

Remind students that they must give the units of their answer and emphasise that area is measured in square units.

## Plenary

Mini whiteboards can be used for a quick-fire quiz to assess students' progress quickly and accurately. Questions can be given as diagrams or simply communicated orally to students. Discuss answers where necessary.

## Exercise commentary

**Questions 1** and **2** – These questions are straightforward. Remind students to use the correct units for area, especially in Question **2**.

**Question 3** – Emphasise the need for accurate measurement. A calculator may be needed.

**Question 4** – Remind students that they are finding the total area.

---

### Answers

1  a  i  12 cm$^2$      ii  6 cm$^2$
   b  i  20 cm$^2$      ii  10 cm$^2$
   c  i  40 cm$^2$      ii  20 cm$^2$
   d  i  42 cm$^2$      ii  21 cm$^2$

2  a  5 cm$^2$    b  9 cm$^2$    c  15 cm$^2$    d  12 mm$^2$
   e  18 cm$^2$    f  45 m$^2$

3  a  12 cm$^2$    b  7.5 cm$^2$

4  7.5 m$^2$

## Objectives

- Deduce and use a formula for the area of a parallelogram. (L6)

| Key ideas | Resources |
|---|---|
| 1  A parallelogram can be made by rearranging a rectangle.<br><br>2  The area of the parallelogram is the same as the rectangle.<br><br>3  The area of the parallelogram is found by multiplying the base by the perpendicular height. | ⊞  Area of a parallelogram (1108)<br>Plastic sheet with a centimetre-squared grid<br>Centimetre-squared paper<br>Scissors<br>Mini whiteboards |

| Simplification | Extension |
|---|---|
| Students write the values that they are going to substitute into the formula before proceeding. They write the formula using words and then using letters.<br><br>Students substitute values for $b$ and $h$ and show their working thereafter. Units need only be shown at the very end in the answer. | Give students further examples where the shapes are compounds of the various shapes that they have met during this chapter. Ask them to explain their methods for working out the areas carefully.<br><br>Introduce the trapezium as a new shape and use the links below to see it used in construction. Look for other shapes used in Inca buildings. |

| Literacy | Links |
|---|---|
| Students often spell 'parallelogram' incorrectly. (To help with spelling, tell students to think of the supermarkets' 'two for one' sales promotions to remind them that there are 'two Ls before one L'.)<br><br>The links with algebra and the use of formulae apply here as they did in the previous lesson. For example, when finding the area with a parallelogram with a base of 10 cm and a perpendicular height of 5 cm, students write:<br><br>Area of parallelogram $= b \times h$<br>$\phantom{Area of parallelogram } = 10 \times 5$<br>$\phantom{Area of parallelogram } = 50 \text{ cm}^2$ | The Inca civilisation built vast cities in South America between 1200 and 1535. Incan architecture used the trapezium shape for windows and doors for decoration and for strength in the event of an earthquake. There are pictures of Incan architecture showing the use of the trapezium at http://www.math.uic.edu/~jbaldwin/pub/incaarch.htm and at www.essential-architecture.com/A-AMERICA-S/PERU/PER-001.htm<br><br>(Note that a trapezium is referred to as a 'trapezoid' in the USA.) |

## Alternative approach

Rather than start with a rectangle and cut a triangular piece from it, you can start with a parallelogram. In a whole-class session, place a transparent centimetre-squared grid over it and find its (approximate) area by counting squares, using the rule 'count more than half as 1; count less than a half as 0'. Then ask if anyone can suggest an exact way of finding the area. Dissect the parallelogram by cutting off a right-angled triangular end and rearranging to make a rectangle. The rest follows as before.

## Checkpoint

Find the area of a parallelogram with base 4cm and perpendicular height 8cm. ($32\text{cm}^2$)

Find the area of a parallelogram with base 3.5cm and perpendicular height 6cm. ($21\text{cm}^2$)

## Starter – Puzzling shapes

Prepare by cutting out a rectangle 30 cm by 10 cm from card. Cut from one corner to the opposite side to make a right-angled triangle and a trapezium.

As a whole-class session, have students describe how the two pieces can come together to make different shapes. Accept unusual shapes. Draw the shapes and ask what it is they all have in common. [They all have the same area.]

Ask if any of the shapes have a particular name. [rectangle and parallelogram] Ask how they can find the area of the rectangle; measure the length and width; calculate the area. [300 cm²] Then ask "What is the area of the parallelogram?" [300 cm²]

## Teaching notes

Remind students that a parallelogram is a quadrilateral and guide them to give a definition using its properties. Ask them to draw an example of a parallelogram on centimetre-squared paper and cut it out.

Students then cut off one right-angled triangle end and place it on the other side of the parallelogram to make a rectangle. Students calculate the area of the rectangle and hence the parallelogram that they started with. Ask for a formula for the area of any parallelogram, emphasising the need to use 'perpendicular height'. Give parallelograms for students to practise the formula using further examples.

## Plenary

Mini whiteboards can be used for a quick-fire quiz. Questions can be given as diagrams or simply communicated orally to students. Set some questions in context. Draw some parallelograms and label both the perpendicular height and the length of one of the sloping sides; discuss students' answers.

## Exercise commentary

**Question 1** – Students can count the squares to find the area but their answers may not be exact; they can use the squares to envisage the original rectangle or they can use the formula. The perpendicular heights are given.

**Question 2** – Students use the formula. The perpendicular heights are given.

**Question 3** – This question requires students to choose the correct length to use. The perpendicular heights and the lengths of the sloping sides are both given. In part **b** the 'base' is vertical for the first time in the exercise.

**Question 4** – Part **a** requires students to find missing lengths. In part **b** students are told that the two parallelograms are congruent. They will therefore have the same area. Students may need to be told that 'congruent' means exactly the same shape and size.

**Question 5** – This is a challenging question. An overall strategy is needed first: the required area is the area of the entire rectangle less the area of the unshaded parallelogram. The length of the base of the parallelogram (with the base shown vertical on the page) has now to be found.

**Question 6** – Part **b** of this question is challenging. The key is to find a pair of values for the base and perpendicular height that multiply together to give 36 cm². Then work from there to find the length of the sloping sides. The diagrams do not need to be to scale.

## Answers

1  a  20 cm²   b  24 cm²   c  25 cm²

2  a  55 cm²   b  30 m²   c  15 cm²

3  a  400 mm²       b  110 cm²

4  a  76 cm²        b  56 cm²

5  52 cm²

6  a  Parallelogram **iii** has a perimeter of 30, not 28, so this cannot be Amir's parallelogram.
   b  Any parallelogram with area 36 cm² and perimeter 28 cm.

## Objectives

- Know and use the formula for the circumference of a circle. (L6)

| Key ideas | Resources |
|---|---|
| 1 The circumference of a circle is the distance all around its edge; the diameter of a circle is the distance across the circle through its centre. <br><br> 2 The circumference of a circle is always a little over three times longer than the diameter of the circle. <br><br> 3 The formula for the circumference of a circle is circumference = π × diameter. | ⊞ Circumference of a circle (1088) <br> Circular objects, compasses and string <br> Calculators <br> Mini whiteboards |

| Simplification | Extension |
|---|---|
| Give the students more practice at working out the circumference of a circle from simple circles before progressing to 'real-life' circles. Estimating the circumference before the use of written methods or a calculator is good practice. Use either the values 3.1 or 3.14 or the π key on the calculator. | Students find perimeters of semicircular shapes (such as protractors) and shapes made from rectangles with semicircles on them (such as stained glass windows). Ensure that they fully explain their methods. |

| Literacy | Links |
|---|---|
| The word 'circumference' comes from two Latin words meaning 'carry round'. The words 'circle' and 'circus' also have the meaning 'round'. <br><br> Approximate values of π were known to the ancient civilisations of Egypt, China and India and its value can be deduced from verses in the Bible. In 1706, William Jones, a Welsh mathematician and friend of Isaac Newton, first used the letter π for the number 3.14… . | A surveyor's wheel is used to measure distances. The circumference of the wheel is an exact length, such as a metre or a yard. As the wheel is rolled along the ground, a mechanical device attached to the wheel counts the revolutions and so measures the distance. There are pictures of surveyors wheels at www.fisco.co.uk/road-meter.html and at www.trumeter.com/Distance_Measuring |

## Alternative approach

A practical approach to find π is strongly recommended. One is to wrap string round various 3D objects, but the means to find the diameter of these objects will need discussion. String can also, more awkwardly, be used to find the circumferences of circles on paper, in which case the diameters can be measured directly – and students can work individually or in pairs. All results can be tabulated under column headings labelled *Diameter*, *Circumference* and *Circumference ÷ Diameter*. An average (mean) value of *Circumference ÷ Diameter* can be found.

## Checkpoint

Find, to one decimal place, the circumference of a circle with diameter 12 cm. (37.7 cm)

Find, to one decimal place, the circumference of a circle with radius 3.6 cm. (22.6 cm)

## Starter – Quick fire

Recap the work of Chapter 1 and this chapter so far. Ask rapid response questions with students responding on mini whiteboards. Discuss answers when there is a need.

## Teaching notes

Remind students what $\pi$ represents and ask them to recall its approximate value. Ask students to say how to find $\pi$ on their calculators and then explain that a value of $\pi$ rounded to one or two decimal places (3.1 or 3.14) will usually be sufficiently accurate when solving problems involving circles.

Give the students an example of a circle of given diameter and ask them to estimate its circumference using a value of 3 for $\pi$. Using calculators, ask the students to calculate a more accurate value for the circumference. Students use mini whiteboards to display their answers.

Give the students further examples as necessary (set some in context) and explain the importance of both units and the accuracy of any necessary rounding of answers.

## Plenary

Mini whiteboards can be used for a quick-fire quiz in order to assess students' progress quickly and accurately. Questions could be to approximate the circumference or to use calculators to get a more accurate answer (or a mixture of both). Questions can be given as diagrams or simply communicated orally to students.

## Exercise commentary

**Question 1** – Students should use $\pi = 3$ to calculate an estimate of the circumference mentally.

**Question 2** – Students should use a written method or a calculator for the multiplication and, in part **d**, discuss if there is a need to round the answer.

**Questions 3** and **4** – These questions look at applying the formula to 'real-life' circles. In Question **4** it is easier to find the circumference of the hole rather than the diameter of the peg.

**Question 5** – Mention that moving heavy objects before the invention of the wheel involved rolling the objects on logs. This question could be extended by considering the turns of a bicycle wheel when cycling, such as "How far do you travel if the wheel of your bike rotates a thousand times?"

**Question 6** – This question requires students to realise that the curved edge of semicircles and quarter-circles are half and one-quarter of the circumference of the circle but that these shapes also have straight sides that must be added to find the total perimeter.

## Answers

1   a   45 cm       b   75 cm       c   21 cm       d   96 mm

2   a   18.6 cm     b   55.8 mm     c   43.4 cm     d   26.04 cm

3   a   17.05 = 17.1 (1 dp)       b   17

4   The peg will not go into the hole. $14.9/\pi = 4.74 > 4.7$
    ($4.7\pi = 14.8$ cm $< 14.9$ cm)

5   a   117.8 cm
    b   1178 cm = 11.78 m

6   a   15.3 cm
    b   14.2 cm

| Key outcomes | Quick check |
|---|---|
| Convert one metric unit to another.     L5 | **a** How many millilitres are in 1.2 litres? (1200) <br> **b** How many centimetres are in 3.4 metres? (340) |
| Convert some metric units to imperial units and vice versa.   L5 | Which is bigger? <br> **a** 12kg or 24 pounds (12kg)         **b** 15km or 10 miles (10 miles) |
| Find the area of a rectangle by using the formula.     L5 | **a** A rectangle has base 20cm and height 30cm. Find the area. ($600cm^2$) <br> **b** A rectangle has area $200cm^2$. If the base is 40cm, find the height. (5cm) |
| Find the area of a triangle by using the formula.     L6 | Find the area of these triangles <br> **a** Base 3cm, height 5cm ($7.5cm^2$) **b** Base 12cm, height 8.5cm ($51cm^2$) |
| Find the area of a parallelogram by using the formula.     L6 | Find the area of a parallelogram with base 12cm and perpendicular height 5cm ($60cm^2$) |
| Find the circumference of a circle by using the formula.     L6 | Find, to one decimal place, the circumference of these circles <br> **a** Diameter 18cm (56.5cm) **b** Radius 8cm (50.3cm) |

## ⊞ MyMaths extra support

| Lesson/online homework | | Description |
|---|---|---|
| Units of length | 1101   L4 | Estimating and using standard units of length |
| Units of capacity | 1104   L4 | Estimating and using standard units of capacity |
| Units of mass | 1105   L4 | Estimating and using standard units of mass |
| Perimeter | 1110   L4 | The perimeter is the distance around the edge of a shape. Practice your measuring skills in this lesson. |
| Imperial measures | 1191   L5 | Learn simple conversions like ounces and grams, miles and km |

# My Review

## Check out

**You should now be able to ...**

**Test it**
Questions

| | | |
|---|---|---|
| ✓ | Convert one metric unit to another. | 1 |
| ✓ | Convert some metric units to imperial units and vice versa. | 2, 3 |
| ✓ | Find the area of a rectangle by using the formula. | 4 |
| ✓ | Find the area of a triangle by using the formula. | 5 |
| ✓ | Find the area of a parallelogram by using the formula. | 6 |
| ✓ | Find the circumference of a circle by using the formula. | 7, 8 |

| Language | Meaning | Example |
|---|---|---|
| Metric units | Metres (m) measure length, grams (g) measure mass and litres (l) measure capacity. | 1000 ml = 1 litre<br>100 cm = 1 m<br>1000 g = 1 kg |
| Imperial | Some of the imperial units are inches, feet, miles, ounces, pounds, stones, pints and gallons. | 5 miles ≈ 8 kilometres<br>1 kilogram ≈ 2.2 pounds<br>1 gallon ≈ 4.5 litres |
| Area | Area is the amount of surface that a shape covers. | Area of rectangle = length × width |
| Circumference and diameter | The circumference of a circle is the distance around its edge.<br>The diameter of a circle is the distance across the circle through the centre. | |

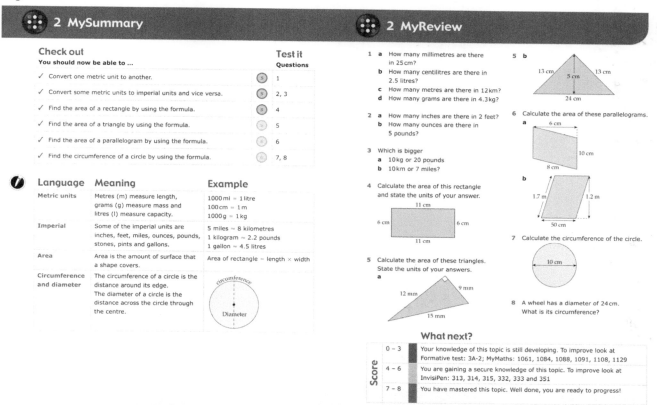

1. a How many millimetres are there in 25 cm?
   b How many centilitres are there in 2.5 litres?
   c How many metres are there in 12 km?
   d How many grams are there in 4.3 kg?

2. a How many inches are there in 2 feet?
   b How many ounces are there in 5 pounds?

3. Which is bigger
   a 10 kg or 20 pounds
   b 10 km or 7 miles?

4. Calculate the area of this rectangle and state the units of your answer.

5. Calculate the area of these triangles. State the units of your answers.
   a

5. b

6. Calculate the area of these parallelograms.
   a
   b

7. Calculate the circumference of the circle.

8. A wheel has a diameter of 24 cm. What is its circumference?

### What next?

| Score | |
|---|---|
| 0 – 3 | Your knowledge of this topic is still developing. To improve look at Formative test: 3A-2; MyMaths: 1061, 1084, 1088, 1091, 1108, 1129 |
| 4 – 6 | You are gaining a secure knowledge of this topic. To improve look at InvisiPen: 313, 314, 315, 332, 333 and 351 |
| 7 – 8 | You have mastered this topic. Well done, you are ready to progress! |

⊕ MyMaths.co.uk      35

## Question commentary

**Questions 1** and **2** – Students may need to refer to the table of conversions.

**Question 3** – Students need to learn the approximate conversions between metric and imperial units.

**Questions 4** to **7** – Students should recall the standard formulae for the areas of these shapes. Check that students are using the perpendicular heights for the triangles and parallelograms.

**Question 8** – A practical application of the formula for the circumference of a circle.

## Answers

| | | | | | | | | |
|---|---|---|---|---|---|---|---|---|
| 1 | a | 250 | b | 250 | c | 12000 | d | 4300 |
| 2 | a | 24 | b | 80 | | | | |
| 3 | a | 10 kg | b | 7 miles | | | | |
| 4 | a | 66 cm$^2$ | | | | | | |
| 5 | a | 54 mm$^2$ | b | 60 cm$^2$ | | | | |
| 6 | a | 60 cm$^2$ | b | 60 cm$^2$ | | | | |
| 7 | | 30 cm | | | | | | |
| 8 | | 72 cm | | | | | | |

# 2 MyPractice

**2a**

1  Convert these.
   a  300 cm into metres
   b  40 mm into centimetres
   c  2000 m into kilometres
   d  4000 ml into litres
   e  8000 g into kilograms
   f  8 km into metres
   g  6 cm into millimetres
   h  4 kg into grams
   i  2 litres into millilitres
   j  5 m into centimetres

**2b**

2  Approximately …
   a  how far is 5 miles in kilometres?
   b  how many pints would 3 litres be equivalent to?
   c  30 centimetres is equivalent to how many inches?
   d  how many ounces are there in 90 grams?
   e  1 metre is equivalent to how many feet?
   f  7 kilograms is the same as how many pounds?

**2c**

3  Use the formula $A = l \times w$ to calculate the areas of these rectangles.
   (Give your answers in cm².)

   a  7 cm × 4 cm
   b  13 cm × 10 cm
   c  16 cm × 9 cm

**2d**

4  Use the formula $A = \frac{1}{2} \times b \times h$ to calculate the areas of these triangles.

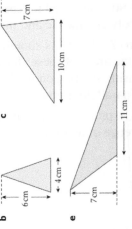

   a  4 cm, 5 cm
   b  6 cm, 4 cm
   c  7 cm, 10 cm
   d  6 cm, 7 cm, 7.7 cm
   e  7 cm, 11 cm

---

**2e**

5  Use the formula $A = b \times h$ to calculate the areas of these parallelograms.

   a  6 cm, 4 cm
   b  5 cm, 7 cm
   c  8 cm, 11 cm
   d  8 cm, 13 cm
   e  9 cm, 4 cm

6  Find the area of these shapes.
   a  2 cm, 5 cm, 4 cm, 8 cm
   b  10 m, 10 m, 5 cm

**2f**

7  Estimate the circumference of each of these circles.
   Use π ≈ 3.1.
   a  8 cm
   b  9.3 mm
   c  15 mm
   d  43 mm

8  Estimate the circumference of each of these circles.
   Use π ≈ 3.1.
   a  6 cm
   b  3.8 cm
   c  21 mm
   d  57 mm

9  The diameter of a wheel is 48 cm.
   a  Find the circumference of the wheel.
   b  How many full revolutions does the wheel need to turn to travel 1 km?

10  The circumference of a circle is 52.7 mm.
    Find the diameter of the circle.

## Question commentary

**Questions 1** and **2** – Students may need to refer to the tables of conversions for these questions.

**Questions 3** to **6** – Students should recall the formulae for the areas of these shapes. In question **6**, extra lengths not marked may need to be found first.

**Questions 7** to **10** – Students are given an approximate value of π to use but calculators could be used to work with the 'exact' value. Check in question **8** that students are doubling the radius. Question **9** is a practical application while question **10** requires the students to work backwards.

## Answers

| | | | |
|---|---|---|---|
| **1** | **a** 3 metres | **b** | 4 centimetres |
| | **c** 2 kilometres | **d** | 4 litres |
| | **e** 8 kilograms | **f** | 8000 metres |
| | **g** 60 millimetres | **h** | 4000 grams |
| | **i** 2000 millilitres | **j** | 500 centimetres |

**2** Accept reasonable approximations
  **a** ≈ 8 kilometres    **b** ≈ 5 pints
  **c** ≈ 12 inches    **d** ≈ 3 ounces
  **e** ≈ 3 feet    **f** ≈ 14 to15 pounds

**3** **a** 28 cm$^2$    **b** 130 cm$^2$    **c** 144 cm$^2$

**4** **a** 10 cm$^2$    **b** 12 cm$^2$    **c** 35 cm$^2$    **d** 21 cm$^2$
  **e** 38.5 cm$^2$

**5** **a** 24 cm$^2$    **b** 35 cm$^2$    **c** 88 cm$^2$    **d** 104 cm$^2$
  **e** 36 cm$^2$

**6** **a** 22 cm$^2$    **b** 75 cm$^2$

**7** **a** 24.8 cm    **b** 28.83 cm
  **c** 46.5 mm    **d** 133.3 mm

**8** **a** 18.6 cm    **b** 11.78 cm
  **c** 65.1 mm    **d** 176.7 mm

**9** **a** 148.8 cm    **b** 672 revolutions

**10** **a** 17 mm

## Learning outcomes

**A1** Use and interpret algebraic notation, including:
- $ab$ in place of $a \times b$
- $a^2$ in place of $a \times a$, $a^3$ in place of $a \times a \times a$; $a^2b$ in place of $a \times a \times b$
- $a/b$ in place of $a \div b$
- $3y$ in place of $y + y + y$ and $3 \times y$
- coefficients written as fractions rather than as decimals
- brackets (L5)

**A2** Substitute numerical values into formulae and expressions, including scientific formulae (L5)

**A3** Understand and use the concepts and vocabulary of expressions, equations, inequalities, terms and factors (L5)

**A4** Simplify and manipulate algebraic expressions to maintain equivalence by:
- collecting like terms
- taking out common factors
- multiplying a single term over a bracket (L5)

**A6** Model situations or procedures by translating them into algebraic expressions or formulae and by using graphs (L5)

## Introduction

The chapter starts by looking at simplifying algebraic expressions by collecting terms and simple multiplication and cancelling before moving on to expanding single brackets. Basic formulae, including substitution into formulae are covered before the final section on writing algebraic expressions from context.

The introduction discusses two very famous equations from the history of mathematics: Newton's formula for gravitation and Einstein's equation $E = mc^2$. Both of these incredibly important scientists and mathematicians led the way in their respective fields and most of modern mathematics and physics is based on the work of one or the other of them. Newton worked with small-scale mechanics and the motion of bodies relative to each other whereas Einstein is more famous for his laws of relativity which apply on a cosmological scale. Biographies of Newton and Einstein can be found at:

http://www-history.mcs.st-andrews.ac.uk/Biographies/Newton.html

http://www-history.mcs.st-andrews.ac.uk/Biographies/Einstein.html

## Prior knowledge

Students should already know how to…
- Perform simple arithmetic including with negative numbers
- Find the perimeter of simple shapes

## Starter problem

The starter problem is an investigation into 'L' numbers, formed by joining five cells on a standard number square to form a 3 by 3 'L' shape. In the example, the 'L' based on square 35 is shown and students are asked to come up with a formula connecting this base number with the sum of the cells.

If we take the base number to be $x$, we can write the two cells to the left as $x - 1$ and $x - 2$. The numbers on the rows above are similarly $x - 12$ and $x - 22$. If we sum these terms algebraically, we get $5x - 37$ as the expression for the total of all the numbers in the 'L'.

For the base number 35, this gives a sum of:

$5 \times 35 - 37 = 138$ which agrees with the arithmetic sum given in the example.

Students could be directed to investigate the sums numerically, or to dive straight into the algebra, depending on their ability and previous knowledge.

## Resources

### MyMaths

| | | | | | |
|---|---|---|---|---|---|
| Rules and formulae | 1158 | Simplifying 2 | 1178 | Simplifying 1 | 1179 |
| Substitution 1 | 1187 | Single brackets | 1247 | | |

| **Online assessment** | | **InvisiPen solutions** | | | |
|---|---|---|---|---|---|
| Chapter test | 3A–3 | Using symbols | 211 | Collecting like terms | 212 |
| Formative test | 3A–3 | Multiplying/dividing terms | 213 | Expanding brackets | 214 |
| Summative test | 3A–3 | Formulae | 251 | Creating a formula | 252 |
| | | Substitution | 254 | Further substitution | 255 |

## Topic scheme

Teaching time = 4 lessons/2 weeks

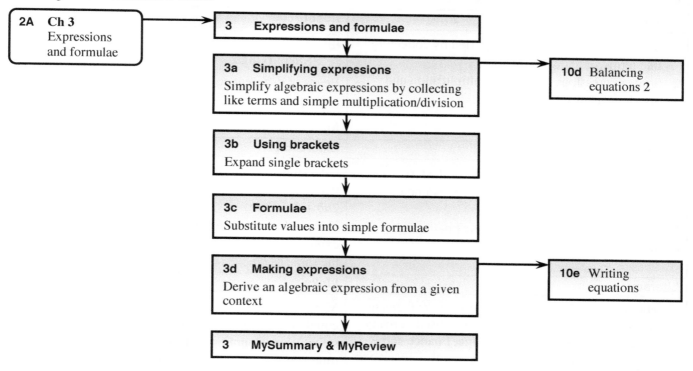

**2A   Ch 3**
Expressions
and formulae

**3      Expressions and formulae**

**3a    Simplifying expressions**
Simplify algebraic expressions by collecting
like terms and simple multiplication/division

**10d**   Balancing
equations 2

**3b    Using brackets**
Expand single brackets

**3c    Formulae**
Substitute values into simple formulae

**3d    Making expressions**
Derive an algebraic expression from a given
context

**10e**   Writing
equations

**3      MySummary & MyReview**

## Differentiation

| **Student book 3A**          38 – 51 | **Student book 3B**          34 – 49 | **Student book 3C**          30 – 51 |
|---|---|---|
| Simplifying expressions<br>Using brackets<br>Formulae<br>Writing algebraic expressions<br>from context | Factorise expressions<br>Simplify algebraic fractions<br>Add and subtract algebraic<br>fractions<br>Substitute into formulae in context<br>Rearranging formulae<br>Deriving formulae<br>Graphing formulae | Index laws<br>Multiplying linear expressions<br>Factorising expressions<br>Identities<br>Formulae in context<br>Rearranging formulae |

## Objectives

- Simplify linear expressions by collecting like terms. (L5)

## Key ideas

1 Some expressions can be simplified by collecting like terms.
2 Some expressions involving multiplication and division can also be simplified.

## Resources

| | |
|---|---|
| ⊞ Simplifying 1 | (1179) |
| Simplifying 2 | (1178) |

Beads of different colours

Flash cards

Mini whiteboards

## Simplification

Students collect like terms where all of the terms are positive and like terms are in order; for example, $4a + 3a + 2b + b$.
Use no more than two different letters in the same expression.

## Extension

Give students examples where the terms are squared or where there are two letters together such as $2ab + 3c + 3ab - c$.
You could reverse the order of the letters, as in the expression $2ab + 3c + 3ba - c$ to demonstrate that $ab$ is the same as $ba$.

## Literacy

Algebra can be said to be the language of mathematics. It expresses ideas succinctly and can be used in many other fields such as science, medicine, finance and engineering. To be literate in mathematics, you have to understand and use algebra.

## Links

Most banks will not accept coins unless they are counted and separated into bags containing coins of the same value. Counting and sorting coins manually is time-consuming, so most shops and businesses use automatic coin-sorters. Coin-sorters separate the coins into piles of each denomination and reject any coins that are damaged or are not of the correct currency. There are pictures of coin sorters at www.safescan.com/uk/productDetail/31/71/coin-counters-and-sorters/safescan-1200-gbp?gclid=CMCOwompxr0CFSUUwwodtKUAyg

## Alternative approach

A brief return to previous introductions is often useful. Use two colours of beads on a string where $b$ and $r$ stand for a blue and a red bead. Use an expression such as $4r + 2b + 3r + 2b$ to represent a string of beads. Ask how the beads can be rearranged and this expression simplified. The beads change places and the expression becomes $7r + 4b$. When negative terms are used, a number line can be used to assist additions and subtractions.

To simplify an expression such as $2 \times 3r$, present students with two identical bags, each containing 3 red beads. The expression represents the contents which, when emptied into one pile, can be simplified as $6r$. This visual display leads to simplifying other expressions such as $15y \div 3$ or $\dfrac{15y}{3} = 5y$.

## Checkpoint

Simplify $6x + 4y - 2x + 3y$ $(4x + 7y)$

Simplify $12a \times 4b$ $(48ab)$

## Starter – I think of a number

Remind students about inverse operations. Pose problems with students responding on mini whiteboards: for example,

I think of a number and add 6. My answer is 10. What is my number?                    [4]

I think of a number. I double it and add 1. My answer is 21. What is my number?     [10]

I think of a number. I halve it and subtract 2. My answer is 3. What is my number?      [10]

I think of a number. I square it and add 2. My answer is 27. What is my number?    [5 or –5]

## Teaching notes

This lesson revisits some earlier work, consolidates it and extends it.

Give the students the following scenario.
Eric, Yasmin and Tom go shopping for fruit. Eric buys three apples and two bananas. Yasmin buys three bananas and an apple. Finally, Tom buys four bananas. The costs of an apple and a banana are $a$ and $b$ pence respectively. How can the total cost be written?
Agree that the total cost, in pence, is:

$3a + 2b + 3b + a + 4b$

Agree that this expression can be simplified by collecting like terms and written as $4a + 9b$.

Discuss collecting like terms when some of the coefficients are negative. Consolidate understanding of collecting like terms with a variety of examples, some of which result in negative coefficients in the answer; for example, $3x + 2y + 4x - 5y$.

## Plenary

Use a selection of flash cards for algebraic simplification. Students respond using mini whiteboards. Tell students that they have, say, 10 seconds to write each answer.
True/False cards can also be used.

## Exercise commentary

**Question 1** – Monitor students in parts **d, e** and **f** as they meet subtraction for the first time in the exercise.

**Questions 2** and **3** – Students meet like terms and unlike terms. In Question **3b**, access to a number line may be useful for directed numbers.

**Question 4** – Check that students recall the meaning of perimeter.

**Question 5** – Remind students that the simplification of letters which are multiplied and divided is not done in the same way as collecting like terms.

**Question 6** – In part **a**, students may need help in translating the written problem into an expression for perimeter. Work with students on part **a** prior to allowing them to tackle part **b** independently.

**Question 7** – Remind students of the formulae for the areas of a rectangle and of a triangle. Make sure they realise these involve multiplication, not collecting like terms.

## Answers

| | | | | | | | |
|---|---|---|---|---|---|---|---|
| **1** | **a** $4h$ | **b** $6j$ | | **c** $5m$ | | **d** $3t$ |
| | **e** $f$ | **f** $5n$ | | | | |

| | | | | |
|---|---|---|---|---|
| **2** | **a** $3w + 4v$ | | **b** $10m + 10n$ |
| | **c** $6y + 10x$ | | **d** $10t + 7q$ |
| | **e** $2e + 7g$ | | **f** $9j - h$ |

**3**  **a** $2b - 4a, 4b + 3a$      **b** $3y - 2x, -4x - 3y$

**4**  **a** $6b + 30$      **b** $2x + 6y$
   **c** $x + 3y + 6$

| | | | | | | | | |
|---|---|---|---|---|---|---|---|---|
| **5** | **a** $10a$ | **b** $30m$ | **c** $15s$ | **d** $40f$ |
| | **e** $24ab$ | **f** $25rs$ | **g** $30mn$ | **h** $56tv$ |
| | **i** $3h$ | **j** $12y$ | **k** $2x$ | **l** $6$ |
| | **m** $72k$ | **n** $0.9v$ | **o** $5$ | **p** $100uv$ |
| | **q** $4$ | **r** $12ab$ | | |

**6**  **a** $-a + 10b$
   **b** Any shape with sides adding to $6x - 12y + 18$

**7**  **a** $4a$
   **b** Rectangle with 2 sides multiplying to $24xy$
   **c** $12u$

## Objectives

- Derive simple expressions. (L6)
- Multiply an expression in brackets by a single numeric term. (L6)
- Substitute numbers into expressions. (L6)

| Key ideas | Resources |
|---|---|
| 1 Expressions use brackets to denote multiplication.<br>2 Brackets can be expanded by multiplying everything in the brackets by the term outside the brackets.<br>3 Letters can be substituted by numbers and the value of an expression calculated. | ⊕ Single brackets (1247)<br>Mini whiteboards |

| Simplification | Extension |
|---|---|
| Progress from collecting like terms in one unknown to two unknowns, from positive terms to negative terms, to expanding brackets. Leave substitution to the end. | Give students examples which have a pair of bracketed terms, such as $3(a + 2b) + 2(3a + 4b)$. Have them expand the brackets before collecting like terms. (Keep terms positive to avoid issues of dealing with negative terms.) |

| Literacy | Links |
|---|---|
| The word 'brackets' comes from the same old English word as 'breeches' meaning 'trousers' which have two legs used in pairs. Brackets are used in pairs in mathematics to denote a multiple of an expression. | There are four types of brackets in use in the English language. The word 'bracket' usually refers to round brackets or parentheses ( ) which are used for explanations. Square brackets [ ] are just called brackets in the U.S. and are often used for comments or corrections. Braces or curly brackets { } are used to link two lines together and are also used in computing and music. Angle brackets < > are used around highlighted phrases. |

## Alternative approach

Adopt a visual approach to introducing brackets. Show students two bags, each containing two gold coins (£1), four silver coins (10p) and six copper coins (1p). The letters $g$, $s$ and $c$ denote the values of the coins in pence. So, in each bag there is $2g + 4s + 6c$ and in two bags there is $2(2g + 4s + 6c)$. When emptied into one pile, there is $2(2g + 4s + 6c) = 4g + 8s + 12c$.

As an example of substitution, the value of one of these bags by substituting $g = 100$, $s = 10$ and $c = 1$, giving the total value of one bag as $2 \times 100 + 4 \times 10 + 6 \times 1 = 246$ pence.

## Checkpoint

Expand the brackets:

a $3(x + 2y)$ $\qquad$ $(3x + 6y)$

b $4(2a - 3b)$ $\qquad$ $(8a - 12b)$

## Starter – Algebraic sums

Draw a 4 × 4 table on the board to form 16 cells. Label the rows with the terms: $7x, 5x, -3x, -x$. Label the columns with the terms: $2x, -3x, 4x, 2y$.

Ask students to fill in each cell of the table by adding its row and column terms together. For example, the top left cell would be $7x + 2x = 9x$.

There can be differentiation by the choice of terms.

## Teaching notes

Give students an example of an expression which has brackets such as $3(x + y)$ and explain that this means 'three lots of both $x$ and $y$', which is the same as 'three lots of $x$ and three lots of $y$'. Give students a practical example of where this type of expression could be used; for example, when buying 'three lots of fish and chips' where $x$ and $y$ are the cost of one portion of fish and one portion of chips.

At a shop, it could express the total weight of three boxes containing a camera ($x$ grams) and its case ($y$ grams).

Explain that we can 'expand' or 'multiply out' the brackets by multiplying each of the terms inside by the number outside. Hence $3(x + y)$ becomes $3x + 3y$.

Explain that if we now know the values of $x$ and $y$, we can evaluate the expression by 'substituting' for $x$ and $y$. Demonstrate that this can be done:

- *either* inside the bracket by evaluating $x + y$ first;
- *or* after the bracket is multiplied out.

The answers should be the same.

## Plenary

As a whole class, give students several expressions to simplify with increasing complexity; for example, from $5x + 3y - 2x$ and $16z \div 2$ to those which involve the expansion of brackets. Include some simple substitutions. Students respond on mini whiteboards.

## Exercise commentary

**Question 1** – This is similar to part **a** of the first example. Parts **a** to **c** could be factorised as in the example.

**Question 2** – In part **c**, ask students to say which is easier to evaluate $2s + 2b + 2t$ or $2(s + b + t)$. They will likely say the second of these.

Using mini whiteboards to display the answers, you could split the class in two and organise a race. Which side finishes first and which side gets the most correct answers?

**Question 3** – Refer students to the second example where brackets are expanded.

**Question 4 –** As a check, ask students to find the perimeter without using algebra.

**Question 5** – A hexagon provides a solution if each of its sides is $x + y$ cm long. Can students find a solution which is not regular, where sides are either $x$ cm or $y$ cm long? [A 12-sided shape with 6 sides each of $x$ and $y$ cm long.]

In part **c**, ask "What must the value of $x + y$ be?" [10]

**Question 6** – Students should recognise that the given side plus the question mark equals half of the given perimeter $(3y + 3x)$.

---

## Answers

1   **a**   $2(c + b)$      **b**   $3(k + t)$
   **c**   $2(s + b + t)$     **d**   $3f + 4c$
   **e**   $4b + 3c$

2   **a**   £3.40    **b**   £6.30    **c**   £4.60    **d**   £18.30
   **e**   £5.60

3   **a**   $3x + 3y$      **b**   $6a - 6b$
   **c**   $10w - 10v$     **d**   $3x + 3y + 3z$
   **e**   $8x + 12y$      **f**   $15p - 10q$
   **g**   $14m - 35n$     **h**   $16t - 24s + 8r$
   **i**   $90u + 36v$     **j**   $6j + 30k$
   **k**   $6 + 4f$       **l**   $20 + 35t$
   **m**   $8r + 32$      **n**   $12r + 24s$
   **o**   $35h + 42i$     **p**   $39q - 15h$

4   **a**   $2x + 2y$      **b**   52 cm

5   **a**   Check students' drawings for regular hexagons
   **b**   Each side should be labelled $x + y$
   **c**   Any combination that equals 10

6   width $= 2x$

## Objectives

- Substitute into formulae. (L6)
- Derive a formula and, in simple cases, change its subject. (L7)

| Key ideas | Resources |
|---|---|
| 1 Numbers can be substituted for letters in a formula to find the value of the subject of the formula. | ⊕ Rules and formulae (1158)<br>Substitution 1 (1187) |
| 2 Formulae can be rearranged to make another letter the subject. | Mini whiteboards |

| Simplification | Extension |
|---|---|
| Give the students examples which refer to contextualised situations. Avoid abstract formulae without context. Ask them to write down what they are doing at each stage in order to enable them to build up a logical process and show their lines of thought. | Give students more complicated formulae to work with such as the conversion between Fahrenheit and Celsius or ones which involve squared terms such as $v^2 = u^2 + 2as$. Suit the complexity of the formulae to students' abilities in this topic. Initially, they calculate the value of the subject of the formulae. Where formulae need rearranging, use formulae they have met before, such as finding the base of a triangle given the area and height. |

| Literacy | Links |
|---|---|
| The word 'formula' is from a Latin word meaning 'rule'. Equations and formulae operate under similar rules, such as "What you do to one side, you must do to the other" to keep the balance. The difference is that, in an equation, the unknown has just one value, whereas, in a formula, many values can be substituted into it. | Formulae are important in many forms of navigation. Navigational satellites move continuously in orbit around the Earth and use solar panels for power. Engineers use formulae to calculate each satellite's future position and to orientate the solar panels to capture the most energy from the sun. There is information about the NavStar GPS system at: http://www.britannica.com/EBchecked/topic/235395/GPS/235218/The-Navstar-system?anchor=ref823338 |

## Alternative approach

When substituing into a formula to find the value of a variable which is *not* the subject (such as using the formula $A = \frac{1}{2} \times b \times h$), there are two methods. One method is to rearrange the formula before substitution. So, for example, to find height $h$, the formula becomes $h = \frac{2A}{b}$ and then substitution takes place.

The other method is to substitute first, simplify the arithmetic and then rearrange. So, for example, to find $h$ when $A = 40$ and $b = 8$, substitute without rearranging to give $40 = \frac{1}{2} \times 8 \times h$ which gives $40 = 4h$ and hence, by dividing both sides by 4, the answer is $h = 10$.

## Checkpoint

$y = a + bx$. Find $y$ if $a = 2$, $b = 7$ and $x = 11$. (79)

Find $x$ if $y = 8$, $a = 4$ and $b = 2$. (2)

## Starter – Match up

Ask students to match up identities from the following expressions.

$3(2x - 6)$,   $2(x + y - 2)$,   $8x - 16$,   $6x - 8$,

$2(3x - 9)$,   $2x + 2y - 4$,   $3(x + 5y)$,   $15x + 5y$,

$2(3x - 4)$,   $4(2x - 4)$,   $3x + 15y$,   $5(3x + y)$

Answers:

$3(2x - 6) = 2(3x - 9)$,

$2(x + y - 2) = 2x + 2y - 4$,

$8x - 16 = 4(2x - 4)$,

$6x - 8 = 2(3x - 4)$,

$3(x + 5y) = 3x + 15y$,

$15x + 5y = 5(3x + y)$

The identities can be differentiated by the choice of expressions or by including extra expressions as red herrings without a pairing.

## Teaching notes

Explain that a formula is like an equation which is used to find an unknown value from known values when solving problems. Give students examples of formulae which they may have encountered such as speed/distance/time, area of a triangle or area of a rectangle. Write them using both words and symbols.

Explain that we use the formulae by 'substituting' known values into them. Give students examples where the formula is used exactly as written to find, say, the area of a rectangle when the length and width are both known.

Explain that, if we know the area of the rectangle but not the width, we can still use the formula by working backwards to find the width. Use the notion of inverse operations to show that the area is divided by the length to find the width.

## Plenary

Give the students a formula (such as for the area of a triangle or the area of a parallelogram) and ask them to use it to find the area given different values for the other unknowns. Mini whiteboards can be used here to get quick feedback. Give them a number of examples where the area is known but one of the other values is not.

## Exercise commentary

Since this exercise is designed for students to substitute values into formulae, check that they do not calculate mentally without written evidence of their methods. They should use the layout used in the examples.

**Question 1** – Support may be needed in part **b**. Use the given formula triangle and explain in terms of inverse operations.

**Question 2** – This question practises previous learning about triangles in the current context of substitution into a formula.

**Questions 3** to **5** – Some students will need support to rearrange the formulae. Help them by using the inverse flow diagram in Question **3** and referring to inverse operations in Questions **4** and **5**.

## Answers

| | | | | |
|---|---|---|---|---|
| 1 | a | i   60 cm² | ii | 54 cm² |
| | | iii   87 cm² | iv | 300 cm² |
| | b | $w = A \div l$ | | |
| | c | i   4 cm | ii | $2\frac{2}{3}$ cm |
| | | iii   9 cm | iv | 3 cm |
| 2 | a | 25 cm² | b | 21 cm² |
| | c | 28 cm² | d | 60 cm² |
| | e | 87.5 cm² | f | 115.5 m² |
| | g | 0.125 cm² | h | 25cm² |
| | i | 4.5cm² | | |
| 3 | a | $h = (A \div b) \times 2$ | b | 60 cm |
| 4 | a | $I = V \div R$ | b | 5 |
| 5 | a | 13   b    2   c | | 3 |

## Objectives

- Derive expressions and formulae from practical contexts (L5)
- Substitute numbers into expressions and formulae (L5)

| Key ideas | Resources |
|---|---|
| 1  Apply reasoning skills in order to derive an expression or formula for a simple situation<br>2  Recognise the generality of the expressions and substitute values in them | Rules and formulae (1158)<br>Marbles (see **Alternative approach**)<br>Mini-whiteboards |

| Simplification | Extension |
|---|---|
| None of the problems in this section are particularly difficult and only question **4** parts **c** and **f** involve more than one letter. These parts could be omitted if necessary. Question **3** part **b** involves more than one step ($\times 6 + 2$) and can similarly be omitted. | Students can devise simple formulae for metric-imperial conversions, such as inches to centimetres. They can also make currency converters for (say) euros to pounds sterling. These conversions could be drawn as graphs. |

| Literacy | Links |
|---|---|
| Expression<br>Formula<br>Being precise with the recording of reasoning is important, with students recognising the need to communicate clearly and accurately. This includes defining their use of any general terms, such as 'let $x$ be the number of cm long', and so on. | Prices for tickets for upcoming concerts and events can be found at http://www.ticketmaster.co.uk or at http://www.seetickets.com<br>A booking fee per ticket and/or a transaction fee are usually charged in addition to the face value of the ticket. Choose an event and select a ticket category. How much would it cost to book one, two, three or four tickets in this category? Can the class derive a formula to calculate the cost of buying tickets? |

## Alternative approach

Since questions **1** and **2** use a bag of marbles, one could actually be used as a practical demonstration tool. You could have the bag on the desk and then present to the class a pile of extra marbles and discuss how the addition (or subtraction) of a specified number of marbles can actually be represented if we don't know how many marbles are actually in the bag. Ask students to decide a letter for the unknown number of marbles (they might chose $n$, but might not) and write expressions on mini-whiteboards to enable quick checking of working and the correct use of algebraic syntax.

## Checkpoint

A rectangle measures $x + 2$ cm by $x$ cm. Write down a formula for the perimeter $P$ cm.   ($P = 4x + 4$))

What is the perimeter of the rectangle if $x = 2$?   (12cm)

## Starter – I think of a number

I think of a number. I halve it. I get the same answer if I subtract five. What is my number? (10)

Similar problems to this could be given or students could be invited to create their own.

## Teaching notes

One of the most common difficulties for students in deriving expressions is that they often do not define their variables precisely and end up using the same symbol to mean more than one thing in a problem. Encourage students to define variables clearly. In each of the examples and throughout the exercise, the variable to be used is given but students should be made aware that it can stand for any number.

## Plenary

Ask students to work in pairs to consider a general formula for the perimeter of a regular polygon with $n$ sides each of length $x$ cm ($P = nx$). They could then be given some quick-fire questions and use mini-whiteboards to write down the answers.

## Exercise commentary

**Question 1** – Students are simply adding an integer value onto their variable.

**Question 2** – Students are now subtracting an integer value.

**Question 3** – Different operations are now required and students may need a bit of guidance on how to represent the multiplication in parts **a** and **c**.

**Question 4** – Here students have to substitute following the derivation of their expressions. An alternative approach could be to place the numbers on a copy of the diagram and simply add them up.

**Question 5** – Not a particularly challenging problem but students will need to understand the context to come up with the answer.

## Answers

1. **a** $n + 2$  **b** $n + 6$  **c** $n + 8$  **d** $n$

2. **a** $m - 2$  **b** $m - 4$  **c** $m - 1$  **d** $m - 6$

3. **a** $3c$  **b** $6c + 2$  **c** $c - 4$  **d** $18$

4. **a** $8n$ cm  **b** $4x$ cm  **c** $h + 2k + 2j$ cm
   **d** $40$ cm  **e** $36$ cm  **f** $27$ cm
   **g** i  $6z$ cm  ii  $21$ cm

5. $2y$

| Key outcomes | | Quick check |
|---|---|---|
| Simplify expressions by collecting like terms. | L5 | Simplify<br>**a** $3x + 5y + 6x - 2y$ $(9x + 3y)$ **b** $2x - y - x + 3y$ $(x + 2y)$ |
| Expand brackets. | L5 | Expand<br>**a** $8(3 + 2x)$ $(24 + 16x)$ **b** $4(5x - 12)$ $(20x - 48)$ |
| Substitute values into expressions with brackets and formulae. | L5 | $A = 2(x + y)$<br>**a** Find $A$ when $x = 7$ and $y = 2$ (18) **b** Find $x$ when $A = 6$ and $y = 1$ (2) |
| Rearrange basic formulae. | L5 | Make $a$ the subject in the formula $y = bx + a$   $(a = y - bx)$ |
| Form expressions. | L5 | A rectangle has lengths $3x$ and $x + y$. Write down an expression for the perimeter. ($2(4x + y)$ or $8x + 2y$) |

## ⊕ MyMaths extra support

| Lesson/online homework | | Description |
|---|---|---|
| Function machines | 1159  L4 | Using function machines to help organise number operations and solve equations |

# My Review

## 3 MySummary

### Check out
**You should now be able to ...**

| | Test it Questions |
|---|---|
| ✓ Simplify expressions by collecting like terms. | ⓢ 1, 2 |
| ✓ Expand brackets. | ⓢ 3 |
| ✓ Substitute values into expressions with brackets and formulae. | ⓢ 4 |
| ✓ Rearrange basic formulae. | ⓢ 5 |
| ✓ Form expressions. | ⓢ 6 |

| Language | Meaning | Example |
|---|---|---|
| Expression | An expression is made up of terms but has no equals sign. | $2x - 6y + 3z$ |
| Simplify | Simplify means to write an expression as simply as possible. | $3x + 5x - x = 7x$ <br> $3a \times 4b = 12ab$ |
| Expand | Expanding brackets means to multiply out the brackets. | $3(2x - 5y) = 6x - 15y$ |
| Formulae | Formulae is plural of formula. A formula is a rule linking two or more variables. | The formula for finding the circumference of a circle is $C = \pi d$ |
| Substitution | Substitution is when you replace the letter in an expression or formula with a number. | $P = 2l + 5w$ <br> Find $P$ when $l = 5$cm and $w = 4$cm. <br> $P = 2 \times 5 + 5 \times 4 = 30$cm |

� 48  **Algebra** Expressions and formulae

## 3 MyReview

1 Simplify these expressions by collecting like terms.
 a $b + 2b + b$
 b $5n + 9m - n + 3m$
 c $11g - 14h + 2h - 10g$
 d $6j + 3 - 2i - 8i + 5j + 2$

2 Simplify these expressions by multiplying and dividing.
 a $2a \times 12$  b $3c \times 4d$
 c $24h \div 8$  d $\dfrac{30v}{15v}$
 e $2 \times 7 \times 3x$  f $\dfrac{9y}{3 \times y}$
 g $5p \times 2 \times 3q$  h $6 \times 4s \div 3s$

3 Expand the brackets.
 a $12(a + b)$  b $4(3v - 4)$
 c $2(3x + 1)$  d $5(2s - 4t)$
 e $3(7 - 4s)$  f $4(p + 2q - 3r)$
 g $6(3 + \frac{1}{2}t)$  h $\frac{1}{2}(8m + 4n)$

4 The formula for the area of a parallelogram is
 $A = b \times h$
 where $b$ is the length of the base and $h$ is the perpendicular height.
 a Find the area of a parallelogram with $b = 9$cm and $h = 11$cm.
 b Find the base of a parallelogram with Area $= 27$cm² and height $= 9$cm.

5 Tim has $t$ apples and Phil has $p$ apples.
 a Write an expression for the number of apples they have all together.
 b Tim eats one of his apples. How many apples does he have now?
 c Katie has twice as many apples as Phil. Write an expression for the number of apples that Katie has.

6 Find a formula for the perimeter, $P$, of each shape. Simplify your answers.
 a
 b
 c
 d

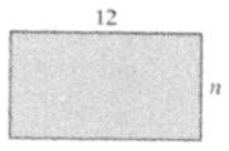

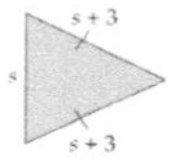

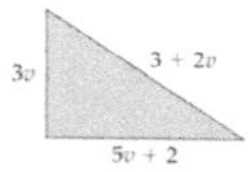

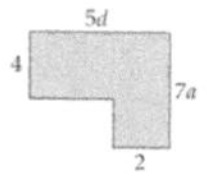

### What next?

| Score | |
|---|---|
| 0 – 2 | Your knowledge of this topic is still developing. To improve look at Formative test: 3A-3; MyMaths: 1158, 1178, 1179, 1187 and 1247 |
| 3 – 5 | You are gaining a secure knowledge of this topic. To improve look at InvisiPen: 211, 212, 213, 214, 251, 252, 254 and 255 |
| 6 | You have mastered this topic. Well done, you are ready to progress! |

 **MyMaths**.co.uk    49

## Question commentary

**Question 1** – Check that students are taking care with negative terms

**Question 2** – Students should be encouraged to simplify the numbers first, then the letters.

**Question 3** – This question should be routine practice.

**Question 4** – Students could tackle part **b** by either rearranging the formula or by substituting and solving a simple equation.

**Question 5** – This question tests the students' comprehension skills. They may need help extracting the information from the word problems.

**Question 6** – Students may need to work out missing side lengths (parts **a** and **d**) before proceeding to write down the required expressions. Encourage them to simplify their expressions by collecting like terms.

## Answers

1 a $4b$  b $4n + 12m$
 c $g - 12h$  d $11j - 10i + 5$

2 a $24a$  b $12cd$  c $3h$  d $2$
 e $42x$  f $3$  g $30pq$  h $8$

3 a $12a + 12b$  b $12v - 16$
 c $6x + 2$  d $10s - 20t$
 e $21 - 12s$  f $4p + 8q - 12r$
 g $18 + 3t$  h $4m + 2n$

4 a $99$ cm²  b $3$ cm

5 a $t + p$  b $t - 1$  c $2p$

6 a $P = 2n + 24$  b $3s + 9$
 c $10v + 5$  d $10d + 14a$

**1** Simplify these expressions.

a $x + x + x + x$  b $2p + 3p$

c $6y - 3y$  d $9a + 2a - 4a$

e $15d - 10d + 2d - 3d$  f $20g - 2g - 10g + 4g$

**2** Simplify these expressions by collecting like terms together.

a $m + 5m + 3n - n$  b $12r + r - 9s + 3r$

c $8x - 6y - x - 4y$  d $12e - 15e + 5f + 3e$

e $8t - 3t + 6u - 6u - 5t$  f $20p + 13q + 7q - p$

**3** Simplify these expressions.

a $4t \times 8$  b $5m \times 6$

c $2a \times b$  d $4x \times 6y$

e $\dfrac{36j}{9}$  f $\dfrac{40n}{8}$

g $\dfrac{15f}{f}$  h $\dfrac{20z}{4z}$

i $2 \times 3 \times 4p$  j $8s \times 7t$

k $\dfrac{4 \times 6p}{8q}$  l $\dfrac{2a \times 8b}{4a}$

**4** Multiply out the brackets in these expressions.

a $6(n + k)$  b $3(f + g)$

c $-2(p + r)$  d $15(x + 2y)$

e $9(2d - 4y)$  f $4(5p - 8q)$

g $5(5f - 4g)$  h $12(5t - 4r + 2)$

i $20(5b + 4c)$  j $15(3m + 6n - 4)$

**5** Use brackets to write an expression for the perimeter of this rectangle.

[rectangle: $5x$, $8y$]

**6 i** Use brackets to write an expression for the area of each rectangle.

**ii** Multiply out the brackets in your expression for the area.

a [rectangle: $x + 6$, $3$]  b [rectangle: $2a + 3b$, $4$]

c [rectangle: $t - 4$, $2$]  d [rectangle: $2a - 3r + 5$, $3$]

---

**7** The formula for the area of a trapezium is

$$\text{Area} = \frac{1}{2} \times (a + b) \times h.$$

Use the formula to calculate the area of each of these trapeziums. All measurements are in centimetres.

a $a = 6$, $b = 5$, $h = 10$

b $a = 8$, $b = 6$, $h = 7$

c $a = 15$, $b = 5$, $h = 9$

d $a = 11$, $b = 8$, $h = 10$

Make sure you use the correct units for your answers.

**8** The formula for converting temperatures from Centigrade to Fahrenheit is $C = \frac{5}{9}(F - 32)$.

a Find the temperature in °C when $F = 95°$

b Find the temperature in °F when $C = -40°$

**9** Write the perimeter of each shape as an expression. Write your answers in their simplest form.

a [Rectangle: $x$, $y$]  b [Kite: $a$, $a$, $b$, $b$]  c [Pentagon: $x$, $x$, $y$, $y$, $x$]

**10** There are $s$ sweets in a bag. How many sweets are there in

a 2 bags?

b 5 full bags and 4 extra sweets?

c 1 bag after 3 have been eaten?

**11 a** A catering company uses this rule to work out the number of sandwiches to make for lunch meetings at an office.

For each group, the number of sandwiches is two per person plus four.

Write this rule as an algebraic formula.

(Let $s$ stand for sandwiches and $p$ stand for people.)

b How many sandwiches need to be made for 12 people?

c How many sandwiches need to be made for 9 people?

d If 36 sandwiches are made, how many people are expected at the meeting?

## Question commentary

**Questions 1** to **3** – Lots of basic practice at algebraic simplification. Check students are dealing with negative terms correctly in questions **1** and **2** while simplifying the numbers first in question **3**.

**Questions 4** to **6** – Question **4** is basic practice while questions **5** and **6** link to the work on forming expressions in **3d**.

**Question 7** – This question also tests students' ability to use BIDMAS (**1c**) so check that they are evaluating the expressions correctly.

**Question 8** – In part **b**, students may find it easier to substitute first and then solve an equation rather than trying to rearrange the given formula.

**Questions 9** to **11** – Students should be encouraged to simplify their answers as fully as possible. They may need help extracting the relevant information for question **11** in particular.

## Answers

**1**  a  $4x$          b  $5p$          c  $3y$          d  $7a$
     e  $4d$          f  $12g$

**2**  a  $6m + 2n$                 b  $16r - 9s$
     c  $7x - 10y$                d  $5f$
     e  $0$                       f  $20q - 19p$

**3**  a  $32t$       b  $30m$      c  $2ab$      d  $24xy$
     e  $4j$        f  $5n$       g  $15$       h  $5$
     i  $24p$       j  $56st$     k  $3p \div q$   l  $4b$

**4**  a  $6n + 6k$                 b  $3f + 3g$
     c  $-2p - 2r$                d  $15x + 30y$
     e  $18d - 36y$               f  $20p - 32q$
     g  $25f - 20g$               h  $60t - 48r + 24$
     i  $100b + 80c$              j  $45m + 90n - 60$

**5**  $2(5x + 8y)$

**6**  a  i  $2(x + 9)$              ii  $2x + 18$
     b  i  $2(2a + 3b + 4)$        ii  $4a + 6b + 8$
     c  i  $2(t - 2)$              ii  $2t - 4$
     d  i  $2(2q - 3r + 8)$        ii  $4q - 6r + 16$

**7**  a  $55$ cm²     b  $49$ cm²    c  $90$ cm²     d  $95$ cm²

**8**  a  $35°C$       b  $-40°F$

**9**  a  $2x + 2y$    b  $2a + 2b$   c  $3x + 2y$

**10** a  $2s$         b  $5s + 4$    c  $s - 3$

**11** a  $s = 2p + 4$                b  $28$
     c  $22$                       d  $16$

| Related lessons | | Resources | |
|---|---|---|---|
| Area | 2c | Circumference of a circle | (1088) |
| Formulae | 3c | Substitution 1 | (1187) |
| Rounding | 1b | Significant figures | (1005) |
| Circumference of a circle | 2f | Catalogues or magazines showing detail of bike sprockets and gears | |
| | | Lego gears | |

| Simplification | Extension |
|---|---|
| The first two tasks link directly into the work in **2d** and should be reasonably straightforward for all students. Calculators will help. The ratios considered in task **3** should also be simple to calculate. It is in tasks **4** and **5** where the main opportunities for simplification arise. | Students could work out the speed ranges for the gears of their own or a friend's bike. |
| | Students could also work out different speed ranges for different sized front sprockets other than the two given in the case study. |
| The initial table is quite straightforward for students to complete if they have the answer to part **a** of task **4** but the calculations of speed in task **5** are both labour-intensive and require conversions. These conversions could be given to the students and/or the task simplified by taking a single value for the number of turns of the pedal, for example 50 turns. Parts **c** and **d** of task **5** could be omitted altogether. | An interesting video clip which covers the principles of mechanical advantage and other things to do with gears can be found at http://www.sciencekids.co.nz/videos/physics/gears.html. Students could be asked to write about other things that they find out from watching the clip. |

| Links |
|---|
| Students who are particularly interested can see a range of information related to power and efficiency when cycling at http://users.frii.com/katana/biketext.html and a detailed consideration of gearing at http://www.phred.org/~alex/kenkifer/www.kenkifer.com/bikepages/touring/gears.htm |

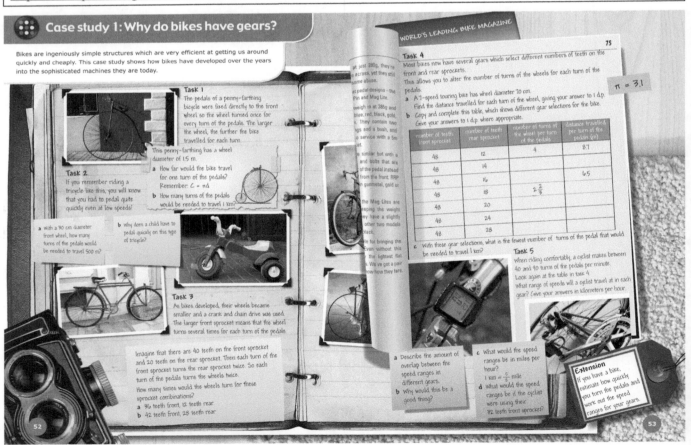

## Teaching notes

This case study starts from a historical point of view with the penny farthing bicycle which, as its pedals were fixed directly to the front wheel, needed a large front wheel in order to reach a reasonable speed. The gearing of a penny farthing was described as the diameter of the wheel (in inches). A fairly normal diameter would be 60 inches. Bike enthusiasts still sometimes refer to the gearing of a bike in inches. A '60 inch gear' means a gear that will make the bike travel the same distance for one turn of the pedals as a penny farthing would with a 60 inch diameter wheel.

Talk to the students about any bicycles they might own. Ask them about the types of bikes they have and whether they have several gears (most touring, racing and mountain bikes) or just a single gear (BMX bikes).

### Task 1

Look at the penny farthing and point out that it has no chain; the pedals are fitted directly to the front wheel. Look also at the picture of the tricycle which also has its pedals attached directly to the front wheel. Students may have had something similar when they were young. Explain that the size of the wheel determines how far the penny farthing travels for each turn of the pedals and ask, how would you work out how far it travels for one turn of the pedals?

### Task 2

Then look together at the bicycle at the bottom of the page. Discuss how the chain and sprockets mean that the wheel doesn't turn at the same rate as the pedals; as the front sprocket is larger, the wheel makes several turns for each turn of the pedals. Some students might find that hard to follow. Using examples with 'easy' numbers such as 40 teeth on the front sprocket and 20 on the rear might help. You could try explaining that each turn of the front sprocket moves 40 links of the chain and 40 links of the chain will turn the rear sprocket twice.

### Task 3

Give students a few minutes to work with a partner through the questions about the bike before looking at the yellow post it note at the bottom of the page, asking how will you work out the speed of the bike? Hear ideas and establish that you need to know how far the bike travels for one turn of the pedals and that the gearing means that for each turn of the pedals the bike moves forward by an amount based on the ratio of the gears and the circumference of the wheels.

### Task 4

Look at the right hand page and talk about the use of gears, asking when and how they use any gears they have on their bike. Talk about the way you can use gears to keep your pedalling rate reasonably constant at different speeds so that it stays within an efficient range.

Look together at the table and ensure that students understand its contents. Discuss how to work out the missing figures from the information given, noting that the sprocket sizes can be used to find the number of times the wheel turns for every turn of the pedals and that the wheel size can then help them find the distance travelled.

### Task 5

Look at the questions about the speed ranges that would be achieved for the given rates of turning the pedals. Make sure that students understand what is being described. Then ask them to work out the speed ranges for each gear. If students work as a group for this they can spread the workload between them.

---

### Answers

1  a  4.71 m   b   212 turns
2  a  529 turns
   b  The pedals are fixed directly to the wheel, which is small so it doesn't travel far for each turn.
3  a  3           b  1.5
4  a  2.20 m
   b  4, 8.80; 3.43, 7.54; 3, 6.60; 2.67, 5.86; 2.4, 5.28; 2, 4.40; 1.71, 3.77
   c  113.64 turns
5  21.11 – 47.50; 18.10 – 40.72; 15.83 – 35.63; 14.07 – 31.67; 12.67 – 28.50; 10.56 – 23.75; 9.05 – 20.36
   a  Students' comments.
   b  Students' comments; highest and lowest gears don't overlap.
   c  13.19 – 29.69; 11.31 – 25.45; 9.90 – 22.27; 8.80 –19.79; 7.92 – 17.81; 6.60 – 14.84; 5.65 – 12.72
   d  14.07 – 31.67 / 8.79 – 19.79; 12.06 – 27.14 / 7.54 – 16.96; 10.56 – 23.75 / 6.60 – 14.84; 9.38 – 21.11 / 5.86 – 13.19; 8.44 – 19.00 / 5.23 – 11.88; 7.04 – 15.83 / 4.40 – 9.90; 6.03 – 13.57/3.77 – 8.48

## Learning outcomes

**N2** Order positive and negative integers, decimals and fractions; use the number line as a model for ordering of the real numbers; use the symbols $=, \neq, <, >, \leq, \geq$ (L5)

**N4** Use the 4 operations, including formal written methods, applied to integers, decimals, proper and improper fractions, and mixed numbers, all both positive and negative (L5/6)

**N9** Work interchangeably with terminating decimals and their corresponding fractions (such as 3.5 and 7/2 or 0.375 and 3/8 (L5)

**N10** Define percentage as 'number of parts per hundred', interpret percentages and percentage changes as a fraction or a decimal, interpret these multiplicatively, express 1 quantity as a percentage of another, compare 2 quantities using percentages, and work with percentages greater than 100% (L5)

**N11** Interpret fractions and percentages as operators (L5)

**SP2** Develop their use of formal mathematical knowledge to interpret and solve problems, including in financial mathematics (L7)

## Introduction

The chapter starts by looking at adding and subtracting fractions with and without a common denominator before a section on finding fractions of an amount. Multiplying and dividing whole numbers by fractions is covered before a spread on converting between fractions and decimals and ordering pairs. Percentages of and percentage problems are covered before the final section which covers the application of percentage change and repeated percentage change.

The introduction discusses the nature of fractals. Fractals occur in nature but can also be generated by computer using simple iterative formulae on a special kind of number called a complex number:

http://www.mathsisfun.com/numbers/complex-numbers.html

Fractals were first developed by Benoit Mandelbrot in the 1960s and since then they have become an important branch of mathematics. The notion of 'self-similarity' has been applied to practical problems such as 'How long is the coastline of Britain?' and they are also used extensively in computer graphics to generate environments for games.

## Prior knowledge

Students should already know how to…

- Work with number lines
- Find simple fractions of amounts

## Starter problem

The starter problem looks at a basic financial scenario. If we consider Andy's purchase decision, it seems sensible to pay £1000 per year. But when we work out the interest at 10%, we discover that it exceeds the payment amount. If we find 10% of £12 000 we see it is £1200 and even if we find 10% of the reduced amount of £11 000 we see it is £1100. It doesn't matter which way we work this, Andy will end up owing more money at the end of each year than at the start…

Understanding financial situations like this, while not immediately relevant to the students, will mean that they are not caught out by similar 'offers' in the future as they engage with more and more financial situations.

## Resources

**MyMaths**

| | | | | | |
|---|---|---|---|---|---|
| Fractions to decimals | 1016 | Adding subtracting fractions | 1017 | Fractions of amounts | 1018 |
| Percentages of amounts 1 | 1030 | Percentages of amounts 2 | 1031 | Equivalent fractions | 1042 |
| Multiply divide fractions | 1046 | Percentage change 1 | 1060 | Comparing fractions | 1075 |

**Online assessment**

| | |
|---|---|
| Chapter test | 3A–4 |
| Formative test | 3A–4 |
| Summative test | 3A–4 |

**InvisiPen solutions**

| | | | |
|---|---|---|---|
| Equivalent fractions | 141 | Fractions of amounts | 142 |
| Adding and subtracting fractions | | | 145 |
| Percentage of an amount | 151 | | |
| Percentage increase and decrease | | | 152 |
| Fractions and decimals | 161 | | |
| Percentages, fractions and decimals | | | 162 |

## Topic scheme

Teaching time = 8 lessons/3 weeks

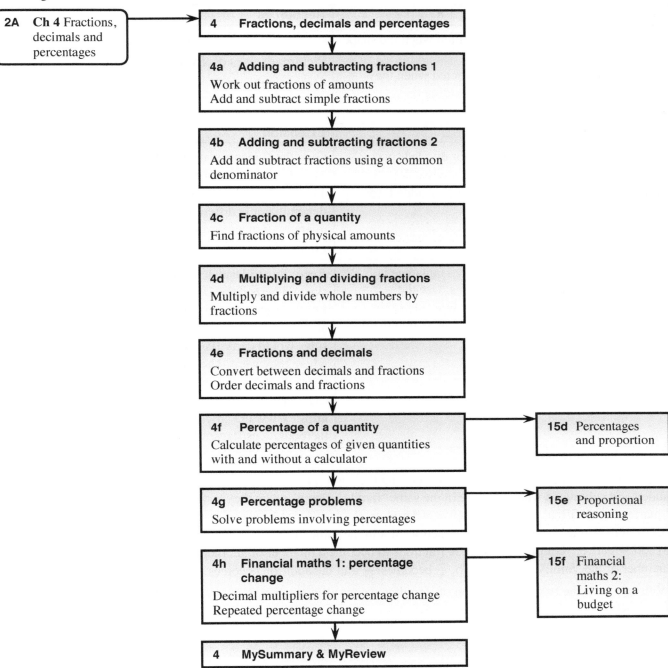

**2A  Ch 4** Fractions, decimals and percentages

**4  Fractions, decimals and percentages**

**4a  Adding and subtracting fractions 1**
Work out fractions of amounts
Add and subtract simple fractions

**4b  Adding and subtracting fractions 2**
Add and subtract fractions using a common denominator

**4c  Fraction of a quantity**
Find fractions of physical amounts

**4d  Multiplying and dividing fractions**
Multiply and divide whole numbers by fractions

**4e  Fractions and decimals**
Convert between decimals and fractions
Order decimals and fractions

**4f  Percentage of a quantity**
Calculate percentages of given quantities with and without a calculator

**15d** Percentages and proportion

**4g  Percentage problems**
Solve problems involving percentages

**15e** Proportional reasoning

**4h  Financial maths 1: percentage change**
Decimal multipliers for percentage change
Repeated percentage change

**15f** Financial maths 2: Living on a budget

**4  MySummary & MyReview**

## Differentiation

| **Student book 3A**      54 – 75 |
| --- |
| Add and subtract fractions |
| Multiply and divide fractions |
| Convert between fractions and decimals |
| Find fractions and percentages of amounts |
| Solve percentage problems |
| Repeated percentage change |

| **Student book 3B**      52 – 71 |
| --- |
| Add and subtract fractions and mixed numbers |
| Multiply and divide by fractions |
| Convert between fractions and decimals |
| Order fractions and decimals |
| Percentage of and percentage increase and decrease |
| Solve percentage problems |
| Repeated percentage change |

| **Student book 3C**      54 – 69 |
| --- |
| Calculate with fractions |
| Recurring decimals and reciprocals |
| Percentage increase and decrease |
| Reverse percentage change |
| Solve percentage problems |

## Objectives

- Add and subtract simple fractions and those with common denominators. (L4)

| Key ideas | Resources |
|---|---|
| 1 A fraction of a shape can be written when the shape is divided into equal parts.<br>2 Fractions can be added or subtracted when they have the same denominator by adding or subtracting the numerators only. | ⊞ Adding subtracting fractions (1017)<br>Pictures of flags or 'fraction diagrams'<br>Mini whiteboards |

| Simplification | Extension |
|---|---|
| Give the students grids of squares or divided 'pizzas' representing various denominators. They colour the parts which represent the fractions being added; for example, $\frac{1}{5} + \frac{2}{5}$ . | Give the students some questions involving simple mixed numbers, for example $1\frac{3}{4} - \frac{1}{4}$ or $2\frac{1}{5} + 1\frac{2}{5}$ . They could also work with simple cases where the denominator is different, for example halves and quarters or quarters and eighths. |

| Literacy | Links |
|---|---|
| The precision of the teacher's spoken language is important in the teaching of fractions. Use the language of 'families' in which fractions are in the same 'family' when they have the same denominator. | According to Danish legend, Dannebrog fell from the sky and helped the Danish forces win the battle of Lyndanisse in Estonia on June 15, 1219. Flags have always been important in battle as the leaders of both sides would carry flags so that their soldiers could see where they were. The battle was often won when the enemy's flag was captured. Flags of the world can be found at https://www.cia.gov/library/publications/the-world-factbook/docs/flagsoftheworld.html |

## Alternative approach

The language of 'families' is useful in describing the addition and subtraction of fractions. Fractions can only be added and subtracted when they are in the same 'family'; that is, when they have the same denominator. The 'quarters' and 'fifths' are two examples of families. So $\frac{1}{5} + \frac{2}{5}$ can be added immediately giving $\frac{3}{5}$, the answer being in the same 'family of fifths'. Fractions not in the same family cannot be added immediately; for example, to add $\frac{2}{5}$ and $\frac{3}{10}$ requires one of these fractions to become a member of another family; $\frac{2}{5}$ has to become a member of the 'family of tenths'. So, $\frac{2}{5}$ becomes $\frac{4}{10}$ and the addition becomes $\frac{4}{10} + \frac{3}{10} = \frac{7}{10}$ .

With an eye to the future, this notion of 'families' is not needed when fractions are multiplied or divided.

## Checkpoint

Find $\frac{1}{6} + \frac{2}{6} + \frac{2}{6}$ $\left(\frac{5}{6}\right)$

Find $\frac{5}{8} - \frac{4}{8}$ $\left(\frac{1}{8}\right)$

**Starter** – Factors and multiples

Write the following list on the board:

$3, 7, 15, 16, 18, 21, 24, 60$

Ask questions; for example,

Which numbers are a multiple of 7?  [7, 21]
Which numbers are not a multiple of 3? [7, 16]
Which numbers have a factor of 4?  [16, 24, 60]

## Teaching notes

Using examples of flags or other geometric shapes which are divided into parts and displayed to the whole class, ask students to identify what fractions of the various diagrams and pictures are various colours. Point out that all the flags and diagrams are divided into parts of equal size; their number gives the denominator of the fraction. The number of pieces of a specific colour gives the numerator of the fraction.

Ask students to draw their own geometric shapes, divide them into equal parts, and colour in several colours. They ask their friends to give the fractions shaded in different ways.

Give a simple example of adding fractions with a common denominator; for example: A chocolate bar has 15 pieces. Two friends eat 3 pieces and 4 pieces. In total they eat $\frac{3}{15} + \frac{4}{15} = \frac{7}{15}$. Explain that subtracting fractions works in the same way. Ensure that students are familiar with and understand that $\frac{x}{x} = 1$. Ask students to complete further examples and check solutions using mini whiteboards.

In the exercise the numbers have been chosen so that, for the most part, the answers will not simplify. Students will probably already know that $\frac{2}{4}$ is equivalent to $\frac{1}{2}$ but you may like to point out other cases where the answer will simplify and explain that it is good practice to write the answers in their simplest form.

## Plenary

Display other pictures or flags showing fractions and ask students to write the fractions on mini whiteboards. Then give examples of adding and subtracting fractions with common denominators.

## Exercise commentary

**Question 1** – Use students' previous experience and knowledge to explain how they know that some flags are not divided into quarters. Use the expressions 'parts of equal size' and 'unequal parts'. In part **c** explain that $\frac{2}{4} = \frac{1}{2}$.

**Question 2** – Check students' understanding of proportion and non-unitary fractions. Point out $\frac{3}{9} = \frac{1}{3}$.

**Questions 3, 4, 6** and **7** – Remind students that fractions 'of the same family' (that is, with the same denominator) can be added or subtracted by adding or subtracting the numerators only.

**Question 3** – Point out that $\frac{2}{8} = \frac{1}{4}$ but to add fractions they need to have the same denominator so they shouldn't simplify the fraction.

**Question 4** – Point out that $\frac{6}{9} = \frac{2}{3}$. Remind students that $\frac{6}{6} = 1$ and that they should write their answer as 1.

**Question 5** – This question provides useful ideas for a class discussion.

**Question 6** – Point out, if you wish, that they can simplify the answers to parts **b, c, d** and **f**.

**Question 7** – Students could work simply with the numerators to find a calculation that works out as 1.

**Question 8** – Remind students how an improper fraction can be written as a mixed number.

---

## Answers

1  a  NATO, Mauritius
   b  The flag is a rectangle, so lines from corner to corner form different sized triangles.
   c  $\frac{1}{2}$
   d  $\frac{3}{4}$

2  a  i  $\frac{4}{9}$  ii  $\frac{1}{3}$  iii  $\frac{2}{9}$

   b  $\frac{5}{9}$

3  a  $\frac{1}{8}$  b  $\frac{7}{8}$  c  $\frac{1}{8}$

4  a  $\frac{4}{5}$  b  $\frac{3}{4}$  c  $\frac{5}{7}$  d  $\frac{2}{3}$
   e  1  f  1

5  a  True  b  False  c  True  d  True

6  a  $\frac{2}{5}$  b  $\frac{1}{4}$  c  $\frac{3}{5}$  d  $\frac{1}{2}$

   e  3/7  f  $\frac{1}{3}$

7  $\frac{3}{10} + \frac{7}{10} - \frac{4}{10} - \frac{5}{10} = \frac{1}{10}$

8  Missing entries top to bottom, left to right
   a  $1\frac{1}{3}, \frac{5}{9}, \frac{7}{9}, \frac{3}{9}, \frac{2}{9}, \frac{1}{9}$  b  $\frac{10}{13}, \frac{5}{13}, \frac{5}{13}, \frac{2}{13}, \frac{3}{13}, \frac{2}{13}$

## Objectives

- Add and subtract fractions with different denominators. (L6)

| Key ideas | Resources |
|---|---|
| 1 You can add or subtract fractions only when they have the same denominator.<br>2 Equivalent fractions are used to add or subtract fractions with different denominators. | ⊕ Adding subtracting fractions (1017)<br>Equivalent fractions (1042)<br>Squared paper<br>Mini whiteboards |

| Simplification | Extension |
|---|---|
| Ensure that students have plenty of practice with equivalent fractions before adding or subtracting fractions with different denominators.<br><br>When the students are adding or subtracting fractions, have squared paper for them to draw fraction diagrams. | Extend the problems in Question **4** to include three (or more) fractions; for example, $\frac{11}{12} - \frac{1}{4} + \frac{1}{6}$ .<br><br>Have students, in pairs, create their own problems and challenge each other. Give students problems involving simple mixed numbers such as $1\frac{5}{12} + 2\frac{1}{6}$. |

| Literacy | Links |
|---|---|
| After reading the section **Links**, compare the English and Latin words 'ounce' and 'uncial'. Also compare the Latin 'semi' with 'semi-detached' and 'semicircle'.<br><br>The precision of the teacher's spoken language is again important and the notion of 'families' in which fractions are in the same 'family' when they have the same denominator can again be used. A clear layout of the steps when adding and subtracting is an aid to clear thinking. | The Romans used words to describe fractions as parts of the whole. In calculations, they used fractions based on the 'as', a unit of weight. As there were twelve 'unciae' in an 'as', the word 'uncia' came to mean one-twelfth of anything. 'Unciae' were added to make halves, thirds and quarters. 'Semis' was six 'unciae' or one half. There is more information about Roman fractions at http://ancienthistory.about.com/od/romannumerals/p/RomanFractions.htm |

## Alternative approach

The language of 'families', as in the previous lesson, can be used here. For the example $\frac{2}{3} + \frac{1}{4}$, quarters and thirds cannot easily become members of each other's family, so they both have to join the family of twelfths. To do so, equivalent fractions are found by multiplying the top and bottom of $\frac{2}{3}$ by 4 and of $\frac{1}{4}$ by 3. The addition is now $\frac{2}{3} + \frac{1}{4} = \frac{8}{12} + \frac{3}{12} = \frac{11}{12}$ .

Students should set out their solution showing all these stages.

## Checkpoint

Work out $\frac{2}{3} + \frac{1}{4}$ $\left(\frac{11}{12}\right)$

Work out $\frac{3}{4} - \frac{1}{5}$ $\left(\frac{11}{20}\right)$

## Starter – Quick fire

Recap work of previous chapters and this chapter so far. Ask rapid-response questions with students responding on mini whiteboards. Discuss answers when there is a need.

## Teaching notes

Students draw a 3 × 4 grid. They shade one-third of the cells in one colour and one-quarter in another colour without shading the same cell twice. They count the total number of shaded cells and express it as the fraction seven-twelfths.

Explain the key term 'equivalent fraction' and explain that one-quarter and one-third have fraction equivalents in twelfths. Use the diagram to find these equivalents. Explain that before you can add two fractions, they must have a common denominator. Use the example to show the correct way to set out the problem and provide further examples as necessary, including examples of subtracting fractions with different denominators.

## Plenary

Students write simple equivalent fractions on their mini whiteboards and, later, add and subtract simple fractions on their mini whiteboards. Discuss their answers where necessary.

## Exercise commentary

**Questions 1 to 4** – Stress that fractions can be added or subtracted only when they have the same denominators. To create the same denominators, discuss equivalent fractions where both the 'top' and 'bottom' of fractions are multiplied by the same number.

**Question 5** – Students could draw a grid similar to the one in Question 4. Point students towards a 4 × 5 grid so that quarters and fifths of the grid are straightforward.

---

## Answers

1 a $\frac{1}{2}$    b $\frac{1}{2}$

2 a Bella    b $\frac{2}{8}$    c $\frac{5}{8}$

3 a $\frac{3}{4}$    b $\frac{1}{4}$

4 a $\frac{9}{12} = \frac{3}{4}$    b $\frac{5}{12}$    c $\frac{5}{12}$    d $\frac{8}{12} = \frac{2}{3}$

   e $\frac{5}{12}$    f $\frac{3}{12} = \frac{1}{4}$    g $\frac{7}{12}$    h $\frac{10}{12} = \frac{5}{6}$

   i $\frac{7}{12}$    j $\frac{1}{6}$    k $\frac{44}{48} = \frac{11}{12}$

5 a $\frac{9}{20}$    b $\frac{11}{20}$

## Objectives

- Calculate fractions of quantities. (L5)

| Key ideas | Resources |
|---|---|
| 1 A unitary fraction of a quantity is found by dividing by the denominator.<br><br>2 A multiple fraction of a quantity is found by dividing by the denominator and then multiplying the result by the numerator. | ⊞ Fractions of amounts (1018)<br>Counters<br>Sheets of card with 3, 4, 5 circles drawn on them<br>Dictionaries<br>Mini whiteboards |

| Simplification | Extension |
|---|---|
| Students use their times table grid to find unitary fractions of a quantity. They learn that finding a unitary fraction is equivalent to doing a division. They then use their times table grid to multiply when finding a multiple fraction of a quantity. | Give students problems where the final answer is not a whole number, for example $\frac{3}{4}$ of 18 or $\frac{1}{5}$ of 11.<br>Accept fractional answers and ask for the decimal equivalents.<br>For example, $\frac{3}{4}$ of $18 = 3 \times 4\frac{1}{2} = 13\frac{1}{2} = 13.5$ |

| Literacy | Links |
|---|---|
| The step-by-step layout of students' work will help their understanding. For example,<br>$\frac{3}{4}$ of $28 = \frac{3}{4} \times 28 = 3 \times 7 = 21$ | Bring dictionaries for the class to use. The word 'fraction' comes from the Latin 'fractio', meaning 'break'. How many other words can the class find beginning or ending with 'fract'? What is the connection between these words and 'break'? |

## Alternative approach

Have sheets of card with 3, 4 or 5 circles drawn on them. Provide a pile of counters for students. If a student has 12 counters, dividing them into two equal piles gives half of 12. Using the 3-circle card, students create three equal piles and find one-third or two-thirds of 12. The 4-circle cards creates quarters to find one-, two- or three-quarters of 12 – and also a discussion about two-quarters being the same as a half. The 5-circle card is used with 15 counters. Repeat with other numbers of counters.

To reinforce the physical division with a calculation, check the answers using a calculator. Emphasise that pressing the ÷ key finds just one-third, quarter or fifth (the unitary fraction) and that pressing the × finds the multiple fraction.

## Checkpoint

Work out $\frac{2}{3}$ of £60 (£40)

Work out $\frac{6}{7}$ of 84kg (72kg)

## Starter – Quick fire

Recap work of previous chapters and this chapter so far. Particularly ask questions about equivalent fractions and adding and subtracting (simple) fractions. Students answer on their mini whiteboards. Discuss questions when their answers indicate a need.

## Teaching notes

Remind students that the denominator and numerator of a fraction are the numbers on the top and bottom, respectively. Use examples in context, such as bad oranges in a bag bought at a supermarket, to find a fraction of a quantity. Show:

- finding a unitary fraction, such as one-third, of a number;
- finding a multiple fraction, such as two-thirds, of a number.

For a unitary fraction, you simply divide the quantity by the denominator.

For a multiple fraction, you find the unitary fraction of the quantity first and then multiply the result by whatever multiple is required.

Have students discuss several examples as a whole class. Then use mini whiteboards to assess their understanding individually.

## Plenary

A quick-fire selection of activities: responses on mini whiteboards to oral questions; a multiple-choice quiz where students have a choice of possible answers; a bingo-style game where students work out answers quickly and eliminate numbers on their grid.

## Exercise commentary

**Question 1** – This question deals only with calculating unitary fractions of quantities. Remind students that when they calculate a fraction of a quantity, they divide the quantity by the fraction's denominator. For example, $\frac{1}{5}$ of £50 means £50 ÷ 5.

**Question 2** – Discuss that, when calculating non-unitary fractions of quantities, students should find the unitary fraction of the quantity first and then multiply by the numerator. For example, as $\frac{1}{5}$ of £50 = £10, then $\frac{2}{5}$ of £50 = 2 × £10.

**Questions 3** and **4** – Ensure that students write the calculation as in Question **2**. For example, in Question **3**, write $\frac{5}{8}$ of 32. Question **4** part **b** is best solved by subtracting their answer to part **a** from 72.

**Question 5** – This question simply requires students to write 29 out of 65 as a fraction.

**Question 6** – If necessary, remind students that a percentage is the number of parts out of 100 and that $50\% = \frac{50}{100} = \frac{1}{2}$ .

## Answers

| 1 | a | £10 | b | £4 | c | 4 mm | d | 8 cm |
|---|---|---|---|---|---|---|---|---|
| | e | 25 kg | f | €5 | g | $4 | h | 30 g |
| | i | 9 tonnes | j | 9 mm | k | 40 m | l | 100 kg |

| 2 | a | £20 | b | $6 | c | 15 g | d | 24 cm |
|---|---|---|---|---|---|---|---|---|
| | e | 18 g | f | £15 | g | 8 m | h | €8 |
| | i | 27 volts | j | 28 mm | k | 25 km | l | 27 kg |

**3** 12

**4** a 54  b 18

**5** $\frac{29}{65}$

**6** They are equal in value.

| Objectives | |
|---|---|
| • Multiply and divide an integer by a fraction. | (L6) |

| Key ideas | Resources |
|---|---|
| 1  Multiplying an integer by a fraction involves a division.<br>2  Dividing an integer by a fraction involves a multiplication. | ⊕ Multiply divide fractions intro    (1046)<br>Circles of cards and scissors<br>Fraction diagrams or 'pizzas'<br>Mini whiteboards |

| Simplification | Extension |
|---|---|
| Give the students fraction diagrams or 'pizzas' to help them visualise the solutions to the problems in Question **2**. For example, a grid of 30 squares will help with part **a**. | Students find 'fractions of fractions' such as one-half of one-quarter of a number. Ask how the answers to the two-stage questions can be found in one step. |

| Literacy | Links |
|---|---|
| The choice of the teacher's words are absolutely crucial.<br><br>For example, 'dividing ten pizzas *into* halves' (to get 20 pieces) is different from 'dividing ten pizzas *in* half (to get 5 whole pizzas).<br><br>'Dividing *into* halves' is the same as 'dividing ten by a half' ($10 \div \frac{1}{2} = 20$). But it is different from 'dividing ten pizzas *in* half' which is the same as 'finding a half of ten pizzas' ($\frac{1}{2} \times 10 = 5$). | American cookery books usually list dry ingredients in terms of fractions of cups, teaspoons and tablespoons. Cups and spoons measure ingredients by volume rather than by weight. There is more information about US cooking measures and conversions at http://www.miketodd.net/encyc/cooking.htm and a typical recipe at http://whatscookingamerica.net/Desserts/ShooflyPie.htm |

**Alternative approach**

This approach for division by a fraction has the same logic as that used with pizzas, but the visual representation is different.

Consider a 2 × 3 rectangle of 6 squares. Cut the rectangle lengthways into two strips of 3 squares. We have divided the rectangle into 2 pieces and we write $6 \div 2 = 3$.

Consider the same rectangle of 6 squares. Divide each square into two halves by drawing along the diagonals of the squares. We have divide the whole rectangle into halves and created 12 pieces and we write $6 \div \frac{1}{2} = 12$.

By dividing each square into halves we have created twice as many pieces as the original six. So dividing into halves has the same effect as multiplying by 2. We write $6 \div \frac{1}{2} = 6 \times 2 = 12$.

This approach works for other rectangles (or squares) such as 3 × 3, so $9 \div \frac{1}{3} = 9 \times 3 = 27$, because dividing 9 squares into 3 pieces each creates 27 pieces.

**Checkpoint**

| | |
|---|---|
| Work out $\frac{1}{8} \times 120$ | (15) |
| Work out $15 \div \frac{1}{2}$ | (30) |

**Starter** – Fraction bingo

Ask students to draw a 3 × 3 grid and enter nine numbers between 5 and 25. Give questions, for example, "What is one-half of 32?" [16], "One-quarter of 28?" [7], "One-fifth of 55?" [11].
The winner is the first student to cross out all nine numbers in their grid.

## Teaching notes

Ask "What is 2 × 3?" [6] and "What is 3 × 2?" [6]. Point out that multiplication can be done in any order so $30 \times \frac{1}{3} = \frac{1}{3} \times 30$. Remind that this is the same calculation that they did to find a fraction of a quantity so to work out $30 \times \frac{1}{3}$ they do a division. So $30 \times \frac{1}{3} = 30 \div 3 = 10$. The fraction has 'flipped', one-third has become 3, and the multiplication has become a division.

Ask students how many people could be fed from 10 pizzas if each person got one-third of a pizza. Explain that the pizzas are being divided by a fraction to give 30 pieces. This division can be written as a multiplication by 3. So $10 \div \frac{1}{3} = 10 \times 3 = 30$. The fraction has 'flipped', one-third has become 3, and the division has become a multiplication. Practise with other examples.

## Plenary

Use mini whiteboards for quick-fire questions to the whole class. Some questions can be asked in succession; for example, "What is $10 \div \frac{1}{3}$?" followed by "What is $10 \times 3$?" Discuss answers where necessary. Bingo or a multiple-choice quiz will give students an element of competition and encourage focused concentration.

## Exercise commentary

**Question 1** – Eight quarters written in two batches of four as: $\frac{1}{4} + \frac{1}{4} + \frac{1}{4} + \frac{1}{4} = 1$ and $\frac{1}{4} + \frac{1}{4} + \frac{1}{4} + \frac{1}{4} = 1$ may give visual help to some students.

**Question 2** – The first example shows how to set out the solutions. Note that the order of the multiplications changes for parts **i**, **j** and **l** to **o**. Point out that multiplication can be done in any order.

**Questions 3** and **4** – Encourage students to calculate rather than count. In Question **3**, write 20 lots of $\frac{1}{5} = 20 \times \frac{1}{5} = 20 \div 5 = 4$ metres.

**Questions 5** and **6** – For students who are not yet secure with division, ask questions such as, "How many halves in one whole?" [2], "So, how many halves in two wholes?" [4] and so on. At this stage, students learn that multiplying by 2 is equivalent to dividing by one-half. Extend to "How many thirds in one whole, two wholes, …?" [3, 6] and beyond.

**Question 7** – Have students discuss their methods. There are different ways of thinking about this problem.

**Question 8** – A calculator could be used to convert the entire distance to yards. An alternative method is to find two-fifths of 26 miles and convert the remainder into yards.

## Answers

| | | | | | | | |
|---|---|---|---|---|---|---|---|
| **1** | **a** | 2 kg | **b** | $2\frac{1}{4}$ kg | | | |

| | | | | | | | | |
|---|---|---|---|---|---|---|---|---|
| **2** | **a** | 10 | **b** | 4 | **c** | 10 | **d** | 5 |
| | **e** | 8 | **f** | 12 | **g** | 60 | **h** | 5 |
| | **i** | 5 | **j** | 5 | **k** | 9 | **l** | 10 |
| | **m** | 6 | **n** | 6 | **o** | 11 | | |

**3**   4 m

**4**   20 strips

| | | | | | | | | |
|---|---|---|---|---|---|---|---|---|
| **5** | **a** | 60 | **b** | 100 | **c** | 3 | **d** | 32 |
| | **e** | 20 | **f** | 24 | **g** | 50 | **h** | 100 |
| | **i** | 245 | **j** | 36 | **k** | 28 | **l** | 1000 |

**6**   32

**7**   40 legs

**8**   18 458 yards = 10 miles, 858 yards

## Objectives

- Recognise that a recurring decimal is a fraction. (L5)
- Use division to convert a fraction to a decimal. (L5)
- Order fractions by writing them with a common denominator or by converting them to decimals. (L5)

| Key ideas | Resources |
|---|---|
| 1 Every fraction can be written as either a recurring or a terminating decimal.<br><br>2 A calculator can be used to convert fractions to decimals. | Fractions to decimals (1016)<br>Comparing fractions (1075)<br>Newspapers and magazines<br>Calculators<br>Matching cards for fractions and decimals<br>Mini whiteboards |

| Simplification | Extension |
|---|---|
| The use of a physical number line will ensure that students have a constant reminder of the simplest of the conversions such as halves, fifths and tenths and help with Question 1. Ensuring that all students have access to similar calculators will enable support to be consistent for the calculator conversions later in the exercise. | Get students to convert harder fractions into decimals without a calculator. For example, ask them to use a logical method to deduce the decimal equivalent for one-eighth from that for one-quarter or the decimal equivalent for one-twentieth from that for one-tenth. Ask them to write other equivalents in the same manner. |

| Literacy | Links |
|---|---|
| The word 'recurring' comes from Latin words meaning 'running on'. A decimal which does not recur is called a 'terminating' decimal, where the word 'terminating' means 'ending'.<br><br>A recurring decimal can be shown using a series of dots, such as 0.3333…. or by rounding the decimal and using the sign $\approx$ meaning 'approximately equal to'. An alternative notation is to write just the first 3 with a dot above it, but it is not dealt with in this chapter. | Bring in some newspapers and magazines for the class to use. Fractions are often used in advertising to express the proportion of the population who claim to prefer a particular brand or who have the need for a particular product. Examples are '1 in 4 people over the age of 40 have high cholesterol' or '8 out of 10 owners said their cat preferred …'. How many examples of fractions can the class find? Can they convert any of these to decimals? |

## Alternative approach

All students need a calculator. They create a table with three headings: *Fraction, Recurring decimal, Terminating decimal*. Starting with $\frac{1}{2}$, they write the fraction and its decimal equivalent in the appropriate columns. They continue with $\frac{1}{3}, \frac{1}{4}, \frac{1}{5}$ … as far as $\frac{1}{25}$. The task is to see if they can spot a pattern which allows them to predict which fractions terminate and which recur. List the prime factors of the denominators of fractions with terminating decimal equivalents. (The denominators of the fractions with terminating decimal equivalents are 2, 4, 5, 8, 10, 20 and 25.) Notice that, if the prime factors are only 2s and 5s, then the fraction will terminate. This is because numbers are based on powers of 10 (recall Th, H, T, U) and the prime factors of 10 are 2 and 5. Now predict whether other fractions will terminate or recur and test the predictions on a calculator.

## Checkpoint

Convert $\frac{9}{20}$ to a decimal (0.45)

Which is larger, 0.4 or $\frac{3}{7}$ ? $\left(\frac{3}{7}\right)$

## Starter – Quick-fire fractions

Students use their mini whiteboards to answer straightforward questions on fractions from earlier in this chapter. Include using the four rules with fractions and finding the fraction of a quantity. The aim is to practise and assess students' competence with fractions rather than ask overly-demanding questions.

## Teaching notes

Students write as many fraction/decimal equivalents as they can. Write them for the whole class to see. Refer to the dual number line in their book which shows some fractions and decimals between 0 and 1.0.

Explain how other fractions can be converted to decimals using a calculator. Ask students to convert examples such as one-eighth and three-twentieths using their calculators. Answers can be shown on mini whiteboards. Show that for some fractions, such as one-third and one-sixth, the decimal equivalents 'go on forever'. Tell students that these are recurring decimals and explain that they should round them. Introduce the 'approximately equal to' sign to use in these cases.

## Plenary

A matching game can be used to assess how well the students have grasped these concepts. Have a number of cards showing fractions and their decimal equivalents and ask students to match them. These cards could also be used to play Fraction Snap.

Use the cards for quick-fire questions (using mini whiteboards for responses) in order to assess all the class.

## Exercise commentary

**Question 1** – This question is basic practice at using the scale given.

**Question 2** – Check students remember the > and < notation. Students find the two numbers on the scale. Check that they know how to choose which is the larger.

**Question 3** – Students need to know that a fraction such as $\frac{3}{20}$ implies the division $3 \div 20$, which they can then enter in their calculators.

**Question 4** – This question builds upon the previous question to compare two fractions.

**Question 5** – Ensure that students can compare two decimals by inspection of the first and, if needed, subsequent decimal places.

**Question 6** – This question could be approached from the point of view of James missing the school record by $\frac{1}{8}$ and Nessi by $\frac{1}{9}$. Comparing these two fractions sees Nessi get *closer* to the record since $\frac{1}{9} < \frac{1}{8}$.

---

## Answers

1.
| | | | |
|---|---|---|---|
| a 0.1 | b 0.5 | c 0.7 | d 0.2 |
| e 0.9 | f 0.6 | g 0.8 | h 0.7 |
| i 0.8 | | | |

2.
| | | | |
|---|---|---|---|
| a > | b = | c < | d = |
| e > | f < | g = | h < |
| i = | | | |

3.
| | | | |
|---|---|---|---|
| a 0.05 | b 0.75 | c 0.625 | d 0.29 |
| e 0.83 | f 0.11 | g 0.18 | h 0.35 |
| i 0.375 | | | |

4.   a,b
   i   $0.375 < 0.4$          ii   $0.8333... > 0.8$
   iii   $0.666... < 0.75$

5.   $1/4 < 3/10 < 2/5 < 1/2$

6.   a   $\frac{7}{8} = 0.875 < 0.888 = \frac{8}{9}$   b   No

## Objectives

- Calculate percentages of a quantity.

| Key ideas | Resources |
|---|---|
| **1** 1% can be found by dividing a quantity by 100. <br> **2** 10% can be found by dividing a quantity by 10. <br> **3** Other percentages can be found from 1% or 10%. | Percentages of amounts 1     (1030) <br> Percentages of amounts 2     (1031) <br> Calculators <br> Dice |

| Simplification | Extension |
|---|---|
| Use a 'hundred square' to emphasise the fact that percentage is 'per hundred'. Find 1% of quantities before finding other percentages by multipication of the answer for 1%. Save finding 10% by dividing by 10 until students are confident with finding percentages via 1%. | Restrict the use of calculators and emphasise that students should be able to work out whole-number percentages by a logical 'splitting' approach such as finding 10%, 5%, 2% and 1% using mental or paper-based methods only. Expect them to work on questions such as in Question **4** without the use of a calculator. Give further, more complicated questions as appropriate. |

| Literacy | Links |
|---|---|
| The word 'percent' means 'out of a hundred' and reinforces the equivalence between, say, $7\%, \frac{7}{100}$ and even 0.07. This is a good opportunity to refresh these equivalences. | National tables of GCSE results are published each year. The tables list the percentage of candidates at each school who passed five or more GCSEs at grades A* to C. Choose a school in the tables at www.education.gov.uk/schools/performance/index.html <br><br> Has the percentage increased or decreased for the chosen school over the last four years? |

### Alternative approach

There are three ways of finding a percentage of a quantity. For example, to find 31% of £240 [£74.40]

- find 1% first and then multiply by the required percentage. Use a calculator and key in $240 \div 100 \times 31$;
- write the equivalent decimal. Use a calculator and key in $0.31 \times 240$;
- partition the 31% into $3 \times 10\%$ and then 1%. $10\% = 240 \div 10 = 24$; $30\% = 3 \times 24 = 72$ and then $1\% = 240 \div 100 = 2.4$; finally, $30\% + 1\% = 72 + 2.4 = £74.40$.

The first of these methods builds on the meaning of 'percentage' as 'hundredth'.

The second method uses the fewest keys on a calculator.

The third method lends itself to a mental approach.

The use of the percentage key on a calculator is not recommended.

### Checkpoint

Calculate 35% of £70        (£24.50)

Calculate 8% of 120 kg        (9.6 kg)

**Starter** – Dice fractions

Ask students to draw four boxes representing the numerators and denominators of two fractions. Throw a dice four times. After each throw, students place the score in one of their boxes. After four shakes, they compare the two fractions (by converting them to decimals using a calculator) and insert the < or > sign between them.

## Teaching notes

Explain that 'percent' means 'out of a hundred' and that one percent is the same as one hundredth.
To find one percent, divide by one hundred and therefore to find X percent, divide by 100 and then multiply by X.

Since $10\% = \frac{10}{100} = \frac{1}{10}$, simply divide by 10. If the percentage is a multiple of 10, then divide by ten and multiply by the multiple. Give a number of examples where students find first 10% and then 20%, 30%, ... of a quantity. Check all answers using mini whiteboards.

Ask students what 21% is as a fraction. Further examples show students that, to find any percentage of a quantity, the first step is to divide the quantity by 100 and the second step is to multiply their answer by the numerator of the fraction. Explain how they can use a calculator to work out a percentage of a quantity using the same steps.

## Plenary

Asking quick-fire questions where the students as a whole class respond on mini whiteboards will enable rapid assessment of progress.

## Exercise commentary

**Questions 1** and **2** – These questions are graded to support a mental approach. In Question **2**, use decomposition for students to work in multiples of 10. For example, 30% = 10% + 10% + 10% = 3 × 10%.

**Question 3** – Discuss that 45% means 'forty-five parts out of 100' and hence can be written as $\frac{45}{100}$ which can be written more simply as $\frac{9}{20}$. Students can also write these percentages as decimals.

**Question 4** – Students should complete this question using a calculator. This can be useful for reinforcing Question **3**. For example, for 65% of 400 cm, use a calculator and work out (65 ÷ 100) × 400. Some students will quickly see and use 45% as its decimal equivalent of 0.45.

**Question 5** – Help students to decode the narrative. By now they should be able to apply their understanding and skills to make the comparisons.

**Question 6** – Students should input the large numbers carefully. They can add their answers as a check.

## Answers

1  a  £5           b  12 g          c  20 kg         d  7.5 cm
   e  $4.60        f  18°

2  a  £10          b  36 g          c  20 m          d  27 litres
   e  63 cm        f  £135

3  a  $\frac{45}{100} = \frac{9}{20}$   b  $\frac{55}{100} = \frac{11}{20}$   c  $\frac{27}{100}$   d  $\frac{90}{100} = \frac{9}{10}$
   e  $\frac{10}{100} = \frac{1}{10}$   f  $\frac{9}{100}$   g  $\frac{5}{100} = \frac{1}{20}$   h  $\frac{1}{100}$

4  a  £20          b  90 kg         c  £19.25        d  260 cm
   e  €140         f  45 g          g  3 volts       h  1 mm
   i  297 miles

5  a  i  Suzi      ii  Suzi         iii  Austin
   b  Suzi is more likely to succeed as she is closer to her targets.

6  a  Land = 147 919 024 km², Water = 362 146 576 km²
   b  Add them up to check they make the total surface area of the Earth, or estimate by dividing the total surface area by 3.

## Objectives

- Express one number as a percentage of another. (L5)
- Calculate percentages and find the outcome of a given percentage increase or decrease. (L6)

| Key ideas | Resources |
|---|---|
| 1 Find a percentage of a quantity by various methods.<br>2 Find one number as a percentage of another. | Percentages of amounts 2 (1031)<br>Percentage change 1 (1060)<br>Calculators<br>Mini whiteboards |

## Simplification

Some students may wish to continue to use a mental method for calculating percentage increase or decrease by finding multiples of 1% and 10%.

To express one number as a percentage of another, keep the numbers simple and use equivalent fractions. For example, to find 3 as a percentage of 25 simply needs a multiplier of 4.

## Extension

Students could extend Question **5** into an investigation by reducing and increasing the price by a different percentage such as 20% or 25% and seeing the effect.

More able students could be introduced to using a single decimal multiplier for finding the final values.

## Literacy

Percentages are a part of daily life; they appear in news headlines and advertisements. Giving students a 'feel' for percentages is as important as giving them the skills to compute accurately.

For example, a news headline says 'annual inflation is 5%' so, if you earn about £19 000 a year, what might you want your annual income to rise by? [about £1000]. If your credit card debt costs you 24.6% a year and your debt is £2000, how much do you pay, in round figures, on your debt? [about £500].

## Links

Council Tax is a local tax levied on households that helps pay for local services such as rubbish collection. The amount that each household is required to pay is based on the estimated value of the property, whether owned or rented, and usually increases each year. The percentage change in average council tax each year from 2000–01 to 2009–10 can be found at www.local.communities.gov.uk/finance/ctax/data/ctax0910t1.pdf

In which year was the increase the highest? [2003–4]

## Alternative approach

Three alternative methods for finding a percentage of a quantity were offered in the previous lesson.

They are

- find 1% first and then multiply by the required percentage using calculator;
- write the equivalent decimal and use a calculator to multiply it by the required percentage;
- partition the percentage into parts that are easy to find mentally, such as 50%, 25%, 10% and 1% and add the parts.

For finding one number as a percentage of another, first write the number as a fraction of the other. After all, a percentage is only a fraction in hundredths. So, for example, if you earn £17 500 and pay £1980 in tax, first write the tax as a fraction of the income, then use a calculator to change it to a decimal (1980 ÷ 17 500 = 0.1131…) and write the hundredths as the percentage 11.3% (rounded to 1 decimal place).

## Checkpoint

A shirt normally costs £32. In a sale the price is reduced by 15%. What is the new price of the shirt? (£27.20)

What percentage of 12 000 is 4500? (37.5%)

## Starter – At the sales!

Have students mentally calculate 1% and 10% of sums of money and easy multiples of 1% and 10%, answering on mini whiteboards. For example, find the reductions when a sale reduces a price of £210 by 1%; another price of £540 is reduced by 2%; a third price of £140 is reduced by 20%; etc.

## Teaching notes

Students explain how to find one-tenth or one-hundredth of an amount. They write their answers on mini whiteboards.

Explain that one-hundredth is one percent and that one-tenth is ten percent. Ask them to use mental methods to find compound percentages; for example 15% of £300 (from 10% and half of 10%) or 22% of 150 kg (from 10% doubled and 1% doubled).

Explain how problems like these can be solved using a calculator.

Ask students to give answers to simple problems asking for one number as a percentage of another number, such as "What is 12 as a percentage of 50?" Students can use mini whiteboards to respond. Explain the process for finding the answer to more complicated examples of this type using a calculator.

## Plenary

Students use mini whiteboards to answer questions of the type 'Find $x$ as a percentage of $y$' where $y$ is 50, 25 or 10. Students mentally multiply $y$ to make 100 and then multiply $x$ by the same number. Discuss answers.

## Exercise commentary

Students can use mental methods, written methods or a calculator.

Only Question 1b involves expressing one number as a percentage of another. All the others ask students to find a percentage of a quantity.

**Question 1** – In part **a**, students use a calculator to find 18% of £3300. In part **b**, students should write the quantities as a fraction which they can then change to a decimal using a calculator.

**Question 2** – Each answer is found from '$p$% of $a$' where $p$% is a percentage and $a$ is an amount. Students have to 'tackle' the language to arrive at the calculation. Parts **a** and **b** can be done using written methods but part **c** probably requires a calculator.

**Question 3** – Students first have to find the increase or decrease. They then have to add or subtract the increase or decrease to find the new value. Part **a** could be done using a written method; parts **b** and **c** probably require a calculator.

**Question 4 –** This is a good question for paired work and discussion. The calculations can be done mentally. Encourage students to give reasons to support their answers.

**Question 5** – The calculation in part **a** can be done using written methods. Part **b** needs careful explanation. Students should be encouraged to see what happens if other items are reduced and, later, increased by 15%.

---

## Answers

**1  a** £594  **b** 16%

**2  a** £7  **b** 84 MB  **c** 792 vowels

**3  a** 172.5 g  **b** £21.45  **c** 64 072 seats

**4  a** There are 412 people in total. If 40% = 160 then 10% should equal 40 people and 60% should equal 240 people. Yes, 38.83%, no, 61.17%.
  **b** No = 240 people

**5  a** £117.30
  **b** Because the increase is 15% of a smaller number.

### Objectives

- Interpret percentages as operators (L7)
- Develop their use of formal mathematical knowledge to interpret and solve problems, including in financial mathematics (L7)

| Key ideas | Resources |
|---|---|
| 1 Compound interest and depreciation<br>2 Decimal multipliers | ⊕ Percentage change 1 (1060)<br>Calculators<br>Mini-whiteboards |

### Simplification

Students who struggle to work with a single multiplier could spend more time practicing the applications of this rather than moving on the problems which have repeated percentage change. Hence questions 5, 6 and 9 could be omitted.

### Extension

Students could investigate how the value of savings under a compound interest scheme differs from the value under a simple interest scheme. Do the values diverge from each other, or does the gap stay the same? A spreadsheet can again be used to help with this investigation. They could also graph the relative values for a given amount saved.

### Literacy

Financial literacy: Words like 'interest' may be new to the students and will need careful explanation.

### Links

There is a wealth of information on financial products and services available to the students. They could investigate actual savings and loan rates by visiting a local bank or going on the internet. Links to the 'credit crunch' and the banking crisis over the last five years can also be developed.

### Alternative approach

While the use of multipliers is by far the simplest method for solving problems of repeated percentage change, an alternative approach (for a small number of time periods) is by systematically calculating the interest earned, adding it to the principal and repeating. Students should get used to the repetitive nature of the calculations and be able to tabulate the outcomes at each stage. An example table might look something like this:

| Year | Start amount | Interest | Finish amount |
|---|---|---|---|
| 1 | | | |
| 2 | | | |
| 3 | | | |
| 4 | | | |

### Checkpoint

£7000 is invested at 8% interest per year. How much is it worth after three years? (£8817.98)

**Starter** – Quick-fire percentages of…

Following on from work in **4f**, students could be asked to calculate different percentages of an amount. For example, what is 50% of 90? What is 30%? What is 70%? What is 25%? Mini-whiteboards can be used to turn this into a speed round.

## Teaching notes

Emphasise the difference between multipliers for percentages of, percentage increase and percentage decrease. It is important at this stage that students 'see' the multiplier in context and can successfully convert the scenario.

When introducing the concept of compound interest emphasise that the interest earned in the first year is added to the *principal* amount so this is the new principal for the second year, etc. This leads on to the concept of repeated multiplication with the multiplier raised to the appropriate power (the number of *periods* of time, usually years). Students will also need to be given some examples of repeated percentage decrease to tackle question **9**.

## Plenary

John invests £3000 at a rate of interest of 4% per year. Alison invests £2500 at a rate of interest of 8% per year. How long will it take Alison to have more money than John? (5 years)

## Exercise commentary

**Question 1** – Revision of percentage to decimal conversions may be necessary.

**Question 2** – Calculators can be used here to encourage students to use the decimal multiplier rather than resorting to an informal method.

**Question 3** – Decimal multipliers that are either added or subtracted from one whole.

**Question 4** – Calculators can be used again here to encourage students to use the decimal multiplier rather than resorting to an informal method.

**Questions 5** and **6** – Ideas of compound interest (and depreciation) are introduced here. Encourage students to use the decimal multiplier if they can or approach the problems using the suggestion in the **Alternative approach**.

**Questions 7** and **8** – Practical applications of percentage calculations. Again, allow calculators and encourage students to use single multipliers where appropriate.

**Question 9** – A compound interest and depreciation (erosion) question similar to questions **5** and **6** but placed firmly in context.

## Answers

1  a  0.66    b  0.23    c  0.77    d  0.5
   e  0.05    f  0.07    g  1.1    h  1.15

2  a  £125 × 0.12 = £15    b  500m × 0.03 = 15m
   c  34kg × 0.57 = 19.38kg    d  £300 × 0.175 = £52.50
   e  4MB × 0.34 = 1.36MB    f  200mm × 0.025 = 5mm

3  a  1.25    b  1.07    c  2.3
   d  0.3    e  0.84    f  0.97

4  a  £300    b  639kg    c  106.25cm   d  £357.21

5  a  $1.4^2$    b  $1.35^5$    c  $0.7^2$    d  $0.94^{10}$

6  a  $£250 × 1.1^4 = £366.03$    b  $£300 × 1.05^6 = £402.03$
   c  $£1000 × 0.8^3 = £512$    d  $£750 × 0.93^6 = £485.24$

7  a  i  2.7GB    ii  3.3GB
   b  1.935
   c  28.8

8  a  227.5g    b  £330 050

9  a  i  £418    ii  £436.81
      iii  £498.47    iv  £621.19
   b  i  £7520    ii  £7068.80
      iii  £5871.23    iv  £4308.92

| Key outcomes | | Quick check |
|---|---|---|
| Add and subtract fractions with the same denominator | L5 | Work out<br>**a** $\frac{2}{10}+\frac{3}{10}+\frac{4}{10}\left(\frac{9}{10}\right)$ **b** $\frac{7}{8}-\frac{4}{8}\left(\frac{3}{8}\right)$ |
| Add and subtract fractions with different denominators | L6 | Work out<br>**a** $\frac{3}{4}+\frac{1}{7}\left(\frac{25}{28}\right)$ **b** $\frac{1}{2}-\frac{4}{9}\left(\frac{1}{18}\right)$ |
| Find the fraction of a quantity | L5 | What is<br>**a** $\frac{1}{3}$ of £66 (£22) **b** $\frac{4}{5}$ of 85 kg (68 kg) |
| Multiply and divide integers by fractions | L6 | Work out<br>**a** $35 \times \frac{1}{7}$ (5) **b** $16 \div \frac{1}{5}$ (80) |
| Convert fractions to decimals and compare them | L5 | **a** Convert $\frac{3}{5}$ to a decimal (0.6)<br>**b** Which is bigger, $\frac{1}{5}$ or 0.21? (0.21) |
| Find the percentage of a quantity | L5 | **a** Work out 45% of 80 (36)<br>**b** Work out 22% of 150 (33) |
| Write one number as a percentage of another | L5 | Write 350 as a percentage of 400 (0.875) |
| Calculate percentage changes | L7 | **a** Increase £450 by 15% (£517.50)<br>**b** Decrease 3,200 kg by 30% (2240 kg) |

## ⊞ MyMaths extra support

| Lesson/online homework | | | Description |
|---|---|---|---|
| Frac dec perc 2 | 1015 | L6 | Converting fractions, decimals and percentages with harder values |
| Frac dec perc 1 | 1029 | L4 | Converting well-known fractions, decimals and percentages |
| Finding fractions | 1062 | L5 | Helps teachers create and discuss fractions of shapes |
| Simple equiv. fractions | 1371 | L4 | Use fractions up to tenths. Start learning about equivalent fractions and decimals |

## My Review

### Check out
**You should now be able to ...**

| | Test it Questions |
|---|---|
| ✓ Add and subtract fractions with the same denominator. | 1 |
| ✓ Add and subtract fractions with different denominators. | 2 |
| ✓ Find a fraction of a quantity. | 3, 4 |
| ✓ Multiply and divide integers by fractions. | 5, 6 |
| ✓ Convert fractions to decimals and compare them. | 7, 8 |
| ✓ Find a percentage of a quantity and a percentage change. | 9 – 12 |
| ✓ Write one number as a percentage of another. | 13 |
| ✓ Calculate percentage changes. | 14, 15 |

### Language

| Language | Meaning | Example |
|---|---|---|
| Denominator | This is the bottom number of a fraction. It tells you how many equal parts are in the whole. | The denominator for $\frac{5}{8}$ is 8. This means the whole is split into 8 equal parts. |
| Numerator | This is the top number of a fraction. It tells you how many parts you have. | The numerator for $\frac{5}{8}$ is 5. This means you have 5 out of the 8 parts. |
| Integer | An integer is zero or any positive or negative whole number. | ... -3, -2, -1, 0, 1, 2, 3, 4 ... |
| Recurring decimal | A recurring decimal has an unlimited number of digits, which form a pattern, after the decimal point. | $\frac{2}{3} = 2 \div 3 = 0.666666...$, the sixes do not stop. |
| Percentage | Percent means out of 100. | 47% means $\frac{47}{100}$ |
| Equivalent decimal | The decimal number that equals a given percentage. | The decimal equivalent of 17.5% is 0.175 |
| Decimal multiplier | The number you multiply by to calculate a percentage change. | To increase by 25% multiply by 1.25. To decrease by 27% multiply by 0.75. |

### 4 MyReview

1 Calculate these and simplify your answer where possible.
 a $\frac{3}{7} - \frac{1}{7}$    b $\frac{2}{11} + \frac{4}{11} + \frac{5}{11}$

2 Calculate these and simplify your answer where possible.
 a $\frac{1}{3} + \frac{1}{6}$   b $\frac{1}{4} - \frac{1}{20}$   c $\frac{2}{3} + \frac{1}{4}$

3 Use a mental method to calculate.
 a $\frac{1}{5}$ of £30    b $\frac{1}{8}$ of 24 students

4 Use a mental or written method to calculate.
 a $\frac{2}{5}$ of 40g    b $\frac{3}{7}$ of 35 cm

5 Work these out, writing your answers as whole numbers.
 a $18 \times \frac{1}{6}$    b $\frac{1}{4} \times 60$

6 Divide these whole numbers by fractions.
 a $50 \div \frac{1}{3}$    b $1 \div \frac{1}{5}$

7 Convert these fractions into decimals without using a calculator.
 a $\frac{3}{10}$   b $\frac{2}{5}$   c $\frac{1}{4}$

8 Use a calculator to convert these fractions into decimals. Round your answers to 2 dp.
 a $\frac{1}{6}$    b $\frac{4}{9}$

9 Calculate these percentages of quantities using a mental method.
 a 10% of 70    b 60% of 120

10 Calculate.
 a 75% of 280    b 3% of 500

11 Increase £76 by 25%.

12 A toaster originally cost £18 but it reduced by 10%, what is the new price?

13 In a class of 25 students, 15 are boys. What percentage are girls?

14 Use a decimal multiplier to
 a increase £300 by 7%
 b decrease £231 by 19%.

15 You invest £740 in a savings account which page 4% interest. How much money do you have after
 a 1 year   b 2 years   c 10 years.

#### What next?

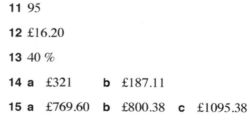

| Score | | |
|---|---|---|
| 0 – 5 | | Your knowledge of this topic is still developing. To improve look at Formative test: 3A-4; MyMaths: 1016, 1017, 1018, 1030, 1031, 1042, 1046, 1060 and 1075 |
| 6 – 12 | | You are gaining a secure knowledge of this topic. To improve look at InvisiPen: 141, 142, 145, 151, 152, 161 and 162 |
| 13 – 15 | | You have mastered this topic. Well done, you are ready to progress! |

## Question commentary

**Question 1** – Students should focus on adding or subtracting the numerators only.

**Question 2** – Students should look for the LCM of the two denominators

**Questions 3 and 4** – Students are guided as to what method to use. Answers could be checked using a calculator.

**Questions 5 and 6** – Encourage students to turn these calculations into division or multiplication by whole numbers.

**Question 7** – Students should be able to recall the equivalent decimals in this case.

**Question 8** – Check the rounding of the final answers.

**Questions 9 and 10** – Mental methods are indicated for question **9** but students could also be encouraged to use a mental method for question **10**.

**Questions 11 to 14** – Encourage students to use a combination of informal and formal methods to solve these problems. They should communicate the methods they use in their written answers.

**Question 15** – Students should be directed to use a decimal multiplier in this question.

## Answers

| | a | b | c |
|---|---|---|---|
| 1 | $\frac{2}{7}$ | 1 | |
| 2 | $\frac{1}{2}$ | $\frac{3}{20}$ | $\frac{11}{12}$ |
| 3 | £6 | 3 students | |
| 4 | 16 g | 15 cm | |
| 5 | 3 | 15 | |
| 6 | 150 | 5 | |
| 7 | 0.3 | 0.4 | 0.25 |
| 8 | 0.17 | 0.44 | |
| 9 | 7 | 72 | |
| 10 | $\frac{57}{100}$ | 15 | |
| 11 | 95 | | |
| 12 | £16.20 | | |
| 13 | 40 % | | |
| 14 | £321 | £187.11 | |
| 15 | £769.60 | £800.38 | £1095.38 |

# 4 MyPractice

**1** Jan and Pauline share a box of chocolates.
There are eight chocolates in the box.
Jan eats $\frac{1}{4}$ of the chocolates and Pauline eats $\frac{3}{8}$.

a Use the picture to calculate the total fraction of the box that they eat.

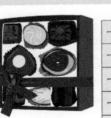

Each chocolate is $\frac{1}{8}$ of the box.

b What fraction of the chocolates is left?

This diagram should help you.

**2** Work these out.

a $\frac{1}{10} + \frac{1}{5}$   b $\frac{2}{5} - \frac{3}{10}$

c $\frac{4}{5} - \frac{2}{5}$   d $\frac{1}{2} + \frac{1}{10}$

**3** Calculate these.

a $\frac{1}{5}$ of £35   b $\frac{1}{8}$ of 40kg

c $\frac{1}{6}$ of 30mm   d $\frac{1}{10}$ of 100cm

e $\frac{1}{3}$ of 24m   f $\frac{1}{9}$ of €36

g $\frac{3}{10}$ of 40cm   h $\frac{5}{6}$ of £30

i $\frac{5}{8}$ of 24cm   j $\frac{7}{8}$ of 24mm

k $\frac{3}{4}$ of 44 kg   l $\frac{9}{16}$ of 32kg

Remember that to find $\frac{1}{4}$ of 20 you work out $20 \div 4$.

Remember that to find $\frac{3}{5}$ of 20 you work out $20 \div 5$ and then multiply the result by 3.

**4** Work these out.

a $\frac{1}{9} \times 90$   b $\frac{1}{4} \times 24$   c $\frac{1}{3} \times 21$   d $\frac{1}{5} \times 30$

e $\frac{1}{8} \times 40$   f $\frac{1}{3} \times 63$   g $\frac{1}{4} \times 120$   h $\frac{1}{8} \times 72$

i $35 \times \frac{1}{5}$   j $45 \times \frac{1}{3}$   k $\frac{1}{8} \times 48$   l $100 \times \frac{1}{4}$

**5** How many halves ($\frac{1}{2}$s) are there in these numbers?

a 1   b 2   c 5   d 10   e 15

**6** Divide these numbers by one-third ($\frac{1}{3}$).

a 1   b 3   c 5   d 10   e 20

**7** Divide these whole numbers by fractions.

a $2 \div \frac{1}{3}$   b $20 \div \frac{1}{5}$   c $5 \div \frac{1}{5}$   d $13 \div \frac{1}{2}$   e $8 \div \frac{1}{4}$   f $5 \div 4$

---

**8** Convert these fractions into decimals. Write your answers to no more than 3 decimal places.

a $\frac{1}{10}$   b $\frac{3}{10}$   c $\frac{7}{10}$   d $\frac{1}{5}$   e $\frac{4}{5}$   f $\frac{2}{5}$

g $\frac{1}{8}$   h $\frac{1}{6}$   i $\frac{4}{11}$   j $\frac{1}{7}$   k $\frac{2}{7}$   l $\frac{3}{7}$

**9** Work out these percentages of quantities.

a 10% of £20   b 20% of £20   c 90% of £20

d 20% of £60   e 30% of 200g   f 70% of 50cm

g 25% of 96kg   h 15% of 360m   i 43% of £62

**10** 10% of £60 is £6.

a What is 5% of £60?   b What is 15% of £60?

**11** Choose the most appropriate method to answer these questions.

a Elliott earns £420 a week.
He spends 29% of his wage each week on his rent.
How much is his rent each week?

b A 180g bar of high-quality cooking chocolate contains 72% cocoa solids.
What is the weight of cocoa solids in this chocolate bar?

**12** a There are 32 people in Evan's class.
26 of them have black hair.
What percentage of Evan's class have black hair?

b Hugh's salary last year was £40000. He had to pay £10000 in tax.
Mandy's salary last year was £32000. She had to pay £6400 in tax.
Who had to pay the higher percentage of their salary in tax?

**13** a A packet of biscuits normally has a weight of 250g.
This week the packets contain 20% extra free.
What is the new weight of the packet of biscuits?

b A DVD normally costs £19.
In an 'up to 50% off' sale the price of the DVD is only reduced by 22%.
What is the sale price of the DVD?

**14** Alex has invested heavily in the price of oil but the price is falling. In January he owned £50 million worth of oil but each month its value falls 2%. How much will Alex's investment be worth in

a February   b March   c September?

**MyMaths**.co.uk

## Question commentary

**Questions 1** and **2** – Emphasise that students should work with a common denominator for these questions.

**Question 3** – The function machines and hint boxes should guide the students through these general practice questions.

**Questions 4** to **7** – Encourage students to think of the questions as dividing or multiplying by a whole number.

**Question 8** – Some of the questions can be done by recall, others will need a calculator. Encourage students to use a calculator only when absolutely necessary.

**Questions 9** and **10** – Encourage students to use informal methods where possible rather than resorting straight away to a calculator.

**Questions 11** and **12** – Students may need help extracting the required information from the word problems. Again, encourage informal methods where possible but emphasise the importance of writing the methods down clearly.

**Questions 13** and **14** – Encourage the use of a decimal multiplier for these questions.

## Answers

**1**  a  $\frac{5}{8}$     b  $\frac{3}{8}$

**2**  a  $\frac{3}{10}$     b  $\frac{1}{10}$     c  $\frac{2}{5}$     d  $\frac{3}{5}$

**3**  a  £7        b  5 kg      c  5 mm      d  10 cm
    e  8 m       f  €4        g  12 cm     h  £25
    i  15 cm     j  21 mm     k  33 kg      l  18 kg

**4**  a  10        b  6         c  7         d  6
    e  5         f  21        g  30        h  9
    i  7         j  15        k  6         l  25

**5**  a  2         b  4         c  10        d  20
    e  30

**6**  a  3         b  9         c  15        d  30
    e  60

**7**  a  6         b  100       c  25        d  26
    e  32        f  20

**8**  a  0.1       b  0.3       c  0.7       d  0.2
    e  0.8       f  0.4       g  0.125     h  0.167
    i  0.364     j  0.143     k  0.286     l  0.429

**9**  a  £2        b  £4        c  £18       d  £12
    e  60 g      f  35 cm     g  24kg      h  54m
    i  £26.66

**10**  a  £3       b  £9

**11**  a  £121.80   b  129.6 g

**12**  a  81.25 %   b  Hugh

**13**  a  300 g     b  £14.82

**14**  a  £49 million          b  £48.02 million
    c  £42.54 million

# MyAssessment 1

These questions will test you on your knowledge of the topics in chapters 1 to 4.
They give you practice in the types of questions that you may see in your GCSE exams.
There are 90 marks in total.

**1** Work these out.

  **a** $15 \times 100$        (1 mark)   **b** $12 \div 0.1$      (1 mark)

  **c** $23 \times 0.01$     (1 mark)   **d** $82 \div 0.01$   (1 mark)

**2** Round these numbers to the degree of accuracy indicated.

  **a** 37.5 (nearest 10)     (1 mark)   **b** 1318 (nearest 100)   (1 mark)

  **c** 14.63 (1 dp)       (1 mark)   **d** 23 895 (nearest 1000)  (1 mark)

**3** **a** Work out these **without** a calculator.

    **i** $3 \times 4^2 - 2$   (1 mark)   **ii** $5^2 + 7 - (3^2 + 1)$   (1 mark)

  **b** Work out these with a calculator.

    **i** $357 - (45 + 4^2) \div 4$   (2 marks)   **ii** $16 \times (5^2 - 12) \times 3$   (2 marks)

**4** **a** What are the common factors of 36 and 52?   (2 marks)

  **b** What are the prime factors of 36 and 52?   (4 marks)

  **c** Find the HCF and LCM of 36 and 52.   (3 marks)

**5** Which two numbers from this list are not divisible by 9?   (2 marks)

  81   261   277   333   627   801

**6** Convert these measurements into the units shown in brackets.

  **a** 3.5 tonnes (kg)     (1 mark)   **b** 4 gallons (pints)   (1 mark)

  **c** 2 miles (feet)      (1 mark)   **d** 2.2 litres (cl)    (1 mark)

**7** Calculate the area of these rectangles.

  **a** A volleyball court 18 m long by 9 m wide   (2 marks)

  **b** A stamp 2.1 cm by 1.8 cm   (2 marks)

  **c** A corn field 232 m by 200 m   (2 marks)

**8** The Vanuatu flag is made from one black triangle
and two identical green and red trapeziums.

  **a** Find the area of the black triangle.   (3 marks)

  **b** Find the area of one of the trapeziums.   (3 marks)

  **c** What is the total area of this model flag?   (1 mark)

Vanuatu flag

6 cm   3 cm   3 cm   10 cm

**9** Stonehenge is a circular prehistoric monument approximately 300 feet across.

  **a** Calculate the circumference of this monument. Take $\pi = 3.14$   (3 marks)

  **b** Each one of the large stones was rolled on circular logs about 12 inches in diameter.
How many whole revolutions of the log would it take to move a stone 22 yards?

    12 inches = 1 foot, 3 feet = 1 yard   (5 marks)

**10** Simplify these expressions by collecting like terms.

  **a** $7x + 2y - x - 5y$   (1 mark)   **b** $12u - v + 5v - u$   (1 mark)

**11** Multiply out these brackets.

  **a** $6(3m - 2)$   (1 mark)   **b** $3(4b + 5c)$   (1 mark)

**12** The sides of the triangle are $(6p - 4)$ cm, $(3p + 1)$ cm and $5p$ cm.

  **a** Find the perimeter of the triangle in terms of $p$.   (3 marks)

  **b** If $p = 2$ work out the lengths of the sides of the triangle.   (3 marks)

**13** The formula for the power (watts) of a circuit is
$P = V \times I$   ($V$ = voltage and $I$ = current)

  **a** Use the formula to calculate the power when $V = 240$ and $I = 3$.   (1 mark)

  **b** Rearrange the formula so that you can calculate the current.   (2 marks)

  **c** Use the rearranged formula to calculate the current when
$V = 240$ and $P = 300$.   (2 marks)

**14** Are these statements true or false?
If they are false then give the correct answer.   (8 marks)

  **a** $\frac{1}{3} + \frac{3}{4} = \frac{13}{12}$   **b** $\frac{5}{8} + \frac{1}{4} = \frac{1}{2}$   **c** $\frac{1}{8} + \frac{5}{8} - \frac{1}{2} = \frac{1}{4}$   **d** $\frac{2}{9} + \frac{1}{3} = \frac{4}{9}$

**15** Calculate these.

  **a** $\frac{1}{3}$ of £39   (1 mark)   **b** $\frac{5}{8} \times 64$ m   (1 mark)

  **c** $22 \div \frac{1}{8}$   (1 mark)   **d** $128 \div \frac{5}{16}$   (2 marks)

**16** **a** Convert these fractions to decimals and decimals to fractions without a calculator.

    **i** $\frac{1}{8}$   (1 mark)   **ii** 0.3   (1 mark)   **iii** $\frac{4}{5}$   (1 mark)

  **b** Use a calculator to convert these fractions to decimals (to 2 dp).

    **i** $\frac{5}{9}$   (1 mark)   **ii** $\frac{4}{11}$   (1 mark)   **iii** $\frac{2}{7}$   (1 mark)

  **c** Use a calculator to convert these decimals to fractions in their simplest form.

    **i** 0.34   (1 mark)   **ii** 0.08   (1 mark)   **iii** 0.96   (1 mark)

**17** Calculate   **a** 56% of 2400 m   (1 mark)

               **b** Increase £271 by 53%   (2 marks)

**MyMaths**.co.uk

# Mark scheme

### Question 1 – 4 marks
**a**   1   1500     **b**   1   120
**c**   1   0.23     **d**   1   0.82

### Question 2 – 4 marks
**a**   1   40     **b**   1   1300
**c**   1   14.6     **d**   1   24 000

### Question 3 – 6 marks
**a i**   1   46     **ii**   1   22
**b i**   2   341.75     **ii**   2   624

### Question 4 – 9 marks
**a**   2   1, 2 and 4
**b**   4   2, 3 (36), 2, 13 (52)
**c**   3   4 (HCF), 468 (LCM); 1 mark for prime factors listed

### Question 5 – 2 marks
    2   277 and 627

### Question 6 – 4 marks
**a**   1   3500 kg     **b**   1   32 pints
**c**   1   10 560 feet     **d**   1   220 cl

### Question 7 – 6 marks
**a**   2   $162 \text{ m}^2$     **b**   2   $3.78 \text{ cm}^2$
**c**   2   $46\ 400 \text{ m}^2$

### Question 8 – 7 marks
**a**   3   $12 \text{cm}^2$ ; $\frac{1}{2} \times (4 \times 6)$ seen for 2 marks
**b**   3   $28.5 \text{cm}^2$ ; $\frac{1}{2} \times 3 \times (10 + 6)$ seen for 2 marks
**c**   1   $69 \text{cm}^2$

### Question 9 – 8 marks
**a**   3   942 feet; 1 mark for $\pi \times d$ or $2\pi \times r$ seen
**b**   5   21 revolutions; 37.68 inches seen 1 mark; 66 feet/792 inches seen 1 mark; 792/37.68 seen 1 mark

### Question 10 – 2 marks
**a**   1   $6x - 3y$     **b**   1   $11u + 4v$

### Question 11 – 2 marks
**a**   1   $18m - 12$     **b**   1   $12b + 15c$

### Question 12 – 6 marks
**a**   3   $14p - 3$ ; 1 mark for $6p - 4 + 3p + 1 + 5p$
**b**   3   perimeter = 25cm; 8cm, 7cm and 10cm

### Question 13 – 5 marks
**a**   1   720 (watts)
**b**   2   I = P/V or I = P ÷ V; accept triangle symbolism
**c**   2   1.25 (amps)

### Question 14 – 8 marks
**a**   2   T; must show evidence
**b**   2   F; 3/8
**c**   2   T; must show evidence
**d**   2   F; 1/3

### Question 15 – 5 marks
**a**   1   £13
**b**   1   40m
**c**   1   2.75
**d**   2   409.6; 128 × 16/5 seen for 1 mark

### Question 16 – 9 marks
**a i**   3   0.125    **b i**   0.56    **c i**   17/50
   **ii**   3   3/10    **ii**   0.36    **ii**   2/25
   **iii**   3   0.8    **iii**   0.29    **iii**   24/25

### Question 17 – 3 marks
**a**   1   1344m; working needs to be seen
**b**   2   £414.63; working needs to be seen

**G5** Describe, sketch and draw using conventional terms and notations: points, lines, parallel lines, perpendicular lines, right angles, regular polygons, and other polygons that are reflectively and rotationally symmetric

(L6)

**G7** Derive and illustrate properties of triangles, quadrilaterals, circles, and other plane figures [for example, equal lengths and angles] using appropriate language and technologies

(L6)

**G10** Apply the properties of angles at a point, angles at a point on a straight line, vertically opposite angles

(L6)

**G12** Derive and use the sum of angles in a triangle and use it to deduce the angle sum in any polygon, and to derive properties of regular polygons

(L6)

**G13** Apply angle facts, triangle congruence, similarity and properties of quadrilaterals to derive results about angles and sides, including Pythagoras' Theorem, and use known results to obtain simple proofs  (L6)

| **Introduction** | **Prior knowledge** |
|---|---|
| The chapter starts by looking at the angle properties of parallel lines before reviewing angles in a triangle and the properties of a triangle. Angles in a quadrilateral and the properties of quadrilaterals are covered in the final two sections. | Students should already know how to… <br> • Measure the length of lines <br> • Calculate missing angles on a straight line, at a point and in a triangle |

| | **Starter problem** |
|---|---|
| The introduction discusses the need for accurate measurement of, and estimation of, angles in real life. It also talks about the different types of angle measure used. The commonly used degrees measure which children learn about from an early age stems from ancient times when geometers were trying to tackle things like measuring distances and angles of places on the globe and in the cosmos. The French attempt to decimalise angles came at a time when every other unit of measure was being turned into metric units (the metre, for example, was devised in France and there are still examples of the 'original' metre dotted around Paris). Grads are still used today in things like artillery targeting, but this was one area where the change to a metric system was largely resisted! | The starter problem is an investigation into quadrilaterals on a 9-pin geo-board. Students are invited to investigate how many different quadrilaterals they can find. Encourage them to think about quadrilaterals that look different, even when rotated and/or reflected. This can lead into a discussion of congruence. <br><br> As an extension, students could be asked to find examples of other polygons on the geo-board, for example different triangles or pentagons. The discussion could develop into finding polygons that are concave as well as the more commonly identifiable convex versions. The geo-board could also be extended to 16-pin or even 25-pin if time and ability allows. |

## Resources

**⊞ MyMaths**

| | | | | | |
|---|---|---|---|---|---|
| Angle reasoning | 1080 | Angle sums | 1082 | Interior exterior angles | 1100 |
| Lines and quadrilaterals | 1102 | Angles in parallel lines | 1109 | Angle proofs | 1141 |

**Online assessment**

**InvisiPen solutions**

| | | | | | |
|---|---|---|---|---|---|
| Chapter test | 3A–5 | Lines and angles | 341 | Calculating angles | 342 |
| Formative test | 3A–5 | Types of triangles and angles | | | 343 |
| Summative test | 3A–5 | Properties of quadrilaterals and angles | | | 344 |
| | | Angles and parallel lines | 345 | | |

## Topic scheme

Teaching time = 5 lessons/2 weeks

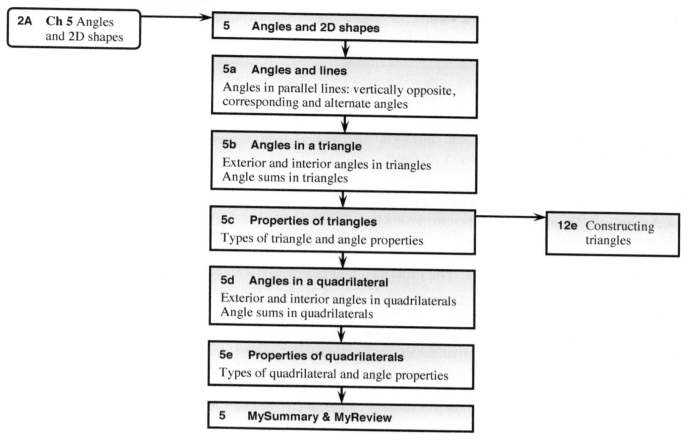

| 2A | Ch 5 Angles and 2D shapes |

**5     Angles and 2D shapes**

**5a    Angles and lines**
Angles in parallel lines: vertically opposite, corresponding and alternate angles

**5b    Angles in a triangle**
Exterior and interior angles in triangles
Angle sums in triangles

**5c    Properties of triangles**
Types of triangle and angle properties

**12e   Constructing triangles**

**5d    Angles in a quadrilateral**
Exterior and interior angles in quadrilaterals
Angle sums in quadrilaterals

**5e    Properties of quadrilaterals**
Types of quadrilateral and angle properties

**5     MySummary & MyReview**

## Differentiation

**Student book 3A     78 – 93**

Angles in parallel lines
Angles and properties of a triangle
Angles and properties of a quadrilateral

**Student book 3B     74 – 89**

Angle properties of triangles
Angles in parallel lines
Properties of quadrilaterals
Angles in quadrilaterals
Interior and exterior angles in regular polygons
Properties of congruent shapes

**Student book 3C     72 – 87**

Angle problems
Angles in a polygon
Properties of a circle
Arcs and sectors
Properties of congruent shapes

## Objectives

- Identify parallel lines. (L4)
- Recognise vertically opposite angles. (L5)
- Identify alternate angles and corresponding angles. (L6)

| Key ideas | Resources |
|---|---|
| 1 Angles are created when two lines cross and when a line crosses two parallel lines.<br><br>2 Angles on a straight line add up to 180°.<br><br>3 Vertically opposite angles are equal; corresponding angles are equal and alternate angles are equal. | ⊞ Angle sums (1082)<br>    Angles in parallel lines (1109)<br><br>Mini whiteboards<br><br>Pre-prepared diagrams |

| Simplification | Extension |
|---|---|
| Provide the students with further numerical examples such as those in Questions **1** and **3** before moving to the more abstract Question **4**. Students should be encouraged to give reasons using the names 'X angles', 'F angles' and 'Z angles' if they find the formal terminology too difficult. | Pairs of students generate examples using their own diagrams and challenge their partner to find the lettered angles. Emphasis should be placed on communicating the rules used using precise mathematical terminology in addition to the informal 'X angles', 'F angles' and 'Z angles'. |

| Literacy | Links |
|---|---|
| The word 'parallel' comes from a Greek word meaning 'beside each other'. Gymnasts use parallel bars.<br><br>The word 'corresponding' means 'being in a similar position to'. The corresponding angles in the diagrams of this lesson lie on the two parallel lines in similar positions.<br><br>The word 'alternate' comes from a Latin word meaning 'by turns'. Note that the adjective is pronounced 'al-ternate'; the verb is pronounced 'alter-nate' and means 'occur in a successive manner'. Alternate angles occur in a successive manner by being in opposite corners of the Z. | Lines of latitude are imaginary lines running around the Earth parallel to the Equator and labelled according to the angular distance north or south from the Equator. The lines are sometimes referred to as parallels; for example, much of the boundary between the USA and Canada runs along the 49th Parallel. In contrast, lines of longitude pass through both poles and are not parallel. There is more information about lines of latitude at<br>http://education.nationalgeographic.com/education/encyclopedia/latitude/?ar_a=1 |

## Alternative approach

A dynamic approach provides an alternative way to the static introduction.

For vertically opposite angles, have two metre rules rotating about a common central point. Watch opposite pairs of angles opening up or closing. Draw pairs of vertically opposite angles. Mark one angle and cut card to fit over it. Show that it also fits exactly on the opposite angle, making an X shape.

For corresponding angles, mark one angle and cut card to fit exactly over it. Slide the card, parallel to the parallel lines and down the line crossing them, to lie exactly on the other corresponding angle, making an F shape.

For alternate angles, have two identical cards lying on top of each other on an angle. Flip one card as for a vertically opposite angle. Slide the other card as for a corresponding angle. The two cards are now in the position of alternate angles within the corners of a Z shape.

## Checkpoint

Two angles lie on a straight line. If one of the angles is 47°, what is the other? (133°)

Is the following statement true or false? 'Alternate angles add up to 180°' (False)

## Starter – How many squares?

Draw a 2 × 2 grid on the board and ask students how many squares they can see. [One large and four small] How many squares are there on a 3 × 3 grid and a 4 × 4 grid? [14, 30]

## Teaching notes

Students list the facts that they already know about angles: angles on a straight line add up to 180°, angles at a point add up to 360° and angles in a triangle add up to 180°.

Define what is meant by parallel lines and show how they are indicated by arrows. Ask how many angles are created if another line intersects two parallel lines [8]. Draw and label a diagram and have students identify any angles which they think are the same size.

Students identify equal angles and name them. They identify them informally and formally as X angles (vertically opposite), Z angles (alternate) and F angles (corresponding).

Students then practise finding angles in different diagrams.

## Plenary

Pairs of students are given a set of matching cards. There are cards with diagrams showing labelled angles, cards with the letters of angles and cards with the sizes of angles in degrees. Students have to group the cards by matching letters with sizes for each diagram.

Students as a whole class find the size of angles in given diagrams and respond using mini whiteboards.

## Exercise commentary

Emphasise that these problems should be solved using mathematical rules rather than by measurement. The diagrams are sketches and are not necessarily drawn accurately.

**Question 1** – Prior whole-class practice should mean this question presents no significant problems.

**Question 2** – Sharp pencils and good quality rulers are needed. Emphasise the need for accuracy in their measurements.

**Question 3** – This question requires simple application of the facts just learnt about angles associated with parallel lines. Students could imagine angles 'sliding' from one parallel line to the other.

**Questions 4** to **6** – Refer students back to the definitions of the types of angles if necessary.

## Answers

| 1 | a | 151° | b | 103° | c | 48° | d | 19° |
|---|---|------|---|------|---|-----|---|-----|

2 **a,b,c**      Check constructions

| 3 | a | $r = 148°$ | b | $s = 32°$ | c | $t = 148°$ | d | $u = 32°$ |
|---|---|-----------|---|----------|---|-----------|---|----------|

| 4 | a | a | b | a | c | b | d | p |
|---|---|---|---|---|---|---|---|---|

5   **a** 72° Alternate angles    **b** 85° Alternate angles
    **c** 61° Alternate angles    **d** 42° Alternate angles

6   **a** Alternate           **b** Corresponding
    **c** Corresponding    **d** Alternate
    **e** Corresponding

## Objectives

- Use side and angle properties of triangles to solve problems. (L6)
- Use the angle sum of a triangle and properties of exterior and interior angles to solve problems. (L6)

| Key ideas | Resources |
|---|---|
| 1 Angles on a straight angle add up to 180° and the angle sum of a triangle is 180°.<br>2 The exterior angle is the angle at a corner between an extended side and the adjacent side at the corner.<br>3 The exterior angle of a triangle is equal to the sum of the two interior opposite angles. | ⊞ Angle reasoning (1080)<br>Angle sums (1082)<br>Pre-prepared paper/card triangles<br>Large triangle<br>Mini whiteboards |

| Simplification | Extension |
|---|---|
| Ensure students know the angle properties of different triangles. Concentrate on the interior angle sum of triangles rather than the properties of exterior angles. When solving multi-step problems, cover up parts of a diagram to emphasise the pertinent part of it. | Students link what they have learned from Lessons **5a** and **5b** to find angles in more complicated diagrams. |

| Literacy | Links |
|---|---|
| A 'theorem' is a word based on Greek meaning 'a statement to be proved'. The statements that 'the angles of a triangle total 180°' and 'the exterior angle of a triangle equals the sum of the two interior opposite angles' are both theorems. They have not been proved in the student's book. Instead, they have been shown or illustrated, a far less rigorous process. | Millions of African slaves were transported to America in the 16th to 19th centuries to work on the plantations. The British trade in slaves was called the Triangular Trade. Ships sailed from Britain to Africa to trade manufactured goods for slaves. The ships then carried the slaves across the Atlantic to America where they were traded for goods such as sugar, cotton and tobacco. These goods were then carried back to Britain and sold for huge profits. There is more about the Triangular Trade at www.nmm.ac.uk/freedom/viewTheme.cfm/theme/triangular |

### Alternative approach

A more demanding way of illustrating that the exterior angle of a triangle equals the sum of the two interior opposite angle requires good agility in using a protractor. Students draw several triangles with all sides longer than 5 cm to allow protractors to be read more easily. Extend one side to make an exterior angle. Measure it and the two interior opposites. Repeat with the other triangles. Enter results in a table with four columns labelled *Exterior angle, An interior opposite angle, Another interior opposite angle, Sum of the interior opposite angles*. Notice the results in the first and last columns. Are they the same? If not, why not?

### Checkpoint

Find the third angle in a triangle with angles 48° and 94°. What type of triangle is it? (48°, Isosceles)

## Starter – Make 180

Give questions orally or in diagrams, for responses on mini whiteboards; for example:

Two angles in a triangle are 34° and 26°, what is the size of the third angle? [120°]

The largest angle in an isosceles triangle is 110°, what are the sizes of the other angles? [35°, 35°]

If one angle in an isosceles triangle is 30°, what sizes are the other angles? [30°, 120° or 75°, 75°]

Discuss responses as necessary.

## Teaching notes

Students name and describe the types of triangle that they know. Say that the angles inside the triangle are called 'interior' angles.

Students are given different triangles made from paper or card. They tear off two of the corners and place them next to the third corner and notice that the three angles of a triangle make a straight line and so add up to 180°.

Ask a volunteer to walk the perimeter of a large triangle drawn on the floor. The class watches what happens each time a corner of the triangle is reached. Explain that the 'exterior' angle of a triangle is the angle the person turns through to go down the next side of the triangle. The angle is more clearly seen if the volunteer points his/her arm in the direction of his/her motion. Indicate on a diagram the three exterior angles of a triangle.

Students are again given different triangles made from card. They tear off two of the corners and place them next to the third corner. This time they see that the two corners make the *exterior* angle at the third corner. This is a demonstration of the rule 'the exterior angle of a triangle equals the sum of the two interior opposite angles'.

## Plenary

Ask students to find angles of triangles using all they know, including the fact about the exterior angle. This can be either as a quiz or a quick-fire response activity using mini whiteboards. Discuss answers as necessary.

## Exercise commentary

**Questions 1 to 3** – Some students may be able to find the angles mentally; others may use a written method or a calculator.

**Question 4** – The triangle is drawn to scale and so students can simply measure the sides if there is any doubt. In part **c**, remind students that angle M is a right angle.

**Question 5** – A deeper understanding comes if students use angles on a straight line and angles in a triangle rather than the fact about the exterior angle of a triangle.

**Question 6** – Students should show their working and give reasons in addition to writing the final answer.

## Answers

1  a  65°       b  72°       c  58°       d  79°

2  a  35°, isosceles       b  87°, scalene
   c  60°, equilateral      d  90°, right-angled
   e  44°, isosceles        f  70°, scalene
   g  18°, isosceles
   h  45°, right-angled, isosceles

3  a  3cm       b  135°       c  23°

4  a  KL                     b  KM
   c  90°. The third angle is a right angle.

5  a  120°       b  103°       c  $p=71.5$  $q=108.5$

6  95°

## Objectives

- Solve geometrical problems using side and angle properties of equilateral, isosceles, scalene and right-angled triangles, explaining reasoning with diagrams and text.                                         (L6)

| Key ideas | Resources |
|---|---|
| 1  Angles in diagrams can be calculated from known facts about the sides and angles of triangles. | Angle reasoning                              (1080)<br>Interior exterior angles                 (1100)<br>Strips of card or straws of varying lengths<br>Commercial construction kits<br>'Yes'/'No' cards |

| Simplification | Extension |
|---|---|
| Students can use physical 'rods' of varying lengths (strips of card, straws, or commercial construction kits) to experiment and show that, for a triangle, the sum of the two shorter sides must be greater than the longest side.<br><br>Ensure that students know the convention for indicating sides of equal length. | Students draw some of the triangles in Question **3** accurately, once they have decided if they are possible. The construction of triangles from the three side lengths could form part of an investigation for these students. Provide a compass and sharp pencil but no instruction in how to use it. |

| Literacy | Links |
|---|---|
| The vocabulary for triangles and angles is extensive and students need to be fluent with it.<br><br>The prefix 'tri-' means 'three' so a triangle has three angles. Other words with the prefix 'tri-' include 'triathlon', 'tricycle', 'triplets' and 'tripod'.<br><br>The name 'equilateral' means having all sides equal. Point out the similarity between 'equal' and 'equi'. '-lateral' means 'side'. Another word students need to know including '-lateral' is 'quadrilateral' meaning 'having four sides'<br><br>The name 'isosceles' comes from Greek and the literal translation is 'having legs of equal length' – we only have two legs so only two of the sides are equal. | Roger Penrose drew the Impossible or Penrose Triangle after attending a lecture by the Dutch artist MC Escher. Escher went on to produce many works of art based on impossible figures including Waterfall (1961), which is based on a Penrose triangle. There is a gallery of Escher's work at www.mcescher.com |

### Alternative approach

A full list of all the facts and statements that students should know and use is a good reference as they tackle a range of problems. Start with a list of the different triangles, giving their names and angle properties. Add the angle sums of angles on a straight line and around a full turn. List the names of angles on parallel lines (the X, F and Z angles), even though they are not needed in this lesson. Finally, list the theorems about the angle sum of a triangle and about exterior angle and the two interior opposite angles. Alongside the list, draw illustrative diagrams, given that 'a picture is worth a thousand words'.

### Checkpoint

Explain why side lengths 4cm, 5cm and 10cm will not make a triangle.    (Sum of shorter two < longest one)

An isosceles triangle has one angle of 112°. Find the other two angles.    (34°, 34°)

**Starter** – How many triangles?

Draw an equilateral triangle. Divide each side into thirds. Draw two lines parallel to each side to connect the points of trisection and so form 9 small triangles. How many triangles are there in this figure?    [13]

## Teaching notes

Restate the facts that the angle sum of a triangle is 180° and the exterior angle of triangle equals the sum of the two interior opposite angles. Restate the properties of isosceles and equilateral triangles.
Ask students to solve some simple angle problems involving these facts.
Discuss the reasoning step-by-step.

To demonstrate the statement that the sum of the two shorter sides of a triangle is greater than the length of the longest side, strips of card or straws of varying lengths (say, 8 pieces ranging in length from 5 cm to 20 cm) can be given to small groups of students. They record any groups of three lengths which they use to construct a triangle. When the students respond with their answers, point out that, in all cases, the sum of the two shorter sides is always longer than the longest one.

## Plenary

Give students quick-fire questions on angles in a triangle using mini whiteboards. The students can also have a piece of card, one side red and the other side green, which they use to indicate 'yes' or 'no' when presented with possible side lengths for triangles.

## Exercise commentary

**Question 1** – Earlier practice with isosceles and equilateral triangles is a prerequisite for this question.

**Question 2** –The problems can all be solved using angles on a straight line and the angle sum of a triangle. The property relating to the exterior angle of a triangle can shorten the working.

**Question 3** – Students need to use the fact that the sum of the two shorter sides of a triangle is greater than the length of the longest side.

**Questions 4** and **5** – These questions combine knowledge of the properties of isosceles triangles with the fact about the angle sum of a triangle.

**Question 6** – Students should work through this problem step-by-step, explaining their reasoning at each stage. The angles which are marked but unlabelled can be given letters to clarify the working.

---

## Answers

1  a   45°       b   60°       c   64°       d   74°
   e   16°       f   94°

2  a   $k = 70°$   b   $w = 95°$   c   $t = 75°, u = 40°$
   d   $d = 58°, g = 32°$

3  b, d, e will not make triangles.

4  a   7 cm       b   34°

5  a   4.5 cm     b   40°

6  a   40°

## Objectives

- Understand a proof that the angle sum of a quadrilateral is 360°.                    (L6)

| Key ideas | Resources |
|---|---|
| 1  Any quadrilateral can be divided into two triangles.<br>2  The angle sum of the four angles of a quadrilateral is 360°. | ⊞  Angle proofs                                    (1141)<br>Quadrilaterals made from card or paper<br>'Yes'/'No' cards<br>Maps of Italy<br>Mini whiteboards |

| Simplification | Extension |
|---|---|
| Two demonstrations (the one in the student's book in which they tear off the corners of a quadrilateral and fit them together to make a full turn and the one using tessellations described in the **Alternative approach**) showing that the angle sum of a quadrilateral is 360° are usually convincing. Provide quadrilaterals with three known angles and use a calculator to find the fourth angle. | Students investigate whether or not there is a rule for exterior and interior angles of quadrilaterals similar to the rule about exterior and interior angles in a triangle. [In general, there isn't one.] |

| Literacy | Links |
|---|---|
| As with angle sums for triangles, so also with quadrilaterals, links can be made with algebra in the way that students write their solutions. For example, a solution may be written as:<br><br>$90 + 120 + 50 + x = 360$<br>$260 + x = 360$<br>$x = 360 - 260$<br>$x = 100$ | Bring some atlases for the class to use. A quadrilateral is also a military term used to describe an area defended by four fortresses supporting each other. The most famous quadrilateral is the Quadrilatero comprising the four fortified towns of Mantua, Peschiera, Verona and Legnago in northern Italy. The area was important during the wars in Italy in 1848. There is a map showing the Quadrilatero at http://commons.wikimedia.org/wiki/File:Quadrilatero Austriaco.png<br><br>Can the class find this area on the map of Italy? |

### Alternative approach

Cut out at least ten congruent quadrilaterals from card. Label the corners *a*, *b*, *c* and *d* for each quadrilateral. Tesselate the quadrilaterals. Look at any point where four quadrilaterals meet. The angles at that point are *a*, *b*, *c* and *d* and they make a full turn of 360°. So $a + b + c + d = 360°$.

### Checkpoint

A quadrilateral has angles 49°, 81°, 120° and *x*°. Work out *x*.                    ($x = 110°$)

An isosceles trapezium has two angles 65° and 115°. Work out the other two angles.           (65°, 115°)

## Starter – Angle bingo

Ask students to draw a 3 × 3 grid and enter nine multiples of 5 between 30 and 120.
Ask questions, for example:
A right-angled triangle has an angle of 55°, what is the size of its third angle?                    [35°]
Two interior angles of a triangle are 45° and 50°, what size is the opposite exterior angle?          [95°]
The winner is the first to cross out their nine numbers.

## Teaching notes

Define a quadrilateral. You could ask students to name different types, giving them 'trapezium' if necessary, but do not spend too long on this as it is the focus of the next lesson.

Show that the angle sum of a quadrilateral is 360° in two ways.

First, students tear off each corner of a quadrilateral made from card or paper. They fit them together to form four angles at a point which make a full turn and add up to 360°.

Second, divide a diagram of a quadrilateral into two triangles and mark their angles. Each triangle contributes 180° to the angles of the quadrilateral. Since 2 × 180° = 360°, the angle sum of a quadrilateral is 360°.

## Plenary

Students respond to questions about the angles in quadrilaterals using mini whiteboards. They could also play a 'true or false' game, showing 'Yes'/'No' cards in response to statements about angles in various quadrilaterals. Discuss responses when needed.

## Exercise commentary

**Question 1** uses the fact that the angle sum of a quadrilateral is 360°. Make the link with algebra in the way that students write their solutions.

**Question 2** – Ensure students have sharp pencils and good quality rulers and protractors. Emphasise the need for accurate measurement. Explain the term 'isosceles' with reference to a trapezium since students will automatically think about isosceles triangles.

**Question 3** – This question is considerably more challenging than Question 1. It could be discussed as a whole-class exercise. Covering parts of the diagram with blank paper may help students concentrate on relevant sections. Ensure they give reasons for each step.

## Answers

| 1 | a | 130° | b | 70° | c | 120° | d | 97° |
|---|---|---|---|---|---|---|---|---|
|   | e | 97° | f | 40° | g | 50° | h | 40° |

| 2 | a | 9cm | b | parallel | c | $g = 60°$ | d | $h = 60°$ |
|---|---|---|---|---|---|---|---|---|
|   | e | 360° | f | 360° | g | 1080° | | |

| 3 | a | 45° | b | 72° |
|---|---|---|---|---|

## Objectives

- Classify quadrilaterals by their geometrical properties. (L6)

| Key ideas | Resources | |
|---|---|---|
| 1 Quadrilaterals can be classified and named according to their properties.<br>2 The properties of quadrilaterals derive from facts about their sides and angles. | Lines and quadrilaterals<br>Angle proofs<br>Sets of quadrilaterals made from card<br>Tracing paper<br>Mini whiteboards | (1102)<br>(1141) |

| Simplification | Extension |
|---|---|
| Students are given blank copies of the different shapes and, on them, mark the properties using the correct symbols to indicate equal sides, equal angles and parallel lines. | Ask students questions such as "Are all squares rectangles?" [Yes] and "Are all rhombuses parallelograms?" [Yes]. This will encourage them to think more about which properties are necessary to define a shape and which are sufficient. They can produce a Venn diagram to illustrate the family of quadrilaterals and how they link to each other. |

| Literacy | Links |
|---|---|
| The prefix 'quad-' comes from the Latin word for 'four' and 'quadrilateral' means 'four sides'. Compare the words 'quadbike', 'quadruped' and 'quadruplet'.<br>In algebra, there are equations called 'quadratic equations' because they can be written in four parts. | Some schools and colleges have a quadrangle, which is a four-sided space or courtyard enclosed by the building. The word 'quadrangle' means 'four angles' and originally was used as an alternative name for a quadrilateral; it is no longer used in this sense. There is a picture of a quadrangle at Christ Church College in Oxford at http://en.wikipedia.org/wiki/Tom_Quad |

## Alternative approach

Symmetry can be used to show that sides and angles of some shapes are equal. The equilateral triangle, square, rectangle and rhombus are some of the shapes with both reflection and rotation symmetry. The isosceles triangle and isosceles trapezium have reflection symmetry showing that these shapes have pairs of sides and angles which are equal. The parallelogram has rotation symmetry showing that opposite pairs of sides and angles are equal. These and other shapes can be cut from card, rotated and folded to show their various equal sides and angles.

Symmetry does not help to show the relationship between adjacent angles of a parallelogram. Draw a parallelogram and cut two adjacent angles from different coloured card. Extend one side of the parallelogram to make an exterior angle. Emphasise the F-shape so formed and identify the two corresponding angles (one inside the shape and the exterior angle outside). Slide the interior corresponding angle onto the exterior corresponding angle to make a straight angle of 180° with the other coloured card. The two interior adjacent angles (the coloured cards) thus add to make 180°.

## Checkpoint

A quadrilateral has two pairs of equal length parallel sides but no right angles. What shape is it? (rhombus)

How many quadrilaterals have all four sides the same length? (2: rhombus, square)

## Starter – Impossible triangles?

Ask students which of the following triangles cannot be constructed and why?

A triangle with sides 3 cm, 6 cm, 10 cm. [Impossible – sum of two shorter sides less than the longest side.]

A triangle containing an angle of 60° and sides of 6 cm, 6 cm. [Possible – it is an equilateral triangle.]

A triangle containing angles of 103°, 89° and a side of 6 cm.
[Impossible – the angle sum is greater than 180°]
A triangle with sides 6 cm, 8 cm, 10 cm. [Possible]

## Teaching notes

Students list the types of quadrilaterals. Explain that quadrilaterals have different names because they have different properties. Give examples of what we mean by properties: pairs of parallel sides, equal angles, equal side lengths, etc.

Students could have sets of quadrilaterals made out of card and, in pairs, write down a list of the properties of the various types. Ask them to feedback what they have discovered to the class.

Students then complete a table showing the family of quadrilaterals matched against the various properties they have investigated. Once recorded, they can compare their results with those printed in the student's book and use the various properties to solve problems involving quadrilaterals.

## Plenary

A visual exercise can be used. Describe a quadrilateral by its properties and ask students to write its name on mini whiteboards when they know it. The description of the shape can be built up in stages to emphasise the need for complete information.

## Exercise commentary

**Questions 1 to 3** – Students can refer to the diagrams given of the quadrilaterals.

**Question 4** – Explain the use of 'isosceles' in this context. This question is easiest solved by using the symmetry of the isosceles trapezium.

**Question 5** – This question can be solved either directly using the properties of a parallelogram or by working from first principles using the angle sum for quadrilaterals in conjunction with angle facts about parallel lines.

**Question 6** – Tracing paper may be needed to match the shapes, or they can be cut out of card and matched directly.

**Question 7** – The sloping lines make two pairs of parallel lines. All the horizontal lines are parallel.

---

## Answers

1   a   trapezium          b   arrowhead
    c   square and rectangle    d   kite and arrowhead
    e   rhombus and square

2   Student should refer to square having 4 right angles.

3   Student should refer to the length of opposite sides.

4   a   $a = 114°$   b   $b = 68°$   c   ST = 5cm

5   a   $w = 47°$              b   $x = 133°$
    c   RS = 8 cm              d   RU = 4 cm

6   a and h = kite, b and e = square, d and g = rectangle, c and f = parallelogram.

7   a   24 trapeziums          b   12 parallelograms

| Key outcomes | Quick check |
|---|---|
| Identify alternate and corresponding angles.    L6 | **a** Is the following statement true or false? 'Corresponding angles are equal.' (True) <br> **b** An angle measures 64°. Write down the size of an angle alternate to this one. (64°) |
| Use side and angle properties of triangles to solve problems.    L5 | Name the type of triangle from the description: <br> **a** All angles different, no right angles (scalene) <br> **b** One right angle, the other two angles equal to each other (right-angled isosceles) |
| Use the angle sum of a triangle and properties of exterior and interior angles to solve problems.    L5 | Find the missing angle in these triangles: <br> **a** 54°, 69°, $x$° (57°) **b** 120°, 35°, $y$° (25°) **c** 48°, $z$°, $z$° (66°, 66°) |
| Use the angle sum of a quadrilateral.    L6 | Find the missing angle in each quadrilateral: <br> **a** 100°, 100°, 60° (100°) **b** 75°, 83°, 94° (108°) |
| Recognise, name and classify different quadrilaterals.    L5 | A quadrilateral has two pairs of adjacent sides equal in length and one pair of equal angles. What is it? (Kite/arrowhead) |

## ⊞ MyMaths extra support

| Lesson/online homework | Description |
|---|---|
| Properties of triangles    1130    L4 | Classifying triangles and solving problems |
| Position and turning    1231    L2 | Turning clockwise and anti-clockwise, quarter and half turns, giving directions and points of a compass |

# My Review

**Check out**

**You should now be able to ...**

| | | Test it Questions |
|---|---|---|
| ✓ | Identify alternate and corresponding angles. | 1 |
| ✓ | Use side and angle properties of triangles to solve problems. | 2 |
| ✓ | Use the angle sum of a triangle and properties of exterior and interior angles to solve problems. | 2 |
| ✓ | Use the angle sum of a quadrilateral. | 3, 5 |
| ✓ | Recognise, name and classify different quadrilaterals. | 4, 5 |

| Language | Meaning | Example |
|---|---|---|
| Parallel lines | Lines which are parallel are always the same distance apart. | |
| Alternate angles | Alternate angles are equal. | |
| Corresponding angles | Corresponding angles are equal. | |
| Vertically opposite | Vertically opposite angles are equal. | |
| Interior and exterior angles | Interior angles are angles inside a shape. Exterior angles are formed when you extend the line of a shape. | |
| Quadrilateral | A quadrilateral is a shape with four straight sides. | |

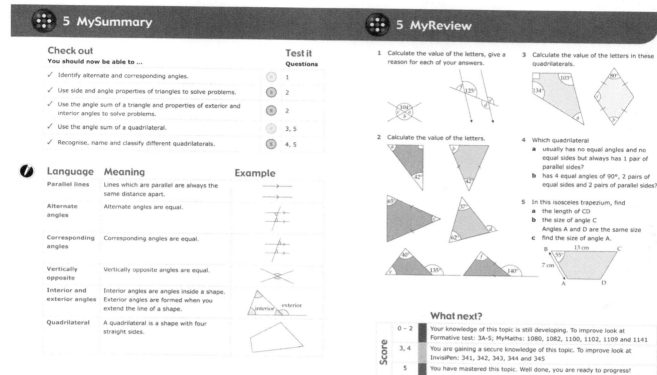

1  Calculate the value of the letters, give a reason for each of your answers.

2  Calculate the value of the letters.

3  Calculate the value of the letters in these quadrilaterals.

4  Which quadrilateral
   a  usually has no equal angles and no equal sides but always has 1 pair of parallel sides?
   b  has 4 equal angles of 90°, 2 pairs of equal sides and 2 pairs of parallel sides?

5  In this isosceles trapezium, find
   a  the length of CD
   b  the size of angle C
      Angles A and D are the same size
   c  find the size of angle A.

**What next?**

| Score | | |
|---|---|---|
| 0 – 2 | Your knowledge of this topic is still developing. To improve look at Formative test: 3A-5; MyMaths: 1080, 1082, 1100, 1102, 1109 and 1141 | |
| 3, 4 | You are gaining a secure knowledge of this topic. To improve look at InvisiPen: 341, 342, 343, 344 and 345 | |
| 5 | You have mastered this topic. Well done, you are ready to progress! | |

**MyMaths**.co.uk                                                                 91

# Question commentary

**Question 1** – The important thing here is the reason for each answer, particularly for the question involving parallel lines. Some of the angles can be worked out using different geometric facts.

**Question 2** – Students should write down the reasons for each deductive step as they work through these problems.

**Question 3** – Students should also know what the quadrilaterals are called.

**Question 4** – Students could be asked to sketch each quadrilateral after identifying it.

**Question 5** – Students will need to recall the properties of an isosceles trapezium to work out the answers to this question.

# Answers

1  a  $a = 76°$ angles on a straight line add up to 180°
   b  $b = 104°$ vertically opposite angles are equal
   c  $c = 76°$ vertically opposite/ straight line/ angles around a point add up to 360°
   d  $d = 125°$ alternate angles are equal
   e  $e = 125°$ vertically opposite/ corresponding angles are equal
   f  $f = 55°$ straight line

2  a  $a = 48°$   b  $b = 69°$   c  $c = 50°$   d  $d = 99°$
   e  $e = 95°$   f  $f = 70°$

3  a  $a = 33°$   b  $b = 80°$   c  $c = 100°$

4  a  trapezium                    b  rectangle

5  a  7 cm     b  55°     c  125°

**5a**

1 a Which is the alternate angle to the one measuring 127°?

b Which is the corresponding angle to the one measuring 127°?

c Which is the alternate angle to the one measuring 53°?

d Which is the corresponding angle to the one measuring 53°?

e What is the size of these angles?

  a angle r    b angle s

  c angle t    d angle u

**5b**

2 Find the missing angle in each triangle.

a    b    c

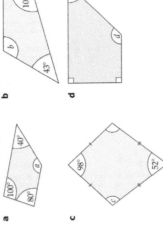
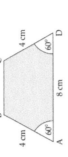

3 Using the rule

'the exterior angle is equal to the sum of the opposite interior angles', calculate the sizes of angles a, b and c.

**5c**

4 Which of these sets of measurements will not make a triangle?

a 4cm, 5cm and 8cm

b 6cm, 11cm and 7cm

c 12cm, 25cm and 20cm

d 3.5cm, 1.1cm and 1.8cm

5 a How long is side AB?

b Find the size of angle x.

---

**5d**

6 Find the missing angle in each quadrilateral.

a    b

c    d

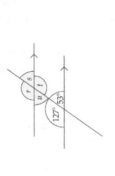

7 a Construct this quadrilateral using a ruler and protractor.

  B  4 cm  C

  4 cm    4 cm

  A  60°  8 cm  60°  D

b What is the mathematical name of the quadrilateral?

c Measure side BC.

d Measure angle ABC and angle BCD.

e If sides AB and DC were extended until they meet what sort of triangle would be formed?

**5e**

8 a Name this quadrilateral.

b Which side is parallel to RS?

c How long is side RU?

d How many degrees is angle TUR?

9 a Name this quadrilateral.

b Which side is parallel to FG?

c How long is side DE?

d How many degrees is angle EFG?

## Question commentary

**Question 1** – Students should recognize that parallel lines are involved and start by identifying pairs of alternate and corresponding angles.

**Questions 2** and **3** – Students might use the formulae for the interior and exterior angles of a triangle to do question **3**. Alternatively, get them to work 'round' the diagram, explaining their reasoning as they go on.

**Questions 4** and **5** – Students should be able to recall the rule required in question **4** and the properties of an isosceles triangle for question **5**.

**Questions 6** and **7** – Students should also be able to name the quadrilaterals in question **5**.

**Questions 8** and **9** – Students should be able to use the properties of the shapes along with the angle sum of a quadrilateral and/or properties of angles in general to solve these problems.

## Answers

1  a  Angle $t$  b  Angle $r$  c  Angle $u$  d  Angle $s$
   e  $r = 127°$, $s = 53°$, $t = 127°$, $u = 53°$

2  a  50°  b  76°  c  36°

3  a  134°  b  126°  c  94°

4  d  will not make a triangle.

5  a  8 cm  b  74°

6  a  140°  b  122°  c  105°  d  135°

7  b  isosceles trapezium  b  4 cm
   c  both are 120°  d  equilateral

8  a  trapezium  b  side UT
   c  4 cm  d  115°

9  a  parallelogram  b  side DE
   c  5 cm  d  55°

**A6** Model situations or procedures by translating them into algebraic expressions or formulae and by using graphs (L6)

**A9** Recognise, sketch and produce graphs of linear and quadratic functions of 1 variable with appropriate scaling, using equations in $x$ and $y$ and the Cartesian plane (L6)

**A10** Interpret mathematical relationships both algebraically and graphically (L6)

**A11** Reduce a given linear equation in two variables to the standard form $y = mx + c$; calculate and interpret gradients and intercepts of graphs of such linear equations numerically, graphically and algebraically (L6)

**A12** Use linear and quadratic graphs to estimate values of $y$ for given values of $x$ and vice versa and to find approximate solutions of simultaneous linear equations (L6)

**A13** Find approximate solutions to contextual problems from given graphs of a variety of functions, including piece-wise linear, exponential and reciprocal graphs (L6)

## Introduction

The chapter starts by looking at horizontal and vertical lines before looking at tables of values worked out from a given function. Plotting straight-line graphs using a table of values is covered before using graphs of two equations to find numerical solutions to pairs of simultaneous equations. Gradient and parallel lines are covered. General real-life graphs and time series graphs are covered in the last two sections.

The introduction discusses how, when you go looking for a new mobile phone, you are bombarded with lots of information about the features of the phone, etc. and then presented with several, often confusing options for the price plans available. The use of straight-line graphs to represent the various alternatives (price v. usage) can often help us to make sense of these plans (but we are never *actually* given the information presented in this way!) Similarly, energy companies use multiple tariffs to give us options but a lot of the time they are equally confusing. We can present their tariffs in a similar way to mobile phone tariffs by using graphs. Students could be encouraged to think about other types of goods and services for which there are multiple pricing options.

## Prior knowledge

Students should already know how to…

- Recognise and plot coordinates
- Work with negative numbers

## Starter problem

The starter problem is a game of 'four-in-a-line' where players use a coordinate grid to place counters and try and gain a winning line of four counters. The counters must all lie in a straight line and this can be used to introduce a discussion of the relationship between the coordinates that make up a straight line graph. In a more general sense, players can be asked to investigate winning lines, rather than just playing the game and seeing what happens.

Winning lines that are not straight up or down, or at 45° might be harder for the players to spot so they could be encouraged to aim for winning lines that are 'unusual'. More able students might be invited to describe winning lines with specific gradients and/or intersections with the $x$- or $y$-axes.

## Resources

### MyMaths

| | | | | | |
|---|---|---|---|---|---|
| Coordinates 2 | 1093 | $y = mx + c$ | 1153 | Drawing graphs | 1168 |
| Real life graphs | 1184 | | | | |

**Online assessment**

| | |
|---|---|
| Chapter test | 3A–6 |
| Formative test | 3A–6 |
| Summative test | 3A–6 |

**InvisiPen solutions**

| | | | |
|---|---|---|---|
| Plotting straight lines from tables | | | 262 |
| Drawing graphs | 264 | Real-life graphs | 275 |
| Line graphs data | 277 | | |

# Topic scheme

Teaching time = 7 lessons/3 weeks

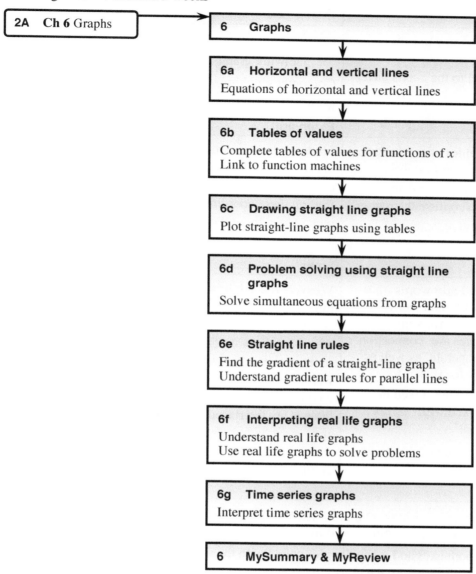

| 2A | Ch 6 Graphs |

**6** **Graphs**

**6a** **Horizontal and vertical lines**
Equations of horizontal and vertical lines

**6b** **Tables of values**
Complete tables of values for functions of $x$
Link to function machines

**6c** **Drawing straight line graphs**
Plot straight-line graphs using tables

**6d** **Problem solving using straight line graphs**
Solve simultaneous equations from graphs

**6e** **Straight line rules**
Find the gradient of a straight-line graph
Understand gradient rules for parallel lines

**6f** **Interpreting real life graphs**
Understand real life graphs
Use real life graphs to solve problems

**6g** **Time series graphs**
Interpret time series graphs

**6** **MySummary & MyReview**

# Differentiation

**Student book 3A**          94 – 113
Horizontal and vertical lines
Plotting straight-line graphs from tables of values
Drawing and using straight-line graphs
Interpreting real-life graphs and time series graphs

**Student book 3B**          90 – 113
Recognise and draw straight-line graphs
Find the gradient, $y$-intercept and equation of a straight-line graph, including those defined implicitly
Draw, understand and use real-life graphs, distance-time graphs and time series graphs

**Student book 3C**          88 – 113
Gradient of a straight-line
Graphs of linear functions
Parallel and perpendicular lines
Recognise and draw quadratic and cubic graphs
Draw, understand and use real-life graphs, distance-time graphs and time series graphs
Exponential and reciprocal graphs

## Objectives

- Recognise straight-line graphs parallel to the $x$-axis or $y$-axis. (L5)

| Key ideas | Resources | |
|---|---|---|
| 1 Vertical straight lines parallel to the $y$-axis have equations of the form $x = a$. <br> 2 Horizontal straight lines parallel to the $x$-axis have equations of the form $y = b$. | Coordinates 2 <br> Drawing graphs <br> Computer graphing software <br> Mini whiteboards | (1093) <br> (1168) |

| Simplification | Extension |
|---|---|
| Use examples where the $x$ and $y$ values of the straight lines are all positive. Emphasise that graphs of the type $x = a$ are vertical and graphs of the type $y = b$ are horizontal. Watch for students who confuse the matter. <br><br> Move to negative values only when students are confident with positive values. | Students draw a rectangle using a combination of two vertical and two horizontal lines and write the coordinates of the corners. They discover a way of finding these coordinates and also the midpoint of the rectangle without drawing a diagram. |

| Literacy | Links |
|---|---|
| The word 'coordinate' comes from Latin words meaning 'ordered together'. Many English words starting with 'co-', 'con-' and 'com-' have some connection with 'together'. Examples are 'connection', 'congregation', 'combine' and 'cooperate' as well as the Co-op shop and the boa constrictor snake. <br><br> The words 'horizontal' and 'horizon' are linked in meaning. The word 'vertical' is linked with 'vertex' which originally meant 'a high point'. | Weavers make fabric or rugs by interlacing long threads that are at right angles to each other. The vertical threads running along the length of the cloth are called the warp threads and the horizontal threads running across the width of the cloth are called the weft threads. Patterns are created by using different coloured threads and by changing the way in which the threads are interlaced. There are rug-weaving diagrams at www.orientalrugcleaning.com/rug%20weaving%20diagrams.htm |

## Alternative approach

Instead of an introduction using computer-generated graphs, points and graphs hand-drawn by the teacher can be used a model for the students' own plotting of points and drawing of graphs.

Use a square grid, draw and label both axes and manually plot points with the same $x$ values. Draw a line (in a different colour to the axes) and label it. Explain the equation used for the label. Repeat for other points having the same $y$ values and other points having negative coordinates.

As a whole-class game, imagine a grid as the street plan of a city. Draw, in a different colour to the grid and axes, a route across the grid using short sections of horizontal and vertical lines. In a whole-class session, students take turns to give the equation of the lines which the route takes from its start to its end.

## Checkpoint

Describe the following lines:

$x = 4$        (Vertical line through coordinates with $x = 4$)

$y = -2$       (Horizontal line through coordinates with $y = -2$)

## Starter – Quick fix

Recap work from previous chapters. Ask rapid response questions from a range of topics. Students reply by writing on their mini whiteboards. Discuss questions when their answers indicate a need.

## Teaching notes

Use computer graph-drawing software to show students graphs of vertical and horizontal lines. Ask them to list the coordinate of points on a selected line, say $y = 2$. Elicit that the $y$-coordinates of all points on this horizontal line are the same and therefore the line can be defined as $y = 2$.

Repeat this activity for a vertical line, say $x = 3$. Students should then be able to give the equation for further examples of horizontal and vertical lines. They can check their work with a partner.

Students now draw other examples of horizontal and vertical lines from given equations. They can check their work with a partner.

Point out that horizontal and vertical lines cross at right angles and ask students to give the coordinates where the lines cross (known as 'points of intersection'). Ask students to describe the shape that is created by two horizontal and two vertical lines crossing each other. [Square or rectangle]

## Plenary

Students draw two axes, labelled only with $x$ and $y$. Give the coordinates of points and the equations of horizontal and veritcal lines. Students sketch the approximate positions of the points and lines. Discuss answers when needed.

## Exercise commentary

**Question 1** – Remind students that the 'coordinate pairs' that the question asks for are the $x$- and $y$-values for any three points on each coloured line.

**Questions 2 and 3** – A common error when asked to draw the line $x = 3$ is to draw the line $y = 3$ instead. Ask students to label the lines they draw with their equations to enable errors to be spotted more readily.

**Question 4** – This task does not require students to draw axes and lines.

## Answers

1  **a**  red: $(x, 5)$, for example, $(-2, 5), (0, 5), (3,5)$
       blue $(4, y)$, for example, $(4,4), (4,2), (4,-1)$
       green $(x, -5)$, for example, $(5,-5), (2,-5), (-1,-5)$
    **b**  red $y = 5$
       blue $x = 4$
       green $y = -5$
    **c**  $(4,5)$              **d**  $(4,-5)$
    **e**  red and green        **f**  $(-3,5), (-3,-5)$

2  **a**  Vertical lines through $x = 6$ and $x = -4$, horizontal lines through $y = 5$ and $y = -3$
    **b**  $(-4, -3), (-4, 5), (6, 5), (6, -3)$
    **c**  perimeter = 28        **d**  area = 48

3  **a**  Vertical lines through $x = 5$ and $x = -5$, horizontal lines through $y = 0$ and $y = 3$
    **b**  $(-5, 3), (-5, 0), (5, 3), (5, -3)$
    **c**  perimeter = 26        **d**  area = 30

4  **a**  Horizontal, $(x, 10)$     **b**  No
    **c**  $y = $ constant         **d**  the $y$-axis

## Objectives

- Generate coordinate pairs that satisfy a simple linear rule. (L5)

| Key ideas | Resources |
|---|---|
| 1 A function machine or an equation can give a rule to find $y$-coordinates given any $x$-coordinate.<br>2 The graphs of these functions slope at an angle to the axes. | ⊞ Drawing graphs (1168)<br>Mini whiteboards |

| Simplification | Extension |
|---|---|
| In the first instance, restrict examples to those which involve only one-stage function machines, such as in Question 1. Extend to function machines and equations as in Question 3. | Students use equations with negatives, either in the constant or in the coefficient of $x$, such as $y = 20 - 2x$. Ask them to explain the effect of using negative values. |

| Literacy | Links |
|---|---|
| The layout of values in a table is common when drawing graphs manually. Each term of the equation has a row to itself and the values of terms in the middle rows can be combined using a number line. The first and last rows are reserved for the values of the $x$- and $y$-coordinates.<br>For simple equations such as $y = x + 3$, the middle rows can be omitted. | The word 'function' comes from the Latin word 'fungi', which means 'perform', so a function machine performs an operation on the input number. The word was first used in mathematics by the German mathematician Leibnitz in the 17th century. |

### Alternative approach

The table of values could be called a 'spreadsheet'. An electronic spreadsheet can be used to set up a formula which gives $y$ values directly from the $x$ values. However, it is instructive (but relatively laborious) to set up an electronic spreadsheet to give a table of values with the intermediate rows exactly like the tables that students create manually. Students can then see the table extended automatically for more values of $x$.

An electronic spreadsheet can also draw a graph from the values it has computed.

### Checkpoint

For the equation $y = 2x + 3$, write down the $y$-coordinates for $x = 0, 2, 4$    (3, 7, 11)

## Starter – 357

Challenge students to make the numbers 1 to 12 using only the digits 3, 5 and 7 in four minutes. A possible solution is:

$1 = 7 - 3 - 3$, $2 = 5 - 3$, 3, $4 = (7 + 5) \div 3$, 5,
$6 = 3 + 3$, 7, $8 = 3 + 5$, $9 = 3 \times 3$, $10 = 5 + 5$,
$11 = 7 + 7 - 3$, $12 = 7 + 5$

This task can be extended by making the numbers up to 20 or by changing the digits.

## Teaching notes

Remind students of what a function is. Explain that an input, $x$, is operated on by the function in order to generate an output, $y$. Explain that the results from a function can be displayed in a table of values. Give students an example of a simple one-step function, say $y = 2x$, and fill in the table of values.

Give an example of a two-step function, say $y = 2x + 5$, and have students, as a whole class, construct a table of values.

Students, in pairs, invent their own functions and ask their partner to fill in the table of values. Students then check each other's solutions.

## Plenary

Have a template of a table of values on the board with $x$ values given. Ask students to copy and complete the table for a given function. Students then check their working and their solutions with a partner or, having written the table on a mini whiteboard, show them to the class.

## Exercise commentary

**Question 1** – These functions are single step functions.

**Question 2** – A two-stage function machine may help some students to use the equation correctly. The values in the table can be combined on a number line.

**Question 3** – Students are directed to use function machines in this question but this element could be left out and they could go straight onto the tables of values.

**Question 4** – The tables for this question are similar in format to those in Question **2**.

**Question 5** – Remind students that $x^2$ means $x \times x$. Justify the examples in the table in part **a** where $x = 0$, $x = 2$ and $x = 10$. Likewise justify the examples in part **b** for negative $x$ values.

## Answers

See master Answers file for this lesson

### Objectives

- Plot the graphs of simple linear functions, where $y$ is given explicitly in terms of $x$, on paper and using ICT.

(L6)

| Key ideas | Resources |
|---|---|
| 1 Tables of values help to calculate the coordinates of points on a straight line.<br>2 Equations of the type $y = 2x + 3$ produce straight line graphs. | Drawing graphs          (1168)<br>Pre-drawn sets of axes<br>Squared paper<br>Graph-drawing software<br>Mini whiteboards |

| Simplification | Extension |
|---|---|
| Restrict examples to those involving only one operation such as + or ×. Provide students with pre-drawn axes. Ask students to check that the points are in line before joining them. | Either give the students examples which involve negative coefficients or give them an example of a function which produces a curve when plotted such as $y = x^2 + 2$. |

| Literacy | Links |
|---|---|
| Students need to 'read' the 'look' of a line from its equation.<br>There are three categories so far: vertical lines of the type $x = a$; horizontal lines of the type $y = b$; and sloping lines of the types $y = 2x$ and $y = 2x + 3$. | Calculators that can plot and display graphs are called graphical calculators. The first graphical calculator was produced in 1985. There is an on-line graphical calculator at www.coolmath.com/graphit/ |

### Alternative approach

As in the previous lesson, an electronic spreadsheet can be used. Set up a spreadsheet using a formula to give $y$ values directly from $x$ values or design a spreadsheet showing the intermediate rows of working. Students can see the table extended automatically for more values of $x$ and an electronic graph drawn.

When negative values of $x$ are introduced, several errors can creep in. Finding a multiple of a negative number, as for $y = 2x - 3$ when $x = -4$, is usually not a problem. Watch that the value for $-3$ does not change across the table, however, and ask students to use a number line when combining the middle values. Occasionally, some students wrongly include the top row (of $x$ values).

### Checkpoint

Write out a table of values for the equation $y = 3x - 1$ for $x = 0$ to 4.      ($y$ values are -1, 2, 5, 8, 11)

## Starter – Algebraic products

Draw a 4 × 4 table on the board to form 16 cells. Label the rows with the terms $2a, 5d, z, 3f$. Label the columns with the terms $c, 3y, 4e, 2x$. Ask students to fill in each cell of the table by multiplying the terms in each row and column together. For example, the top left cell reads $2ac$ because it is the product of $2a$ and $c$.

This task can be differentiated by choosing different terms.

## Teaching notes

As a whole class, construct a table of values and provide pre-drawn axes for students on squared paper. Students label the axes $x$ and $y$ and add the scales with equally spaced numbering.

Students plot points from the table of values and join them to give a straight line. Students then practise further examples.

Students invent their own functions and create tables of values. They then ask a partner to plot points and draw graphs. They check each other's points and graphs.

## Plenary

Give students a new function and ask them to draw up a table of values for given values of $x$ on their mini whiteboards. On axes which are pre-drawn on squared paper, they use the table to draw a straight line and label it. Discuss the line and ask for the coordinates of other points on it.

## Exercise commentary

**Question 1** – Explain the three completed sets of values in the table, for $x = 0, 3$ and 5. Ensure the students understand that the middle rows are the 'working' which combine to give the final $y$-values.

**Question 2** – This question introduces negative values of $x$ for the first time in the exercise.

**Question 3** – Explain the two completed sets of values in the table, for $x = -3$ and 1. Possibly display a number line for students to use when combining the middle two rows of the table.

**Question 4** – Parts **a** and **b** are straightforward. Part **c** may be best done by drawing the lines for questions **2** and **3** on the axes for this question.

## Answers

**1  a**

| $x$ | 0 | 1 | 2 | 3 | 4 | 5 | 6 |
|---|---|---|---|---|---|---|---|
| $2x$ | 0 | 2 | 4 | 6 | 8 | 10 | 12 |
| + 1 | + 1 | + 1 | + 1 | + 1 | + 1 | + 1 | + 1 |
| $y$ | 1 | 3 | 5 | 7 | 9 | 11 | 13 |

  **b**  Straight line drawn through (0, 1) and (5, 11)

**2  a**

| $x$ | -3 | -2 | -1 | 0 | 1 | 2 | 3 |
|---|---|---|---|---|---|---|---|
| $y$ | -6 | -4 | -2 | 0 | 2 | 4 | 6 |

  **b**  Straight line through the origin, gradient 2

**3  a**

| $x$ | -4 | -3 | -2 | -1 | 0 | 1 | 2 | 3 | 4 |
|---|---|---|---|---|---|---|---|---|---|
| $2x$ | -8 | -6 | -4 | -2 | 0 | 2 | 4 | 6 | 8 |
| - 2 | - 2 | - 2 | - 2 | - 2 | - 2 | - 2 | - 2 | - 2 | - 2 |
| $y$ | -10 | -8 | -6 | -4 | -2 | 0 | 2 | 4 | 6 |

  **b**  Straight line through (0, -2), gradient 2

**4  a**

| $x$ | -2 | -1 | 0 | 1 | 2 | 3 |
|---|---|---|---|---|---|---|
| $3x$ | -6 | -3 | 0 | 3 | 6 | 9 |
| - 4 | - 4 | - 4 | - 4 | - 4 | - 4 | - 4 |
| $y$ | -10 | -7 | -4 | -1 | 2 | 5 |

  **b**  Straight line through (0, -4) and (2, 2)

  **c**  (4, 8), (2, 2)

## Objectives

- Plot the graphs of simple linear functions, where $y$ is given explicitly in terms of $x$, on paper and using ICT. **(L6)**
- Solve simultaneous equations using graphical methods. **(L6)**

| Key ideas | Resources |
|---|---|
| 1  Plot graphs of linear functions<br>2  Plot pairs of linear functions to find the intersection (solve them simultaneously) | ⊕  Drawing graphs                    (1168)<br>Prepared axes/graph paper<br>Graph-drawing program |

| Simplification | Extension |
|---|---|
| Students can be given prepared axes and/or tables which are more complete than the ones given in the exercise. The important element to the lesson is to find the intersection points and understand the basics of simultaneous equations so a set of pre-drawn graphs could also be used where the students simply read off various intersection points. | Remove the scaffolding of the pre-drawn tables. In addition, students could be given further examples that are not quite so straight-forward such as $y = 3x + 4$ and $y = 1 - 3x$. These give non-integer solutions (-0.5, 2.5).<br>A basic introduction to algebraic methods could also be given to students. |

| Literacy | Links |
|---|---|
| Straight-line graph<br>Simultaneous (equations)<br>Reference can be made to other contexts where the word simultaneous occurs such as 'the two TV programmes were shown simultaneously'. | Links to work on spreadsheets can be developed with students attempting to create formulae that generate the coordinate points for given equations. Likewise, drawing graphs using a spreadsheet (or graph-drawing program) can also be developed.<br>Point out contexts where finding the intersection of two linear graphs might be useful such as comparing different mobile phone tariffs or energy suppliers. |

| Alternative approach |
|---|
| Straight-line graphs drawn using a computer program can be used to quickly demonstrate the principles here. It will also help the students visualise the graphs (slope, etc.) before they proceed to draw their own. |

| Checkpoint |
|---|
| The graphs of the equations $y = 2x - 1$ and $y = x + 3$ intersect at (4, 7). True or false?                    (True) |

## Starter – Missing coordinates

Give students an equation of a line and either an $x$-coordinate or a $y$-coordinate and ask them to find the missing coordinate. For example

$y = 2x - 7$  (-1,  )  (  ,7)  (-5,  )  (1.5,  )  (  ,-1)

Solutions: (-1, -9) (7, 7) (-5, -17) (1.5, -4) (3, -1)

The task can be differentiated by the choice of equation and coordinates.

## Teaching notes

It is important that the students develop a visual awareness of straight-line graphs so reference to the worked example and/or other prepared graphs will be useful. Check throughout that the students are correctly completing the tables of values (to give *straight* lines) before attempting to plot the graphs. Emphasise that the intersection of the two graphs represent a unique solution where both equations are true.

## Plenary

Link forward to the next section and ask students to plot the graphs of $y = 2x + 1$ and $y = 2x + 2$. Focus on students using the word 'parallel' to describe the two lines.

## Exercise commentary

**Question 1**– This question is fully scaffolded including the axes required so students should simply follow the steps. They may need reminding that the line $y = 4$ is horizontal.

**Question 2** – The scaffolding has been removed and students will need to generate their own tables of values and appropriate axes. They may need reminding that the line $x = -1$ is vertical.

**Questions 3** and **4** – In these two questions, the lines are both sloping. Prepared axes might be given to speed up the work.

## Answers

**1  a**

| $x$ | -2 | -1 | 0 | 1 | 2 | 3 |
|---|---|---|---|---|---|---|
| $y$ | -4 | -2 | 0 | 2 | 4 | 6 |

   **b**  Straight line through the origin, gradient 2

   **c**  Horizontal line through $y = 4$

   **d**  (2, 4)

**2  a**

| $x$ | -2 | -1 | 0 | 1 | 2 | 3 |
|---|---|---|---|---|---|---|
| $y$ | 6 | 5 | 4 | 3 | 2 | 1 |

   **b**  Straight line through (0, 4), gradient -1

   **c**  Vertical line though $x = -1$

   **d**  (-1, 5)

**3  a**

| $x$ | -2 | -1 | 0 | 1 | 2 | 3 |
|---|---|---|---|---|---|---|
| $2x$ | -4 | -2 | 0 | 2 | 4 | 6 |
| $+1$ | $+1$ | $+1$ | $+1$ | $+1$ | $+1$ | $+1$ |
| $y$ | -3 | -1 | 1 | 3 | 5 | 7 |

   **b**  Straight line through (0, 1), gradient 2

   **c**

| $x$ | -2 | -1 | 0 | 1 | 2 | 3 |
|---|---|---|---|---|---|---|
| $y$ | 3 | 2 | 1 | 0 | -1 | -2 |

      Straight line through (0, 1), gradient -1

   **d**  (0, 1)

**4  a**

| $x$ | -2 | -1 | 0 | 1 | 2 | 3 |
|---|---|---|---|---|---|---|
| $y$ | 7 | 6 | 5 | 4 | 3 | 2 |

   **b**  Straight line through (0, 5), gradient -1

   **c**

| $x$ | -2 | -1 | 0 | 1 | 2 | 3 |
|---|---|---|---|---|---|---|
| $2x$ | -4 | -2 | 0 | 2 | 4 | 6 |
| $-1$ | $-1$ | $-1$ | $-1$ | $-1$ | $-1$ | $+1$ |
| $y$ | -5 | -3 | -1 | 1 | 3 | 5 |

   **d**  Straight line through (0, -1), gradient 2

   **e**  (2, 3)

## Objectives

- Recognise that equations of the form $y = mx + c$ correspond to straight line graphs. (L6)

| Key ideas | Resources |
|---|---|
| 1  The value of $m$ gives the gradient of the line. <br> 2  The value of $c$ gives the point where the line intersects the $y$-axis. | ⊞  $y = mx + c$ (1153) <br> Graphing software <br> Mini whiteboards |

| Simplification | Extension |
|---|---|
| Keep with functions of the type $y = kx$ until students understand the concept. Encourage them to draw triangles on the diagrams and physically count the squares. | Extend the graphs to those of the type $y = b - ax$. <br> Introduce students to lines sloping downwards. |

| Literacy | Links |
|---|---|
| The steepness of a straight line is a new concept. Steepness is measured by finding the gradient of the line and the word 'gradient' can be introduced to students. <br><br> Whereas gradient is often written as, for example, 1 in 5, it is increasingly expressed as a percentage which, for '1 in 5' is 20%. | Ordnance Survey maps indicate steep roads by marking them with arrows. One arrow indicates a gradient of 1 in 7 to 1 in 5 and two arrows indicate a gradient of 1 in 5 or steeper. A gradient of 1 in 5 means that for every 5 metres that a vehicle travels along horizontally, it climbs one metre vertically. There is an example of an Ordnance Survey map showing steep roads at www.bbc.co.uk/schools/gcsebitesize/geography/geographical_skills/maps_rev3.shtml |

## Alternative approach

Spend time on working just with gradients before introducing lines that do not pass through the origin.

Use a simple one-stage function machine for lines of the type $y = \square \times x$. Construct tables of values for $y = x$, $y = 2x$, $y = 3x$, $y = \frac{1}{2}x$ and $y = -x$, $y = -2x$, $y = -3x$, $y = -\frac{1}{2}x$. On axes labelled from –3 to 3 and –10 to 10, draw all eight lines. On each line, draw a staircase where each step moves one square to the right (always to the right – some students may move to the left!). Find how many squares upwards the staircase rises for each graph. Make the connection between the multipliers in the equations and the gradients of the lines. Also make the connection that rising lines have positive gradients and falling lines have negative gradients.

Now consider a one-stage function machine of the type $y = 2x + \square$. Construct tables of values for $y = 2x$, $y = 2x + 1$, $y = 2x + 3$, $y = 2x + 4$ and $y = 2x + 6$. On axes labelled from 0 to 6 and from 0 to 20, draw all five lines. Notice that they all have the same gradient, which is 2 in each case. Compare each line with the graph of $y = 2x$. Notice that, for $y = 2x + 1$, all points on $y = 2x$ have moved up the grid by one square. A similar result applies to the other lines.

Summarise the results by saying that:

- when $y = \square \times x$, the multiplier of $x$ gives the gradient of the line;
- when $y = x + \square$, the number added gives the upward movement of the line.

## Checkpoint

| | |
|---|---|
| Are the following lines parallel? $y = 4x + 2$ and $y = 4x - 3$ | (yes) |
| Are the following lines parallel? $y = 3x - 1$ and $y = -3x - 1$ | (no) |

## Starter – Rectangles

Draw a rectangle on a square grid with the lines $y = 1$, $y = 4$, $x = 2$ and $x = 6$ as sides. Ask students to give the equation for each of the four sides. If available, check responses with a graphing software.

Extend with lines in different quadrants.

## Teaching notes

Give students some examples of straight line graphs through the origin using computer graphing software.

From a starting point, they describe the stepping process to get to the next point on the grid. They find the numbers of squares the line rises for each square moved to the right. Point out that the number of squares risen is the same as the number multiplying $x$ in the equation. Students write the equation in the form $y = kx$.

Students check this result by completing further examples.

Explain that graphs which do not go through the origin undergo another stage of working. Explain that, for $y = 3x$ for example, the graph does pass through the origin, but if it is moved upwards by two squares at every point along its length, then the equation of the new graph is $y = 3x + 2$.

## Plenary

Present an equation to students, such as $y = 3x + 1$. Ask questions about the graph of this equation, with students responding on mini whiteboards, such as:

Is the graph a straight line?

Does it pass through the origin?

If $x = 2$, what is the value of $y$?

Does the point $(5, 15)$ lies on the graph?

For every one square moved to the right, how many squares upwards does the graph rise?

Discuss answers as necessary.

## Exercise commentary

**Question 1** – Reinforce the language used in part **a**, that is 'the points on the lines move □ squares up for every one square across'. The link is a multiplication.

**Question 2** – This question provides for a whole-class discussion. Students could discuss that the red line has been translated vertically by two units. Show how two units have been added to each red $y$-coordinate to obtain a blue $y$-coordinate. Students should come to the conclusion that the 'one across, two up' relationship remains, but now two units have been added to each $y$-coordinate so the new (blue) relationship is $y = 2x + 2$.
The function machine makes the relationship more explicit.

**Question 3** – Draw the graph of $y = 3x$ first, using the first stage of the function machine and checking that the points on the line move three squares up for every one square across. Then discuss the effect of adding the extra 1.

## Answers

1 **ai** The line moves 4 squares up for every 1 square across.
 **ii** The line moves 6 squares up for every 1 square across
 **iii** The line moves 2 squares up for every 1 square across
 **iv** The line moves ½ square up for every 1 square across
 **b i** ×4    **ii** ×6     **iii** ×2      **iv** ×$\frac{1}{2}$
 **c i** $y = 4x$      **ii** $y = 6x$
 **iii** $y = 2x$      **iv** $y = x/2$

2 **a** ×2
 **b** $y = 2x$
 **c** ×2, + 2
 **d** $y = 2x + 2$

3 **a** $3x$, + 1. The line moves 3 squares up for every one square across. It crosses the $y$-axis at $(0, 1)$

4 Straight line through $(0, 7)$ and $(8, -1)$

## Objectives

- Discuss and interpret graphs arising from real situations, including distance–time graphs. (L6)

| Key ideas | Resources |
|---|---|
| 1  On distance–time graphs, the steeper the graph, the faster the speed.<br><br>2  On distance–time graphs, horizontal parts of the graph indicate being at rest. | ⊞  Real life graphs                                      (1184)<br><br>Graphing software<br><br>Empty bottles and jars of various shapes |

| Simplification | Extension |
|---|---|
| Restrict distance–time graphs to those which involve very simple 'there-and-back' scenarios rather than those which incorporate breaks. Avoid curved sections to graphs.<br><br>Practical demonstrations of liquids filling various containers help students visualise how depth of liquid changes with time. | Ask students to consider a range of more complicated containers and draw the depth–time graphs for them. Students then invent their own unusual containers and challenge a partner to draw the graph of depth against time. |

| Literacy | Links |
|---|---|
| Time always moves forwards, but distance can move forwards and backwards, so distance–time graphs always move to the right in the direction of increasing time, but can move both up and down the distance axis.<br><br>But beware! Sometimes distance is measured as how far you have travelled regardless of the direction, so that graph always has distance increasing and the graph rising. At other times, distance is measured from a fixed point (such as home), so when you are returning home, the distance from home is falling.<br><br>Understanding information presenting graphically, including graphs, is called 'graphicacy' which is part of 'numeracy' and all part of being 'mathematically literate'. | Earthquake activity causes shock waves to move through the Earth. A seismograph detects the vibrations caused by the shock waves and represents them as a graph called a seismogram. Seismograms from stations around the World can be viewed at http://rev.seis.sc.edu/<br>and there is an animation of a seismogram at www.yenka.com/freecontent/attachment. action?quick=9w&att=704 |

## Alternative approach

When a student goes on a journey by car, he/she re-sets the trip meter to zero and records how far they have gone every quarter of a hour until they reach their destination. Back at school, the class decides what scale is needed on their axes to plot a point for each quarter of an hour of the jounrey. The points are joined with straight lines.

Questions to ask are "Does the shape of the graph give the bends in the road?", "Does the graph show the car at rest for part of the time?", "When was the car travelling at its fastest and what kind of road was it on at this time?", "How long was the total jounrey in time and in distance?"

## Checkpoint

Steven cycles for 2 hours at a speed of 30 km/h. How far does he travel?                              (60 km)

If his ride home takes 2 ½ hours, what is his speed on the return journey?                              (24 km/h)

## Starter – More rectangles

Students write four equations that, if plotted as graphs, will make a rectangle with an area of 15 squares. Challenge students to find different possibilities.

[Possible answers are: $x = 0$, $y = 0$, $x = 5$, $y = 3$ and $x = 1$, $y = 2$, $x = 4$, $y = 7$ and $x = -1$, $y = 8$, $x = -2$, $y = -7$]

## Teaching notes

Describe a journey to students and explain that the journey can be represented using a graph. Describe the journey again and, using a pre-drawn distance–time graph, work through the various stages of the journey explaining how to work out the speeds at various points.

Give the students another example of a distance–time graph and ask them to write down the story of this journey themselves. Emphasise the need for correct English and correct mathematical words and phrases.

Using a series of differently-shaped bottles and jars, ask students to explain in words what happens to the rate of increase of the depth of the water as they fill up from a steady flow of water. Introduce the notion of a sketch graph which can be used to represent changes in depth over time, where the horizontal axis is time and the vertical axis is depth of water.

## Plenary

Ask students to plan their own short journey and write a description of each stage of it. They draw a distance–time graph of their journey and exchange graphs with a partner. Their partner checks the graph against the description and they discuss any discrepancies.

## Exercise commentary

**Question 1** – Ask how far Gabriella cycled in 1 hour and explain that this gives her speed in km per hour for the first leg of her journey. Discuss how the graphs show that Gabriella arrives home at the end of each trip.

**Question 2** – Refer firstly to the previous page of the student's book and discuss the example there. Discuss the rate of fill. Ask students how the rate of fill will change as the width of the container increases and decreases. Show students how to break down the flask into different shaped components.

**Question 3** – Discuss how to plan the axes, starting at 10:00 a.m. on the horizontal axis. Discuss the scales of the axes. Note that the time axis only needs half-hour divisions.

## Answers

1  **a**  A = 25 km/hr        B = 12 km/hr
   **b**  C                   **c**  1 hour
   **d**  It is increasing.   **e**  B

2  i – B, ii – A, iii – C

3  Check students' drawings

## Objectives

- Understand and construct graphs of time series.                                    (L6)

| Key ideas | Resources |
|---|---|
| 1  Know how to 'tell the story' of a time series.<br>2  Know how to see and describe a trend. | Real life graphs                              (1184)<br>Data taken from real life situations<br>Spreadsheet software<br>Mini whiteboards |

| Simplification | Extension |
|---|---|
| Offer a simple time series graph, for example, of temperature in a room in winter. Ask students to 'tell the story' of the graph over time.<br><br>Repeat with a graph of, say, house prices over a period of years when prices fluctuated. Encourage students to try to summarise the data and look for trends. | Ask students to find examples of time series graphs from the Internet or newspapers. Ask them to describe what these graphs are showing and explain their findings to a partner. |

| Literacy | Links |
|---|---|
| The word 'trend' is from an old word from northern Europe meaning 'to bend in different directions'. It now means the general direction in which something is moving. Graphically, the trend ignores the minor ups and downs and looks for the overall direction of the graph. Of course, there doesn't always have to be a trend. | There are an infinite number of prime numbers and various prizes are offered to anyone who discovers a prime number larger than those already known. A prime number with 13 million digits was discovered in August 2008. There is a time series graph showing the number of digits in the largest known prime number at http://primes.utm.edu/notes/by_year.html |

## Alternative approach

As in the previous lesson, an alternative approach takes data from a real life scenario.  For example, a student could read the electricity meter at home or school each hour of the day for one day (or at the same time each day over a few weeks).  Graphs drawn from such data show the changes in usage over time.

A particularly interesting set of data is to measure the length of the shadow of a vertical metre rule at the same time and place each day for several weeks (and especially if the weeks include the 21st June or 21st December). Draw a time series graph and note how the lengths varies.

## Checkpoint

Describe the possible trends in these situations:

**a** Ice cream sales from January to August.                                    (Probably increasing)

**b** The temperature on a particular day from 4pm to midnight.                   (Probably decreasing)

**Starter** – Quick fire

Recap work of previous chapters and this chapter so far. Ask rapid response questions with students responding on mini whiteboards. Include questions about plotting points and drawing graphs. Discuss answers when there is a need.

## Teaching notes

Students offer scenarios for which time series graphs would be appropriate; such as, recording the temperature in a garden over the course of a day, the number of ice creams sold throughout the months of a year. Pre-prepared examples (using computer spreadsheet software) could be shown to the students and discussed.

If students need to draw a time series graph, they should draw axes with time along the horizontal axis and the measured variable on the vertical axis. Give students a set of data and ask them to plot the coordinate points on a set of axes. Explain that the points are now joined with straight line segments to create the line graph.

Explain that such a graph can show trends over time.

## Plenary

Give students a set of data and ask them, working in pairs, to draw the resulting graph.

Show a time series graph to the whole class and ask question about it with students responding on mini whiteboards.

## Exercise commentary

**Questions 1 and 2** – Ensure students pay careful attention to the scales, particularly when the time axis uses times of day (a.m. and p.m.)

In Question **2**, note the false origin on the temperature axis, indicated by a zigzag in the axis.

**Question 3** – The temperature axis here also has a false origin. Students can write down any patterns or trends that they see when they have plotted the graph.

## Answers

1  **a**  5 people       **b**  12 o'clock (noon)
   **c**  2 pm 31 visitors  **d**  11 am and 4 pm

2  **a**  28°C   **b**  25°C   **c**  23°C   **d**  2 pm
   **e**  3 pm   **f**  9 am

3

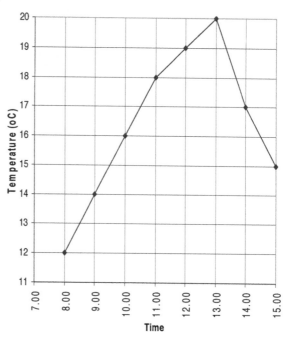

**b**  Reference should be made to the increase in temperature until 13:00 followed by a sharp decrease in temperature.

| Key outcomes | Quick check |
|---|---|
| Identify and draw horizontal and vertical lines on a graph. L6 | Describe the following lines: <br> **a** $y = 3$ (Horizontal through $y = 3$) **b** $x = -4$ (Vertical through $x = -4$) |
| Construct tables of values for graphs. L6 | Write down the $y$ values for the equation $y = 2x - 5$ for $x = 0$ to 4 <br> (-5, -3, -1, 1, 3) |
| Draw and understand straight-line graphs. L6 | Give two examples of straight-line graphs that are parallel to $y = 3x + 2$ <br> (Students' answers, in the form $y = 3x + c, c \neq 2$) |
| Read and interpret real-life graphs. L6 | A graph of Simon's journey to school indicates he travels 1.4 miles in 20 minutes. What is his speed? (4.2 miles per hour) |
| Understand and draw time-series graphs. L6 | Describe the possible trends in a time-series graph showing average monthly rainfall in the UK. (Possibly decreasing then increasing, but accept justified alternatives) |

## ⊕ MyMaths extra support

| Lesson/online homework | Description |
|---|---|
| Conversion graphs 1059 L6 | Using conversion graphs; converting units such as miles to kilometers, pounds to kilograms, GBP to Euros and also temperatures. |

## My Review

### Check out
**You should now be able to ...**

Test it ➡
Questions

| | | Test it |
|---|---|---|
| ✓ | Identify and draw horizontal and vertical lines on a graph. | 1 |
| ✓ | Construct tables of values for graphs. | 2 |
| ✓ | Draw and understand straight line graphs. | 2, 3 |
| ✓ | Read and interpret real life graphs. | 4 |
| ✓ | Understand and draw time series graphs. | 5 |

| Language | Meaning | Example |
|---|---|---|
| Coordinates | Coordinates are two numbers which show the position of a point. They are written in brackets, separated by a comma. | (4, 7) This is 4 units right and 7 units up from (0, 0). (-3, -2) This is 3 units left and 2 units down from (0, 0) |
| Vertical | A vertical line is a line going straight up. A vertical line is parallel to the $y$-axis and has the equation $x$ = something. | |
| Horizontal | A horizontal line is a line going straight across. A horizontal line is parallel to the $x$-axis and has the equation $y$ = something. | |
| Equation | An equation is where an expression is equal to another expression. | $x = 3$, $y = -2$ and $y = 2x - 1$ are all equations of lines. |
| Trend | A trend is the general direction for a set of data. | The trend for a set of data would increase, decrease or stay the same. |

110 Algebra Graphs

1 Write the equations of lines A, B, C and D

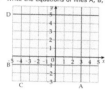

2 For the equation $y = 2x + 1$
  a copy and complete the table

| x | 0 | 1 | 2 | 3 | 4 |
|---|---|---|---|---|---|
| 2x | | | | | |
| +1 | +1 | +1 | +1 | +1 | +1 |
| y | | | | | |

  b draw axes with $x$ from 0 to 5 and $y$ from 0 to 10 then draw the graph.

3

  a Write the rule that links the $x$- and $y$-coordinates in the graph above.
  b What is the equation of the line?

4 The graph shows Jim's journey to work.

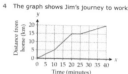

  a At what speed was Jim travelling during the first 10 minutes of his journey?
  b How far is Jim's journey to work?
  c What happens 20 minutes into Jim's journey?

5 The time-series shows the takings in the previous hour by a newsagent, for example between 7 and 8 a.m. £300 was made.

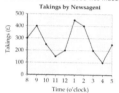

  a What takings were made between 2 and 3 p.m.?
  b During which hour did the newsagent take the most money?
  c When do you think the newsagent is the quietest?

### What next?

| Score | | |
|---|---|---|
| | 0 – 2 | Your knowledge of this topic is still developing. To improve look at Formative test: 3A-6; MyMaths: 1093, 1153, 1168 and 1184 |
| | 3 – 4 | You are gaining a secure knowledge of this topic. To improve look at InvisiPen: 262, 264, 275, 276 and 277 |
| | 5 | You have mastered this topic. Well done, you are ready to progress! |

⚙ **MyMaths**.co.uk

111

## Question commentary

**Question 1** – Check students give the vertical lines as $x = \square$ and the horizontal lines as $y = \square$.

**Question 2** – This question should pose few problems.

**Question 3** – Make sure students take into account the fact that the scales on the two axes are different. Some might just 'count the squares'.

**Question 4** – Students could describe Jim's journey in its entirety rather than following the structure of the question.

**Question 5** – Check that the students are reading from the scale correctly on the takings axis. They could also describe the trends over the course of the day.

## Answers

1 Yellow: $x = -4$, Red: $x = 3$, Green: $y = -1$, Purple: $y = 5$

2 a

| x | 0 | 1 | 2 | 3 | 4 |
|---|---|---|---|---|---|
| 2x | 0 | 2 | 4 | 6 | 8 |
| +1 | +1 | +1 | +1 | +1 | +1 |
| y | 1 | 3 | 5 | 7 | 9 |

  b Straight line, starting at (0, 1), which goes up two squares for every one square across.

3 a $x \rightarrow \times 3 \rightarrow y$     b $y = 3x$

4 a 30 km/hr     b 20 km
  c He stops

5 a £200     b 12 – 1pm
  c 3 – 4 pm

# 6 MyPractice

**1** Copy these axes.
Plot each set of coordinates.
Join each set with a straight line.

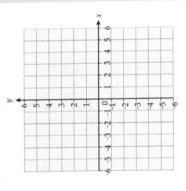

| a | (5, 5) | (3, 5) | (0, 5) |
| | (-2, 5) | (-6, 5) | |
| b | (-4, 5) | (-4, 1) | (-4, 0) |
| | (-4, -3) | (-4, -6) | |
| c | (-5, -4) | (-1, -4) | (0, -4) |
| | (1, -4) | (5, -4) | |
| d | (3, 6) | (3, 4) | (3, 0) |
| | (3, -3) | (3, -5) | |

**2** Write the equation of each of the lines
in question **1**.

**3** Copy and complete the tables of values for these relationships.

**a** $y = 2x - 2$

| x | 0 | 1 | 2 | 3 | 4 | 5 |
|---|---|---|---|---|---|---|
| 2x | 0 | 2 | 4 | | | |
| -2 | -2 | -2 | -2 | -2 | -2 | -2 |
| y | | -2 | 2 | | | |

**b** $y = 5 - x$

| x | 0 | 1 | 2 | 3 | 4 | 5 |
|---|---|---|---|---|---|---|
| +5 | +5 | +5 | +5 | +5 | +5 | +5 |
| -x | 0 | -1 | -2 | | | -4 |
| y | 5 | 4 | | | | |

**4** Copy the axes.
Plot the points from the two tables in question **3**.
Join each set of points with a straight line.

**5 a** Draw a set of axes with x from 0 to 5 and y from
0 to 13.

**b** Plot these four lines on your axes.
$y = 2x$    $y = 2x + 4$    $x = 2$    $x = 4$

**c** What is the mathematical name of the shape made
by these lines?

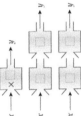

**Algebra** Graphs

---

**6** Write the coordinates of the point where the lines $y = 2x - 2$ and
$y = 5 - x$ intersect.

**7** For each of the lines on the graph, write the rule that links
the x- and y-coordinates.

**a**
**b**
**c**

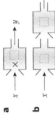

**8** The graphs show how the depth of liquid changes in three flasks
as liquid is poured into them.
Match the flasks to the graphs.

**A**
**B**
**C**

**i**
**ii**
**iii**

**9** The temperature in a vegetable cold store
is recorded every hour.
The results are recorded on a line graph.

**a** What is the temperature at 9 a.m.?

**b** The cold store is switched off for one hour
for cleaning. What time was this?

**c** What is the difference in temperature
between 12 p.m. and 5 p.m.?

**d** How many degrees difference are there
between the warmest and coolest temperatures?

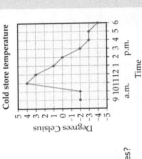

Cold store temperature

## Question commentary

**Questions 1** and **2** – **(6a)** Check that the students are joining the points up for each part separately before moving on. In question **2**, check they have the horizontal and vertical lines classified correctly.

**Question 3** – **(6b)** Students may quickly pick up a pattern in the $y$-values but encourage them to check by using a complete method.

**Questions 4** and **5** – **(6c)** Check the students have got the correct tables for question **3** first before proceeding. In question **5**, discourage the drawing of tables of values.

**Question 6** – **(6d)** Students will need to draw the graphs of the two equations. Tables of values may be required.

**Question 7** – **(6e)** This question could be done by asking the students for the equation of the line directly, rather than the function machines.

**Question 8** – **(6f)** Students could be asked to justify their answers.

**Question 9** – **(6g)** Students could be asked to describe, in detail, the changes in temperature throughout the day.

## Answers

**1**  **a**  Horizontal line through (0, 5)
    **b**  Vertical line through (-4, 0)
    **c**  Horizontal line through (0, -4)
    **d**  Vertical line through (3, 0)

**2**  **a**  $y = 5$   **b**  $x = -4$   **c**  $y = -4$   **d**  $x = 3$

**3**  **a**

| $x$ | 0 | 1 | 2 | 3 | 4 | 5 |
|---|---|---|---|---|---|---|
| $2x$ | 0 | 2 | 4 | 6 | 8 | 10 |
| -2 | -2 | -2 | -2 | -2 | -2 | -2 |
| $y$ | -2 | 0 | 2 | 4 | 6 | 8 |

    **b**

| $x$ | 0 | 1 | 2 | 3 | 4 | 5 |
|---|---|---|---|---|---|---|
| +5 | +5 | +5 | +5 | +5 | +5 | +5 |
| -x | 0 | -1 | -2 | -3 | -4 | -5 |
| $y$ | 5 | 4 | 3 | 2 | 1 | 0 |

**4**  straight lines through (0, -2) and (2, 2) and (0, 5) and (1, 4)

**5**  parallelogram

**6**  $(2\frac{1}{3}, 2\frac{2}{3})$

**7**  **a**  $\times 1$   **b**  $\times \frac{8}{3}, -1$   **c**  $\times 2, +3$

**8**  A – iii, B – i, C – ii

**9**  **a**  -2°C       **b**  10-11 am
    **c**  6°C       **d**  8°C

| Related lessons | | Resources | |
|---|---|---|---|
| Order of operations | 1c |  Order of operations | (1167) |
| Fractions and decimals | 4e | Multiply two decimals | (1011) |
| Using a calculator | 7f | String; beads; padded envelopes | |
| Estimating and approximating | 7e | Postal rate leaflets; scales | |

| Simplification | Extension |
|---|---|
| The bulk purchasing elements could be ignored and the beads and thread just priced by the unit. Likewise, the online auction costings can be simplified to include just a listing fee or a selling fee.<br><br>Alternatively, ask the students to work out the number of beads that can fit on each piece of jewellery first and then price up the beads for each necklace and bracelet before working out how many they can make per metre of the thread/cord. | Students could consider diversifying their range. They would need to research the cost of materials, either from catalogues that you provide or from online suppliers.<br><br>Students could be encouraged to find other suppliers in order to compare costs and secure the best deal. Students could also repeat the whole process for a different product of their choosing, maybe in response to the question, what business would you try if you could? |

### Links

One example of an online supplier is http://www.the-beadshop.co.uk/

For Royal mail postage costs see
http://sg.royalmail.com/portal/rm/PriceFinder?catId=23500532&gear=pricingcalc

## Teaching notes

Start with a general discussion about buying on-line. Have you or your family ever bought or sold anything by online auction? Ask students who have experience of this to describe what it involves.

Read through the start of the case study to see that two friends are setting up a small business selling bracelets and necklaces through an online auction site. Discuss how, before they can start selling, they will need to buy in supplies to make their bracelets and necklaces, so will be spending some money at the outset. What would they need to think about when deciding what materials to buy? Hear students' suggestions and discuss how the group will want to make sure that they don't lose a lot of money, so will need to think about how much to spend and what profit they are likely to make.

### Tasks 1, 2 and 3

Make sure the students are clear that there are two possible suppliers and then give them time, working with a partner, to tackle the questions relating to the beads.

### Tasks 4 and 5

Move on to the right hand page to consider the costs involved in the auction. Make sure that students understand the charges involved: a charge for putting an item on sale (the listing fee) and a commission charged if the item sells (selling fee). Also point out that there is a choice of two ways of selling: either using an auction where people bid against one another, steadily raising the price or as a fixed price sale, where the seller sets the price they want and any buyer will pay that price. Give students time to answer the questions about the auction. They could create a spreadsheet to find out at what price fixed price fees become less than auction fees.

### Task 6

Finally the students should work with their partner to produce a detailed business plan that they think should provide a profit. It should contain reasons for their decisions and an estimate of the costing involved and predicted income, including an estimate of the number they will need to sell to break even. They should also give examples of ideas that they rejected along the way, explaining why they rejected them. When complete, it would be interesting for the students to compare their decisions.

### Answers to Tasks

1 a, b

|  |  | NBC | B-e-l |
|---|---|---|---|
| **2000** | **8 × 16** | £64.00 | £76.00 |
|  | **12 × 9** | £40.00 | £43.00 |
|  | **P & P** | £3.50 | free |
|  | **Total** | £107.50 | £119.00 |
|  |  |  |  |
|  | **50m leather thread** | £11.95 | £22.50 |
|  | **50m waxed cord** | £5.00 | £5.00 |
|  | **Grand total** | £124.45 | £146.50 |

2 a  7.5 long beads (so 7 actual beads)

  b  13 round beads

  c  312

3 a  12.5 long beads (so 12 actual beads)

  b  22 round beads

  c  166

4  Students' answers: for – no listing fee, may tempt buyers; against – could sell for 99p.

5 a  By auction (15 + 50 = 65p < 40 + 42 = 82p)

  b  Fees coincide at £10, so lowest theoretical price is £10.01 However if prices are rounded to nearest penny, then £10.35 (127.975 p fixed price < 128.5 p auction).

6  Students' answers

## Learning outcomes

**N1** Understand and use place value for decimals, measures and integers of any size (L5)

**N4** Use the 4 operations, including formal written methods, applied to integers, decimals, proper and improper fractions, and mixed numbers, all both positive and negative (L5/6)

**N5** Use conventional notation for the priority of operations, including brackets, powers, roots and reciprocals (L5)

**N14** use approximation through rounding to estimate answers and calculate possible resulting errors expressed using inequality notation $a < x \le b$ (L5)

**N15** Use a calculator and other technologies to calculate results accurately and then interpret them appropriately (L5)

## Introduction

The chapter starts by looking at mental and written methods for adding and subtracting before looking at similar methods for multiplying and dividing. Estimating and approximating from real life contexts is covered before a section on the use of a calculator (including the appropriate order of operations) to solve problems.

The introduction discusses the use of the binary number system in computing. By converting numbers into binary, computers can recognise the on/off state of the various electronic switches and understand the numbers. They can then perform arithmetic using logic gates.

As of July 2013, the fastest computer has been developed in China and can work out over 33 000 trillion calculations per second. This number is getting so difficult to represent using our standard language of large numbers so computer scientists have invented another number to represent 1000 trillion – the 'Petaflop'. 33 000 trillion is therefore 33 petaflops. In reality, the 'flop' part stands for floating point operation which is the standard type of calculation carried out by a computer processor.

http://www.petaflop.info/

Students could be invited to investigate other large numbers such as the google or the googleplex.

## Prior knowledge

Students should already know how to…

- Carry out simple arithmetic
- Round numbers to nearest whole or ten

## Starter problem

The starter problem considers three different methods of carrying out the same calculation.

Method 1 is essentially a binary calculation where successive 'powers of two' multiples of 21 are written down and then the 13 is formed by adding the terms that start '1 ×…', '4 ×…' and '8 ×…'.

Method 2 sees the 13 successively doubled and the 21 successively halved (rounding down). When the halving leaves a remainder, the multiple of 13 is circled and the answer to the calculation is the sum of the circled numbers. This is probably the most complicated of the methods.

Method 3 is a grid method where the answer is found by adding up the numbers in each diagonal, running top right to bottom left. For example, the '7' is found by adding the 1, the 0 and the 6 in the longest diagonal. This method requires only the skills of single digit multiplication and adding.

All of the methods are easily adaptable for the new calculation given at the end of the problem.

## Resources

**MyMaths**

| | | | | | |
|---|---|---|---|---|---|
| Estimating introduction | 1002 | Adding in columns | 1020 | Division chunking | 1021 |
| Subtraction columns | 1028 | Long division | 1041 | Estimating calculations | 1043 |
| Mixed sums all numbers | 1345 | Mixed tables 2 to 12 | 1367 | | |

**Online assessment**

| | | |
|---|---|---|
| Chapter test | 3A–7 | |
| Formative test | 3A–7 | |
| Summative test | 3A–7 | |

**InvisiPen solutions**

| | | | |
|---|---|---|---|
| Mental addition/subtraction | 121 | Mental multiplication | 122 |
| Mental division | 123 | Written addition/subtraction | 125 |
| Written multiplication | 126 | Written division | 127 |
| Calculator methods | 128 | | |

# Topic scheme

Teaching time = 6 lessons/2 weeks

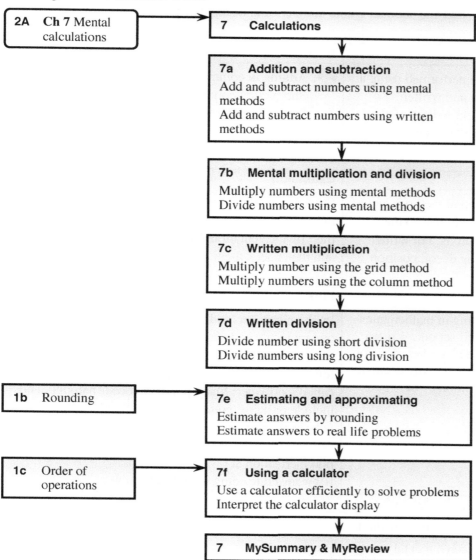

**2A   Ch 7** Mental calculations

**7   Calculations**

**7a   Addition and subtraction**
Add and subtract numbers using mental methods
Add and subtract numbers using written methods

**7b   Mental multiplication and division**
Multiply numbers using mental methods
Divide numbers using mental methods

**7c   Written multiplication**
Multiply number using the grid method
Multiply numbers using the column method

**7d   Written division**
Divide number using short division
Divide numbers using long division

**1b   Rounding**

**7e   Estimating and approximating**
Estimate answers by rounding
Estimate answers to real life problems

**1c   Order of operations**

**7f   Using a calculator**
Use a calculator efficiently to solve problems
Interpret the calculator display

**7   MySummary & MyReview**

# Differentiation

**Student book 3A**        116 – 133

Addition and subtraction
Mental and written methods for
multiplication and division
Estimating and approximating
Use a calculator efficiently

**Student book 3B**        116 – 131

Add, subtract, multiply and divide
decimals using efficient mental
and written methods
Use a calculator efficiently,
including the correct order of
operations
Interpret the calculator display

**Student book 3C**        116 – 129

Order of operations
Calculating with decimals
Use a calculator efficiently,
including the correct order of
operations
Interpret the calculator display

## Objectives

- Use efficient written methods to add and subtract whole numbers and decimals with up to two decimal places.
  (L4)

| Key ideas | Resources |
|---|---|
| 1 Addition and subtraction can be performed using a variety of methods, both mental and written.<br>2 The column method is an efficient written method for both addition and subtraction of integers and decimals. | Adding in columns (1020)<br>Subtraction columns (1028)<br>Mixed sums all numbers (1345)<br>A 100 square<br>Mini whiteboards |

| Simplification | Extension |
|---|---|
| In the first instance, work using mental methods and a 100 square for two-digit numbers. Progress to the column method for three-digit additions. For written subtractions, keep examples needing decomposition straightforward. | Students calculate by adding and subtracting decimal numbers having up to 2 decimal places. They devise their own calculations, have a partner find the answers, and then check them. |

| Literacy | Links |
|---|---|
| As with writing in English, so writing in mathematics is most easily understood if it is well set out. Written calculations using the column method are best done on squared paper with one digit to a square. Any decimal points can either have their own column or be positioned on a grid line. | In chemistry, an 'addition reaction' is a reaction where one molecule adds on to another. When two or more identical molecules undergo an addition reaction, a long chain molecule with repeating links is formed called a polymer. Many polymers occur naturally and include proteins, cotton and natural rubber. But polymers, including most plastics, are also made synthetically There is an animation illustrating addition polymerisation at www.ausetute.com.au/polymers.html |

## Alternative approach

Before doing a calculation, decide on the best method:

- for additions, the choice is between a mental or written method;
- for subtractions if a mental method is chosen, the next choice is between 'taking away' from the larger number or 'adding onto' the smaller number;
- for subtractions if a written method is chosen, the next choice is whether to use the column method with possible decomposition or to use complementary addition starting from the smaller number.

## Checkpoint

Work out:

a $17.1 + 52.3$       (69.4)

b $124.8 - 81.3$       (43.5)

## Starter – Quick fire

Recap work of previous chapters, especially Chapters 1 and 4. Ask rapid response questions with students responding on mini whiteboards. Discuss answers when there is a need.

## Teaching notes

Ask students to complete a number of quick fire additions and subtractions of single-digit numbers, using their mini whiteboards to show answers.

Explain that, when numbers get longer and more complicated, adding or subtracting them mentally gets more difficult. Demonstrate the 'number line' method for addition and subtraction of two-digit numbers and possibly three-digit numbers. Point out that this method requires a new number line for each calculation and that the column method of addition and subtraction is more efficient. Give an example of adding using the column method and then ask students to practise with further questions.

Give the students examples which involve adding and subtracting decimal numbers and explain that the method is exactly the same except that the decimal points must be lined up vertically in the column method.

When subtracting with a top digit smaller than the bottom digit, show how to use decomposition in the column method.

Show that, for some subtractions, such as 212 – 198, complementary addition is the best method.

## Plenary

Students find answers to similar calculations and show them on mini whiteboards. A time limit for each question is set as speed and accuracy are both important. Discuss answers and methods where necessary.

## Exercise commentary

**Question 1** – This question could be done as a whole-class activity with mini-whiteboards. It is usually best to start with the larger number when adding.

**Questions 2 to 5** – These questions test students' basic skills. They could also be done in the form of a timed 'race' or whole-class activity.

**Questions 6 and 7** – Ensure students line up the decimal points before proceeding.

## Answers

| | | | | | | | | |
|---|---|---|---|---|---|---|---|---|
| **1** | a | 15 | b | 11 | c | 25 | d | 13 |
| | e | 22 | f | 11 | g | 17 | h | 29 |
| | i | 15 | j | 21 | k | 18 | l | 20 |
| | m | 15 | n | 24 | o | 30 | p | 20 |
| | q | 23 | r | 25 | s | 27 | t | 35 |
| **2** | a | 84 | b | 79 | c | 69 | d | 53 |
| | e | 77 | f | 91 | g | 131 | h | 141 |
| **3** | a | 12 | b | 33 | c | 25 | d | 30 |
| | e | 37 | f | 38 | g | 112 | h | 57 |
| **4** | a | 55 | b | 49 | c | 70 | d | 59 |
| | e | 287 | f | 317 | g | 455 | h | 528 |
| **5** | a | 34 | b | 40 | c | 36 | d | 25 |
| | e | 324 | f | 152 | g | 104 | h | 66 |
| **6** | a | 24.7 | b | 9.5 | c | 51.8 | d | 22.9 |
| | e | 272.8 | f | 145 | g | 222.2 | h | 41.6 |
| **7** | a | 5.2 | b | 17.5 | c | 11.5 | d | 5.5 |
| | e | 24 | f | 182.5 | g | 88 | h | 203.7 |

## Objectives

- Strengthen and extend mental methods of calculation and include decimals. (L4)
- Multiply and divide integers and decimals by 10 and 100. (L5)

## Key ideas

1 There are a variety of mental methods to use when multiplying and dividing.
2 Multiplying and dividing by 10 and 100 uses the idea of place value.

## Resources

Division chunking (1021)
Mixed tables 2 to 12 (1367)
Mini whiteboards

## Simplification

Concentrate on students' basic mental arithmetic skills such as using multiplication tables for × and ÷ and knowing simple addition and subtraction bonds before progressing to formal mental methods.

Give priority to multiplying and dividing integers by 10 and 100.

## Extension

Students complete simple mental multiplications using decimals; such as $4 \times 3.5$ and $5 \times 1.2$. Ask them to explain a method by which they could do these calculations using mental methods.

## Literacy

A love of language comes with the enjoyment of language in all its forms: speaking and listening, reading and writing. A love of numbers comes with confident use and a feel for their size and how they can be used. Mental methods need practice and confidence and are an essential tool in getting a feel for numbers.

## Links

'Partitioning' means 'splitting something into parts'. Many computer hard drives are partitioned into two or more parts. Each section behaves as its own hard drive, so that directories and files of different categories can be stored in different partitions. For example, operating system files and/or program files can be kept separate from data files. If one partition becomes corrupted, the files in the other partition are still recoverable. There is more about partitioning hard drives at www.aboutpartition.com

## Alternative approach

The first decision is to choose the best method.

For mental multiplications, some can be done quickly straight from the times tables; others need partitioning. For mental divisions, some are done using the times tables in reverse (for example, because $6 \times 7 = 42$, then $42 \div 7 = 6$); others might need 'chunking' (repeated subtractions with jottings). For multiplication or division by 10 or 100, imagine the digits changing columns by moving left or right.

## Checkpoint

Work out:

**a** $33 \times 4$ (132)

**b** $84 \div 6$ (14)

**Starter** – One, two, three, four

Ask students to make as many numbers up to 20 as they can by using all the digits 1, 2, 3, 4 and any operations for each number.

For example,

$(4 - 1) \times 3 + 2 = 11, 4 \div 2 \times 3 + 1 = 7$

## Teaching notes

Use mini whiteboards for quick fire questions to recall multiplications from times tables. Adopt mental strategies for times-tables answers which are not easily recalled; such as, finding $8 \times 7$ from $7 \times 7 = 49$ or finding $9 \times 7$ from $10 \times 7 = 70$.

Extend to mental partitioning; for example, $14 \times 8$ is seen as $10 \times 8$ and $4 \times 8$.

Revise multiplying and dividing integers and decimals by 10 and 100. Use mini whiteboards to gauge proficiency.

Recall the column headings Th , H , T , U , t , h.

Return to times tables to do simple divisions, such as $32 \div 8$. Extend to $84 \div 7$ using chunking (repeated subtraction).

## Plenary

Give a series of quick fire calculations, with students responding on mini whiteboards. Assess their proficiency. Discuss questions where needed. Have similar sessions over the followings days and regularly thereafter. Set some questions in context.

## Exercise commentary

**Questions 1** and **2** – Quick-fire recall should be expected here.

**Question 3** – Students should think of the digits moving left or right, not the decimal point moving.

**Questions 4** and **5** – Mental partitioning is generally the best mental method; for $3 \times 14$ work out $3 \times 10$ and $3 \times 4$. Encourage students to use other valid mental methods when they are more appropriate; for example, $9 \times 12$ may be known by immediate recall or may be found by subtracting 12 from $10 \times 12$.

**Questions 6** and **7** – Students may use chunking but they could also use the quicker method of short division.

**Question 8** – A nice problem-solving question for students to experiment with. Suitable for paired work, perhaps in the form of a challenge.

## Answers

| | | | | | | | | |
|---|---|---|---|---|---|---|---|---|
| 1 | a | 15 | b | 18 | c | 24 | d | 28 |
| | e | 24 | f | 35 | g | 27 | h | 32 |
| 2 | a | 4 | b | 4 | c | 3 | d | 6 |
| | e | 6 | f | 6 | g | 5 | h | 4 |
| 3 | a | 80 | b | 12 | c | 28 | d | 410 |
| | e | 900 | f | 15 | g | 2600 | h | 71 |
| | i | 28 | j | 6.3 | k | 140 | l | 0.85 |
| | m | 8 | n | 0.06 | o | 60 | p | 0.115 |
| 4 | a | 42 | b | 78 | c | 108 | d | 90 |
| | e | 108 | f | 120 | g | 102 | h | 126 |
| 5 | a | 105 | b | 92 | c | 176 | d | 104 |
| | e | 123 | f | 210 | g | 162 | h | 222 |
| 6 | a | 11 r 2 | b | 21 | c | 13 | d | 12 |
| | e | 16 | f | 12 | g | 15 | h | 18 |
| 7 | a | 19 | b | 13 | c | 14 r 3 | d | 13 r 4 |
| | e | 11 | f | 12 | g | 13 r 6 | h | 14 r 8 |
| 8 | 7884 | | | | | | | |

## Objectives

- Use efficient written methods for multiplication of integers and decimals. (L5)

| Key ideas | Resources |
|---|---|
| 1 Two written methods are the grid method and long multiplication.<br>2 Estimating the answer is one method for placing the decimal point in the answer. | Mini whiteboards<br>Calculators |

| Simplification | Extension |
|---|---|
| Restrict examples to those involving one- and two-digit numbers. Avoid multiplying decimals until work with integers is secure. Concentrate on the column method for long multiplication at the expense of the grid method. | Students multiple two decimals such as $1.2 \times 13.6$ and discuss where to place the decimal point in the answer. They test if they are correct using a calculator. |

| Literacy | Links |
|---|---|
| There are several ways of multiplying two integers together. Two writen methods are dealt with in the student's book: the grid method, which uses partitioning and the column method for long multiplication. In the end, it is better that a student is totally proficient in one method than partially proficient in two. The currently favoured method is the column method for long multiplication. | Pyramid selling is an illegal scam that operates like a chain letter. People are asked to invest money and are then rewarded for recruiting more people to join the scheme. The numbers of people involved in the scheme can be worked out using multiplication. If an investor recruits ten friends who each recruit ten (different) friends and so on, after eight levels, there has to be one hundred million recruits, more than the population of the UK! All these schemes eventually run out of recruits and then everyone loses their money. |

## Alternative approach

Two alternative approaches for multiplication are already offered: partitioning and long multiplication. It is very likely that the column method for long multiplication will be the more efficient use of students' time. They will likely get answers more quickly and more accurately using this method.

A policy of working on squared paper with 'one digit to one square' helps with control over columns.

## Checkpoint

Work out:

a $24 \times 81$ (1944)

b $7 \times 11.3$ (79.1)

## Starter – Match up

Ask students to find the pairs in the following:

| | | |
|---|---|---|
| $2 \times 10 + 8$ | $10 \times 4 \div 5$ | $4 + 4 \times 4 - 4$ |
| $20 \div (3 + 2)$ | $(3 + 1) \times (7 - 2)$ | $(3 + 4) \times 4$ |
| $8 - 2 \times 2$ | $32 \div 2$ | $3 \times 2 + 2$ |
| $4 + 8 \times 2$ | | |

$[2 \times 10 + 8 = (3 + 4) \times 4 = 28;$

$10 \times 4 \div 5 = 3 \times 2 + 2 = 8;$

$4 + 4 \times 4 - 4 = 32 \div 2 = 16;$

$20 \div (3 + 2) = 8 - 2 \times 2 = 4;$

$(3 + 1) \times (7 - 2) = 4 + 8 \times 2 = 20]$

Pairings can be differentiated by the choice of calculations.

## Teaching notes

Give students some simple multiplications which they can solve mentally before introducing a more complex problem like $142 \times 23$.

Explain that there are two methods:

- the numbers can be partitioned and a grid used to find the answer;
- the numbers can be written in columns and long multiplication used.

Demonstrate both methods. Give students a similar multiplication, say $234 \times 32$. Time the students for both methods and see which is quicker and which is more accurate.

Use long multiplication to multiply a decimal by a single-digit integer and then a two-digit integer. Explain where the decimal point is placed in the answer and why.

## Plenary

Suggest real life situations where people may have to use long multiplication; such as "A man buys 14 televisions for £132 each at a wholesalers. How much does he spend?" Students use mini whiteboards to show their working and find their answers.

## Exercise commentary

**Question 1** – To get a more balanced estimate, approximate one number on the high side and the other on the low side. For example, in part **a**, an estimate can be found from $10 \times 140 = 1400$ or $15 \times 100 = 1500$).

**Questions 2 and 4** – Either the grid method or long multiplication can be used, with long multiplication requiring less written work.

**Question 3** – Watch that students place a zero on the right-hand end of the line when multiplying by 10.

**Questions 5 and 6** – Ensure that students place the decimal point correctly.

**Question 7** – An opportunity for class or paired discussion of the solution.

**Question 8** – Practical problems that test the skills covered.

## Answers

| | | | | | | | | |
|---|---|---|---|---|---|---|---|---|
| **1** | **a** | 1716 | **b** | 1716 | **c** | 3125 | **d** | 3840 |
| **2** | **a** | 1968 | **b** | 2964 | **c** | 2430 | **d** | 2430 |
| | **e** | 3611 | **f** | 6324 | **g** | 7392 | **h** | 9216 |
| **3** | **a** | 1716 | **b** | 1500 | **c** | 2884 | **d** | 11016 |
| **4** | **a** | 2145 | **b** | 2821 | **c** | 2160 | **d** | 5950 |
| | **e** | 8126 | **f** | 28974 | | | | |
| **5** | **a** | 45.6 | **b** | 57.2 | **c** | 64.5 | **d** | 177 |
| **6** | **a** | 34.8 | **b** | 62.5 | **c** | 115.5 | **d** | 189.6 |
| | **e** | 122.4 | **f** | 97.6 | | | | |

**7** Alan is correct

**8**
- **a** $18 \times 32 = 576$ biscuits
- **b** $174 \times 7 = 1218$ passengers
- **c** $22.5 \times 6 = 135$ g
- **d** $26 \times 8 = 208$ crates
- **e** $37.4 \times 6 = 224.4$ cm

## Objectives

- Use efficient written methods for division of integers. (L4)

| Key ideas | Resources |
|---|---|
| **1** Short and long division are two methods of dividing integers. | ⊞ Long division (1041) <br> Mini whiteboards |

| Simplification | Extension |
|---|---|
| In the first instance, concentrate on short division by a single-digit number without remainders. Progress to divisions with remainders. Then divide by straightforward double-digit integers (such as 11, 12, 20) using short division without (and, later, with) remainders. | When a division of two integers leads to a remainder, students write the answer in three ways: (a) giving the remainder, (b) writing the remainder as a fraction, (c) continuing the division into decimals and giving the answer as a terminating decimal and, later, as a recurring decimal. |

| Literacy | Links |
|---|---|
| Adopting the policy of writing computations on squared paper with one digit to a square helps keep the columns aligned correctly. | Human cells divide in two ways. Cells not involved in reproduction divide by a process called mitosis to produce cells identical to the original cell. Reproductive cells divide by a process called meiosis during which gametes are formed containing half the number of chromosomes of the original cell. There is more about mitosis and meiosis at www.pbs.org/wgbh/nova/miracle/divide.html and an interactive activity at www.biologyinmotion.com/cell_division/index.html |

### Alternative approach

Some students find long division confusing. Short division provides an alternative. Short division is not as confusing on paper but, when dividing by a number beyond the times tables, there is a need to make jottings on the side to work out multiples. For example, $701 \div 17$, when set out using short division, becomes:

$\underline{\phantom{00}4\ 1}$ r 4 and jottings on the side are the multiples $17, 34, 51, 68$, showing that $70 \div 17 = 4$ remainder 2.

$17\ )\ 7\ 0^2 1$

### Checkpoint

Work out:

**a** $287 \div 7$ (41)

**b** $528 \div 16$ (33)

## Starter – Quick fire

Revise the previous lesson by having students using mini whiteboards show their working for written multiplications such as $132 \times 24$ and $32.4 \times 2$.

They show answers and discuss results as necessary.

## Teaching notes

Give students some quick-fire divisions taken from the times tables; they write their answers on mini whiteboards. Introduce two written methods for more complex divisions. Demonstrate short division for dividing by a one-digit number with an example such as $96 \div 6$. Demonstrate long division for dividing by a two-digit number with an example such as $156 \div 13$.

Students first estimate the size of the answer before they proceed and, later, make a comparison with their final written answer.

Consider a problem which has a remainder, say $173 \div 14$, and work through the problem using long division. Explain the correct notation for remainder.

## Plenary

Present students with a problem in context, such as "A woman goes into a shop and buys 17 identical items. The total bill comes to £204. How much was each item?" Give the students sufficient time to find the answer on their mini whiteboards. Repeat for other problems. Discuss answers when needed.

## Exercise commentary

**Questions 1** and **2** – These questions could be done as a quick-fire whole-class exercise.

**Question 3** – As with earlier written computation on squared paper, a policy of one square for one digit should be used.

**Question 4** – Students have a choice. They can use long division or they can use short division with jottings to help with the working.

**Question 5** – The answers have remainders. Students make their own choice of the most appropriate method.

**Question 6** – These questions are practical applications. Again, students make their own choice of method.

## Answers

| | | | | | | | | |
|---|---|---|---|---|---|---|---|---|
| 1 | a | 4 | b | 10 | c | 2 | d | 3 |
| | e | 7 | f | 5 | g | 6 | h | 4 |
| | i | 6 | j | 9 | k | 9 | l | 9 |
| 2 | a | 10 | b | 6 | c | 16 | d | 20 |
| | e | 23 | f | 9 | g | 12 | h | 9 |
| 3 | a | 17 | b | 16 | c | 23 | d | 21 |
| | e | 23 | f | 22 | | | | |
| 4 | a | 22 | b | 21 | c | 23 | d | 31 |
| | e | 23 | f | 25 | g | 27 | h | 13 |
| | i | 29 | j | 53 | | | | |
| 5 | a | 23 r 1 | b | 15 r 4 | c | 15 r 5 | d | 23 r 4 |
| | e | 24 r 4 | f | 21 r 5 | g | 24 r 10 | h | 13 r 11 |
| | i | 23 r 12 | j | 23 r 5 | | | | |

6   a   $253 \div 11 = £23$ each

     b   $324 \div 6 = 54$ hens

     c   $360 \div 15 = 24$ lengths

     d   $189 \div 7 = 27$ weeks

     e   $408 \div 12 = 34$ years

## Objectives

- Use rounding to make estimates. (L5)

| Key ideas | Resources | |
|---|---|---|
| 1 An estimate is found by using approximate values for numbers.<br>2 Approximate values are found by rounding. | ⊕ Estimating introduction<br>  Estimating calculations<br>Mini whiteboards | (1002)<br>(1043) |

| Simplification | Extension |
|---|---|
| Refresh previous work done on rounding. Discuss when to round up and when to round down. Some students may need to practise rounding numbers to the nearest 1, 10, 100 and 1000. | Students could extend Question **4** by describing other scenarios and making estimates of their own. For example, how long would it take to walk to around the Earth? |

| Literacy | Links |
|---|---|
| Rounding produces an approximate value of a number.<br>To approximate a number is to replace it with a less accurate value.<br>To estimate means to perform a numerical calculation using approximate values. (To estimate can also mean to guage the length, weight, etc. of an object without measuring it.) | Students estimate their ages to the nearest year, nearest day and nearest second. There is an accurate age calculator online at www.onlineconversion.com/howold.htm How accurate are their estimates? |

### Alternative approach

When estimating a calculation, it is often possible to balance the effects of any approximations. For example, estimating $126 \times 48$ by using $130 \times 50$ will definitely give an overestimate and by using $120 \times 40$ will definitely give an underestimate. Using $120 \times 50$ or $130 \times 40$ will give intermediate values. The same line of thought applies to addition.

When subtracting or dividing, more care is needed and the methods are beyond the scope of this book.

### Checkpoint

Estimate the answers to these calculations:

**a** $32\ 154 \times 1.92$  $(30\ 000 \times 2 = 60\ 000)$

**b** $885 \div 9.31$  $(900 \div 9 = 100)$

## Starter – Quick fire

Recap work of previous chapters and this chapter so far. Ask rapid response questions with students responding on mini whiteboards. Discuss answers when there is a need. Include simple long multiplications and short divisions.

## Teaching notes

Remind students that they can round numbers to any given power of 10. Remind them when to round up and when to round down. Students can practise rounding using mini whiteboards.

Explain that rounding numbers to the nearest ten or hundred can be useful for estimating the answers where the exact answer is unnecessary. Give students practice at this type of rounding. Describe problems in context where rounding is necessary; such as estimating the weight of chocolate eaten by students in the school each week.

## Plenary

Give students quick fire questions involving rounding and estimation. They write their solutions on mini whiteboards. Discuss as necessary.

## Exercise commentary

**Question 1** – This question is a good opportunity for student discussion. It reinforces visually how to round a number to the nearest £10.

**Question 2** – Part **b** needs students to estimate the number of weeks in a month.

**Question 3** – Students may need some help choosing suitable approximations. In part **a**, a good estimate for the mass of a chocolate bar is 250 g and for Siobhan's mass is 42 000 g. In part **b**, use 50 kg and 25 000 kg or 28 000 kg

**Question 4** – This is a good question for paired work and discussion. Encourage students to explain how they have made their estimates. Students could do a survey to work out the average amount of pocket money received by the class.

## Answers

1   Britain - £130, Chad - £0, Greenland - £140, Egypt - £30 USA - £170, Japan - £160

2   **a**   Sam              **b**   Hugh

3   **a**   84 days          **b**   500 times heavier

4   **a,b**          Check student answers

## Objectives

- Carry out complex calculations effectively and efficiently using the function keys for powers and roots.(L6)
- Use brackets and the memory. (L5)
- Interpret the display in different contexts. (L6)

| Key ideas | Resources |
|---|---|
| 1 Brackets can be used to ensure the right priority is given to operations within a calculation. <br> 2 Alternatively, complex calculations can be worked out piecemeal. | Money calculations (1014) <br> Calculators and emulator software <br> Mini whiteboards |

| Simplification | Extension |
|---|---|
| Students should be encouraged to write down each step of a complex calculation. This should help them keep track of the whole calculation. | Students, in pairs, could write complex calculations to which they find answers. Each student exchanges their calculation with their partner who also works it out. They compare their answers and discuss any discrepancies. |

| Literacy | Links |
|---|---|
| The answer to a calculation may need to be interpreted differently depending on the context from which it arose. Consider $32 \div 5 = 6.4$. <br><br> Finding the cost of one article if 5 of them cost £32, uses $32 \div 5 = 6.4$ and the cost of one article is £6.40. <br><br> A car can carry 5 passengers and there are 32 people to transport. How many trips are needed? 6.4 is not a sensible answer. The number of trips is 7 (with a few spare places on the last trip). <br><br> A bottle holds 5 litres. How many bottles can be completely filled from 32 litres. Again, 6.4 is not a sensible answer. There can be only 6 full bottles (with 2 litres of liquid left over). <br><br> So, the answer to the calculation $3.2 \div 5$ has been interpreted in three different ways: 6.40, 7 and 6. Understanding the context is essential. | Charles Babbage (1791–1871) was the first person to design a mechanical computer that could store information. He invented his analytical engine in 1834 but only part of it was ever built. Another of his calculating machines, the Difference Engine No. 2, was built to his original designs at the Science Museum in London in 2002. There is a video of the Difference Engine at work at www.computerhistory.org/babbage/ |

## Alternative approach

Question **5** can be used to test the efficiency of two methods when using a calculator with complex calculations. Have some students calculate by using brackets to enter the entire calculation. Have other students calculate piecemeal, making jottings of parts of the calculation on the way. Explore how long each method takes and which method more often gives the correct answer.

## Checkpoint

Work out, using a calculator, the following:

**a** The number of 22 kg sacks needed to store 853 kg of grain. (39)

**b** The total cost of 8 music tracks at 69 pence each. (£5.52)

## Starter – Forgotten numbers

Given that $a \div b = 1.352\,941\,176$ where $a$ and $b$ are both two-digit integers, find the values of $a$ and $b$.

$$[a = 23, b = 17]$$

A possible whole-class approach is to multiply $1.352\,941\,176$ by all integers from 11 upwards, allocating increasing values of $b$ to different students. Can this method be teased out of the class by discussion?

## Teaching notes

Ensure students have access to a scientific calculator (preferably all the same type) and if possible have an emulator displayed on the board.

Give students some simple calculations to do in order to practise their basic skills and have them display their answers on mini whiteboards.

Explain that the way we write our answer is important; for example 6.25 hours is better written as 6 hours and 15 minutes. Compare problems involving time with those involving people. For example, 1000 minutes converted into hours would be 16 hours and 40 minutes whereas 1000 people divided into 60 groups would be 16 groups and 40 people remaining.

Explain how to convert the decimal part of an answer to a whole number by first subtracting the whole number part of the answer and then multiplying the decimal remainder by the original divisor. Students need to practise interpreting remainders in context.

A second feature of calculators is the use of brackets in long calculations. With some calculators, the entire calculation can be keyed in by using brackets appropriately. At other times, a complex calculation is better found in separate parts, which may or may not be placed in the calculator's memory.

## Plenary

Give the students a number of quick-fire calculations to do on their calculators and ask them to display their answers on mini whiteboards to enable easy assessment of responses.

## Exercise commentary

**Question 1** – Check that students convert all the amounts to the same units, either pounds or pence. They should also do a mental estimate to check the size of their answer.

**Question 2** – This is a good question for use as a paired activity. Students could discuss the interpretation of each of the remainders in their answers.

**Question 3** – Students will probably need some help in using their calculators to convert the divisor into a whole number. You may need to start with more simple examples such as how many weeks and days are there in 12 days.

**Question 4** – Encourage students to write down all of their working here and take care with remainders at each step.

**Question 5** – Either the use of brackets around the divisor and dividend will need to be explained, or students should work out the dividend and divisor separately and then divide. The second of these methods is more likely to result in a final correct answer. For greater accuracy, the calculator's memory can be used to store intermediate values.

## Answers

1  a  £8.92
   b  A writing pad and 3 erasers

2  a  24 bundles, 4 CDs left over
   b  £1142.85          c  5 coaches
   d  29.1 kg           e  8.2 minutes

3  a  33 hours, 20 minutes    b  216 days, 16 hours
   c  75 minutes             d  45 weeks, 5 days
   e  27 years, 145 days

4  114 years, 56 days, 16 hours

5  a  21.62    b  9.17    c  114.33

| Key outcomes | Quick check |
|---|---|
| Use mental methods to calculate with whole numbers.    L5 | Work out: <br> **a** $7 \times 25$ (175)         **b** $68 \div 100$ (0.68) |
| Use a standard column method to do addition and subtraction.    L5 | Work out: <br> **a** $158 + 745$ (903)       **b** $731 - 287$ (444) |
| Use long multiplication.    L6 | Calculate: <br> **a** $21 \times 43$ (903)       **b** $135 \times 61$ (8235) |
| Multiply decimals by a single-digit number.    L5 | Work out: <br> **a** $6 \times 14.2$ (85.2)     **b** $23.8 \times 4$ (95.2) |
| Use short and long division.    L5 | Work out: <br> **a** $581 \div 7$ (83)      **b** $1196 \div 13$ (92) |
| Use rounding to estimate and approximate.    L5 | Estimate the answer to this calculation: <br> $31\,926 \div 158 + 894$ ($32\,000 \div 160 + 900 = 1100$) |
| Interpret the remainder in a division calculation.    L5 | How many days are there in 1000 hours? (Give the remainder in hours) (41 days, 16 hours) |

## ⊕ MyMaths extra support

| Lesson/online homework | | | Description |
|---|---|---|---|
| Doubling and halving | 1023 | L4 | Doubling numbers where there is a carry-over can be quite tricky. |
| Order of operations | 1167 | L5 | Dealing with brackets and BIDMAS |
| Introducing money | 1226 | L3 | Counting up money using coins and giving change |
| Best buys and value | 1226 | L5 | How to make sure you are getting the best buy and real value for your money |
| Money problems | 1377 | L4 | Solving shopping problems |

# My Review

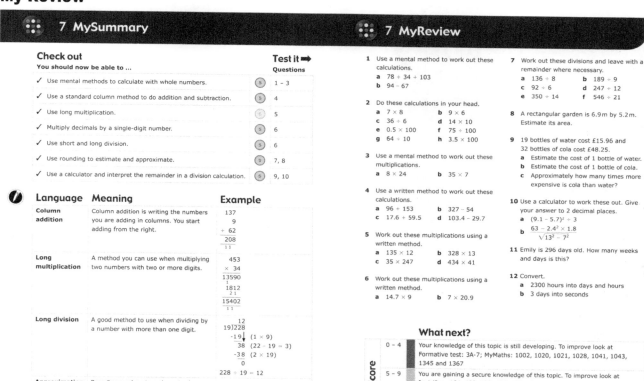

## Check out
**You should now be able to ...**

**Test it ➡**
**Questions**

| | | |
|---|---|---|
| ✓ | Use mental methods to calculate with whole numbers. | ⑤ 1 – 3 |
| ✓ | Use a standard column method to do addition and subtraction. | ⑤ 4 |
| ✓ | Use long multiplication. | ⑥ 5 |
| ✓ | Multiply decimals by a single-digit number. | ⑤ 6 |
| ✓ | Use short and long division. | ⑤ 6 |
| ✓ | Use rounding to estimate and approximate. | ⑨ 7, 8 |
| ✓ | Use a calculator and interpret the remainder in a division calculation. | ⑤ 9, 10 |

| Language | Meaning | Example |
|---|---|---|
| **Column addition** | Column addition is writing the numbers you are adding in columns. You start adding from the right. | 137<br>9<br>+ 62<br>208<br>1 1 |
| **Long multiplication** | A method you can use when multiplying two numbers with two or more digits. | 453<br>× 34<br>13590<br>1812<br>2 1<br>15402<br>1 1 |
| **Long division** | A good method to use when dividing by a number with more than one digit. | 12<br>19)228<br>-19↓ (1 × 9)<br>38 (22 − 19 = 3)<br>-38 (2 × 19)<br>0<br>228 ÷ 19 = 12 |
| **Approximation** | Rounding numbers to make a simpler calculation that is close to the exact answer | 68.4 + 33.2 ≈ 70 + 30<br>≈ 100 |

**1** Use a mental method to work out these calculations.
 **a** 78 + 34 + 103
 **b** 94 − 67

**2** Do these calculations in your head.
 **a** 7 × 8   **b** 9 × 6
 **c** 36 ÷ 6   **d** 14 × 10
 **e** 0.5 × 100   **f** 75 + 100
 **g** 64 ÷ 10   **h** 3.5 × 100

**3** Use a mental method to work out these multiplications.
 **a** 8 × 24   **b** 35 × 7

**4** Use a written method to work out these calculations.
 **a** 96 + 153   **b** 327 − 54
 **c** 17.6 + 59.5   **d** 103.4 − 29.7

**5** Work out these multiplications using a written method.
 **a** 135 × 12   **b** 328 × 13
 **c** 35 × 247   **d** 434 × 41

**6** Work out these multiplications using a written method.
 **a** 14.7 × 9   **b** 7 × 20.9

**7** Work out these divisions and leave with a remainder where necessary.
 **a** 136 ÷ 8   **b** 189 ÷ 9
 **c** 92 ÷ 6   **d** 247 ÷ 12
 **e** 350 ÷ 14   **f** 546 ÷ 21

**8** A rectangular garden is 6.9 m by 5.2 m. Estimate its area.

**9** 19 bottles of water cost £15.96 and 32 bottles of cola cost £48.25.
 **a** Estimate the cost of 1 bottle of water.
 **b** Estimate the cost of 1 bottle of cola.
 **c** Approximately how many times more expensive is cola than water?

**10** Use a calculator to work these out. Give your answer to 2 decimal places.
 **a** $(9.1 - 5.7)^2 \div 3$
 **b** $\dfrac{63 - 2.4^2 \times 1.8}{\sqrt{13^2 - 7^2}}$

**11** Emily is 296 days old. How many weeks and days is this?

**12** Convert.
 **a** 2300 hours into days and hours
 **b** 3 days into seconds

### What next?

| Score | | |
|---|---|---|
| 0 – 4 | | Your knowledge of this topic is still developing. To improve look at Formative test: 3A-7; MyMaths: 1002, 1020, 1021, 1028, 1041, 1043, 1345 and 1367 |
| 5 – 9 | | You are gaining a secure knowledge of this topic. To improve look at InvisiPen: 121, 122, 123, 125, 126, 127 and 128 |
| 10 – 12 | | You have mastered this topic. Well done, you are ready to progress! |

**MyMaths**.co.uk

## Question commentary

**Questions 1** to **3** – Mental methods should enable quick-fire completion of these questions.

**Questions 4** to **7** – Each of these questions requires the use of a formal written method. Allow students to choose the one they feel most comfortable with and check the magnitude of their answers using an estimate.

**Questions 8** and **9** – Estimates should be to one significant figure unless an obvious (easy to use) alternative is apparent.

**Question 10** – Students could be advised to break the calculations down and write their working.

**Questions 11** and **12** – Ensure students are giving their remainders in the correct form after using the calculator.

## Answers

**1** **a** 215   **b** 27

**2** **a** 56   **b** 54   **c** 6   **d** 140
   **e** 50   **f** 0.75   **g** 6.4   **h** 350

**3** **a** 192   **b** 245

**4** **a** 249   **b** 273   **c** 77.1   **d** 73.7

**5** **a** 1620   **b** 4264   **c** 8645   **d** 17794

**6** **a** 132.3   **b** 146.3

**7** **a** 17   **b** 21   **c** 15 r 2   **d** 20 r 7
   **e** 25   **f** 26

**8** 35 m²

**9** **a** 80 p   **b** £1.50   **c** 2

**10** **a** 3.85   **b** 4.80

**11** 42 weeks, 2 days

**12** **a** 95 days, 20 hours   **b** 259 200 seconds

**1** Work out these additions by writing the calculations in columns.

| | | | | | | |
|---|---|---|---|---|---|---|
| **a** 198 + 331 | | **b** 61 + 180 | | **c** 272 + 94 | |
| **d** 37 + 73 + 152 | | **e** 19 + 160 + 271 | | **f** 337 + 148 + 22 | |
| **g** 218 + 29 + 267 | | **h** 195 + 73 + 362 | | **i** 88 + 357 + 457 | |

**2** Work out these subtractions by writing the calculations in columns.

| | | | |
|---|---|---|---|
| **a** 171 − 124 | **b** 368 − 198 | **c** 435 − 365 | |
| **d** 308 − 178 | **e** 430 − 124 | **f** 216 − 96 | |
| **g** 101 − 73 | **h** 360 − 225 | **i** 253 − 88 | |

**3** Work out these calculations using a mental method.
Make an estimate of the answer before you start each calculation.

| | | | |
|---|---|---|---|
| **a** 32 × 5 | **b** 3 × 71 | **c** 8 × 81 | |
| **d** 49 × 6 | **e** 78 × 4 | **f** 123 × 4 | |
| **g** 96 ÷ 3 | **h** 152 ÷ 8 | **i** 144 ÷ 6 | |
| **j** 145 ÷ 6 | **k** 272 ÷ 3 | **l** 763 ÷ 5 | |

(**j**, **k** and **l** will leave a remainder.)

**4** Use the standard method to complete these.

| | | | |
|---|---|---|---|
| **a** 135 × 6 | **b** 238 × 5 | **c** 239 × 4 | |
| **d** 132 × 23 | **e** 253 × 14 | **f** 143 × 32 | |
| **g** 203 × 27 | **h** 152 × 51 | **i** 246 × 38 | |
| **j** 4037 × 6 | **k** 1032 × 23 | **l** 4263 × 17 | |

**5** Use a suitable method to complete these division problems.

| | | | |
|---|---|---|---|
| **a** 138 ÷ 6 | **b** 184 ÷ 8 | **c** 273 ÷ 13 | |
| **d** 372 ÷ 12 | **e** 504 ÷ 7 | **f** 504 ÷ 9 | |

(These problems will leave a remainder.)

| | | | |
|---|---|---|---|
| **g** 107 ÷ 4 | **h** 164 ÷ 7 | **i** 189 ÷ 12 | |
| **j** 361 ÷ 14 | **k** 5236 ÷ 6 | **l** 9999 ÷ 8 | |

**6** Solve each of the following problems by making an approximation.

**a** Aoife buys 58 trays of plants at £1.59 a tray.
Antony buys 72 trays of plants at £1.10 a tray.
Who spends more?

**b** Nadeem eats two packets of crisps a day for a year.
Each packet costs 43p.
Horratio eats one box of cereal a week.
Each box costs £3.89.
Who spends more over one year?

**7** Estimate the answers to each of these problems using rounding. Do not use a calculator.

**a** A robin weighs 18g.
It has to eat its own body weight in seeds each day.
How much seed will the robin eat in a month?

**b** Bird seed costs £1.23 per 250g.
How much would it cost to feed a robin for a year?

**8** These are costs of different cat foods.
Pouch 32p    Tin 63p    Biscuits £1.49    Treats 75p

**a** Axel the cat eats two pouches a day, one packet of biscuits a week and one packet of treats a month. How much does it cost to feed Axel each year?

**b** Mittens the cat eats one tin a day, two packets of biscuits a month and one packet of treats each week. How much does it cost to feed Mittens each year?

**9** Convert these measurements of time to the units indicated in brackets.

**a** 1312 minutes      (into hours and minutes)
**b** 87 hours           (into days and hours)
**c** 24420 seconds      (into minutes and seconds)

**10** Use a calculator to work these out.
Give your answers to 2 decimal places where appropriate.

**a** $(5 + 4.7)^2 \div 3$

**b** $\dfrac{58.2 - 1.3^2 \times 3}{\sqrt{4.06} + 9.2}$

**c** $\dfrac{5.2 \times (16.3 - 4.2)^2}{\sqrt{13^2 - 5^2}}$

**d** $\dfrac{\sqrt{12.7 - 5^2} + 14.3}{91 - (18.2 + 7.6)^2}$

**MyMaths**.co.uk

## Question commentary

**Questions 1** and **2** – Lots of basic practice questions on adding and subtracting in columns.

**Question 3** – This question could be done as a speed challenge.

**Question 4** – Students could be encouraged to use the column method but allow alternatives such as the grid method if students prefer.

**Question 5** – Short or long division is suitable in each case.

**Questions 6** and **7** – Students are not expected to work the answers out but to estimate. Encourage one significant figure rounding.

**Questions 8** to **10** – Check students are converting remainders correctly and encourage them to break multi-stage calculations down and show intermediate steps in working.

## Answers

| | | | | | | | | |
|---|---|---|---|---|---|---|---|---|
| **1** | **a** 529 | **b** 241 | **c** 366 | **d** 262 |
| | **e** 450 | **f** 507 | **g** 514 | **h** 630 |
| | **i** 902 | | | |
| **2** | **a** 47 | **b** 170 | **c** 70 | **d** 130 |
| | **e** 306 | **f** 120 | **g** 28 | **h** 135 |
| | **i** 165 | | | |
| **3** | **a** 160 | **b** 213 | **c** 648 | **d** 294 |
| | **e** 312 | **f** 492 | **g** 32 | **h** 19 |
| | **i** 24 | **j** 24 r 1 | **k** 90 r 2 | **l** 152 r 3 |
| **4** | **a** 810 | **b** 1190 | **c** 956 | **d** 3036 |
| | **e** 3542 | **f** 4576 | **g** 5481 | **h** 7752 |
| | **i** 9348 | **j** 24222 | **k** 23736 | **l** 72471 |
| **5** | **a** 23 | **b** 23 | **c** 21 | **d** 31 |
| | **e** 72 | **f** 56 | **g** 26 r 3 | **h** 23 r 3 |
| | **i** 15 r 9 | **j** 25 r 11 | **k** 872 r 4 | **l** 1249 r 7 |
| **6** | **a** Aoife | **b** Nadeem | | |
| **7** | **a** 600 g | **b** £ 360 | | |
| **8** | **a** £ 320.08 | **b** £ 304.71 | | |
| **9** | **a** 21 hours, 52 minutes | | **b** 3 days, 15 hours | |
| | **c** 407 minutes | | | |
| **10** | **a** 31.36 | **b** 14.59 | **c** 63.44 | **d** 0.61 |

## Learning outcomes

**S1** Describe, interpret and compare observed distributions of a single variable through: appropriate graphical representation involving discrete, continuous and grouped data; and appropriate measures of central tendency (mean, mode, median) and spread (range, consideration of outliers) (L5/6)

**S2** Construct and interpret appropriate tables, charts, and diagrams, including frequency tables, bar charts, pie charts, and pictograms for categorical data, and vertical line (or bar) charts for ungrouped and grouped numerical data (L5/6)

**S3** Describe simple mathematical relationships between 2 variables (bivariate data) in observational and experimental contexts and illustrate using scatter graphs (L6)

## Introduction

The chapter starts by looking at designing a survey and then moves on to methods of data collection. Drawing up frequency tables, statistical diagrams and the calculation of averages are all covered before sections on scatter graphs and stem-and-leaf diagrams. Basic frequency diagrams from grouped data (histograms) are covered before the final section on communicating the findings from a statistical enquiry.

The introduction discusses the spurious use of statistics by politicians and advertisers to support their policies or products. In fact the majority of 'statistical' claims made in newspapers and in advertisements are based on very little supportive data and evidence. Small sample sizes, hidden alternative results and a lack of controlled conditions allow the claims to be made but we should always take time to consider the nature of these claims.

More rigorous statistical testing takes place over longer periods of time with large, unbiased samples and a high degree of control over the conditions. Medical testing, for example, uses what are called 'control groups' of people who think they are getting the drug on trial but are in fact getting a placebo.

## Prior knowledge

Students should already know how to…

- Interpret simple statistical diagrams

## Starter problem

The starter problem is about correlation. If we consider the possible reasons for such a claim, such as 'taller people have longer legs', 'taller people have a bigger stride', etc. we can see where such a hypothesis might come from.

The students are invited to investigate the truth of this statement and can therefore set up a practical investigation. Heights can be measured in class and the jumping part can also take part in class or outdoors as appropriate. A standing jump is probably the easiest to control since running speed is obviously a factor in the distance someone can jump (just look at the speed the long and triple jumpers get to on the runway in an athletics event).

You can also use an investigation like this to discuss data collection methods, the validity of the sample and how we might process the results in order to prevent false or dubious conclusions being reached.

## Resources

### MyMaths

| | | | | | |
|---|---|---|---|---|---|
| All averages | 1192 | Frequency tables and bar charts | | | 1193 |
| Grouping data | 1196 | Mean and mode | 1200 | Median and range | 1203 |
| Pictograms and bar charts | 1205 | Reading pie charts | 1206 | Drawing pie charts | 1207 |
| Sampling | 1212 | Scatter graphs | 1213 | Stem-and-leaf | 1215 |
| Types of data | 1248 | | | | |

### Online assessment

| | |
|---|---|
| Chapter test | 3A–8 |
| Formative test | 3A–8 |
| Summative test | 3A–8 |

### InvisiPen solutions

| | | | |
|---|---|---|---|
| Organising data | 411 | Planning an enquiry | 414 |
| Questionnaires | 415 | Bar charts | 422 |
| Pie charts | 423 | Histograms | 426 |
| Scatter graphs | 427 | Stem and leaf diagrams | 431 |
| Averages of a list | 441 | Writing statistical reports | 448 |

# Topic scheme

Teaching time = 10 lessons/4 weeks

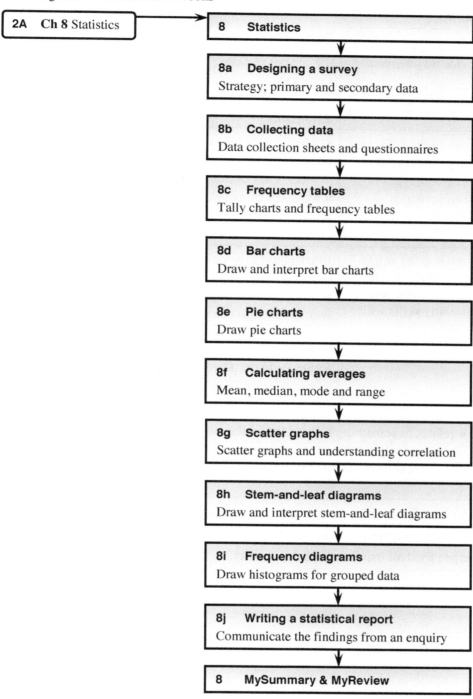

| 2A | Ch 8 Statistics |
| --- | --- |

**8    Statistics**

**8a    Designing a survey**
Strategy; primary and secondary data

**8b    Collecting data**
Data collection sheets and questionnaires

**8c    Frequency tables**
Tally charts and frequency tables

**8d    Bar charts**
Draw and interpret bar charts

**8e    Pie charts**
Draw pie charts

**8f    Calculating averages**
Mean, median, mode and range

**8g    Scatter graphs**
Scatter graphs and understanding correlation

**8h    Stem-and-leaf diagrams**
Draw and interpret stem-and-leaf diagrams

**8i    Frequency diagrams**
Draw histograms for grouped data

**8j    Writing a statistical report**
Communicate the findings from an enquiry

**8    MySummary & MyReview**

# Differentiation

**Student book 3A          134 – 159**

Planning projects and collecting data
Two-way tables, statistical diagrams and the interpretation thereof
Scatter diagrams and correlation
Averages and range
Writing statistical reports

**Student book 3B          132 – 159**

Planning projects and collecting data
Two-way tables, statistical diagrams and the interpretation thereof
Scatter diagrams and correlation
Averages and range
Writing statistical reports

**Student book 3C          130 – 155**

Planning projects and collecting data
Statistical diagrams and the interpretation thereof
Scatter diagrams and correlation
Averages and range
Cumulative frequency and box plots

## Objectives

- Discuss a problem that can be addressed by statistical methods and identify questions to explore. (L5)
- Identify possible sources of data. (L5)

| Key ideas | Resources |
|---|---|
| 1  A data-handling cycle helps provide a systematic approach.<br>2  Both primary and secondary data can be used. | ⊕  Types of Data  (1248)<br>Mini whiteboards |

| Simplification | Extension |
|---|---|
| Give students many examples of types of data; discuss whether it can be classified as primary or secondary data. Ask them to suggest examples of both types of data which could be collected in given scenarios. | Students suggest a possible area for investigation within their school; for example, the quality of school dinners. They decide what data to collect and whether it would be primary data or secondary data. They devise possible questions. |

| Literacy | Links |
|---|---|
| This lesson involves much discussion. It gives ample opportunity for students to gather their ideas, organise them and articulate them in pairs, groups and whole-class session. Their speaking and listening skills will be very evident. | Blackgang Chine on the Isle of Wight is the oldest existing theme park in the UK. It was opened in 1843 and is still owned by the same family. The park was built around a scenic chine, or steep-sided gully leading to the sea, and original attractions included a waterfall, landscaped paths leading to the beach, and a whale skeleton. There is more about the theme park today at  www.blackgangchine.com |

## Alternative approach

This topic comes more alive when it relates to something beyond the mathematics classroom. Other subjects may be embarking on an investigation. The school might have an issue that needs exploration. The work of the textbook can run alongside the real life context from outside the classroom.

## Checkpoint

Does the data in the following cases come from a primary or a secondary source?

**a** John asks the members of his class how many brothers and sisters they have. (Primary)

**b** Josie collects data on Premier League football matches from the internet. (Secondary)

**Starter** – Quick fire

Recap work of previous chapters. Include recent work on mental and written methods of calculation. Ask rapid response questions with students responding on mini whiteboards. Discuss answers when there is a need.

## Teaching notes

Explain that data handling can be used to explore real life situations and help to solve problems or investigate hypotheses. Explain that there are four key aspects to the data-handing cycle. Students discuss each stage in turn and also the 'Evaluate results' stage. In each case, they explain what each stage entails.

Explain that the first thing to do is specify the problem and the plan. Ask students to think of some problematic examples for which handling data might be useful. Possible examples can come from the fields of sports, music or television.

Explain that once the problem has been specified, the next stage of the plan is to decide what data to collect and how to collect it. Distinguish between primary data and secondary data, giving examples of each.

Discuss the need for reliable data and how secondary data might be unreliable. Discuss the part played by the 'Evaluate results' stage.

## Plenary

Students write what they understand by the data-handling cycle in their own words. They give examples of primary data and secondary data and share these with the class.

## Exercise commentary

This exercise provides much opportunity for paired, group and whole-class discussion.

**Question 1** – Emphasise that the reasoning used in deciding which suggestions are good is important.

**Question 2** – You may need to restate what primary and secondary data sources are.

**Question 3** – The question asks students to match four statements to the four stages of the data-handling cycle. Discuss if 'Evaluate results' should be within the cycle itself or, as here, in a bubble outside the cycle.

## Answers

1 Good suggestions: **b, f, g, i**
Weak suggestions: **a, c, d, e, h**

2 primary sources: **a, c, d, g**
secondary sources: **b, e, f, h**

3 **a** Stage 4 **b** Stage 3 **c** Stage 1 **d** Stage 2

## Objectives

- Plan how to collect and organise sets of data from surveys and experiments.   (L4)
- Design questionnaires and data-collection sheets.   (L5)
- Decide which data to collect and the degree of accuracy needed.   (L5)

| Key ideas | Resources |
|---|---|
| 1  Data can be collected and recorded in different ways.<br>2  The quality of the data depends on the quality of how it was collected. | ⊞ Sampling   (1212)<br>Examples of questionnaires and data-collection sheets<br>Mini whiteboards |

| Simplification | Extension |
|---|---|
| Give the students clear guidance as to what constitutes a good question. Limit the complexity of the questions which are used as examples. | Ask students to design their own questionnaire about a topic that interests them, concentrating on designing good questions. These can be given to others in the group to assess for suitability. |

| Literacy | Links |
|---|---|
| Relevant words include: 'survey', 'sample', 'biased', 'unbiased', 'questionnaire', 'representative', 'population', 'census', 'random'.<br>Note that a 'population' in mathematics is not just about people. A mathematical population is the set of the entire group of items being studied in a survey. For example, when rolling a dice, the population of possible scores is 1, 2, 3, 4, 5 and 6. | The British Crime Survey has been carried out every year since 1982 and measures the amount of crime experienced in England and Wales. It differs from police records because it includes crimes that have not been reported to the police. The survey aims to collect data from around 1000 members of the public in each of the 20 Police Force areas. Since January 2009, the survey has included young people aged 11 – 15. There is more about the British Crime Survey at www.ons.gov.uk/ons/guide-method/method-quality/specific/crime-statistics-methodology/guide-to-finding-crime-statistics/crime-survey-for-england-and-wales--csew-/index.html |

### Alternative approach

Highlight the differences between a survey which is:

- a census in which every member of a population is involved;
- a sample in which only some members of a population are involved.

Note that a sample can be biased or random. Explain the difference.

Data is either primary data or secondary data. Primary data can be collected using a questionnaire, observation or an experiment as in science. It can be recorded on a data-collection sheet.

### Checkpoint

Criticise the following question and suggest two improvements:

"How many hours of TV do you watch?"

(No time scale and too vague: Improvements will be to include a time scale, e.g. "How many hours of TV do you watch per week?" and include response boxes)

## Starter – Quick fire

Recap work of previous chapters and especially number work. Ask rapid response questions with students responding on mini whiteboards. Discuss answers when there is a need.

## Teaching notes

Explain that secondary data can be collected from a number of sources, such as books or the internet. Explain that primary data must be collected first-hand and will usually be collected using either a survey or a questionnaire. Explain that a data collection sheet is used to carry out a survey and give examples. These could include studying the frequency of car colours passing down the road. Ask students to suggest their own examples of where they might use a data collection sheet.

Describe the key features of a questionnaire and the idea of closed and open questions. Explain that closed questions are easier to analyse and give examples of these such as 'yes'/'no' and tick boxes.

Explain that, when carrying out a survey, it is important to collect data from enough people and that the sample chosen is representative.

Students can then devise (or be given) a problem of their own (chosen individually or in small groups), for which they design their own questionnaires.

## Plenary

Ask students to give examples of questions from their own questionnaires. Ask the class to say whether they are open questions or closed questions. Ask the class to say whether they think the questions are likely to be effective in helping to solve the problems they are associated with, ensuring that criticism is constructive.

## Exercise commentary

This exercise provides much opportunity for paired, group and whole-class discussion.

**Question 1** – Explain the difference between an irrelevant question and a question which is useful but poorly expressed (and thus in need of rewording and refining).

**Question 2** – Remind the students that questions should be free from bias and simple to answer.

**Question 3** – There are no right and wrong answers as long as the response is justified by clear reasons.

## Answers

1.  a  sample too small
    b  sample unrepresentative
    c  question is inappropriate
    d  reasonable question
    e  question is inappropriate
    f  reasonable question
    g  question is inappropriate
    h  reasonable question
    i  reasonable question

2.  Check questions that are generated by this problem.

3.  a  Any reasonable suggestions
    b  Check questions that are generated by this problem.

## Objectives

- Plan how to collect data. (L4)
- Construct frequency tables with equal class intervals for gathering and recording data. (L5)

| Key ideas | Resources |
|---|---|
| 1 Data can be collated using tally charts and represented in frequency tables.<br>2 Numerical data can be collated using class intervals. | Frequency tables and bar charts (1193)<br>Mini whiteboards |

| Simplification | Extension |
|---|---|
| Students should concentrate on tallying discrete data such as colour, gender, etc. before moving on to consider the tallying of numerical data in groups. | Students conduct their own survey, decide on an appropriate data-collection sheet, tally their results and construct a frequency table. |

| Literacy | Links |
|---|---|
| The word 'tally' comes a Latin word meaning 'stick', referring to the sticks used to keep a record of loans and payments. (See **Links** for more about tally sticks.) The word 'collate' also comes from Latin, it means 'bring together'. | Tally sticks were used to keep a record of loans and payments, especially in Medieval Britain when many people could not read or write. A stick was marked with notches to show relevant information such as the amount owed. It was then split lengthwise with one half given to the lender and the other to the receiver. When the debt was due to be repaid, the two halves of the stick were held together to make sure that they tallied. There is a picture of tally sticks at www.nationalarchives.gov.uk/museum/item.asp?item_id=6 |

## Alternative approach

This topic has more purpose when it relates to something beyond the mathematics classroom. Other subjects or the school itself may be embarking on an investigation that needs data to be collected. Science is often a fertile area for data-handling.

## Checkpoint

Data relating to the ages of 50 people travelling on a train is collected. Suggest suitable groupings to make tallying the people easier.          (four groups, 0-20, 21-40, 41-60, 60+, or alternative justified groupings)

**Starter** – Quick fire

Recap work of this chapter. Include questions about the design and collection of data. Ask rapid response questions with students responding on mini whiteboards. Discuss answers when there is a need.

## Teaching notes

Explain that either during a survey or after collecting responses from a questionnaire, data needs to be recorded and collated in a way which enables an analysis to be carried out effectively.

A data collection sheet is a useful way of recording raw data. Tally charts are a useful way of grouping data in a way that leads to showing the data in frequency tables.

Give examples of situations (such as the number of goals scored in football matches or colour of students' eyes) and ask students to suggest the format of suitable data-collection sheets.

Explain that, if the range of possible responses is large, data can be grouped into classes over a narrow range of values known as the class interval. Give examples of appropriate classes that could be used, for example, with the ages of people attending a football match, the number of hours of TV watched in a week. Students can suggest their own examples.

Students can then carry out a survey of their fellow students, working in small groups on a problem of interest. They collect the resulting data using appropriate data-collection sheets, decide on class intervals and construct a frequency table.

## Plenary

Students respond 'true' or 'false' on mini whiteboards to statements, such as:

- It was on the Internet, so it must be true!
- Rhakesh collected the data from the Internet, so it is secondary data.
- Emma surveyed her friends using a questionnaire, so she collected primary data.

Then ask students to give examples of the questions they have asked in their survey. Ask other groups to suggest what the data-collection sheets should look like and compare these suggestions. Students can provide a positive critique of other examples.

## Exercise commentary

**Question 1** – Point out the key at the top of the diagram. Ensure students realise that the figures in the key are not part of the data set.

**Question 2** – The missing numbers in the first column of the table can be found by assuming that the class intervals are equal.

**Question 3** – This question differs as students decide on their own class intervals. Different frequency tables are likely.

---

## Answers

**1 a**

| Visitors | Tally | Frequency |
|---|---|---|
| Man | ‖‖‖ ‖‖‖ ‖‖ | 11 |
| Woman | ‖‖‖ ‖‖ | 7 |
| Boy | ‖‖‖ ‖‖‖ ‖‖‖ ‖‖ | 17 |
| Girl | ‖‖‖ ‖‖‖ ‖ | 11 |

    **b** 46 people     **c** Boys

**2 a,b**

| Money spent | Tally | Frequency |
|---|---|---|
| 0 – 4.99 | ‖‖ | 3 |
| 5 – 9.99 | ‖‖‖ ‖‖‖ | 10 |
| 10 – 14.99 | ‖‖‖ ‖‖‖ | 9 |
| 15 – 19.99 | ‖‖‖ ‖ | 6 |
| 20 – 24.99 | ‖‖‖ | 5 |
| 25+ | ‖ | 2 |

**3**

| km travelled | Frequency |
|---|---|
| 0 – 9 | 13 |
| 10 – 19 | 13 |
| 20 – 29 | 9 |
| 30 – 39 | 7 |
| 40 – 49 | 4 |
| 50 – 59 | 4 |

## Objectives

- Construct and interpret bar charts. (L5)

| Key ideas | Resources |
|---|---|
| **1** Bar charts can represent discrete data.<br>**2** Comparative bar charts compare the distributions of two sets of data on the same chart. | ⊞ Pictograms and bar charts (1205)<br>Pre-drawn axes<br>Real life examples of bar charts<br>Computer spreadsheets<br>Mini whiteboards |

| Simplification | Extension |
|---|---|
| Concentrate on bar charts of simple discrete data with small frequencies; such as the number of goals scored in the matches of football's Premier League last week. | Students consider how they might deal with data that is numerical. Is there a difference between how you deal with discrete numerical data and continuous numerical data? Ask them to write a brief description of any differences in their methods and discuss them with others. |

| Literacy | Links |
|---|---|
| There are two kinds of data. Discrete data is data that is counted in categories, such as colour, goals, pets. Continuous data is data that is measured, such length, mass, volume. Bar charts use only discrete data.<br><br>Beware the spellings of 'discrete' and 'discreet'. The spelling 'discrete' means 'in separate distinct parts', but the spelling 'discreet' means 'tactful'. | A Gantt Chart (invented in the 1910s by Henry Gantt, an American engineer) is a special type of bar chart used in industry to manage a project. The chart shows the project broken up into individual tasks. It is used to plan and coordinate the task schedule and to keep track of which tasks are completed. There are examples of Gantt charts at<br><br>www.ganttchart.com/index.html |

## Alternative approach

Bar charts can be constructed in different ways. Here are two other ways.

The simplest way, often used with young children in primary school, is to give each child a square which they stick to form columns on blank paper with a horizontal axis labelled with their current interest; such as favourite type of pet.

An electronic method is to use a speadsheet with a column for the names of the categories and the adjacent column for their frequencies. The frequencies are highlighted and the toolbar is used to draw a bar chart.

## Checkpoint

A bar chart showing the eye colour of a class of 30 students is drawn. The bars for 'blue', 'green' and 'hazel' eyes are of height 6, 7 and 3 respectively. The bars for 'brown' and 'blue-green' are of equal heights. There are no other colours. How high are the bars for 'brown' and 'blue-green'? (both 7)

## Starter – Two-way table

Draw this two-way table on the board.

|  | Football | Swimming | Tennis |
|---|---|---|---|
| **Girls** | 3 | 4 | 1 |
| **Boys** | 7 | 2 | 3 |

Ask questions; for example,

How many students were surveyed? [20]

What percentage of students prefer football? [50%]

What proportion of all the students are girls who favour swimming? $[\frac{4}{20} = \frac{1}{5}]$

Discuss any assumptions made.

## Teaching notes

A bar chart is one way of displaying statistical data. The data must be discrete data and the bars, which may be horizontal or vertical, do not touch each other.

Construct a bar chart with students using known data on pre-drawn axes. Explain, giving an example, that if the bars are all going to have high frequencies, then a broken scale can be used on the vertical axis to make the drawing of the chart more manageable.

Examples of bar charts abound on the Internet and several could be displayed in order to show students real life examples. Explain that the tallest bar shows the most frequent result. This result is the mode (or modal result).

Students should practise drawing simple bar charts using their own data.

Explain what is meant by a comparative bar chart and provide an example, such as the split being boys/girls and the data being 'favourite subject'. Students again practise by drawing charts from their own data.

## Plenary

Provide examples of bar charts and comparative bar charts and ask questions about them. Students respond on their mini whiteboards. Discuss answers where appropriate.

## Exercise commentary

**Question 1** – The vertical axis has a broken scale. Ask students what it means.

**Questions 2** and **3** – All bars on the same chart must have the same width and be separated by the same distance. Make sure students include the titles of the charts.

**Question 4** – This chart can be thought of as a bar chart on its side.

## Answers

**1 a** 30 people      **b** Go Karts
   **c** Glider          **d** 131 people

**2**

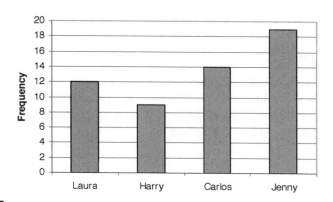

**3**

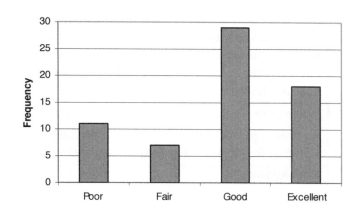

**4 a** The survey is about the number and type of lunchtime snacks eaten by visitors.
   **b** Fish and chips      **c** 17
   **d** Hot dogs         **e** 101
   **f** 'Other' covers snack foods other than those listed.

## Objectives

- Construct pie charts on paper and using ICT for discrete data. (L6)

| Key ideas | Resources |
|---|---|
| 1  A pie chart uses sectors of a circle to represent different categories of data.<br>2  The angles of the sectors are proportional to the frequencies of the categories. | ⊕  Reading pie charts (1206)<br>Dice<br>Pre-prepared circles of radii just over 5 cm.<br>Protractors<br>Computer spreadsheets<br>Mini whiteboards |

| Simplification | Extension |
|---|---|
| Students are given the angles in degrees to practise measuring the angles and drawing the pie charts without concern about calculating the angles.<br><br>Later, ensure that all examples have total frequencies that are, initially, 360, 180 or 90 and then progress to other total frequencies that divide exactly into 360°. | Students draw a pie chart where the frequency does not divide exactly into 360°. For example, a total of 100 for all frequencies will give an angle of 3.6° for each of the 100. |

| Literacy | Links |
|---|---|
| A pie chart, sometimes known as a circle diagram, is divided into sectors. Words which include 'sect-', such as 'bisect', 'disect', 'insect', 'section' all come from a Latin word meaning 'cut'. | Although they convey the same information, computer-generated pie charts are often more elaborate than those drawn by hand. Many software packages offer a collection of different types of pie chart including 3D charts and charts with a slice of the pie pulled out. There are examples of different charts available in Excel at http://office.microsoft.com/en-gb/help/HA102118481033.aspx |

### Alternative approach

An alternative way of calculating the angles of the sectors is to work with fractions. For example, if there are three categories with frequencies of 6, 12 and 9 (which total 27), then the three sectors are $\frac{6}{27}$ , $\frac{12}{27}$ and $\frac{9}{27}$ of the circle. As the full circle is 360°, the angles are 80°, 160° and 120° (which total 360°). Awkward numbers will need a calculator.

When drawing the circle, be sure to make the radius just over 5 cm. School protractors will then fit easily.

To draw a pie chart using a computer spreadsheet, construct it with two columns for the names of the categories and their frequencies. The frequencies are highlighted and the toolbar is used to draw a pie chart.

### Checkpoint

Data is collected on the type of pet the students in a class of 30 have. There are 12 cats, 10 dogs, 6 rabbits and 2 'other'. What size would each sector be in a pie chart displaying this data? (144°, 120°, 72°, 24°)

## Starter – High fives!

Students draw five squares in a line and enter a multiplication sign into any one of the central three boxes. Throw a dice four times. After each throw, the students write the score in an empty box. They use long multiplication to multiple the two numbers they have created. The winner is the person with the highest result. Repeat.

## Teaching notes

Once data has been collected and collated, it needs to be analysed. An analysis is helped by having statistical diagrams. There are many kinds of these diagrams. Ask students to give examples of the types of diagrams they might use; such as bar chart, pictogram, pie chart.

Using an example, work through the process of creating a pie chart with the students. Pre-drawn circles can be used to save time. The circle needs to be divided into 'slices' according to the frequencies of the various categories. Remind students that 'slices' of a circle are called sectors. Take great care when explaining how the angles of the sectors are calculated.

The pie chart needs a key. Adding all the angles together serves as a check; they should total 360°.

If students have already collected data in categories through their own surveys, then they can use it to draw further examples of pie charts. If the total number of items in the data set is not a factor of 360, then a calculator will be needed and the angles will be more awkward to draw accurately.

## Plenary

Provide a frequency table with simple frequencies (such as 8, 10, 12, 6 which total 36) and ask students for the total of the frequencies and the number of degrees needed for each sector. Students respond on mini whiteboards. Discuss the answers.

## Exercise commentary

Remind students how to use a protractor. There is a particular difficulty with pie charts as the re-positioning of the protractor for each angle will confuse some students.

**Question 1** – As a whole-class, find the angle for one child in degrees. Emphasise the need for accurate measurement of angles.

**Questions 2 to 4** – Students have to calculate the angles. Give assistance only after they have tried for themselves.

**Question 5** – Allow students to discuss their answers to this question. Try to get them to explain their methods and show their working out.

## Answers

**1**

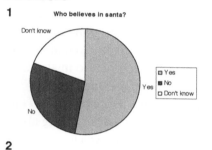

**2**

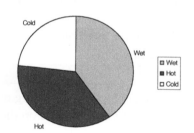

**3**

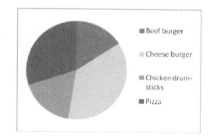

**4**

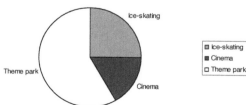

**5**  23 people said yes

## Objectives

- Calculate statistics for small sets of discrete data:
  - find the mode, median and range         (L4)
  - calculate the mean.         (L5)

| Key ideas | Resources | |
|---|---|---|
| **1** An average is a typical value for the data set. It can be the mode, median or mean.<br>**2** The range is a measure of the spread of the data. | ⊞ All averages<br>    Mean and mode<br>Computer spreadsheet<br>Calculator<br>Mini whiteboards | (1192)<br>(1200) |

| Simplification | Extension |
|---|---|
| Work with small data sets of single-digit numbers which have been ordered, have an odd number of data points and for which the total is easily divisible by the frequency. | Students analyse numerical data which is unordered, has two modes, has an even number of data points, and for which the total does not easily divide by the number of data points. |

| Literacy | Links |
|---|---|
| Statistics are everywhere and to understand them is part of being numerate – and especially to understand when they are being misused into order to mislead. Advertisers and politicians often use and misuse statistics to their own advantage. For example, '9 out of 10 dieters said they lost weight' says nothing about the sample size or how much weight was lost.<br><br>The alliteration of the three averages can confuse. Remind students that the 'mode' is 'the most common' result (with all the **o**'s) and the '**med**ian' is the '**mid**dle' result (with the **m** and **d**). | The highest roller coaster in the world is the Kingda Ka at Six Flags Great Adventure amusement park in New Jersey, USA with a height of 139 metres. It was also the fastest in the world at 128 mph until the Ring°racer was built at the Nürburgring race track in Nürburg, Germany in 2009 with a top speed of 134.8 mph. There is more information about the Kingda Ka at www.sixflags.com/greatAdventure/rides/Kingdaka.aspx |

## Alternative approach

A computer spreadsheet can help with handling data. Enter the data set in a column of the spreadsheet and highlight it. Use the *data* and *formulas* tabs on the toolbar to order the data set by size and so find the mode, median and range more quickly and also to find the total of the data set to help find the mean.

## Checkpoint

Calculate the mean, median, mode and range for this set of data:

$3, 6, 7, 8, 3, 5, 3, 7, 9, 10, 3, 5, 6$         $(5.77, 6, 3, 7)$

## Starter – Pizza

A pizza is cut into three unequal slices. The second slice is twice the size of the first slice. The third slice is three times the size of the first. What is the angle of each sector?                    [60°, 120°, 180°]

Continue to recap previous work by asking rapid response questions with students replying on their mini whiteboards.

## Teaching notes

Explain that, when analysing a set of numerical data, it is usual to summarise the data by finding a typical value, known as an average, and a measure of the spread of the data. There are three averages, the mode, median and mean, and the spread is measured by the range.

Using a simple data set, say

   1  2  2  2  2  3  3  5  7

show that the **mode** is the most frequent [2] and that the **median** is the middle value when the data is arranged in order (as here) [2]. When there is an even number of data, the median lies halfway between the middle values.

To calculate the **mean**, add up all the data values and divide by how many of them there are [27 ÷ 9 = 3]. The three averages usually give different values and sometimes one average is clearly more typical of the whole data set than the others.

The **range** is the difference between the largest value and the smallest value [7 – 1 = 6]. It is not an average; it measures the spread of the data.

## Plenary

Show various sets of data. Students write the mean, median, mode and range on their mini whiteboards. Assess responses and discuss them as necessary.

## Exercise commentary

**Question 1** – Students are instructed to order the data first before proceeding.

**Questions 2** and **3** – As in Question 1, first write the data in ascending order.

**Question 4** – Since only the mean is required, the data need not be ordered in this question.

**Question 5** – The information is not used in the order that it is given. This question also provides the framework for further extension questions. Students could be asked to make up their own problem of a similar type.

## Answers

**1**   **a**   16, 17, 18, 18, 18, 19, 20, 21, 23, 27, 34
    **b**   18 years       **c**   18 years
    **d**   19 years

**2**   **a**   17 years       **b**   20 years
    **c**   17 years

**3**   **a**   45 points       **b**   7
    **c**   5               **d**   5

**4**   4.9hrs

**5**   **a**   2 kg, 2 kg, 4 kg, 5 kg    **b**   20 kg

| Objectives | |
|---|---|
| • Construct and interpret scatter graphs. | (L6) |

| Key ideas | Resources | |
|---|---|---|
| 1  Scatter graphs can show whether there is a link between two variables.<br>2  A widespread scatter shows there is no link; a scatter lying roughly in a line shows a link; the closer to a straight line it lies, the stronger the link. | Scatter graphs<br>Squared paper<br>Spreadsheet software<br>Graph-drawing software<br>Pre-labelled axes | (1213) |

| Simplification | Extension |
|---|---|
| Students are given scatter diagrams and they concentrate on describing the patterns and trends. Have early examples with strong correlation. Examples that they plot themselves can initially avoid broken scales. | Students calculate the means of the two sets of data (say, $m_1$ and $m_2$) and plot the point $(m_1, m_2)$ on diagrams that they draw. Explain that a line of best fit can be drawn on the graphs in order to better illustrate the trend and that it must go through this mean point. |

| Literacy | Links |
|---|---|
| When drawing conclusions from a scatter diagram, students can use a 'writing frame' with missing words. Students complete the sentences by choosing words from a list of likely possibilities. | Broadband speed is affected by how far your home lies from the telephone exchange; the further your home from the exchange, the slower the broadband speed. There is a scatter graph showing the correlation between broadband speed and telephone line length (distance from the exchange) at www.ispreview.co.uk/news/ EkFyVApuAEXICMaXax.html |

**Alternative approach**

As an introduction and avoiding the sensitivities of measuring students' heights and weights, construct a whole-class scatter graph by plotting 'span' (the distance between the tips of the little finger and thumb when the hand is stretched) and 'cubit' (the distance from the tip of the middle finger to the point of the elbow) as a point for each student in turn. Students see the graph appear before their eyes. A discussion about the strength of any link ('correlation') and about 'cause and effect' can take place.

Contrasting graphs where there is no correlation and negative correlation need to be drawn.

**Checkpoint**

A scatter diagram of the age of a certain type of car against the value of the car is drawn. Suggest the type of correlation that might be shown.                    (Negative – with justification)

## Starter – Prime calculations

Students list the prime numbers up to at least 35.

[2, 3, 5, 7, 11, 13, 17, 19, 23, 29, 31]

They make each of the numbers 1 to 20 using exactly two prime numbers. For example,

$1 = 3 - 2$        $2 = 19 - 17$        $3 = 5 - 2$
$4 = 11 - 7$        $5 = 3 + 2$        $6 = 3 \times 2$

## Teaching notes

Suggest various scenarios for students to decide if a scatter diagram is appropriate. Examples could include height against weight, exam performance against time spent doing revision. Prepared examples using squared paper, spreadsheet software or graph-drawing software could be used to illustrate these examples.

Explain that the two 'variables' of a scenario may or may not be linked. They can be plotted as a series of data points. Students are given a set of data and plot the data points on diagrams with labelled axes. Explain that the data points *should not* be joined to each other.

Students discuss and then make a statement relating to the relationship between the two variables. Explain that we can use the scatter graph to suggest a link between the variables (called 'correlation') and use this link to make predictions.

## Plenary

Give students a set of data. Display a set of pre-labelled axes. As a class, students take turns to plot points and discuss whether there is a correlation between the two variables and whether it is a stong correlation.

## Exercise commentary

**Questions 1** and **2** – Ensure that students pay careful attention to the scales and note the broken axis in **1**. Ask students to give as much detail in their answers as possible.

**Question 3** – Students should realise that each pair of entries in the table, such as (5, 50), refer to one adult on the course.

## Answers

1  a   Yes, when the weather is cold more students visit the library.

   b   Approximately 6 students.

2  a   True        b   False        c   True        d   False

3  a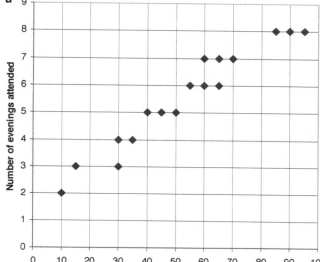

   b   Yes

| Objectives | |
|---|---|
| • Construct and interpret stem-and-leaf diagrams. | (L4) |
| • Find the mode, median, range and modal class from stem-and-leaf diagrams. | (L6) |

| Key ideas | Resources | |
|---|---|---|
| **1** A stem-and-leaf diagram orders data vertically on a stem and horizontally on several leaves.<br>**2** The mode, modal group, median and range are straightforward to find from a stem-and-leaf diagram. | ⊞ Stem and leaf<br><br>Mini whiteboards | (1215) |

| Simplification | Extension |
|---|---|
| Concentrate on the accurate construction of stem-and-leaf diagrams for small data sets comprising integer values. Ensure students cross off the data they have entered on the diagram to avoid 'double-plotting'. Ordering within the leaves is a secondary task. | Students construct stem-and-leaf diagrams for decimal data (similar to that in Question **4**). Students find the mode, median and mean. They compare the three averages. |

| Literacy | Links |
|---|---|
| The stem is invariably vertical. The leaves are horizontal and usually to the right of the stem.<br>When comparing two distributions (as has already been done using comparative bar charts), the leaves are to the right of the stem for one data set and to the left of the stem for the other.<br>The name 'stem-and-leaf diagram' is usually written with hyphens. | The stem-and-leaf diagram was invented in the late 1960s by the American statistician John Tukey to display information clearly and without losing the individual data. Stem-and-leaf diagrams can be used to create timetables that show bus or train times at a certain stop or station. There is an example of a stem-and-leaf bus timetable at www.redwoodtransit.org/schedules/ stop_times.php?stop_id=1260&service_id=1 |

| Alternative approach |
|---|
| As a whole-class introduction, data can be taken from each student in the class in turn and entered on a stem-and-leaf diagram. No explanation is given. Students see the diagram appear before them. They then have to describe what has happened, how information is entered and what the advantages of this diagram are. A useful data set is the length of time (in minutes) that it takes students to get to school.<br>Students are asked how the diagram can be improved. Ordering of data within each leaf is the desired response. |

| Checkpoint |
|---|
| Explain what the entry 1 | 5 would mean in a stem-and-leaf diagram showing the ages of students at secondary school.                                                    (The student is 15 years old) |

## Starter – Quick fire

Recap work of previous chapters and this chapter so far. Ask rapid response questions with students responding on mini whiteboards. Discuss answers when there is a need.

## Teaching notes

Students already know that once they have collected data, they need to summarise it in a way that is easy to interpret. This lesson shows another way of doing this.

Collect some appropriate data from the students, such as how many hours of TV they watch in a week, and record the responses as a list. Explain the process for drawing a stem-and-leaf diagram from the data. Emphasis should be on the numbers in the stem being evenly spaced and the numbers in the leaves being (eventually) ordered. Explain that a key is essential. Students can then draw the stem-and-leaf diagram.

Explain that the diagram now shows the data *in order* and that both the modal value and the modal group can be easily found. Also show how the range can be determined and how the median value can be found directly from the diagram.

Students can then practise drawing and interpreting further examples of stem-and-leaf diagrams.

## Plenary

Present the whole class with several stem-and-leaf diagrams. Ask students for the mode, the modal group and the range, with responses being shown on mini whiteboards. Discuss responses where necessary. Also ask students for the median in small data sets.

## Exercise commentary

**Question 1** – Students should look first to see that the data is in ascending order from bottom to top (the stem) and also ordered from left to right (the leaves).

**Question 2** – Students should ensure their stem-and-leaf diagram is ordered. The framework is given.

**Question 3** – Here, the students will need to design their own framework for the stem-and-leaf diagram.

**Question 4** – Here, the data is decimal. Ensure that students follow the examples for 1.7 and 1.8 to complete the diagram. A key is also needed.

## Answers

1  a  21 people          b  54
   c  9                  d  45
   e  3 people           f  20 – 29
   g  29

2  a

**Results of science test**

| 50 | 1 3 5 |
|----|-------|
| 40 | 0 1 6 7 9 9 |
| 30 | 1 2 4 4 4 4 5 7 8 8 9 |
| 20 | 0 3 5 7 |
| 10 | 6 8 |
| 0  | 8 9 |

| Key | 50 | 5 | stands for 55 |

   b  34          c  47

3  a, b, c

**Merits earned by 9H**

| 70 | 4 6 |
|----|-----|
| 60 | 2 4 6 |
| 50 | 0 4 7 |
| 40 | 4 7 8 9 |
| 30 | 3 5 6 7 7 8 9 |
| 20 | 1 4 8 |
| 10 | 2 7 9 |

| Key | 20 | 1 | stands for 21 |

   d  64          e  30 – 39    f  39

4

**Record of growth**

| 5 | 2 8 8 9 |
|---|---------|
| 4 | 3 6 7 7 7 7 9 |
| 3 | 0 8 |
| 2 | 3 8 8 |
| 1 | 7 8 |

| Key | 5 | 2 | stands for 5.2 |

## Objectives

- Construct and interpret frequency diagrams for continuous data. (L5)
- Find the modal class from a frequency diagram. (L5)

| Key ideas | Resources |
|---|---|
| 1 A frequency diagram displays continous data.<br>2 The modal class can be found from a frequency diagram. | ⊞ Grouping data (1196)<br>Blank frequency tables and pre-labelled axes<br>Graphing software<br>Mini whiteboards |

| Simplification | Extension |
|---|---|
| Compare bar charts with frequency diagrams. Bar charts are for discrete (counted) data and frequency diagrams are for continuous (measured) data. Show how tally charts are different for discrete and continuous data and how there are gaps/no gaps between columns on the chart/diagram.<br>It can be instructive to draw a bar chart and a frequency diagram at the same time and explain the differences as they are drawn. | Give the students raw data that is not yet tabulated and ask them to decide their own class intervals, draw up their tally charts and frequency tables, and then draw their frequency diagrams using sensible scales. |

| Literacy | Links |
|---|---|
| Names of diagrams can be confusing.<br>Bar charts are for discrete data and frequency diagrams are for continuous data. There are no gaps between the columns in a frequency chart as the data is continuous.<br>Also beware the use of the word 'histogram'. A histogram is *not* a frequency diagram. A histogram has as a vertical axes labelled 'frequency density' (not frequency) and its use is beyond the scope of this book. | Frequency diagrams are often used in scientific papers to display continuous data obtained by scientific experiment. There are frequency diagrams showing the distribution of eye weight, lens weight and retinal area in the 'Methods' section of a scientific paper analysing variation in eye size in adult mice at www.nervenet.org/papers/OVSMyopia.html |

### Alternative approach

The labelling of the horizontal axis can cause confusion. It is usual to label this axis in one of two ways:

- *either* with the class interval under each column; for example, 0–5, 5–10, 10–15, and so on;
- *or* in the usual way with single integers on the grid lines; for example, 0, 5, 10, 15, and so on.

### Checkpoint

Describe some of the key features of a frequency diagram.

(Responses may include 'used for continuous data', 'bars touch', 'frequency goes up', 'class intervals are equal', etc.)

**Starter** – Quick fire

Recap work of previous chapters and this chapter so far. Ask rapid response questions with students responding on mini whiteboards. Discuss answers when there is a need.

## Teaching notes

Explain to students that continuous data is data which can take any value, such as height, length or weight. It is data that is found by measuring rather than counting and it is usually rounded.

Show the students a frequency table of data (which could have been collected in class; for example, students' heights). Point out that the data is grouped into classes and explain the use of inequality symbols in this context.

Explain that the table of data can now be converted into a frequency diagram. The horizontal axis is always labelled with a continuous scale; the vertical axis always gives the frequency. Students draw bars on their own axes.

Further examples could be shown using graph-drawing software.

## Plenary

Give each student a frequency table and pre-labelled axes as in Question 1, but with no tallies, no frequencies and no columns on the axes. Students complete the tables by inventing their own tallies and frequencies. In pairs, they exchange tables and their partners draw the frequency diagram. They check each other's diagrams and discuss the results.

## Exercise commentary

**Question 1** – Finding the range from the raw data is straightforward. Ask if there is an odd or even number of data – students need not count, as the vertical pairing in the table indicates a single value on the end. Discuss the implications of the inequality signs.

**Question 2** – This can be extended to discuss what might happen as a consequence of the difference between the two classes. How would students explore any hypothesis?

## Answers

**1 a i** 4 cm  **ii** 5.9 cm

**b**

| Growth (g cm) | Tally | Frequency |
|---|---|---|
| $4 \leq g < 5$ | III | 3 |
| $5 \leq g < 6$ | ЖII | 8 |
| $6 \leq g < 7$ | IIII | 4 |
| $7 \leq g < 8$ | IIII | 4 |
| $8 \leq g < 9$ | II | 2 |

**c**

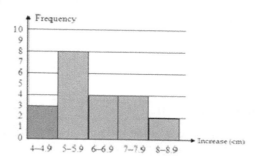

**d** 11 students      **e** 6 students

**f** $5 \leq g < 6$

**2 a** 10 students      **b** 16 students

**c** 9K: 30-59 minutes, 9M: 60-90 minutes

## Objectives

- Interpret tables, graphs and diagrams for discrete and continuous data, relating summary statistics and findings to the questions being explored. (L5)
- Write about and discuss the results of a statistical enquiry using ICT as appropriate. (L6)

| Key ideas | Resources |
|---|---|
| 1 A statistical report needs an overall structure based on the data-handling cycle and including conclusions. | ⊞ Reading pie charts (1206) <br><br> Writing frames <br><br> ICT facilities <br><br> Mini whiteboards |

| Simplification | Extension |
|---|---|
| Give students a clear writing frame to use, with prompts and questions to guide them through the process of writing their reports. | Students look at reports in newspapers or on the Internet which involve statistics. Ask them to be critical of the way they are used and to comment on the articles. |

| Literacy | Links |
|---|---|
| Writing a report requires student to combine their literacy and numeracy skills. Spelling, punctuation and grammar are important, as are numerical accuracy, appropriate graphicacy and evidenced-based argument and conclusions. | Many different organisations, including the government, the pharmaceutical industry, manufacturing industries, research facilities and the NHS, employ statisticians to analyse and interpret data. Statisticians provide information and advice to help the government, business and the wider population make informed decisions. There is information about becoming a statistician at www.rss.org.uk/careers |

### Alternative approach

The report can also include an evaluation of the data-handling process, the limitations encountered and any further or future lines of enquiry that may be needed.

### Checkpoint

Explain the four main stages of the data-handling cycle.

(Planning, collecting/recording, analyzing, interpreting/concluding – student responses should include reference to these main elements)

## Starter – Four in a line

Ask students to draw a $5 \times 5$ grid and enter the numbers 6 to 30 in any order.

Ask students questions such as:

What is the median of 11, 15, 29, 43, 50? [29]

If the smallest value of the data is 9 and the largest value is 22. What is the range? [13]

The mean of four numbers is 5. What is the total of these four numbers? [20]

The winner is the first student to cross out four numbers in any line, horizontal, vertical or diagonal.

Note that this activity has less assessment potential that the use of mini whiteboards.

## Teaching notes

At the end of the data-handing cycle, a report is written to summarise the findings. Students suggest what they think should be in the report. An appropriate structure for the final report is decided, possibly using a writing frame.

Discuss possible ways of drawing conclusions with the class and emphasise the need for these conclusions to be based solely on the data that has been analysed.

If students have been working on their own projects, they can write their own reports at this stage. The use of ICT for the graphs could be encouraged and the whole report could be completed on a computer for a more professional look. If they have been working through the case study in the text book, they could write up the final report for the theme park in a similar way.

## Plenary

Ask students to write down in their own words the four steps in the data-handling cycle. Ask them to write down the key features of the final report and give examples of their findings and conclusions.

## Exercise commentary

**Question 1** – It must be relevant to Max's investigation and, if possible, summarise it.

**Questions 2 to 4** – Explain the need for evidence from the data to support the findings.

## Answers

1  Title should refer to fall in visitor numbers.
2  a  Reasonable suggestions
   b  The chart shows attendance figures have fallen (this year, approximately 177 000; last year, approximately 217 000)
   c  August                   d  September
   e  20 000 visitors          f  15 000 visitors
3  a  Answer should refer to use of primary and secondary data collection.
   b  Students should comment that rainfall during this year was significantly greater than previous years.
4  a  The majority, more than 50% think Thunderworld is poor value for money.
   b  Reasonable suggestions

| Key outcomes | | Quick check |
|---|---|---|
| Plan how to collect data and use a suitable method to collect it. | L4 | Criticise this question: "You are certain, aren't you, that you like the new plans for the ring-road?" (It is leading/biased and suggests that they *should* like it) |
| Construct frequency tables for discrete data. | L4 | Construct a frequency table for this data:<br>Number of brothers and sisters: 2, 3, 0, 4, 1, 3, 5, 2, 1, 0, 2, 2<br>(Frequencies are: 2, 2, 4, 2, 1, 1) |
| Interpret and draw bar charts. | L5 | Draw a bar chart for the data in the previous question.<br>(Heights as per the frequencies, bars not touching, labelled 0 to 5) |
| Draw pie charts. | L6 | Draw a pie chart for the data.<br>(Angles are 60°, 60°, 120°, 60°, 30°, 30°) |
| Find the mode, median, mean and range of a set of data. | L5 | Find the mean, median, mode and range for the data.<br>(2.08, 2, 2, 5) |
| Construct and interpret scatter graphs. | L6 | Describe the correlation that might be present in a scatter diagram displaying the temperature of the day and the number of ice creams sold. (Positive) |
| Construct and use stem-and-leaf diagrams. | L6 | Draw a stem-and-leaf diagram for this data on test scores in science:<br>4, 6, 8, 11, 15, 17, 18, 18, 21, 21, 22, 27, 28, 30, 31, 32, 35, 36<br>(Stems from 0 to 3, leaves placed correctly in ascending order: 4, 6, 8; 1, 5, 7, 8, 8; 1, 1, 2, 7, 8; 0, 1, 2, 5, 6, key given) |

## ⊕ MyMaths extra support

| Lesson/online homework | | | Description |
|---|---|---|---|
| Median Mode from freq table | 1202 | L7 | Introduction to the idea of cumulative frequency |
| Introducing data | 1235 | L3 | Sorting data into groups using Venn diagrams and tally charts. Bar charts and pictograms |

# My Review

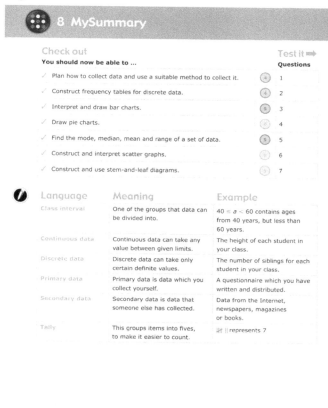

**Check out**

**You should now be able to ...**

| | Test it ➡ Questions |
|---|---|
| ✓ Plan how to collect data and use a suitable method to collect it. | 1 |
| ✓ Construct frequency tables for discrete data. | 2 |
| ✓ Interpret and draw bar charts. | 3 |
| ✓ Draw pie charts. | 4 |
| ✓ Find the mode, median, mean and range of a set of data. | 5 |
| ✓ Construct and interpret scatter graphs. | 6 |
| ✓ Construct and use stem-and-leaf diagrams. | 7 |

| Language | Meaning | Example |
|---|---|---|
| Class interval | One of the groups that data can be divided into. | $40 \leq a < 60$ contains ages from 40 years, but less than 60 years. |
| Continuous data | Continuous data can take any value between given limits. | The height of each student in your class. |
| Discrete data | Discrete data can take only certain definite values. | The number of siblings for each student in your class. |
| Primary data | Primary data is data which you collect yourself. | A questionnaire which you have written and distributed. |
| Secondary data | Secondary data is data that someone else has collected. | Data from the Internet, newspapers, magazines or books. |
| Tally | This groups items into fives, to make it easier to count. | ⦀⦀ represents 7 |

1 Pippa is going to stand at the entrance to a supermarket and record whether the shoppers
– are male or female and
– have brought their own shopping bags.
Design a data-collection sheet for her to use.

2 Pippa also asks people leaving the supermarket how much they have spent and records the answers.

| | | | |
|---|---|---|---|
| £69 | £34 | £55 | £18.42 |
| £4.50 | £9.99 | £75 | £25.13 |
| £37 | £48 | £62 | £8.45 |
| £15 | £22 | £37 | £18.99 |

Copy and complete the frequency table

| Amount Spent (£) | Tally | Frequency |
|---|---|---|
| 0–9.99 | | |
| 10–19.99 | | |
| 20–29.99 | | |
| 30–39.99 | | |
| 40–49.99 | | |
| 50–59.99 | | |
| 60–69.99 | | |
| 70–79.99 | | |

3 Out of the 20 people Pippa asked, 13 had brought their own shopping bags and 7 had not.
Draw a bar chart to display this data.

4 Children have a choice of three dinners in a school canteen. The table shows what they chose to eat.

| Food | Frequency |
|---|---|
| Roast Chicken | 35 |
| Chilli | 15 |
| Vegetable Lasagne | 10 |

Draw a pie chart to show this information.

5 The age of children in a playground were

    1 3 2 5 4 6
    1 1 1 3 2 1

a Find the mode.
b Calculate the mean.
c Find the median.
d Calculate the range.

6 The number of sandwiches and packs of crisps sold at a cafe on different days is shown in the table.

| Sandwiches | 55 | 30 | 40 | 20 | 10 | 25 | 50 |
|---|---|---|---|---|---|---|---|
| Crisps | 25 | 15 | 20 | 5 | 2 | 15 | 20 |

a Draw a scatter diagram for this data.
b Describe the correlation.

7 Here are the scores of students in a maths test.

    4  18 23 28 31 32 32 34
    36 38 40 42 43 43 43 47

Draw a stem-and-leaf diagram to display this data.

**What next?**

| Score | | |
|---|---|---|
| 0 – 3 | Your knowledge of this topic is still developing. To improve look at Formative test: 3A-8; MyMaths: 1192, 1193, 1196, 1200, 1203, 1205, 1206, 1207, 1212, 1213, 1215 and 1248 |
| 4 – 6 | You are gaining a secure knowledge of this topic. To improve look at InvisiPen: 411, 414, 415, 422, 423, 426, 427, 431, 441 and 448 |
| 7 | You have mastered this topic. Well done, you are ready to progress! |

**⊕ MyMaths.co.uk**

## Question commentary

**Question 1** – Students often confuse data collection sheets with questionnaires.

**Question 2** – The groupings are given so this is just an exercise in filling in the table correctly. Encourage students to work through the list in order.

**Question 3** – Check the bars do not touch.

**Question 4** – Students will need to use a sharp pencil, ruler and protractor, they will also need a pair of compasses or something circular to draw around. The sections of the pie chart should either be labelled or coloured in and a key provided. Allow 2° tolerance on angles.

**Question 5** – Suggest that the students write the numbers in order first. Ensure students understand that the range is not a type of average.

**Question 6** – Check that students have drawn the axes and written the scales accurately. You could provide these for students who might struggle.

**Question 7** – Students must also provide a key. The data for each stem should be in numerical order. It is given in the question in order so their diagrams should automatically be ordered.

## Answers

See master Answers file for this lesson

**8a**

1 Decide whether each source of data is primary or secondary.
 a Surveying the students in your class about their favourite food.
 b Data from a newspaper about popular takeaway companies.

**8b**

2 Andrea surveys the students in her class. She wants to find out their age, gender and if they are vegetarian. Design a data-collection sheet for her to use.

**8c**

3 Students on a field trip are asked to vote for what they want to eat on the final night of their visit. Copy and complete this frequency table from the data.

Burgers    Burgers    Fish & chips
Chinese    Fish & chips    Fish & chips
Curry    Chinese    Burgers    Kebab    Burgers
Burgers    Curry    Vegetarian    Burgers    Curry
Curry    Fish & chips    Fish & chips    Burgers
Fish and chips    Burgers    Fish & chips
Vegetarian    Curry    Vegetarian    Burgers
Fish & chips    Chinese    Fish & chips

| Food | Tally | Frequency |
|---|---|---|
| Burgers | | |
| Fish & chips | | |
| Kebab | | |
| Chinese | | |
| Vegetarian | | |
| Curry | | |

**8d**

4 a Draw a bar chart from the frequency table in question 3.
 b How many people voted in total?
 c What was the modal choice of food?

**8e**

5 Andrea wants to display the data from question 3 as a pie chart.
 a Complete the sentence: 'Each student is _____ of the pie chart.'
 b Draw the pie chart. Use a colour code or key to explain each sector.

**8f**

6 These are the sizes of shoes sold in one day in the men's shoe department.

Shoe sizes
6  8  8  7  10
8  10  9  9  12
7  10  11  8  8
9  9  8  9  9
6  10  11  7  8

 a Write out the shoe sizes in order, smallest to largest.
 b What is the modal size?
 c What is the median size?
 d What is the range of sizes?

7 Leon and Ben play for the school basketball team.
 In matches Leon has scored 4, 10, 4, 5, 7 and 6.
 In matches Ben has scored 5, 9, 8 and 6. Who has the best mean score?

---

**8g**

8 Ms DaCosta uses taxis to travel around.
 The scatter diagram shows the relationship between distance and cost.
 a What distance was the longest trip she took?
 b What is the most she has paid for a journey?
 How much might she expect to pay if she travels
 c 3.5km?    d 10km?

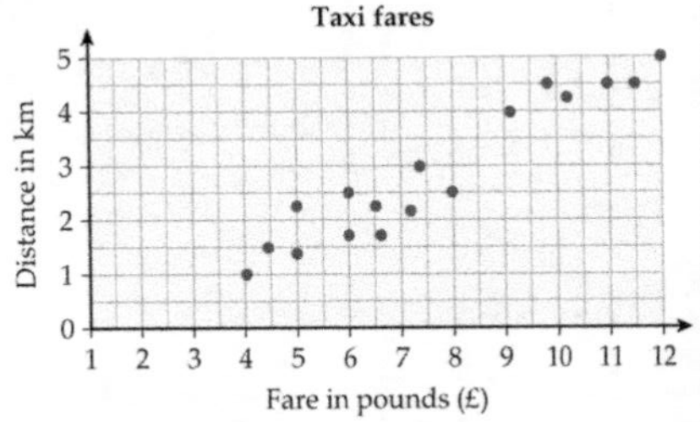

Taxi fares

**8h**

9 The BusCo bus company records the number of passengers on the Route 13 bus for one day. The bus makes 30 trips. The stem-and-leaf diagram shows the data.
 a Which was the modal group?
 b What was the median number of passengers?
 c What was the range of passenger numbers?

Passengers on Route 13

```
5 | 2 3 5
4 | 1 3 3 5 6 9
3 | 0 0 2 4 6 6 7 8 8 9
2 | 0 3 7
1 | 4 5 5 5 8
0 | 5 7
```
Key 5 | 5 = 55

**8i**

10 Thirty students took a history test. Their marks are shown in the table.

| 48 | 44 | 43 | 41 | 40 | 39 | 39 | 39 | 36 | 34 |
| 31 | 31 | 29 | 28 | 27 | 26 | 25 | 25 | 23 |
| 22 | 21 | 20 | 19 | 18 | 17 | 16 | 15 | 11 |

Draw a stem-and-leaf diagram to display the data.

**8j**

11 The data from question 10 is organised in a frequency table.
 a Copy and complete the frequency table.
 b Draw a frequency diagram.

| Marks, $m$ | Frequency |
|---|---|
| $10 \leq m < 20$ | 7 |
| $20 \leq m < 30$ | |
| $30 \leq m < 40$ | |
| $40 \leq m < 50$ | |

**8j**

12 The BusCo bus company recorded the number of passengers on the Route 13 bus on the same day during the previous year. During the 30 trips the largest number of passengers was 42 and the median was 27. Does the data support the claim that the number of passengers using the Route 13 bus has increased?

**MyMaths**.co.uk

## Question commentary

**Question 1** – Students may need reminding of the definitions of primary and secondary data.

**Question 2** – Students should design a data collection sheet and not a questionnaire.

**Question 3** – Check that the students add up the total frequency at the end to cross-check against the raw data total.

**Question 4** – Check that the bars do not touch.

**Question 5** – Check the students are using a sharp pencil and that the angles are within 2° tolerance.

**Questions 6** and **7** – The data will need to be ordered first for question **6** but need not be ordered for question **7**.

**Question 8** – Check that the answers to parts **c** and **d** are sensibly within the range of the data.

**Questions 9** and **10** – Question **9** requires students to read from the stem-and-leaf diagram while question **10** requires them to draw their own. Ensure sensible stems (0 – 4) and that the data is in order and a key given.

**Question 11** – Check that the bars touch and the $x$-axis is labelled with a continuous scale.

**Question 12** – Lots of answers are possible, but emphasise that claims must be justified by reference to the data.

## Answers

see master Answers file

## MyAssessment 2

These questions will test you on your knowledge of the topics in chapters 5 to 8.
They give you practice in the types of questions that you may see in your GCSE exams.
There are 90 marks in total.

1  a  Which are the corresponding angles to angle *a*
      and angle *b*? (2 marks)

   b  Which angles are vertically opposite angles *v*
      and *x*? (2 marks)

   c  Which are the alternate angles to angles *c* and *d*? (2 marks)

   d  If angle *a* = 50° calculate angles *b*, *u*, *v*, *w* and *x*. (5 marks)

2  a  Find the size of the angles marked with letters. (2 marks)

   b  What names do we give to these triangles? (2 marks)

3  This is an isosceles trapezium.

   a  Give three properties of an isosceles trapezium. (3 marks)

   b  Find the sizes of angles *x*, *y* and *z*. (2 marks)

4  a  Draw *x*- and *y*-axes from -5 to +5 on square grid paper and plot
      the points (-5, 4) (-3, 4) (-1, 4) (1, 4) and (3, 4). (2 marks)

   b  What is the equation of the line that joins these points together? (1 mark)

   c  Draw the line that corresponds to the equation *x* = -3 on your graph. (2 marks)

   d  What is the coordinate of the point where the two lines cross? (2 marks)

5  Use the same axes as above.

   a  Complete the table of values for the equation *y* = *x* − 3 (3 marks)

| *x* | -2 | -1 | 0 | 1 | 2 | 3 | 4 | 5 |
|-----|----|----|----|----|----|----|----|----|
| *y* |    |    |    |    |    |    |    |    |

   b  Plot these coordinates on your graph and join the points with a
      straight line. (3 marks)

   c  What are the coordinates of the point where the straight line meets
      the line *y* = 0? (2 marks)

   d  Complete this sentence.
      'The points move ... square up for every ... square across' (2 marks)

---

6  This perfume bottle is filled at a steady rate.
   Draw a sketch of the height of the perfume versus time. (3 marks)

7  Work out these calculations using a mental method.

   a  21 + 13 ÷ 7    b  86 − 38    c  87.6 + 124.2    d  543.7 − 349.1 (4 marks)

8  Work out these calculations using a mental method.
   Make an estimate of the answer before you start each calculation.

   a  18 × 7    b  6 × 46    c  78 ÷ 3    d  216 ÷ 9 (4 marks)

9  Work out these calculations using a written method.

   a  145 × 26    b  43.7 × 9    c  16)464    d  572 ÷ 12 (8 marks)

10  Solve each of these problems using your calculator.

    a  Convert 256 hours into days and hours. (4 marks)

    b  The cost of 46 seats on a coach at £5.68 per person. (2 marks)

    c  The annual salary of a worker who works 40 hours per week for
       48 weeks at £13.56 per hour. (3 marks)

11  What is the difference between **primary** and **secondary** data? (2 marks)

12  Design a questionnaire to collect this information.

    a  How did you travel to school today? (2 marks)

    b  How old are you? (2 marks)

13  The masses (in grams) of 20 plum tomatoes were recorded as follows.

    52  49  46  51  46  45  41  40  60  37
    50  46  46  51  44  42  51  52  42  39

    a  Construct a frequency table to show this data using class intervals
       36–40, 41–45, 46–50, 51–55 and 56–60. (3 marks)

    b  Draw a bar chart to represent this information. (3 marks)

    c  Determine the mode, median and range for this data. (3 marks)

    d  Calculate the mean mass for this set of tomatoes. (2 marks)

14  In a local health clinic study the results of weight (kg) versus blood pressure
    (mm of mercury) was studied in eight men with these results.

| Weight (kg) | 67.2 | 66.8 | 76.2 | 75.0 | 89.8 | 100.4 | 55.8 | 72.8 |
|-------------|------|------|------|------|------|-------|------|------|
| Blood pressure (mm of mercury) | 70 | 65 | 80 | 75 | 85 | 90 | 60 | 70 |

    a  Draw a scatter graph for this data. The *x*-axis is taken from
       50 to 110kg and the *y*-axis from 50 to 100mm of mercury. (5 marks)

    b  Draw the best straight line through the points. (1 mark)

    c  Comment on the correlation. (2 marks)

🔷 **MyMaths**.co.uk

# Mark scheme

**Question 1** – 11 marks

a   2   angles $a$ and $u$, $b$ and $w$

b   2   angles $v$ and $w$, $x$ and $u$

c   2   angles $a$ and $x$, $b$ and $v$

d   5   $b = 130°, u = 50°, v = 130°, w = 130°$ and $x = 50°$

**Question 2** – 4 marks

a   2   $128°$

b   2   $52°$

**Question 3** – 5 marks

a   3   2 pairs of equal angles, 1 pair of equal sides, 1 set of parallel sides (-1 mark for each omission)

b   2   $x = 73°, y = 107°, z = 73°$

**Question 4** – 7 marks

a   2   Correct $x$ and $y$ grid drawn and labeled, all points correctly plotted

b   1   $y = 4$

c   2   Correct line drawn; 1 mark for any other vertical line

d   2   $(-3, 4)$

**Question 5** – 10 marks

a   3   -5, -4, -3, -2, -1, 0, 1, 2, 3; -1 mark each error or omission

b   3   All points correctly plotted; straight line (ruled) drawn

c   2   $(0, -3)$

d   2   The points move **one** square up for every **one** square across

**Question 6** – 3 marks

    3   Graph showing slope decreasing then increasing, similar to below.

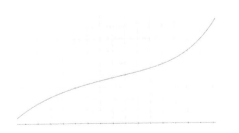

**Question 7** – 4 marks

a   1   41       b   1   48

c   1   211.8       d   1   194.6

**Question 8** – 4 marks

a   1   140, 126       b   1   300, 276

c   1   25, 26       d   1   20, 24

**Question 9** – 8 marks

a   2   3779       b   2   393.3

c   2   29       d   2   47 r 8

**Question 10** – 9 marks

a   4   10 days 16 hours; 2 marks if 10.6666 seen

b   2   £227.20; 1 mark if $5.68 \times 46$ seen

c   3   £26 035.20; 1 mark if $13.56 \times 40$; 1 mark if $542.5 \times 48$ seen

**Question 11** – 2 marks

    1   Primary data is data you collect yourself

    1   Secondary data is someone else's data

**Question 12** – 4 marks

a   2   Minimum of 45 students, 45 – 75 is a sensible range

b   2   Sample has to be representative; ratio of boys to girls considered

**Question 13** – 11 marks

a   3   Frequencies are 3, 5, 6, 5, 1; tally chart drawn; total checked

b   3   Correct bar chart constructed; frequency on $y$-axis and correct grouping shown on $x$-axis

c   3   Mode 46-50, median 46-50, range 13g

d   2   46.5g; 1 mark for 930 seen

**Question 14** – 8 marks

a   5   Correct axes drawn; correct scales; all points plotted correctly; axes labeled

b   1   Ruled correct straight line drawn

c   2   Shows a reasonably strong correlation despite small sample size

## Learning outcomes

**G3** Draw and measure line segments and angles in geometric figures, including interpreting scale drawings
(L6)

**G8** Identify properties of, and describe the results of, translations, rotations and reflections applied to given figures
(L5)

**G9** Identify and construct congruent triangles, and construct similar shapes by enlargement, with and without coordinate grids
(L6)

## Introduction

The chapter starts by looking at reflection and rotation symmetry before sections on reflection, translation and rotation. Enlargements in general and then through a given centre are covered. The final section covers scale drawing.

The introduction discusses how 15th century artists started to use the concept of perspective to draw three-dimensional objects to scale and develop a sense of depth in their pictures. Before this time, perspective was largely ignored and most paintings looked 'flat'. A history of, and some excellent examples of, perspectival paintings can be found at:

http://www.op-art.co.uk/history/perspective/

The link to the concept of enlargement using ray lines can be made explicit to the students or they could be directed to investigate these themselves, as in the starter problem.

## Prior knowledge

Students should already know how to...

- Understand simple symmetry
- Estimate angles of turn
- Recognise changes in size

## Starter problem

The starter problem asks students to look at the general effects on coordinates following a simple transformation. The example given of reflecting in the $y$-axis has the effect of changing the sign of the $x$-coordinate. Further investigation is suggested and students should look at other straight line reflections, for example in the $x$-axis (the $y$-coordinate changes sign) or the line $y = x$ (the coordinates 'swap').

The rules for rotations are more difficult to describe but more able students could be asked to try this for simple shapes.

## Resources

**MyMaths**

| | | | | | |
|---|---|---|---|---|---|
| Enlarging shapes | 1099 | Map scales | 1103 | Reflecting shapes | 1113 |
| Lines of symmetry | 1114 | Rotating shapes | 1115 | Rotation symmetry | 1116 |
| Scale drawing | 1117 | All transformations | 1125 | Translating shapes | 1127 |

**Online assessment**

| | |
|---|---|
| Chapter test | 3A–9 |
| Formative test | 3A–9 |
| Summative test | 3A–9 |

**InvisiPen solutions**

| | | | |
|---|---|---|---|
| Reflection and rotation symmetry | | | 361 |
| Reflection | 362 | Translation | 363 |
| Enlargements | 366 | Scale drawings | 372 |

# Topic scheme

Teaching time = 7 lessons/3 weeks

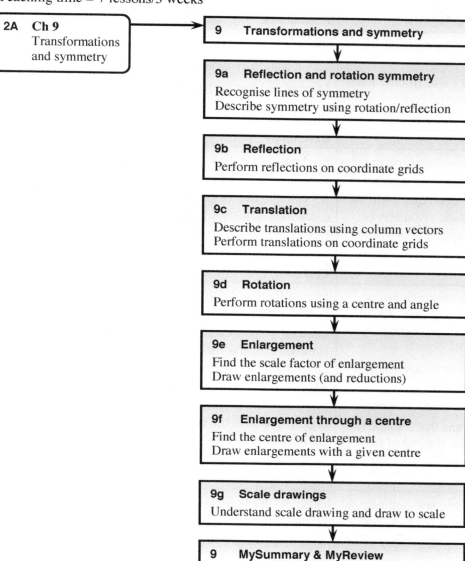

| 2A   Ch 9 |
| Transformations and symmetry |

**9    Transformations and symmetry**

**9a    Reflection and rotation symmetry**
Recognise lines of symmetry
Describe symmetry using rotation/reflection

**9b    Reflection**
Perform reflections on coordinate grids

**9c    Translation**
Describe translations using column vectors
Perform translations on coordinate grids

**9d    Rotation**
Perform rotations using a centre and angle

**9e    Enlargement**
Find the scale factor of enlargement
Draw enlargements (and reductions)

**9f    Enlargement through a centre**
Find the centre of enlargement
Draw enlargements with a given centre

**9g    Scale drawings**
Understand scale drawing and draw to scale

**9    MySummary & MyReview**

# Differentiation

**Student book 3A          162 – 181**

Rotation and reflection symmetry
Reflection, rotations and
translations
Enlargements using a scale factor
with and without a centre of
enlargement
Scale drawings

**Student book 3B          162 – 177**

Rotations, reflections and
translations, including
combinations thereof
Enlargements using a scale factor
and centre of enlargement
Map scales and scale drawings
Bearings

**Student book 3C          158 – 173**

Transformations and combinations
of transformations
Enlargements using a scale factor
and centre of enlargement
Map scales and scale drawings
Enlargements and similar shapes

## Objectives

- Identify reflection and rotational symmetry of 2D shapes.                                    (L5)

| Key ideas | Resources |
|---|---|
| 1  A shape with reflection symmetry has at least one line of symmetry.<br><br>2  A shape with rotational symmetry will fit onto itself at least once before it completes a full turn about a point. | ⊕  Lines of symmetry                                    (1114)<br>    Rotation symmetry                                    (1116)<br>Mirrors and tracing paper<br>Mini whiteboards |

| Simplification | Extension |
|---|---|
| Ensure students understand that the *order* of rotational symmetry could be described simply as 'the number of times a shape fits onto itself during a full turn'. Mirrors will help them to identify the reflection symmetry of symmetrical shapes while tracing paper will help with rotational symmetry. | Students group the letters of the alphabet according the symmetry properties they possess. This could be using a Venn diagram or simply by listing letters in various categories. Can they make words which have either type of symmetry? |

| Literacy | Links |
|---|---|
| The word 'symmetry' comes from a combination of Latin and Greek meaning 'measured together'. Other words where 'sym-' means 'together' are 'sympathy' and 'symphony'.<br><br>A 'line of symmetry' is also less formally known as a 'mirror line'.<br><br>'Reflection symmetry' is also called 'line symmetry'.<br><br>Rotational symmetry of order 1 means that a shape fits onto itself *only once* in a full 360° (at the end of the turn), so it has no rotational symmetry. | Many plants and animals are highly symmetrical to the extent that exceptions are rare. Mammals are bilaterally symmetrical, worms are radially symmetrical, star fish have rotational symmetry of order 5 whilst corals have rotational symmetry of either order 6 or order 8. Most flowers also show symmetry. Biologists use symmetry to help classify an organism within the animal or plant kingdom. There are examples of bilaterally symmetrical butterflies and moths at www.wmnh.com/wmiab000.htm |

## Alternative approach

A kaleidoscope is a good instrument to see symmetrical shapes. With squared paper, students can imitate a kaleidoscope by using coloured pencils to shade squares and make patterns that are designed to have one or two lines of symmetry or to have rotational symmetry of order 2 or 4. Shading triangles on isometric paper can give shapes with three lines of symmetry or rotational symmetry of order 3.

In addition, website such as http://nrich.maths.org/1840 provide investigative approaches.

## Checkpoint

| | |
|---|---|
| How many lines of symmetry does a regular pentagon have? | (5) |
| State the order of rotational symmetry of a regular octagon. | (8) |

**Starter** – Today's number is ... 161

Ask questions based on 161. For example:

| | |
|---|---|
| What is half of 161? | [80.5] |
| What is the tenth multiple of 161? | [1610] |
| What is 1% of 161? | [1.61] |
| What is 10% of 161? | [16.1] |
| What number is it, if turns 161 through 180°? | [191] |

Follow the above with other work of previous chapters. Ask rapid response questions. Students reply by writing on their mini whiteboards. Discuss questions when their answers indicate a need.

## Teaching notes

Explain to students that symmetry is the property of a shape that enables it to fit on itself when moved. Distinguish between reflection symmetry, when the shape fits on itself after being 'folded', and rotational symmetry when the shape fits on itself after being turned. Give examples of shapes that have either (or both) symmetries. (Letters of the alphabet can be used to show the two types of symmetry.)

Define the terminology 'order of rotational symmetry'. Students find the symmetry properties of various letters and other shapes. They could work in groups or pairs with a set of letters in different styles. Address issues such as "Does the letter Q have a line of symmetry?" [It depends on the style of lettering but not usually].

Ask them to describe the symmetry of other shapes and to draw shapes with given symmetries.

## Plenary

Ask students to identify the lines of symmetry (mirror lines) for shapes shown to them. Students record their answers on mini whiteboards to enable quick assessment. Also ask students to identify the order of rotational symmetry of shapes shown to them.

## Exercise commentary

This topic is more enjoyable with the provision of mirrors and tracing paper for exploring reflection and rotational symmetry respectively.

**Question 1** – Beware of students who say that an order of rotational symmetry is zero. If the shape has no rotational symmetry then the order of rotational symmetry is 1.

**Question 2** – Reflection symmetry can be checked with a mirror.

**Question 3** – It may help to make an exact copy of the shape which can be folded over to convince students of the equality of corresponding angles. If necessary, remind students that the diagonals cross at 90° (two folds of the shape can show this) and that the sum of the angles in a triangle is 180°.

**Question 4** – Beware of students claiming that the parallelogram in part **d** has a line of symmetry. Folding the parallelogram will convince them that it hasn't.

**Question 5** – This question is more difficult to do without access to a mirror. Students will need to visualise the shapes carefully.

**Question 6** – Students could be directed to Question **4** for inspiration.

---

## Answers

1. **a** Vertical line through centre of arrow, order 1
   **b** Vertical line through centre, order 1
   **c** Vertical and horizontal lines through centre, order 2
   **d** Horizontal line through centre, order 1
   **e** Vertical line through centre, order 1
   **f** Vertical and horizontal lines through centre, order 2
2. **a** Two lines of reflection symmetry (vertical and horizontal through centre), rotational symmetry of order 2
   **b** Four lines of reflection symmetry (vertical and horizontal, both diagonals, through centre), and rotational symmetry of order 4
   **c** Two lines of reflection symmetry (vertical and horizontal through centre), rotational symmetry of order 2
   **d** One line of reflection symmetry (diagonal from top left to bottom right), rotational symmetry of order 1
3. Top and bottom: 80° each
   Left and right: 100° each
6. Parallelograms have no reflection symmetry, but they have rotational symmetry. Kites have reflection symmetry but no rotational symmetry.

## Objectives

- Transform 2D shapes by reflection on paper and using ICT. (L5)

| Key ideas | Resources |
|---|---|
| **1** A reflection maintains the size and shape but changes the position of an shape. <br><br> **2** The object and image are equidistant from the line of reflection. <br><br> **3** A line joining corresponding points on the object and image is perpendicular to the line of reflection. | Reflecting shapes (1113) <br> Graph-drawing software <br> Pre-drawn axes <br> Mini whiteboards |

| Simplification | Extension |
|---|---|
| Restrict examples to those involving simple geometrical shapes such as rectangles and triangles. (Avoid squares because of their particular symmetry which can mask the overall effect.) Only consider reflections in the axes. | Students draw more complicated examples of geometrical shapes on axes and challenge a partner to draw their reflections when reflected in each axis. Ask them to fill in the shape for the fourth quadrant too by a further reflection. |

| Literacy | Links |
|---|---|
| The 'line of symmetry' is also less formally known as the 'mirror line'. <br><br> In these lesson on symmetry, watch for the common misspelling of 'symmetry' with a single 'm'. | Distorting mirrors are popular as fairground attractions and can make a person appear taller, shorter, thinner or fatter. Most mirrors are flat, but a distorting mirror has a curved surface, usually in one direction only. A good discussion on mirrors can be found at: http://science.howstuffworks.com/mirror-info.htm |

## Alternative approach

Investigations can free the topic from drawing shapes on axes. The website http://nrich.maths.org/5458 provides various investigative activities, this one involving two reflections in parallel mirrors. Ask students if any have stood between two parallel mirrors and seen their multiple reflections running away from them.

Computer-generated transformations add further interest.

## Checkpoint

Write down the coordinates of the image of point (2, 3)

**a** After being reflected in the $y$-axis (-2, 3)

**b** After a reflection in the line $y = 1$ (2, -1)

## Starter – Four in a line

Ask students to draw a 5 × 5 grid and enter the numbers 1 to 25 in any order. Ask questions such as:

How many lines of symmetry does an isosceles triangle have?                    [1]

What is the order of rotational symmetry of a rectangle?                    [2]

Include questions from earlier chapters, especially number concepts and skills. The winner is the first student to cross out four in a line.

## Teaching notes

Using an example, possibly drawn using graph-drawing software, explain what happens when a shape is reflected in the $y$-axis. Explain that the $x$-coordinates change sign. Students draw a shape given the coordinates of its vertices. Pre-drawn axes can speed this up. Students reflect the shape in the $y$-axis and note the coordinates of the image.

Using the same example as before, show the reflection in the $x$-axis. Students reflect their shape in the $x$-axis and note the coordinates of the image.

Give students examples where the vertical or horizontal mirror line is not either of the axes and ask them to identify the equations of the mirror lines.

Demonstrate the effect of a reflection in the line $y = x$. Show that the $x$- and $y$-coordinates interchange. Students complete their own example.

## Plenary

Using prepared examples, ask students to identify the mirror lines used in various situations. Students record their answers on mini whiteboards to enable quick assessment.

## Exercise commentary

Some students may benefit from pre-drawn grids and axes.

**Question 1** – Review negative coordinates. The mirror line is the $y$-axis and students may need the equation $x = 0$ explaining.

**Question 2** – Recap key concepts: reflections are always perpendicular to the mirror line; objects and images are equidistant from the mirror line.

**Question 3** – Discuss the equation $y = x$ and review ideas from Question **2**.

**Question 4** – Recap equations of lines parallel to the $x$-axis; for example, $y = 3$.

## Answers

1  **a,b,d,f**        Check students drawings
   **c**  $x = 0$        **e**  (-4, -1), (-1, -1), (-3, -4)
   **g**  (1, -1), (4, -1), (3, -4)
   **h**  Reflect in the line $x = 0$

2  **a,b,d**
   **c**  $y = x$
   **e**  $A^2$ (-4, 7), $B^2$ (-4 9), $C^2$ (-1, 9), $D^2$ (-1, 7)

3  **a**  (-5, 8)      **b**  (2, -6)      **c**  (5, 3)

4  **a**  (4, 1)      **b**  (-2, 3)      **c**  (-2, -4)

| Objectives | |
|---|---|
| • Transform 2D shapes by translation on paper and using ICT. | (L5) |

| Key ideas | Resources | |
|---|---|---|
| 1  A translation maintains the shape and size of a shape but changes its position.<br>2  A translation moves an object onto into image by a slide without any rotation. The slide is defined by a vector. | ⊞ Translating shapes<br>Graphing software<br>Pre-drawn axes on squared paper<br>Mini whiteboards | (1127) |

| Simplification | Extension |
|---|---|
| Students describe translations in words before using directed numbers.<br><br>Secure basic understanding using positive components only in vectors. Once secure, introduce negative components in one direction at a time. | Students draw a shape and transform it under two (or more) successive translations. They find one translation equivalent to the two successive translations. Can they see any connections between the vectors involved? |

| Literacy | Links |
|---|---|
| The words 'transformation' and 'translation' are often confused. Thinking of 'translation' as moving 'sideways' from one language to another helps to make the distinction.<br><br>The words 'vector' and 'vehicle' come from the same Latin word meaning 'carry'. There are various notations for a vector. The one used here is the column vector:<br><br>$\begin{pmatrix} x \\ y \end{pmatrix}$  for horizontal movement<br>for vertical movement<br><br>When the movement is right or up, the signs of $x$ and $y$ are positive; when left and down, they are negative. | The first Ferris wheel was designed by George Ferris in 1893 for the World Fair in Chicago. A Ferris wheel rotates around a central axis but the individual gondolas rotate by gravity in the opposite direction around their own axes of rotation. As a result, the gondolas and the people inside are translated around the edge of a large circle and do not rotate at all. There is a picture of the first Ferris wheel at www.hydeparkhistory.org/newsletter.html |

| Alternative approach |
|---|
| Investigations can free the topic from drawing shapes on axes. The website http://nrich.maths.org/9350 provides various investigative activities involving different transformations. Computer-generated transformations add further interest. |

| Checkpoint | |
|---|---|
| Describe the translation that maps A(2, 1) to B(4, 7). | $\begin{pmatrix} 2 \\ 6 \end{pmatrix}$ |
| What vector is needed to translate B back to A? | $\begin{pmatrix} -2 \\ -6 \end{pmatrix}$ |

## Starter – Reflective maths

Write the word MATHEMATICS on the board. Ask students to describe the symmetry of each letter. Draw a mirror line and challenge students to reflect the word in it.

Follow with questions from earlier chapters, especially questions about number concepts and skills.

## Teaching notes

Explain to students that a translation is a transformation which keeps the shape exactly the same in terms of orientation but moves its position.
A vector is used to describe the translation. It consists of a column of two numbers where the top number gives the units moved horizontally and the bottom number gives the units moved vertically. Positive numbers indicate a move to the right and upwards. Negative numbers indicate a move to the left and downwards.

Students draw shapes and their images on pre-drawn axes and describe translations. Use graph-drawing software to draw shapes and their images.

Students draw shapes and, given the vectors for translations, draw their images under the translations.

## Plenary

Show students objects and images under translations on square grids. Students write the vectors of the various translations. Include both positive and negative components of vectors. Students respond using mini whiteboards to allow quick assessment.

## Exercise commentary

Some students may benefit from using pre-drawn axes.

**Questions 1 to 3** – Ensure that students understand the difference between the notation $(x, y)$ for a point and the vector notation.

$\begin{pmatrix} x \\ y \end{pmatrix}$  for horizontal movement
  for vertical movement

Check that students are secure in using negative components in vectors.

**Question 4** – Remind students that the vectors give movement instructions:

$x \leftrightarrow$ horizontal        and        $y \updownarrow$ vertical.

## Answers

**1  a,b**

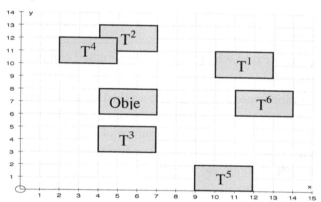

**2  a** $\begin{pmatrix} -6 \\ 0 \end{pmatrix}$  **b** $\begin{pmatrix} 6 \\ 1 \end{pmatrix}$  **c** $\begin{pmatrix} -6 \\ -1 \end{pmatrix}$  **d** $\begin{pmatrix} 6 \\ 10 \end{pmatrix}$

**e** $\begin{pmatrix} 0 \\ 5 \end{pmatrix}$  **f** $\begin{pmatrix} 5 \\ 3 \end{pmatrix}$  **g** $\begin{pmatrix} 0 \\ 9 \end{pmatrix}$  **h** $\begin{pmatrix} 10 \\ 2 \end{pmatrix}$

**i** $\begin{pmatrix} 7 \\ 2 \end{pmatrix}$  **j** $\begin{pmatrix} 6 \\ 0 \end{pmatrix}$  **k** $\begin{pmatrix} 11 \\ 3 \end{pmatrix}$  **l** $\begin{pmatrix} 0 \\ -5 \end{pmatrix}$

**m** $\begin{pmatrix} 5 \\ -5 \end{pmatrix}$  **n** $\begin{pmatrix} 0 \\ 4 \end{pmatrix}$

**3  a,b,c,d**        Check students drawings

**4**  No, adding the vectors, we see that the robot ends up 1 to the right of where it began.

## Objectives

- Transform 2D shapes by rotation on paper and using ICT. (L5)

| Key ideas | Resources |
|---|---|
| 1 A rotation maintains the shape and size of an object but alters its position.<br>2 A rotation is defined by an angle and direction of rotation and a centre of rotation. | Rotating shapes (1115)<br>Tracing paper<br>Protractors<br>Pre-drawn axes<br>Graphing software<br>Mini whiteboards |

| Simplification | Extension |
|---|---|
| Restrict examples to 180° and 90° rotations in the first instance and use a grid where the centre of rotation is the origin. Use tracing paper. The angle of a rotation can be clockwise or anticlockwise. | Students draw a more complicated geometrical shape and challenge a partner to draw its images after rotations of 90°, 180° and 270°.<br><br>Students combine transformations, say, a reflection in in the *x*-axis following by a rotation of 180° about the origin, and then describe the overall result as a single transformation. |

| Literacy | Links |
|---|---|
| The context in which rotations are studied can be widened.<br><br>Rotations need not always be studied on grids with axes. For example, a tessellation of regular hexagons can be created using only rotations of one hexagon onto another. Bicycle wheels can be investigated for the number of turns one wheel makes when the other rotates just once. | An aeroplane (or ship) can rotate in three dimensions and the principle rotations of an aircraft are called pitch, roll and yaw. Pitch is a rotation involving raising or lowering the nose of the plane, roll is a rotation towards one of the wings and yaw is a horizontal rotation. Pitch, roll and yaw are illustrated at www.flyingsites.co.uk/newcomers/controls/primaryflight1.htm |

## Alternative approach

Rather than take several shapes and different roations, it can be more interesting to take one irregular shape and see how it moves for different positions of the centre of rotation. The centre can be a point outside the shape, a point on the edge of the shape or a point within the shape.

Polar graph paper is a simple way of rotating shapes plotted on it. Shapes can be likened to images seen on a radar screen.

Interlocking cog wheels with different numbers of teeth can be investigated for the number of turns taken for different numbers of teeth.

Given a object and image and a centre of rotation, a compass can be used to draw an arc from a point on the object shape to the corresponding point on the image. Computer-generated rotations often show the path traced out by a point as it rotates.

## Checkpoint

Write down the coordinates of the image of the point (4, 1)

**a** After a 180° rotation about the origin (-4, -1)

**b** After a rotation of 90° clockwise about the origin (1, -4)

## Starter – Transforming pentominoes

Students draw pentominoes (which are shapes made from 5 squares touching edge to edge) on squared paper and reflect them in a mirror line. They then translate the pentominoes. Do any reflected images look the same as the translated images?

## Teaching notes

Explain that a rotation is described using three key facts: the angle and direction of rotation together with the centre of rotation.

Using an example, show how to apply a rotation of 180°. Give students the coordinates of a shape which they draw on labelled axes. They carry out a 180° rotation of their shape using tracing paper and draw the image.

Repeat with rotations of 90°, both clockwise and anticlockwise. Note that an anticlockwise rotation of 90° is the same as a clockwise one of 270°.

The next task is to find the centre of rotation when the positions of the object and image are known. Provide students with several objects and images under various rotations on either plain or squared paper. Students use tracing paper to find the positions of the centres of rotation. This task can be surprisingly difficult even for straightforward rotations.

## Plenary

Show a selection of object and image shapes. For each pair, students indicate whether the transformation is a rotations are not and, if it is, to write the angle and direction of rotation. Students can give their answers using mini whiteboards to enable quick assessment.

## Exercise commentary

Some students may benefit from using pre-drawn axes.

Ensure that students understand the terms 'clockwise' and 'anticlockwise'.

**Question 1** – Remind students that the dotted lines in parts **a** and **b** are the 'ray' lines which rotate about the centre, O. Ask students to see how the horizontal and vertical sides of the object shape change their orientations under different degrees of rotation.

**Question 2** – Students should confirm their answer by actually performing the rotation using tracing paper.

**Questions 3 and 4** – One method is for students to use tracing paper. Another method, not requiring tracing paper, is to count the horizontal and vertical distances from the centre O to any vertex of the triangle – and then count the same distances but starting off in a different direction as given by the required rotation.

**Question 5** – The position of the image can be checked by using a pair of compasses to draw the arcs of the circles along which the vertices of the object shape travel.

---

## Answers

1 **a,b**

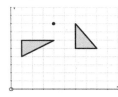 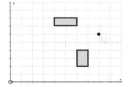

**c, d**

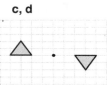 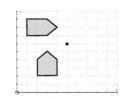

2 **a**   (6, 6)      **b**   clockwise      **c**   90°

3

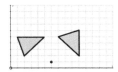

4 **a,d**    Check students' drawings
   **b**   Vertices at (1, -1), (5, -1), (2, -4)
   **c**   Vertices at (-1, -1), (-1, -5), (-4, -2)
5   Check students' drawings

## Objectives

- Understand and use the language and notation associated with enlargement. (L5)

| Key ideas | Resources |
|---|---|
| **1** An enlargement alters the size but not the shape of an object. <br><br> **2** An enlargment is defined by a scale factor (and a also a centre, as in the next lesson). | ⊞ Enlarging shapes (1099) <br> Projector and screen <br> Graph-drawing software <br> Squared paper <br> Mini whiteboards |

| Simplification | Extension |
|---|---|
| Restrict examples to shapes which have been enlarged using integer scale factors. Use simple shapes, such as rectangles and triangles. Ensure that students enlarge each of the sides using the same scale factor. | Ask students to enlarge a given shape by scale factors which are not integers (for example, by $1\frac{1}{2}$). <br><br> Students find the areas of objects and their images and try and find a connection between the scale factor of enlargement and the ratio of areas. |

| Literacy | Links |
|---|---|
| The word 'enlargement' in everyday English means that an object has grown in size. In mathematics, the word 'enlargement' also applies when the size is reduced, in which case the scale factor is a fraction (less than 1). | File sizes for images captured using a digital camera are usually too big to email or to post on a website, so the images have to be resized. Digital images are made up of pixels, one pixel being the smallest picture element. To resize an image, the resolution of the picture is changed so that it is displayed using fewer pixels. The more pixels that are used to represent an image, the more closely the image will resemble the original. There are examples of resized images at www.shrinkpictures.com/examples.php |

## Alternative approach

Place a rectangular piece of card in the beam of light from a projector onto a screen. Measure the sides of the rectangle and its image on the screen and calculate the scale factor of the enlargement. Alter the position of the card and repeat. Discuss how position affects scale factor. Discuss how the screen needs to be at right-angles to the light to get the same scale factor for all sides of the rectangle, which is a requirement for a true enlargment.

Use the enlargment facility on a computer to enlarge an image. Find the scale factor.

## Checkpoint

A rectangle measures 3cm by 5cm. It is enlarged by scale factor 2.5.

What are the dimensions are the enlargement? (7.5cm by 12.5cm)

What scale factor of enlargement would be needed to return the enlarged triangle back to its original size? (0.4)

**Starter** – Number rotations

Use these digits 0, 0, 1, 1, 6, 8, 8, 8, 9 to find:

• the highest number that can be made which reads the same when turned upside down; [981080186]

• the lowest odd number that can be made which reads the same when turned upside down.

[106888901]

Follow with questions from earlier chapters, especially questions about number concepts and skills.

## Teaching notes

Show the students two shapes, one an enlargement of the other. Explain that the 'scale factor' of enlargement is the number of times that one shape is bigger than the other. Find this scale factor by finding the multiplier which gives the image lengths from the object lengths. (The multiplier will likely be found by division but the use of the word 'multiplier' helps the concept of enlargement.)

Now do the opposite by using a given scale factor to draw an enlargement of a given shape. Repeat with different scale factors on the one diagram.

Explain that a reduction in the size of the object shape is obtained by performing an enlargement with a fractional scale factor. Demonstrate this with an example and then students draw the image of their shape under simple fractional enlargements. Choose object shapes with lengths of sides that divide easily (as in Question **4** of the exercise).

## Plenary

Using prepared examples, students identify the scale factors of various enlargements. They record their answers on mini whiteboards to enable quick assessment.

## Exercise commentary

Access to squared paper is useful.

**Question 1** – Students should not start to draw near the edge of their squared paper; they need to leave enough space to fit the images.

**Question 2** – Remind students that the diagrams are not drawn to scale.

**Question 3** – This question relates to enlargements where images are smaller than the objects, so the scale factors are fractions. Talk through the purpose of the calculations; for example, reducing the size by 2 is the same as halving the lengths, so $\div 2$ is the same as $\times \frac{1}{2}$.

**Question 4** – Students can count the squares along the perpendicular edges of the object triangle and calculate these lengths on the reduced triangle.

**Question 5** – Remind students that a mathematical enlargement enlarges all the lengths of a shape by the same scale factor.

## Answers

1 Check students' drawings
   a $3 \times 2 \rightarrow 6 \times 4$ rectangle
   b $2 \times 3 \rightarrow 6 \times 9$ triangle
   c $3 \times 3 \rightarrow 12 \times 12$ parallelogram
   d $3 \times 4 \rightarrow 6 \times 8$ arrow

2 a 3      b 4

3 a $\frac{1}{2}$      b $\frac{1}{3}$      c $\frac{1}{5}$

4 a Check students' drawings
   $12 \times 8 \rightarrow 3 \times 2$ triangle
   b 4

5 original $5 \times 15 \rightarrow$ enlargement $15 \times 45$

## Objectives

- Enlarge 2D shapes given a centre of enlargement and a positive integer scale factor. (L6)

| Key ideas | Resources |
|---|---|
| 1  Under an enlargement, the vertices of an object shape travel along 'rays' outwards from the centre.<br>2  The distances travelled along a 'ray' are determined by the scale factor of the enlargment. | Enlarging shapes  (1099)<br>Graph-drawing software<br>A pantograph<br>Squared paper<br>Mini whiteboards |

| Simplification | Extension |
|---|---|
| Students should work with simple geometrical shapes such as triangles and rectangles. Initially, provide pairs of object and image shapes so that they practise drawing rays to identify the centres of enlargement.<br><br>Then, they draw image shapes, given the object shape, a centre of enlargement and a scale factor. | Students draw a more complicated geometrical shape and challenge a partner to enlarge it by a given scale factor using a given centre.<br><br>Students explore enlargements with fractional scale factors. |

| Literacy | Links |
|---|---|
| The word 'ray' draws on the idea of light rays. If students saw a projector used in the previous lesson to create an image, remind them that the 'rays' of this lesson can be thought of as light rays.<br><br>The word 'pantograph' (which is an instrument for copying a drawing to a different scale) comes from Greek and means 'draws everything'. | Artists sometimes use a projector to enlarge a design to a required size and project it onto the surface to be painted. The size of the projected image depends on the distance of the projector lens from the design and on the distance from the projector to the image. The artist can then draw around the outline or paint over the image and thus transfer it to the surface to be decorated. There is a guide to using an artist's projector at www.art-is-fun.com/art-projector.html |

## Alternative approach

A pantograph is an instrument for copying a drawing to a different scale by using a system of hinged and jointed rods. (It is also the name given to the mechanical linkage above a tram or electric train to provide it with electricity.) Enter 'images of pantograph' into a search engine to see many different kinds. A simple pantograph can be bought cheaply and used in class to draw enlargements with integer and fractional scale factors.

## Checkpoint

A point P(2, 3) on an object shape is mapped to a point Q(3, 6) under an enlargement of scale factor two. Find the centre of enlargement. (A sketch or neat drawing may be useful)  (1, 0)

## Starter – Symmetry here and there

Challenge students to draw quadrilaterals where the order of rotational symmetry equals the number of lines of symmetry. [Possible solutions: 1 = isosceles trapezium, 2 = rectangle, 3 is impossible, 4 = square]

Continue with questions on earlier topics such as mental calculations and number work with decimals, fractions and percentages. Students respond on mini whiteboards.

## Teaching notes

Explain how to draw an enlargement using a given scale factor and centre of enlargement. Use 'rays' emanating from the centre through the vertices of the object and then multiplying the distances along the 'rays' by the given scale factors to find vertices of the image. Students draw their own images using squared paper.

The next task is to find the centre of enlargement given the positions of the object and image. Students draw the 'rays' through corresponding vertices of the object and image and extend them back until they all meet at one point. This point is the centre of the enlargement. They also find the scale factor of the enlargement either by measuring the sides of the object and image, or measuring how far corresponding points on the object and image are from the centre of enlargement.

## Plenary

Show students enlargements (with 'rays') which are drawn with labelled axes on grids. Students find the scale factor and the coordiantes of the centre of enlargement. They record their answers on mini whiteboards to enable easy assessment.

## Exercise commentary

Some students may benefit from using pre-drawn axes. Sharp pencils are required.

**Question 1** – When copying the diagram make sure students leave enough space to fit the images on their paper. Stress that all the distances measured from the centre of enlargement are doubled. The doubling can be done either by using a ruler, the results of which are not always accurate, or by counting squares across and up (that is, using the idea of a vector) and doubling the count.

**Question 2** – When copying the diagram make sure students leave enough space to fit the images on their paper. In this case the distances are trebled rather than doubled.

**Questions 3** and **4** – The questions need diagrams with sufficient space to find the centre (in question **3**) and the image (in question **4**).

**Question 5** – In this question the scale factor is a fraction. Allow students to ponder on this question before offering intervention. The question provides a good assessment opportunity.

## Answers

**1**

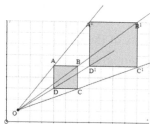

**2**

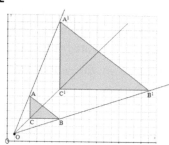

**3**  **a**  3          **b**  (6.5, 3)
**4**  Rectangle with vertices at (2,1), (-4, 1), (2, -3), (-4, -3)
**5**  **a**  0.5
       **b**

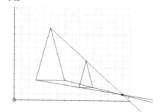

## Objectives

- Make and use scale drawings. (L6)

| Key ideas | Resources |
|---|---|
| 1  A scale drawing can represent an object which is larger or smaller than the scale drawing.<br><br>2  A scale is needed, but not a centre of enlargement. | Map scales (1103)<br>Scale drawing (1117)<br>Squared paper<br>Metre rules and tape measures<br>Maps of the local area<br>Mini whiteboards |

| Simplification | Extension |
|---|---|
| Give students simple examples of shapes which they are to make scale drawings of. These could be as simple as rectangles of various lengths needing to be drawn accurately up to stylized garden plots or rooms. Ensure that the scales given are easy to use, such as 1 : 10. | Students complete a scale drawing which requires the use of a pair of compasses, for example a garden design which contains a pond, trees, even sections of the border which are arcs from circles. |

| Literacy | Links |
|---|---|
| A scale drawing is an accurate plan but, technically, it is not a mathematical enlargement as it doesn't need a centre of enlargement.<br><br>The scale can be written in two ways.<br>One way is to use an 'equals sign' with units, such as 1 cm = 5 metres.<br>The other way is to use a colon, as in the student's book, for example, 1cm : 5 metres. Often no units are given with this method, as with 1 : 500, because the same units are used on both sides of the colon.<br><br>Maps have scales called 'representative fractions' (which is sortened to just 'RF') which are written as either 1 : 50 000 or 1/50 000. | The Angel of the North is a steel sculpture of an angel which overlooks the A1 main road at Gateshead on Tyneside. The sculpture was unveiled in 1988 and was designed by Antony Gormley. It stands 20 m tall and has a wingspan of 54 m. The 1 : 16 scale model originally used for fundraising for the statue was the first item ever to be valued at £1million on the BBC television programme *Antiques Roadshow* in 2008. There is more information about the Angel of the North at www.gateshead.gov.uk/Leisure%20and%20Culture/attractions/Angel/Home.aspx |

## Alternative approach

Maps are a fertile source of real life material. Using maps of the local area may involve a scale such as 1 : 10 000. It is good revision to convert this scale to 1 cm = 100 metres or 1 mm = 10 metres. Groups of students can be given maps (perhaps borrowed from the geography department) to measure in millimetres and convert to metres, or whatever units are appropriate for the maps being used. Calculators may need to be used.

Students can measure the classroom, the school hall or a room at home, decide on a scale and make a scale drawing.

## Checkpoint

A scale drawing of a rectangular room is made to a scale of 1: 20. If the drawing is 20 cm by 15 cm, find, in metres, the dimensions of the room.                    (4 m by 3 m)

## Starter – Growing letters

Ask students to draw the initial letter of their first or last name using straight lines. Then ask them to mark a centre of enlargement and, using ray lines, enlarge their letter by a scale factor of 2.

## Teaching notes

Explain to students that a scale drawing is simply an enlargement (or reduction) of an object or shape.

Organise students into groups or pairs and explain that they are going to produce scale drawings of various items within the classroom, possibly even the room itself.

Provide the students with metre rules or tape measures and ask them to select various things in the room and produce scale drawings. The scales used in each case should be appropriate and students can be advised as to what scales to use. Typically 1 m : 1 cm or 10 cm : 1 cm will be appropriate for objects in and around the classroom.

Students could even complete a full scale drawing of the classroom and its contents.

## Plenary

Give students various examples of scale drawings and ask them to identify the scales used. Students can record their answers on mini whiteboards to enable easy assessment.

## Exercise commentary

Provide general support by discussing examples of scale drawings and the purpose they serve.

**Question 1** – Make sure that students do not miss the scale which is stated under each drawing. Draw attention to the different scale in each question. Students do not need to draw the scale drawing.

**Question 2** – Make sure that students are secure in multiplying decimals.

**Question 3** – Students can find the required length by division or use a 'couplet' to spot the factor.

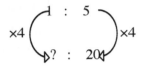

**Question 4** – Provide students with centimetre-squared paper.

## Answers

see master Answers file

| Key outcomes | Quick check |
|---|---|
| Recognise reflection and rotational symmetry of 2D shapes.          L5 | Write down the number of lines of symmetry and the order of rotational symmetry for a regular decagon.          (10, 10) |
| Reflect shapes in mirror lines.          L5 | Write down the image of the point (-2, 1) after<br><br>**a** A reflection in the *x*-axis (-2, -1) **b** A reflection in the line *y* = *x* (-1, -2) |
| Use vectors to translate shapes in any direction.          L5 | Write the image of the point (4, 1) after a translation by vector $\begin{pmatrix} 5 \\ -2 \end{pmatrix}$<br><br>(9, -1) |
| Rotate shapes from a centre of rotation.          L5 | Write down the image of the point (-1, 0) after<br><br>**a** A 180° rotation about the origin (1, 0) **b** A 90° anti-clockwise rotation about the origin (0, -1) |
| Enlarge shapes using whole number and fractional scale factors.          L5 | A rectangle is enlarged from 2.5cm by 6cm to one 7.5cm by 18cm. What is the scale factor of enlargement? (3)<br><br>What scale factor would be required to return the enlargement to the original size? ($\frac{1}{3}$) |
| Enlarge shapes from a centre of enlargement.          L6 | A triangle A(2, 1), B(4, 1) and C(4, 3) is enlarged by scale factor 2 about the origin. Write down the coordinates of the image. (A'(4, 2), B'(8, 2) and C'(8, 6)) |
| Use ratio and draw scale drawings.          L6 | How long would the following roads be on a map drawn to the scale 1: 25000?<br><br>**a** 2km (8cm) **b** 1.6km (6.4cm) **c** 0.5km (2cm) |

## ⊕ MyMaths extra support

| Lesson/online homework | Description |
|---|---|
| Symmetry          1230   L3 | Looking at shapes that are symmetrical. Simple reflection in a mirror line |
| Tessellation tool          6001   L4 | Make your own tessellations with this lesson |

# My Review

## Check out

**You should now be able to ...**

**Test it**
Questions

✓ Recognise reflection and rotational symmetry of 2D shapes.  (5)  1

✓ Reflect shapes in mirror lines.  (5)  2

✓ Use vectors to translate shapes in any direction.  (5)  3

✓ Rotate shapes from a centre of rotation.  (5)  4

✓ Enlarge shapes using whole number and fractional scale factors.  (5)  5

✓ Enlarge shapes from a centre of enlargement.  (5)  6

✓ Use and draw scale drawings.  (3)  7

| Language | Meaning | Example |
|---|---|---|
| Clockwise/ Anticlockwise | These are directions you can turn. It is the same/opposite direction to the hands on a clock. | clockwise  anticlockwise |
| Line of symmetry | A line which divides a shape into two halves which are the mirror image of each other. | A rectangle has 2 lines of symmetry. |
| Mirror line | A line in which you reflect a shape. | |
| Order of rotational symmetry | The number of times a shape looks exactly the same as itself during a complete turn. | A rectangle has rotational symmetry order 2. |
| Scale factor | Tells you by how many times to change each side of the shape. | A scale factor 2 tells you to draw each side twice as long. |
| Vector | A vector tells you how far to move a shape. | $\binom{4}{-5}$ move shape 4 units right move shape 5 units down |

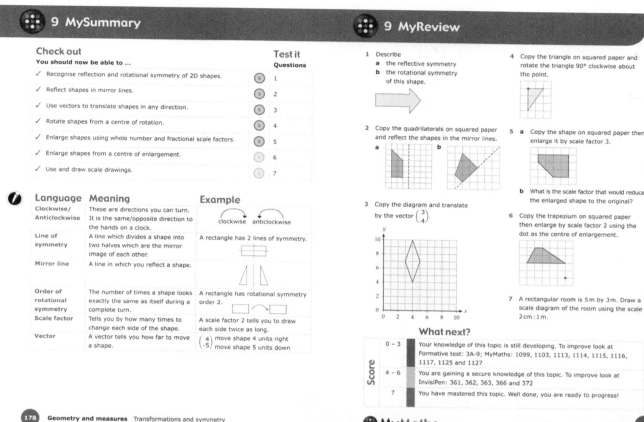

1 Describe
   a the reflective symmetry
   b the rotational symmetry of this shape.

2 Copy the quadrilaterals on squared paper and reflect the shapes in the mirror lines.
   a      b

3 Copy the diagram and translate by the vector $\binom{3}{-4}$.

4 Copy the triangle on squared paper and rotate the triangle 90° clockwise about the point.

5 a Copy the shape on squared paper then enlarge it by scale factor 3.
   b What is the scale factor that would reduce the enlarged shape to the original?

6 Copy the trapezium on squared paper then enlarge by scale factor 2 using the dot as the centre of enlargement.

7 A rectangular room is 5m by 3m. Draw a scale diagram of the room using the scale 2cm:1m.

### What next?

| Score | | |
|---|---|---|
| | 0 – 3 | Your knowledge of this topic is still developing. To improve look at Formative test: 3A-9; MyMaths: 1099, 1103, 1113, 1114, 1115, 1116, 1117, 1125 and 1127 |
| | 4 – 6 | You are gaining a secure knowledge of this topic. To improve look at InvisiPen: 361, 362, 363, 366 and 372 |
| | 7 | You have mastered this topic. Well done, you are ready to progress! |

**MyMaths**.co.uk

## Question commentary

**Question 1** – Check students do not give the order of rotational symmetry as zero.

**Question 2** – Students should check their mirror line is a line of symmetry of the finished diagram

**Question 3** – Check that students correctly move the shape *down* in the *y* direction.

**Question 4** – Tracing paper can be used in this question.

**Question 5** – No centre of enlargement is given so students can draw their image anywhere on their page.

**Question 6** – Ensure sufficient room is left in which to draw the image of this enlargement.

**Question 7** – Check that students are working in consistent units since the scale is given in mixed units.

## Answers

see master Answers file

# 9 MyPractice

**9a**

1  a  Describe the reflection and rotation symmetry of the shape.
   b  Shade two more squares on the shape so that it has rotation symmetry of order 4.
   c  How many lines of symmetry does the shape in part **b** have?

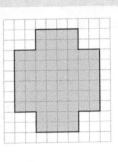

**9b**

2  a  Reflect the triangle A, in the *x*-axis. Label the image B.
   b  Reflect the new image B in the *y*-axis. Label this new image C.
   c  What are the coordinates of image C?

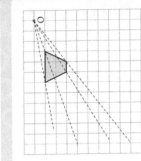

**9c**

3  Write down the vector which translates the YELLOW dot to the positions of the other coloured dots.

Write,  yellow to black  →  $\binom{4}{5}$

yellow to green  → .........
yellow to white  → .........
yellow to brown  → .........
yellow to purple  → .........
yellow to blue  → .........
yellow to orange  → .........
yellow to red  → .........

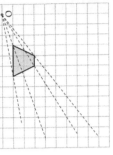

**9d**

4  a  Copy the 'T' shape and position the centre of rotation O. Rotate the 'T' shape through 180°. Label the image T₁.
   b  Reflect the image, T₁ in the blue dotted mirror line. Label the image T₂.

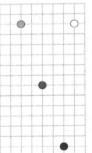

---

**9e**

5  a  What is the perimeter of the shape?
   b  Reduce the shape by a scale factor of $\frac{1}{2}$.
   c  What is the perimeter of the reduced image?

**9f**

6  Copy the trapezium carefully.
   Position the centre of enlargement in exactly the right place.
   By drawing lines from the centre O, enlarge the shape by a scale factor of 2.

**9g**

7  Draw straight lines to these scales.
   a  36m to a scale of 1cm : 6m
   b  200m to a scale of 1cm : 40m
   c  40km to a scale of 2cm : 5km
   d  100m to a scale of 3cm : 25m
   e  28m to a scale of 3cm : 7m

8  a  Measure the lengths of this 'L' shape to the nearest millimetre.

   b  Calculate the true perimeter of this shape if the scale of the drawing is 1cm : 4m.

**MyMaths**.co.uk

## Question commentary

**Question 1** – A printed copy of the diagram might be useful for part **b**.

**Question 2** – Students could be asked to give the equations of the mirror lines used in parts **a** and **b** to reinforce work on horizontal and vertical lines in **6a**.

**Question 3** – Check students are writing the vectors the right way up and using negative signs as appropriate.

**Question 4 –** Students could be asked to describe the transformation that takes the final image back to the original shape.

vector translation of $\begin{pmatrix} 5 \\ -1 \end{pmatrix}$

**Question 5** – Students could work out the dimensions of the image by counting squares.

**Question 6** – The ray lines are already drawn on the diagram so students could simply be given a printed copy of the diagram.

**Questions 7** and **8** – Check that students are working in consistent units where the scale is mixed.

## Answers

see master Answers file

| Related lessons | | Resources | |
|---|---|---|---|
| Percentage of a quantity | 4f | Percentage change | (1060) |
| Percentage problems | 4g | Change as a percentage | (1302) |
| Interpreting real-life graphs | 6f | Conversion graphs | (1059) |
| Time series graphs | 6g | Real life graphs | (1184) |
| Pie charts | 8e | Drawing pie charts | (1207) |
| Calculating averages | 8f | Mean and mode | (1200) |
| | | Median and range | (1203) |
| | | Literature on global warming | |

| Simplification | Extension |
|---|---|
| Often students are vague with their justifications in data tasks like this. A writing frame could be used for tasks **3a**, **4c** and **4d** to help students structure their answers. Making sensible predictions is often difficult and in this repect students may need guidance on how to approach task **2c**. The values given in the table in task **4** can be rounded to the nearest whole number to make it easier for the students to calculate the ranges and means. | Ask if two sets of data are really sufficient to draw conclusions. Discuss how one or both of the years chosen might have freak temperatures, maybe having a particularly warm summer or cold winter. Looking at the data, do they think this is the case? Establish that you could compare other pairs of years that are 100 years apart, such as 1907 and 2007. Students could also research information about carbon footprints, maybe using one of the online calculators to measure their own footprint. |

**Links**

New Scientist magazine has lots of interesting articles on climate change on their website:
http://www.newscientist.com/topic/climate-change

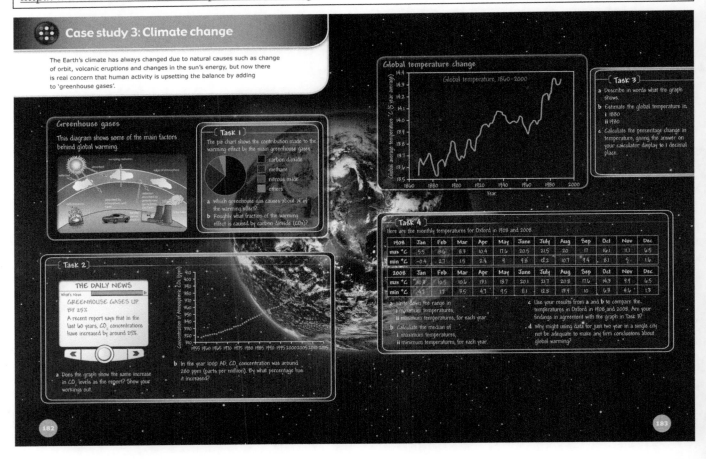

## Teaching notes

This case study provides a limited amount of information about greenhouse gases and temperatures, leaving students to draw their own conclusions from the data.

Discuss how the greenhouse effect is needed to keep the Earth at a habitable temperature. Use the diagram to talk about the main processes involved:

– Most of the energy that the Earth receives from the Sun is in the form of visible light.

– Some of the energy is directly absorbed by the atmosphere and some is reflected off the top of the atmosphere, but as the atmosphere is fairly transparent to visible light, most of the energy passes through the atmosphere.

– The heat absorbed by the Earth warms it up. The warmed Earth radiates heat back to the atmosphere, but this time in the infrared range rather than as visible light.

– The infrared energy radiated from the Earth does not pass through the atmosphere. Instead, the energy is absorbed by the atmosphere, heating it up.

– The warmed atmosphere then radiates some of its heat back to Earth and some of it out into space.

A balance of heat gains and heat losses maintains the Earth at a habitable temperature. Ensure that students realise that the greenhouse effect is not a bad thing. Without it, Earth would be too cold to sustain life. Much reporting of climate change makes it sound as if the greenhouse effect is in some way bad, rather than the problem being that the balance of heat gains and losses could be changing.

### Task 1

Look at the pie chart and establish that carbon dioxide has the greatest effect on warming. Then look at the report describing how $CO_2$ levels have risen. Introduce the idea of human activity altering the levels of greenhouse gases. Ask questions such as; what things do you know about that increase the $CO_2$ levels in the atmosphere?

### Task 2

Give students a few minutes to work on the questions relating to the report and $CO_2$ levels graph before asking: if $CO_2$ levels have increased, what is likely to have happened to temperatures? Hear students' thoughts. Establish that it is likely that temperatures will have risen as $CO_2$ has the greatest warming effect of the greenhouse gases.

### Task 3

Look at the global temperatures graph and ask; what does the vertical axis show? What do you think is happening with the temperature? Some may mention that temperatures went down steadily for several years beginning about 1915, despite greater industrial activity and increasing motorised transport at the time.

### Task 4

Looking quickly at the data, do you think there has been much change in Oxford's temperatures in the past 100 years? They could argue that temperatures have increased, giving reasons such as Jan 2008 being much warmer than Jan 1908. They could argue that temperatures haven't changed very much, giving

reasons such as July in both years being very similar and December in both years being very similar.

What could we do with the data to get a better idea of any changes? Talk about their answers and decide as a class whether you think there is any change in Oxford temperatures and whether this mirrors the change in global temperatures.

### Answers

1  a  Methane  b  $\frac{5}{8}$ or 60%

2  a  Yes, there was about a 30% increase.

   b  43%

   c  Students' own answers but somewhere in the region of 2115.

3  a  There is a general upward trend. Temperatures appear to be rising.

   b  i 13.6°C      ii 14.2°C

   c  4.4%

4  a  i 1908: 16°C, 2008: 15.2°C

     ii 1908: 12.6°C, 2008: 12.6°C

   b  i  1908: 13.59 °C, 2008: 14.51 °C

     ii  1908: 6.00°C, 2008: 7.01 °C

   c  Students' opinions: generally yes, both have increased.

   d  Students' opinions: The two years could be 'freak' years and looking at more pairs across more cities would improve reliability.

**A3** Understand and use the concepts and vocabulary of expressions, equations, inequalities, terms and factors
(L5)

**A4** Simplify and manipulate algebraic expressions to maintain equivalence by:
- collecting like terms
- multiplying a single term over a bracket
- taking out common factors
(L5/6)

**A6** Model situations or procedures by translating them into algebraic expressions or formulae and by using graphs
(L6)

**A7** Use algebraic methods to solve linear equations in 1 variable (including all forms that require rearrangement)
(L5/6)

## Introduction

The chapter starts by looking at the mathematical principles of equality and inequality. Solving simple one-step and two-step equations are the covered, including ones which require simplification first. Constructing equations from a given context (and solving them) is covered in the final section.

The introduction discusses the widespread use of equations in everyday, scientific contexts. The use of equations and mathematical formulae is an essential part of any scientific research and modelling. In fact Eric Temple Bell wrote a book in 1931 entitled 'The Queen of the Sciences' in which the importance of mathematics in a scientific context was discussed. He followed this up with the sequel 'The Handmaiden of the Sciences' in 1937. This book rather looked at mathematics as a tool which is used by scientists rather than as a fundamental underpinning what is necessary for science to even exist. Whatever your view, there is no doubt that the examples given in the introduction are all important cases for the scientific and other fields mentioned. Further examples can be given as part of the discussion of these ideas as required.

## Prior knowledge

Students should already know how to…
- Perform simple arithmetic
- Write down simple functions shown as machines

## Starter problem

The starter problem is a spider diagram showing a simple equation which has been modified in six different ways. Students are invited to describe the six changes and continue each one a further step.

In order, clockwise from top left:

- 1 has been subtracted from both sides
- both sides have been doubled
- 1 has been added to both sides
- $x$ has been added to both sides
- both sides have been halved
- $x$ has been subtracted from both sides

Students are then directed to invent some changes of their own. These could be further examples of changes to the original equation given, or they could be invited to make up their own equation and complete a similar exercise to this one.

## Resources

**MyMaths**

| | | | | | |
|---|---|---|---|---|---|
| Simple equations | 1154 | Rules and formulae | 1158 | Solving equations | 1182 |

| **Online assessment** | | **InvisiPen solutions** | | | |
|---|---|---|---|---|---|
| Chapter test | 3A–10 | Making equations | 231 | Inequality symbols | 232 |
| Formative test | 3A–10 | Balancing equations | 233 | One-step equations | 234 |
| Summative test | 3A–10 | Two-step equations | 235 | Unknowns on both sides | 237 |

# Topic scheme

Teaching time = 5 lessons/2 weeks

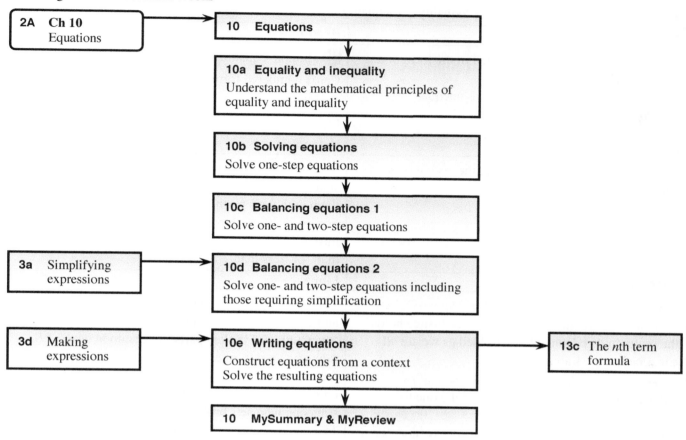

**2A Ch 10**
Equations

**10 Equations**

**10a Equality and inequality**
Understand the mathematical principles of equality and inequality

**10b Solving equations**
Solve one-step equations

**10c Balancing equations 1**
Solve one- and two-step equations

**3a Simplifying expressions**

**10d Balancing equations 2**
Solve one- and two-step equations including those requiring simplification

**3d Making expressions**

**10e Writing equations**
Construct equations from a context
Solve the resulting equations

**13c** The $n$th term formula

**10 MySummary & MyReview**

# Differentiation

| Student book 3A 184 – 199 | Student book 3B 180 – 195 | Student book 3C 176 – 195 |
|---|---|---|
| Equality and inequality<br>Solving simple equations<br>Solve equations by balancing<br>Write down and solve equations given in context | Solve one- and two- step equations<br>Solve equations involving brackets<br>Solve equations with the unknown on both sides<br>Construct equations from contexts and solve them<br>Solve equations using trial and improvement | Consolidation of linear equations<br>Forming and solving pairs of simultaneous equations<br>Solving simultaneous equations graphically<br>Solving inequalities<br>Solving equations using trial and improvement |

| Objectives | |
|---|---|
| • Know the meaning of the words 'equality', 'inequality' and 'equation'. | (L4) |

| Key ideas | Resources |
|---|---|
| **1** An equation is a relation written in the form of an equality of two expressions. <br> **2** An inequality is a relation of two unequal expressions. | ⊕ Simple equations       (1154) <br> Cards numbered form 1 to 20 <br> True/False cards <br> Mini whiteboards |

| Simplification | Extension |
|---|---|
| Keep the arithmetic simple so that the notion of two equal expressions has priority. | Students work in pairs and make their own equality statements such as those in Question **4**. They exchange them with their partners who find the missing numbers. For inequalities, they find the range of values for the missing number to make the statement either 'greater than' or 'less than'. |

| Literacy | Links |
|---|---|
| The balanced scales are a symbol of 'equality'. See also the statue on the Old Bailey. Lady Justice holds the scales and is depicted blindfolded as we are all equal before the Law. <br><br> It may not be obvious to some students that, for unbalanced scales, the heavier pan is the one to descend. <br><br> The prefix 'in-' used in 'inequality' means 'not', as in other words such as 'invalid', 'inadequate', 'inaction'. Compare with words where 'in-' means 'in', such as 'inside', 'inhabit', 'ingredient'. | The word 'algebra' is only used today in mathematics and comes from the Arabic word *al jabr*, which means 'the reunion of broken parts'. In common usage, *al-jabr* was used to refer to a bonesetter, or someone who reunited broken bones. In the book *Don Quixote*, completed in 1615, the author Cervantes refers to someone who sets broken bones as an *algebrista*. There is more about Don Quixote at http://en.wikipedia.org/wiki/Don_Quixote |

| Alternative approach |
|---|
| Students work in pairs. Each has a set of cards numbered from 1 to 20. One student selects two cards and writes the values as an addition sum (that is □ + □ ). The second student selects one card and completes the equality by finding mentally the fourth value which adds or subtracts to make the equality; that is □ + □ = □ … . They change roles and repeat the activity. <br><br> A second activity is where both students select two cards each. They each add their cards and agree how to complete the statement □ + □ … □ + □ by inserting one of the symbols <, > or =. |

| Checkpoint | |
|---|---|
| Find the missing numbers in these equations: | |
| **a** $13 + 7 = 6 + \square$ | (14) |
| **b** $7 \times 6 = \square \div 2$ | (84) |

## Starter – True or false

Write the following on the board and ask students which are true and which are false.

$m + n + m + n = 2m + 2n$ [T]    $8a - 5a = 5$ [F]
$g + g + g + g = 4g$ [T]    $3c \times 2d = 6cd$ [T]
$e + 2f + 3e + 4f = 4e + 6f$ [T]    $a - 2a + 3a = 2a$ [T]
$m + 2n - m - n = 5$ [F]    $10c \div 5 = 2$ [F]

These can be followed by questions on other algebra topics, such as simple substitutions and expansion of brackets.

## Teaching notes

Define 'equality' and 'inequality' using a series of numerical examples; for example $2 \times 3 = 1 \times 6$ and $3 \times 4 \neq 2 \times 7$. Emphasise the correct use of the 'equal to' sign and the 'not equal to' sign. Use inequality symbols when comparing two values; for example $3 \times 4 < 2 \times 7$. Recall that the open end of the $<$ and $>$ signs indicate the larger side. Explain that when two things are equal, we get an 'equation'.

Use mini white boards in a whole-class session to insert one of the signs $<$, $>$ or $=$ into statements such as $12 \times 2 \ \square \ 18 + 5$. Also ask true/false questions. Students' responses indicate the degree of their understanding.

## Plenary

As earlier in the lesson, so also in the plenary session, true/false quick-fire questions can be used with responses written on mini whiteboards.

Students can also do quick-fire 'fill in the blanks' questions on mini whiteboards.

## Exercise commentary

This exercise is used to prepare students for solving equations. Use the exercise to consolidate the notion of balancing the LHS and RHS.

**Questions 1** and **3** – Students must know the meaning of the signs $=$, $\neq$, $>$ and $<$.

**Questions 2** and **5** – Mental number skills may be sufficient to find the answers; if not, then students should practise their written methods.

**Question 4** – This question requires students to balance the equation by adding the correct number to the box. Generally, they should work out the calculation on the left hand side and then use inverse operations.

## Answers

| | | | | | | | | |
|---|---|---|---|---|---|---|---|---|
| **1** | a | $=$ | b | $\neq$ | c | $=$ | d | $\neq$ |
| | e | $\neq$ | f | $=$ | g | $=$ | h | $=$ |
| | i | $\neq$ | | | | | | |

| | | | | |
|---|---|---|---|---|
| **2** | a | No | b | Yes |

| | | | | | | | | |
|---|---|---|---|---|---|---|---|---|
| **3** | a | True | b | True | c | False | d | False |
| | e | False | f | True | g | True | h | False |
| | i | True | | | | | | |

| | | | | | | | | |
|---|---|---|---|---|---|---|---|---|
| **4** | a | 6 | b | 2 | c | 5 | d | 4 |
| | e | 12 | f | 5 | g | 20 | h | 5 |
| | i | 5 | | | | | | |

| | | | | |
|---|---|---|---|---|
| **5** | a | 18 on the left | b | 7 on the left |
| | c | 4 on the right | d | 1 on the left |

| | | |
|---|---|---|
| **6** | a | Move 2 from the left to the right |
| | b | Move 3 from the right to the left |

## Objectives

- Construct and solve simple linear equations with integer coefficients with the unknown on one side only using an appropriate inverse operation. (L5)

| Key ideas | Resources |
|---|---|
| 1  An equation can be thought of as function machine.<br>2  Solving an equation uses inverse operations. | ⊞  Simple equations (1154)<br><br>Dice<br><br>Computer spreadsheet<br><br>Mini whiteboards |

| Simplification | Extension |
|---|---|
| Ensure the arithmetic is straightforward so that the focus is on solving equations rather than doing the arithmetic. Students draw the diagram before solving the equation. | Give the students problems which do not have integer solutions and expect them to work in either fractions or decimals.<br>Have students use two-stage function machines. |

| Literacy | Links |
|---|---|
| The 'language' of mathematics in this lesson involves the use of a diagrammatic representation which is equivalent to an algebraic representation involving an unknown value.<br><br>The letters LHS and RHS are common abbreviations for 'left-hand side' and 'right-hand' side. | Secret messages are usually written in code to prevent anyone who intercepts the message from being able to read it. Ciphering and deciphering a message are examples of inverse operations. There is an introduction to ciphers at www.quadibloc.com/crypto/intro.htm |

## Alternative approach

An alternative, if rather a sledgehammer approach is to set up a spreadsheet for multiple inputs and see which input gives the required output. Though a long method, it shows a spreadsheet at work and shows how simple, by comparison, the inverse function is as a method. So, enter 1 into cell A1 and set up a formula with cell A2 = A1 + 1, dragged down by, say, 40 cells. Then set up a formula with cell B1 = A1 + 19 (for Question **2i**) or B1 = A1*2 (for Question **2ii**) and drag it down. Column B gives the outputs. Select the input for the required output.

## Checkpoint

Solve:

**a** $15 + x = 27$ (12)

**b** $12y = 84$ (7)

**Starter** – Dice challenge

Ask students to draw five boxes in a line representing two pairs of unknown values separated by the middle box. Throw a dice four times. After each throw, ask students to place the score in one of the four boxes allocated for numbers. Students then work out the sum of the first and second box and the product of the fourth and fifth box, finally entering <, > or = in the middle box; for example, $4 + 6 > 2 \times 4$.

Repeat using a dice with more sides.

## Teaching notes

Explain that, if two expressions are equal to each other, they can be written as an equation. Introduce the idea of a function machine where an unknown input value becomes a known output value. When this operation is reversed, it is known as an 'inverse operation'. Students should know the inverse of each of the four standard operations.

Write down a simple equation such as $x + 12 = 20$ and explain that the objective is to find the value of the 'unknown $x$'. Use an inverse operation. On the left-hand side, there is '+12', so we need the inverse operation '−12'. Draw a function machine for both operations and so find the value of $x$ as 8.

Students can create their own simple equations and ask a partner to solve them.

## Plenary

Students in turn create equations for the class to solve. Mini whiteboards are used to display answers. Discuss answers where appropriate.

## Exercise commentary

**Questions 1** and **2** – Check the answers to these questions before students begin on question **3**.

**Questions 3** and **4** – Students should still use inverse operations. In question **4**, explain that the order on the left-hand side of parts **a**, **b** and **e** makes no difference to the method, because, for example, $12 + t$ has the same value as $t + 12$.

**Question 5** – This question is a good one to develop as a class discussion on appropriate inverse operations.

**Question 6** – The operations in these equations are multiplication and division. Students need to know the inverse operations.

**Question 7** – Can students write the situation as an equation before they solve it? Part **b** may be found naturally through solving part **a**.

## Answers

| | | | | | | | | |
|---|---|---|---|---|---|---|---|---|
| **1** | **i** | $-21$ | **ii** | $\times 9$ | **iii** | $\div 10$ | **iv** | $+25$ |
| **2** | **i** | 21 | **ii** | 15 | **iii** | 100 | **iv** | 100 |
| | **v** | 10 | **vi** | 0 | | | | |
| **3** | **a** | 3 | **b** | 9 | **c** | 30 | **d** | 8 |
| | **e** | 50 | **f** | 20 | | | | |
| **4** | **a** | 8 | **b** | 22 | **c** | 21 | **d** | 15 |
| | **e** | 40 | **f** | 30 | | | | |

**5** Sammy is right because $56 \div 8 = 7$

| | | | | | | | | |
|---|---|---|---|---|---|---|---|---|
| **6** | **a** | 10 | **b** | 3 | **c** | 16 | **d** | 4 |
| | **e** | 15 | **f** | 50 | **g** | 4 | **h** | 6 |
| | **i** | 8 | **j** | 15 | **k** | 3 | **l** | 60 |
| **7** | **a** | 45 g | **b** | 15 g | | | | |

## Objectives

- Solve simple linear equations with integer coefficients and the unknown on one side only using the method of 'balancing'. (L5)

| Key ideas | Resources |
|---|---|
| 1  An equation can be represented by two scale pans balancing.<br>2  Any operation on one side must be balanced by the same operation on the other side. | Solving equations (1182)<br>Old-style kitchen scales<br>Mini whiteboards |

| Simplification | Extension |
|---|---|
| Ensure the arithmetic is straightforward so that the focus is on solving equations rather than doing the arithmetic.<br><br>Students solve one-stage problems before moving on to simple two-stage problems. Restrict examples to those using multiplication and addition. | Ask students how they might physically represent, using a balance, an equation involving a subtraction, such as $3x - 2 = 10$. [One idea is a helium balloon fixed to one scale.]<br><br>They solve equations which require manipulation of fractions or decimals. |

| Literacy | Links |
|---|---|
| The worked example in the student's book has the steps $3x + 1 = 10$, $3x + 1 - 1 = 10 - 1$, $3x = 9$, $3x \div 3 = 9 \div 3$, $x = 3$.<br><br>Once the process of inverse operations is understood, the working can be condensed by doing the inverse operation mentally. The steps then become: $3x + 1 = 10$, $3x = 9$, $x = 3$ with the associated oral patter of 'Subtract 1 from both sides' and 'Divide both sides by 3'. | One of the events that female gymnasts perform is the balance beam. The balance beam is a rail 10 cm wide and 5 m long that is raised 1.2 m above the floor. Gymnasts perform a routine of leaps, turns and tumbling moves while balancing on the beam. There is a video of gymnast Olga Korbut on a balance beam during the 1972 Olympic games at www.olgakorbut.com/videos/ |

## Alternative approach

An alternative is to have a set of scales where objects and weights can accompany the oral explanation of the written symbols. Even if no physical scales are available (and a metre rule balanced on a pencil might suffice), then diagrams of scales alongside the algebraic working, as drawn in the student's book, will help students to understand what is happening with the symbols.

## Checkpoint

Solve:

a $2x + 5 = 23$ (9)

b $8a - 7 = 9$ (2)

## Starter – Match up

Ask students to match up six identities from the following twelve expressions. They could be written on cards with students working in pairs.

$$x + y + 3 + x - y + 1 \qquad 1 + 2x - 4 + 2x$$
$$3x + 3x + 3y - 3x \qquad 4x + 2 - 2x + 2$$
$$2x - 4x + 4 \qquad 2x + y + x + 3y$$
$$2y + 2 + y - 2 + 3x \qquad x - y + x$$
$$4x + 2y - 2x - 3y \qquad 2y - x + 2y + 4x$$
$$3 - x + 1 - x \qquad 2x + x - 1 + x - 2$$

$[x + y + 3 + x - y + 1 = 4x + 2 - 2x + 2 \; (= 2x + 4);$
$1 + 2x - 4 + 2x = 2x + x - 1 + x - 2 \; (= 4x - 3);$
$3x + 3x + 3y - 3x = 2y + 2 + y - 2 + 3x \; (= 3x + 3y);$
$2x - 4x + 4 = 3 - x + 1 - x \; (= 4 - 2x)$
$2x + y + x + 3y = 2y - x + 2y + 4x \; (= 3x + 4y)$
$x - y + x = 4x + 2y - 2x - 3y \; (= 2x - y)]$

## Teaching notes

Recap what an equation is and how to solve simple ones using inverse operations. Start with a few word problems such as "I think of a number …".

Then introduce a more complicated equation involving two operations and written in the standard way, such as $3x + 2 = 14$. Describe it in words as "Three lots of $x$ add an extra 2 equals 14" or in context as "Three identical boxes of unknown weight and an extra 2 kg balance with 14 kg".

Explain that, in order to solve equations of this type, we still use inverse operations but we do so in two steps. Emphasise that they should first get the term with the unknown ($3x$ in this case) by itself. To get rid of the 2 on the LHS, ask students for the inverse of '+ 2'. They perform the inverse on both sides of the equation to keep it balanced. Set the working out as in the example in the student's book.

The second stage is to get the unknown by itself. Remind students that $3x = 12$ means $3 \times x = 12$ and to get rid of the 3 requires another inverse operation. Ask students for the inverse of '×3'.

## Plenary

Recap the key points about the use of inverse operations on both sides of the equation to keep it balanced. Provide one-stage and then two-stage equations for students to solve mentally. Mini whiteboards are used for answers and immediate feedback.

## Exercise commentary

**Question 1** – Students will benefit from expressing at least one of the problems as a formal equation. For example, for part **a**, students should write $3 \times l = 60$, where $l$ for the cost of one lemon. The simplicity of the problems will allow the teacher to explain how to divide the LHS and the RHS by the same number.

**Question 2** – abstract examples with the same structure as question **1**.

**Question 3** – Some students may not be familiar with physical balances. It would be good to show them an old-style kitchen balance. Write the steps for each equation as shown in the example in the student book. Doing so is a good introduction to Question **4**.

**Question 4** – Students must realise that there are two operations involved: multiplication and addition/subtraction. Diagrams of balances, as in question **3**, might be needed.

**Question 5** – This is a good question to stimulate class discussion on selecting the appropriate inverse operation.

**Question 6** – The equation could be written as $n + n + 1 + 1 + 1 + 1 + 1 = 35$ if students do not instantly see it as $2n + 5 = 35$.

## Answers

| 1 | a | 20p | b | £60 | c | 15 cm | d | 12.5kg |
|---|---|-----|---|-----|---|-------|---|--------|

| 2 | a | 4 | b | 4 | c | 7 | d | 15 |
|---|---|---|---|---|---|---|---|----|
|   | e | 2 | f | 3 | g | 5 | h | 5 |

| 3 | a | $3n = 9, n = 3$ | b | $4m = 20, m = 5$ |
|---|---|-----------------|---|------------------|
|   | c | $5x = 10, x = 2$ | d | $2t + 3 = 7, t = 2$ |
|   | e | $3x + 1 = 10, x = 3$ | f | $3p + 5 = 20, p = 5$ |

| 4 | a | 5 | b | 9 | c | 3 | d | 3 |
|---|---|---|---|---|---|---|---|---|
|   | e | 3 | f | 5 | g | 4 | h | 6 |
|   | i | 10 | j | 4 | k | 3 | l | 2 |

**5** She is wrong – she should have added 3 to both sides instead of subtracting 3.

| 6 | a | $2n + 5 = 35$ | b | 15 litres |
|---|---|---------------|---|-----------|

## Objectives

- Construct and solve linear equations with integer coefficients with unknowns on either or both sides using the method of 'balancing'. (L6)

| Key ideas | Resources |
|---|---|
| 1 Equations can have knowns and unknowns on both sides.<br>2 Any operation on one side must be balanced by the same operation on the other side. | Rotating shapes (1115)<br>Computer spreadsheet<br>Mini whiteboards |

| Simplification | Extension |
|---|---|
| In the first instance, restrict examples to those involving unknowns on only one side. Collect 'like terms' before looking to solve the equation. Once unknowns are introduced on both sides, aim to 'balance out' the unknowns by taking from both sides in equal quantities. | Introduce examples which involve negative terms, either letters or numbers; for example, $x + 2x - x + 6 = 12 - 4$ extending to $3x - 2 = x + 4$. |

| Literacy | Links |
|---|---|
| The overall strategy for solving equations with unknowns on both sides affects how the solution is set out.<br>The first step is to note which side has the most unknowns (it is usually the LHS) and eliminate as many unknowns from both sides so that one side no longer has any.<br>The second step is to eliminate whatever value is added or subtracted from the remaining unknowns, so that remaining unknowns are by themselves.<br>The last step is to reduce the number of unknowns by division so that only one is left. | Equations are used in chemistry as a form of shorthand to describe the changes that occur during a chemical reaction. The substances reacting (reactants) are shown on the left-hand side of the equation with an arrow pointing to the chemicals formed (products) on the right. The equation must account for every atom that is used, so there must be the same number of atoms of each element on both sides of the equation.<br>There is more information about chemical equations at www.chemtutor.com/react.htm |

## Alternative approach

A heavy-handed method to solve an equation is to use a spreadsheet. For example, to solve Question **2e**, label three columns $n$, $2n + 20$, $n + 35$ in row A. Put the value 1 into cell A2. Set up a formula so that cell A3 = A2 + 1 and drag it down to give increasing values of $n$. Then set up formulae for cells B1 and C1 using the value in cell A1 – these formulae are the LHS and RHS of the equation. Drag these formulae down. Look down columns B and C for the same value and column A gives the solution, $n = 15$.

## Checkpoint

Solve:

**a** $3x + 2 = x + 8$ (3)

**b** $4x - 5 = 9x - 10$ (1)

## Starter – Quick fire

Recap work of previous chapters and this chapter so far. Ask students to solve simple equations such as $2x = 14$, $x - 5 = 2$ and $2x + 1 = 11$. Ask other rapid response questions with students responding on mini whiteboards. Discuss answers when there is a need.

## Teaching notes

Recap the idea of solving equations by balancing. Give an example of an equation which has the unknown on both sides of the equation such as $3x + 2 = x + 6$. Draw a picture of scales on a balance for this equation and explain that we first need to deal with the unknowns. There are three lots of $x$ on the left and only one on the right. So, we remove the one on the right and, to keep the balance, we also remove one of those on the left.

Once the equation is reduced to the form $2x + 2 = 6$, it is solved in the same way as the ones in the previous lesson, using inverse operations.

Each student, in pairs, invents an equation of this type and exchanges it for their partner to solve. They then agree or resolve any disagreement about the solutions.

## Plenary

Recap the key points for solving equations of this form. Give students equations to solve. They respond using mini whiteboards to display their working and their answers. Discuss any methods and solutions when necessary.

## Exercise commentary

**Question 1** – Students sketch the scales and then cross out, from both sides, the items which can be taken away while maintaining a balance. In part **c** for the first time, there are more unknowns on the RHS.

**Question 2** – Exemplify by demonstrating how to balance both sides by using the same inverse operation on each side. Discuss how to choose the most appropriate inverse to use and in the most efficient order. Discuss at some point that, no matter what operation is used, it is vital to treat both sides equally; that is, 'do the same to both sides'. In parts **a** to **d**, allow students to solve without collecting 'like terms' on both sides.

**Questions 3** and **4** – Continue the same strategies.

**Question 5** – The number of mints in a full tube is unknown. This is a useful question for assessment.

## Answers

1. 
   a $5x + 2 = 4x + 6$, $x = 4$    b $4t + 3 = 3t + 7$, $t = 4$
   c $3t + 5 = 4t$, $t = 5$    d $n + 10 = 2n + 4$, $n = 6$

2. 
   a $n = -7$    b $x = 4$    c $y = 6$    d $h = 7$
   e $n = 15$    f $t = 6$    g $k = 5$    h $y = 8$
   i $b = 7$    j $v = 21$

3. 
   a $2c + 5 = 11$, $c = 3$    b $4t + 2 = 2t + 6$, $t = 2$
   c $4n + 3 = n + 10$, $n = \frac{7}{3}$

4. 
   a $n = 4$    b $h = 4$    c $t = 15$    d $m = \frac{20}{3}$
   e $k = 3$    f $t = 3$    g $t = 9$    h $d = 3$
   i $x = 4$    j $x = 5$    k $x = 7$    l $x = 3$

5. There are 6 mints in a tube. Andy and Jo each have 33 mints.

## Objectives

- Write equations to describe situations given in words or diagrams. Solve the equations and check the solutions in context.                                                                      (L6)

| Key ideas | Resources |
|---|---|
| 1  Situations can sometimes be summarised in an equation which describes key information.<br>2  The equation can be solved and the solution checked in context. | ⊕  Rules and formulae                              (1158)<br>Pairs of cards with equivalent algebraic expressions<br>Mini whiteboards |

| Simplification | Extension |
|---|---|
| Simplify the process of creating equations to involve just 'one-step' equations, such as 'I have a total of 18 jam tarts which are packed in 6 small boxes. Each box holds $n$ jam tarts. How many jam tarts are in each box?' | Students challenge each other by making up their own word problems and asking a partner to solve them. Students can also work collaboratively to devise further problems which require three or four stages of working to find the solution. |

| Literacy | Links |
|---|---|
| Creating an equation from a scenario described in words is not straightforward for many students.<br>The student can imagine that the unknown quantity is a known value and ask themselves "What would I now do to work out the answer?". Whatever arithmetic operation they choose for the arithmetic is the same operation that is needed for the algebra. | Equations are used to model and predict the behaviour of natural hazards including avalanche prediction. Avalanches occur when the weight of snow is greater than the strength of a layer in the snow or the strength of the force which is holding the snow to the ground. Scientists use equations that take account of the weather conditions, wind speed, temperature, precipitation and terrain to predict whether or not the snow is stable and whether an avalanche is likely. More information about avalanche forecasts in Scotland can be found at www.sais.gov.uk |

## Alternative approach

Students generally find that equations that arise from a spatial context (such as finding perimeters or areas or angles in diagrams) are easier to 'see' than equation which arise from worded contexts. That being the case, it is worthwhile having students gain experience with spatial problems first; for example, more like Question **2** in the exercise before moving on to Question **3**.

## Checkpoint

The perimeter of a rectangle is 16cm. If the sides are of length $2.5x$ and $1.5x$, form an equation and solve it to find the value of $x$ and the lengths of the sides of the rectangle.          ($8x = 16$, $x = 2$, 5cm by 3cm)

## Starter – Make fifteen

Give students the values $a = 2$, $b = 3$, $c = 5$. They find expressions that have a value of 15; for example, $bc$ and $4c - a - b$.

Then recap work of previous chapters and this chapter so far. Ask rapid response questions. Students reply by writing on their mini whiteboards. Discuss questions when their answers indicate a need.

## Teaching notes

Make a pack of cards of algebraic expressions which can be paired together; for example, $x + x + x$ and $3 \times x$; $y + y + 5 - 3$ and $2y + 2$. Have students in a whole-class session choose pairs and display them with an = sign between them.

Pose a problem to the students such as "If a rectangle has length $3x$, a width $x$ and a perimeter of 16 cm, what are its dimensions?". Write an expression for the perimeter $[3x + x + 3x + x]$, simplify it $[8x]$, form an equation $[8x = 16]$ and solve it $[x = 2$ so they length is 6 cm and the width is 2 cm]. Check that the solution does indeed give a perimeter of 16 cm $[6 + 2 + 6 + 2 = 16]$. Students can now practise forming and solving equations.

## Plenary

Students use mini whiteboards to show equations that they have formed from situations described in words or pictures. They solve them, again displaying their answers on the mini whiteboards. Discuss their solutions.

## Exercise commentary

**Question 1** – This could be done as a pairs game or a class activity.

**Question 2** – Check that students are familiar with the terms 'expression' and 'perimeter'. Highlight that the perimeter of each shape is 60 cm.

**Question 3** – Converting worded scenarios into algebra is not straightforward for many students – expect some difficulties. Monitor especially those students with weaker literacy skills.

**Question 4** – This is a useful question to assess a student's progress in this topic.

---

1. $(42 + 7) = (7 \times 7)$
   $(5 \times 20) = (17 + 83)$
   $(42 \div 1) = 6 \times 7$
   $(90 \div 2) = (3 \times 15)$
   $(90 \div 3) = (5 \times 6)$
   $(9 + 5) = (2 \times 7)$
   $(3 \times 20) = (15 \times 4)$

2. **a** $4x = 60$, $x = 15$ cm    **b** $12y = 60$, $y = 5$ cm
   **c** $6n = 60$, $n = 10$ cm    **d** $3t = 60$, $t = 20$ cm

3. **a** $15 + 35 = y$, $y = £50$    **b** $70 = 2x$, $x = 35$ kg
   **c** $210 - 120 = p$, $p = £90$    **d** $(20 - 5) \div 5 = c$, $c = £3$

4. **a** $2t + 5 = 11$    **b** $t = 3$
   **c** $15$

| Key outcomes | Quick check |
| --- | --- |
| Understand what an equation is.   L5 | **a** Is the following true? $25 \div 2 = 15 - 2.5$ (yes) <br> **b** Fill in the missing number: $30 \div 6 = 18 - \square$ (13) |
| Calculate the unknown value in equations.   L5 | Solve: <br> **a** $3 + x = 11$ (8) **b** $7a = 42$ (6) |
| Use balancing to solve equations. L6 | Solve: <br> **a** $2x - 7 = 9$ (8) **b** $3x + 11 = 8$ (-1) |
| Solve equations with unknowns on both sides.   L6 | Solve: <br> **a** $3x + 7 = 2x + 11$ (4) **b** $2x - 9 = 5x + 6$ (-5) |
| Write equations from real life situations.   L6 | A triangle has sides $3x$, $2x$ and $x + 1$. If the perimeter is 19cm, form and solve an equation to find $x$. ($6x + 1 = 19$, $x = 3$) <br> What is the length of the longest side of the triangle? (9cm) |

# My Review

## Check out

**You should now be able to ...**

**Test it**
**Questions**

✓ Understand what an equation is.    ⑤ 1, 2

✓ Calculate the unknown value in equations.    ⑤ 3

✓ Use balancing to solve equations.    ④ 4, 5

✓ Solve equations with unknowns on both sides.    ⑥ 6

✓ Write equations from real-life situations.    ⑥ 7

| Language | Meaning | Example |
|---|---|---|
| Equation | An equation is true for particular values. For any equation, the left-hand side is equal to the right-hand side. | $2x - 5 = 13$ True for $x = 9$ |
| Expression | An expression is a group of terms but no equals sign. | $2a - 3b$ |
| Inequality | An inequality is where one side is greater than the other. | $7 < 8$ is the same as $8 > 7$ |
| Solve | To solve an equation means to find the value of the unknown. | Solve $2x - 5 = 13$<br>$2x - 5 + 5 = 13 + 5$<br>$2x = 18$<br>$2x \div 2 = 18 \div 2$<br>$x = 9$ |
| Unknown | The letter in an equation represents the unknown value. | In the equation $2x - 5 = 13$ the unknown is represented by the letter $x$. |

1. Do these pairs of calculations make equations? Use = for an equation and ≠ for not an equation.
   a $5 \times 7$ and $70 \div 2$
   b $24 + 17$ and $8 \times 5$
   c $14 \times 3$ and $50 - 9$

2. Write > or < in-between the calculations to make inequalities.
   a $25 \div 5 \quad 4 \times 2$
   b $42 \div 3 \quad 3 \times 4$
   c $5 \times 11 \quad 7 \times 8$

3. Solve these equations.
   a $a + 16 = 29$
   b $b - 14 = 31$
   c $3 + c = 13$
   d $2 \times d = 30$
   e $e + 5 = 9$
   f $3f = 27$
   g $\frac{g}{2} = 8$

4. Solve these equations by balancing.
   a $3x + 6 = 27$
   b $5x - 7 = 48$
   c $6x + 4 = 10$
   d $32 = 3x - 4$

5. a Write an equation for these scales.

   b Solve the equation to calculate the value of $p$.

6. Solve these equations.
   a $n + n + 7 = n + n + n + 5$
   b $m + m + m + m = m + 18$
   c $3q + 7 = 13$
   d $5x - 12 = 4x - 10$
   e $4x - 13 = x + 5$
   f $6x - 8 = 4x - 2$

7. The perimeter of this rectangle is 32 cm

   a Write an equation for the perimeter of the rectangle.
   b Solve the equation.
   c Find the lengths of each side of the rectangle.

### What next?

| Score | | |
|---|---|---|
| 0 – 3 | Your knowledge of this topic is still developing. To improve look at Formative test: 3A-10; MyMaths: 1154, 1158 and 1182 |
| 4 – 6 | You are gaining a secure knowledge of this topic. To improve look at InvisiPen: 231, 232, 233, 234, 235 and 237 |
| 7 | You have mastered this topic. Well done, you are ready to progress! |

## Question commentary

**Questions 1** and **2** – Students should be able to do the required calculations mentally.

**Questions 3** to **6** – Graded questions with the equations getting harder. Ensure students are getting the first ones right before moving on.

**Question 7** – Check that students are completing the question and not just settling on an answer for $x$.

## Answers

1. a =    b ≠    c ≠

2. a <    b >    c <

3. a 13   b 45   c 10   d 15
   e 45   f 9   g 16

4. a 7   b 11   c 1   d 12

5. a $5p + 4 = 39$    b $p = 7$

6. a $n = 2$   b $m = 6$   c $q = 2$   d $x = 2$
   e $x = 6$   f $x = 3$

7. a $16x = 32$   b $x = 2$cm   c $5x = 10$cm, $3x = 6$cm

1 a Are these scales balanced?
  b What could you do to the left-hand side to make the scales balance?
  c What could you do to the right-hand side?

2 Copy these and complete them with >, < or = to make the statements true.
  a $90 ÷ 3 \;\square\; 30$
  b $32 ÷ 8 \;\square\; 9$
  c $12 \;\square\; 33 ÷ 11$
  d $19 − 6 \;\square\; 6 + 7$
  e $24 \;\square\; 5 × 4$
  f $35 ÷ 5 \;\square\; 7$

3 Copy these and fill in the missing numbers to make the statements true.
  a $15 = 3 × \square$
  b $12 = \square × 3$
  c $25 = 5 × \square$
  d $10 = 40 ÷ \square$
  e $15 + \square = 21$
  f $36 = \square × 6$
  g $12 + 3 = 6 + \square$
  h $21 − 4 = 9 + \square$
  i $32 ÷ 4 = 2 × \square$
  j $26 − 5 = 7 × \square$
  k $45 ÷ 9 = 5 × \square$
  l $28 + 8 = 6 × \square$

4 Find the value of the unknown in each of these equations.
  a $b + 22 = 29$
  b $t − 30 = 40$
  c $f − 19 = 9$
  d $m + 56 = 63$
  e $g − 18 = 2$
  f $k − 6 = 0$
  g $2t = 16$
  h $5t = 30$
  i $10j = 70$
  j $\frac{t}{2} = 5$
  k $\frac{t}{5} = 4$
  l $6d = 36$
  m $\frac{u}{10} = 2$
  n $8n = 24$
  o $\frac{v}{3} = 5$

5 i Write an equation for each of these scales.
  ii Find the weight of one parcel on each of the scales by solving the equations.

a    b    c

6 Solve these equations.
  a $5x + 34 = 19$
  b $3b + 7 = 19$
  c $8t − 5 = 11$
  d $6s − 3 = 21$
  e $7q + 7 = 35$
  f $8r − 6 = 18$
  g $8j − 7 = 25$
  h $20a − 2 = 18$
  i $2z + 30 = 50$
  j $9f − 4 = 14$
  k $11q + 3 = 36$
  l $12k + 15 = 39$

7 i Write an equation for each of these scales.
  ii Find the weight of one parcel on each of the scales by solving the equations.

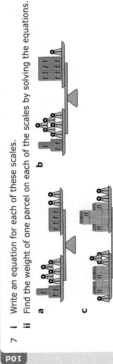

a    b

c

8 Solve these equations.
  a $d + d + d + 7 = d + d + 15$
  b $c + c + c + c + 10 = c + c + c + 20$
  c $v + v + v + 35 = v + 55$
  d $m + m + m + 30 = m + 40$
  e $3e + 3 = e + 19$
  f $5f + 6 = 2f + 18$
  g $6h + 4 = 2h + 24$
  h $8u + 12 = u + 26$

9 i Write an expression for the perimeter of each shape. Use the symbols given.
  ii The perimeter of each shape is 40cm. Write an equation and solve it to find the length of the sides of each shape.

  a [rectangle, $3n$ cm]
  b [triangle, $3x$ cm, $4x$ cm, $3x$ cm]
  c [pentagon, all sides are $p$ cm]
  d [octagon, all sides are $h$ cm]

10 The perimeter of this hexagon is 56cm.
  a Write an expression for the perimeter using $y$.
  b Write an equation and solve it to find the value of $y$.

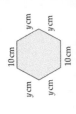

[hexagon with sides $y$ cm, $y$ cm, $y$ cm, $y$ cm, 10 cm, 10 cm]

## Question commentary

**Questions 1** to **3** – Students should be able to do the calculations required mentally. Check they are happy with the symbols in question **2**.

**Question 4** – Single-step equations that many students may be able to solve informally.

**Questions 5** and **6** – Two-step equations. Check the students are applying the correct inverse operations in the correct order. Answers can be checked by substituting back.

**Questions 7** and **8** – Equations with the unknown on both sides. Encourage students to balance towards the side with the most unknowns on and check their answers at the end by substituting back.

**Questions 9** and **10** – Problem-solving with equations. Some of the problems may be solvable with informal methods but encourage students to write down an equation representing the problem anyway.

## Answers

**1**  **a** No  **b** Add 5  **c** Take away 5

**2**  **a** $=$  **b** $<$  **c** $>$  **d** $=$
    **e** $>$  **f** $=$

**3**  **a** 5  **b** 4  **c** 5  **d** 4
    **e** 6  **f** 6  **g** 9  **h** 8
    **i** 4  **j** 3  **k** 1  **l** 6

**4**  **a** 7  **b** 70  **c** 28  **d** 7
    **e** 20  **f** 6  **g** 8  **h** 6
    **i** 7  **j** 10  **k** 20  **l** 6
    **m** 20  **n** 3  **o** 15

**5**  **a** $4n = 12, n = 3$  **b** $2p + 3 = 11, p = 4$
    **c** $3t + 3 = 15, t = 4$

**6**  **a** $x = -3$  **b** $b = 4$  **c** $t = 2$  **d** $s = 4$
    **e** $q = 4$  **f** $r = 3$  **g** $j = 4$  **h** $a = 1$
    **i** $z = 10$  **j** $f = 2$  **k** $q = 3$  **l** $k = 2$

**7**  **a** $3t + 5 = 4t + 2, t = 3$  **b** $3t + 6 = 8t + 1, t = 1$
    **c** $2n + 4 = 3n + 2, n = 2$

**8**  **a** $d = 8$  **b** $c = 10$  **c** $v = 10$  **d** $m = 5$
    **e** $e = 8$  **f** $f = 4$  **g** $h = 5$  **h** $u = 2$

**9**  **a** $3n + n + 3n + n, 8n = 40, n = 5$ cm
    **b** $4x + 3x + 3x, 10x = 40, x = 4$ cm
    **c** $p + p + p + p + p, 5p = 40, p = 8$ cm
    **d** $h + h + h + h + h + h + h + h, 8h = 40, h = 5$ cm

**10 a** $y + y + y + y + 10 + 10$
    **b** $4y + 20 = 56, y = 9$ cm

## Learning outcomes

**N5**  Use conventional notation for the priority of operations, including brackets, powers, roots and reciprocals

(L6)

**N7**  Use integer powers and associated real roots (square, cube and higher), recognise powers of 2, 3, 4, 5 and distinguish between exact representations of roots and their decimal approximations

(L5/6)

**N8**  Interpret and compare numbers in standard form $a \times 10^n$  $1 \leq a < 10$, where $n$ is a positive or negative integer or 0

(L6)

## Introduction

The chapter starts by looking at square numbers and square roots, both exact and found using a calculator. Using square numbers and square roots in practical contexts is covered before some of the rules of indices are looked at. The final section covers standard index form for large and small numbers.

The introduction discusses how standard index form can be used to represent the large number 24,000,000,000,000,000,000 more efficiently (as $2.4 \times 10^{19}$). The 'need' for scientists and astronomers to use this kind of notation arises not from any absolute necessity, but to simplify the written calculations and the way the numbers are written.

There is an excellent website which shows how the sizes of things in our universe *really* relate to each other. This website is called 'The Scale of the Universe' and can be found at http://htwins.net/scale/ or http://htwins.net/scale2/.

Thinking about massive numbers or minute numbers is really quite difficult and something like this interactive 'zooming' universe can help us to relate to these quantities. Alternatively, consider things like football stadiums: How many people is 'one million people'? Well, a crowd that size would fill Wembley Stadium 11 times over!

## Prior knowledge

Students should already know how to…
- Perform simple arithmetic
- Multiply and divide by powers of ten

## Starter problem

The starter problem requires students to work out the square root of 70 to two decimal places. Since the 'square root' key of their calculator is not working, they need to use a trial and improvement method.

Students should be able to identify that the value lies between 8 and 9 since $8^2 = 64$ and $9^2 = 81$.

It makes sense to choose 8.5 as the starting value in the decimal search: $8.5^2 = 72.25$

So our search begins:

$8.4^2 = 70.56$

$8.3^2 = 68.89$

$8.35^2 = 69.7225$

$8.36^2 = 69.8896$

$8.37^2 = 70.0569$

Since we have identified a two decimal place interval, all that remains is to check to see if it is closer to 8.36 or 8.37. We try 8.365: $8.365^2 = 69.97…$

So our value of the square root of 70, correct to two decimal places, is 8.37.

Students could be given further approximate square roots to find (or cube roots) if time and ability permit.

## Resources

**MyMaths**

| | | | | | |
|---|---|---|---|---|---|
| Indices 1 | 1033 | Standard form large | 1051 | Squares and cubes | 1053 |

**Online assessment**

| | | | |
|---|---|---|---|
| Chapter test | 3A–11 | | |
| Formative test | 3A–11 | | |
| Summative test | 3A–11 | | |

**InvisiPen solutions**

| | | | |
|---|---|---|---|
| Squares and square roots | 181 | Powers of 10 | 182 |
| Standard form | 183 | | |

# Topic scheme

Teaching time = 4 lessons/2 weeks

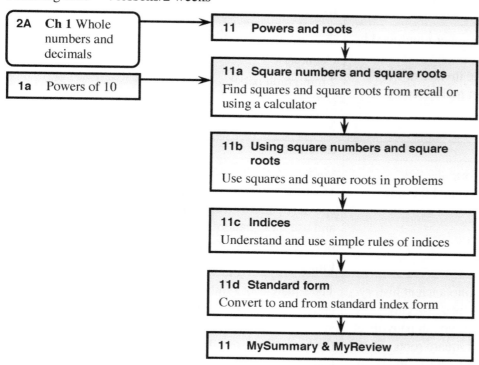

**2A** **Ch 1** Whole numbers and decimals

**1a** Powers of 10

**11** Powers and roots

**11a** Square numbers and square roots
Find squares and square roots from recall or using a calculator

**11b** Using square numbers and square roots
Use squares and square roots in problems

**11c** Indices
Understand and use simple rules of indices

**11d** Standard form
Convert to and from standard index form

**11** MySummary & MyReview

# Differentiation

**Student book 3A**   200 – 213

Understand and use square numbers and square roots
Understand basic rules of indices
Understand standard index form

**Student book 3B**   196 – 211

Find square and cube roots using a variety of methods
Work with rules of indices including fractional indexes
Simplify using indices and surds
Work with standard index form for large and small numbers
Calculate using standard index form

**Student book 3C**   196 – 209

Work with standard index form for large and small numbers
Calculate using standard index form
Understand powers and operations
Work with rules for indices and surds

## Objectives

- Recognise the squares of numbers to at least 12 × 12 and the corresponding square roots. (L4)

| Key ideas | Resources |
|---|---|
| 1  The square of a number is the number multiplied by itself.<br>2  The square root of number is the inverse of the square. It is the value that, when multiplied by itself, gives the number. | Squares and cubes (1053)<br>Counters<br>2 mm graph paper<br>Calculators<br>Mini whiteboards |

| Simplification | Extension |
|---|---|
| Work with squares of counters to form the link between the total number of counters and the side length of the square. | Students find the squares of numbers ending in 5, say 15 up to 45 using a calculator. Ask them if they can spot any patterns (for example, they all end in '25') and use these patterns to find the squares of larger numbers such as 75 and 85. |

| Literacy | Links |
|---|---|
| The use of square roots goes back into ancient history. The Ancient Babylonians wrote about $\sqrt{2}$ on clay tablets about 1700BC. There is an Egyptian papyrus of the same time showing how to find square roots. There are writings from India dated around 700BC and from China dated about 200BC, which also tell how to find them. | The square root symbol is called the radical symbol and the line across the top is called the vinculum. The symbol without the vinculum first appeared in 1525 in the book 'Die Coss' by the German mathematician Christoff Rudolff. It is thought that Rudolff chose the symbol because it is similar to the way a small letter "r", the initial of the Latin word 'radix' (meaning 'root'), was written at the time. The vinculum was later added by Rene Descartes (the inventor of Cartesian coordinates) in 1637. |

### Alternative approach

Write all the factor pairs for 64. They are $1 \times 64, 2 \times 32, 4 \times 16, 8 \times 8, 16 \times 4, 32 \times 2, 64 \times 1$.
As the first factors decreases, the second factors increase and they cross each other at $8 \times 8$.

So $8^2 = 64$ or $\sqrt{64} = 8$.

When repeated for 40, the factor pairs are $1 \times 40, 2 \times 20, 4 \times 10, 8 \times 5, 5 \times 8, 4 \times 10, 2 \times 20, 1 \times 40$. The factors cross between $8 \times 5$ and $5 \times 8$, so $\sqrt{40}$ lies between 5 and 8. The average of 5 and 8 is 6.5 and $40 \div 6.5 = 6.2$ (to 1 dp), so $\sqrt{40}$ lies between 6.2 and 6.5, which have an average of 6.35 giving
$40 \div 6.35 = 6.30$. So $\sqrt{40}$ lies between 6.30 and 6.35. These iterations continue until there is the required accuracy.

Then use the method for $\sqrt{32}$ and $\sqrt{28}$. [Check using the square root key on a calculator – so much quicker!]

### Checkpoint

| | |
|---|---|
| What is $8^2$? | (64) |
| What is $\sqrt{81}$? | (9) |
| What is $\sqrt{900}$? | (30) |

## Starter – Quick fire

Recap work of previous chapters. Particularly include previous number work on mental and written computation. Ask rapid response questions with students responding on mini whiteboards. Discuss answers when there is a need.

## Teaching notes

Students arrange counters into square arrays with side lengths of 1, 2, 3, ..., and note the total number of counters used in each array. Explain that the numbers of counters represent 'square numbers' and introduce the correct notation for representing a square number, for example $3^2 = 9$. Students write the first ten square numbers, either from knowledge of tables or from arranging further counters, and learn them by heart.

Explain that if we know the square number, we can work backwards to find what number has been squared. Introduce the idea of a square root and its symbol. Students write the square root of the various square numbers alongside the list of squares above.

Explain to students that there are many numbers which do not have an exact (integer) square root. On pre-drawn axes, get students to draw a graph of the first ten square numbers and use this to estimate, say $2.5^2$ or the square root of 40.

## Plenary

Ask students to write an explanation, in their own words, of what a square number is. Ask them to also write what a square root is. Give the students several numbers and ask them to say whether the numbers are square numbers or not and, if so, ask them to write the square root of the number.

## Exercise commentary

**Questions 5** and **6** – Calculators are allowed here but students might check their answers by either squaring or square rooting their answer to go back.

**Question 7** – Explain that the graph cannot be very accurate but that it will give a useful answer. Discuss how the relationship is not linear, so the slope of the graph gets steeper.

**Question 8** – Students should evaluate the elements of the calculations and use operations before deducing the answer from recall.

## Answers

1  a  square, square root    b  square root, square
   c  square, square root    d  square root, square

2  a  6   b  8, 64   c  0, 0, 0   d  9, 9, 81
   e  7, 49   f  10, 10, 100

2  a  3   b  4   c  6   d  7
3  e  9   f  2   g  1   h  8
   i  10   j  0

4  a  25   b  9   c  144   d  4
   e  11   f  20   g  81   h  12
   i  25

5  a  289   b  676   c  22.09   d  51
   e  27   f  86.49   g  9.61   h  41
   i  32

6  a  12.2   b  8.8   c  16.1   d  127.0
   e  1.4   f  85.9   g  467.9   h  17.3
   i  1.7

7  a

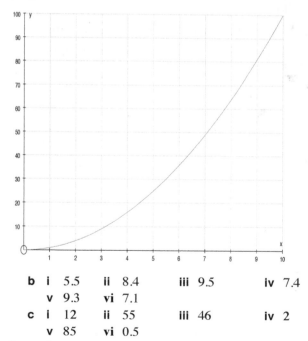

   b  i  5.5   ii  8.4   iii  9.5   iv  7.4
     v  9.3   vi  7.1
   c  i  12   ii  55   iii  46   iv  2
     v  85   vi  0.5

8  a  2   b  1   c  3   d  1
   e  3   f  2   g  5   h  17

9  a  6,7   b  7,8   c  8,9   d  11,12

## Objectives

- Use squares and positive square roots of positive integers. (L5)

| Key ideas | Resources | |
|---|---|---|
| **1** A square number has an integer square root.<br>**2** A non-square number has a decimal square root which can be rounded. | Squares and cubes<br><br>Counters<br><br>Calculators<br><br>Mini whiteboards | (1053) |

| Simplification | Extension |
|---|---|
| Explain that square numbers can be used to determine the number of whole tiles or slabs that are needed for building square patios, etc. Work with square arrays only at first. Avoid any links with perimeter. | Explain that square numbers can be of further use when working out if a number is prime. One test for 'prime-ness' is to divide the number by all prime numbers less than the square root of the number. For example, to test if 183 is prime, try dividing it by 2, 3, 5, 7, 11 and 13, since 183 lies between $13^2$ and $14^2$. |

| Literacy | Links |
|---|---|
| Links between various mathematical notations can be made in the search for square roots.<br>For example, the factor pairs of, say, 36 can be written as coordinates $(1, 36), (2, 18), (3, 12), \ldots$, which can be plotted to draw the graph of $x \times y = 36$. Finding the point where $x = y$ gives the value of $\sqrt{36}$.<br>Repeat for the number 12 to find a decimal answer. | The Ancient Babylonians used square numbers in their calculations and could also calculate square roots. A picture of a clay tablet dating from between 1800BC and 1600BC showing the calculation of the square root of two can be found at<br>www.math.ubc.ca/~cass/Euclid/ybc/ybc.html |

### Alternative approach

For some numbers, their square root can be found from their prime factors.
For example, $1936 = 2 \times 2 \times 2 \times 2 \times 11 \times 11 = (2 \times 2 \times 11) \times (2 \times 2 \times 11)$
So, $\sqrt{1936} = 2 \times 2 \times 11 = 44$

### Checkpoint

A square field has an area of 400 m². How long is each side? (20 metres)

Alex wishes to tile a square wall measuring 6 m by 6 m. How many 50 cm square tiles will be need? (144)

## Starter – Four in a line

Ask students to draw a 5 × 5 grid and enter the numbers 1 to 25 in any order. Give questions, for example:

| | |
|---|---|
| Five squared? | [25] |
| Square root of 36? | [6] |
| Double eleven? | [22] |
| A multiple of both eight and three? | [24, 48, …] |
| A factor common to 6 and 9? | [3] |

The winner is the first to cross out four in a line.

## Teaching notes

Ask students, working in pairs, to arrange a number of counters into rectangular arrays in as many ways as possible. Start with 12 or 16 counters. No matter how hard they try, 12 counters cannot be arranged into a square array, while 16 counters can. So 16 is a square number but 12 is not. Students give further examples of whole numbers which can and cannot be arranged into squares.

For numbers that cannot, the length of the side of the square is not a whole number, but it can be found by using the 'square root' key on a calculator and rounding the display appropriately. Students practise finding and rounding square roots on their calculators to ensure each student knows how to use their calculator.

## Plenary

Give students a list of square numbers and ask them to write the square roots on their mini whiteboards. Then give several integer numbers which are not square and they use their calculators to find the square roots, rounded to 2 decimal places.

## Exercise commentary

**Questions 1** and **2** – For the slabs to be arranged into a square pattern, they must have a single factor which, multiplied by itself, gives the number of tiles in the pile. For example, $15 = 1 \times 15$ or $3 \times 5$; so there is no one single factor. The number 15 is not square.

**Questions 3** and **4** –Students could use their calculators to explore factors of these numbers.

**Question 5** – Students can explore the square root of 130 on their calculators.

## Answers

1 **a** **i** No    **ii** Yes    **iii** No    **iv** Yes
    **v** Yes   **vi** No
  **b** **i** $1 \times 15$ or $3 \times 5$
    **iii** $1 \times 48, 2 \times 24, 3 \times 16, 4 \times 12$ or $6 \times 8$
    **v** $1 \times 80, 2 \times 40, 4 \times 20, 5 \times 16$ or $8 \times 10$

2   Because 30 is not a square number.

3   **a**   A is false and B is false.
   **b**   $7.7 \times 7.7 = 59.29 < 60$ and $11 \times 11 = 121$

4   **a**   15 m    **b**   No

5   46 cm

## Objectives

- Use squares, positive and negative square roots, cubes and cube roots, and index notation for small positive integer powers (L6)
- Know and use the index laws for multiplication of positive integer powers (L6)

| Key ideas | Resources |
|---|---|
| 1  Familiarity with indices and their meaning | ⊞ Indices 1 (1033) |
| 2  Apply indices knowledge to simplify both number and algebraic expressions. | Mini-whiteboards |

| Simplification | Extension |
|---|---|
| Simplifications of the kind offered in questions **3** to **5** can initially be undertaken by students writing their answers on mini-whiteboards. This use of whiteboards, prior to attempting the exercise, allows assessment of students' understanding early in the activity. | There are many words, other than *million* and *billion*, for large numbers. Students could draw up a list of them. Alternatively students could compare $2^4 \times 2^{-1}$ and $2^4 \times \frac{1}{2}$ to give meaning to the index -1. |

| Literacy | Links |
|---|---|
| Check the notation and how to read these values. Include the notation used on calculators and also on computers, including ^ for raising a power. | In recent years, Britain has adopted the American system for naming large numbers. Traditionally, one billion referred to $10^{12}$ but the term is now used to refer to $10^9$, that is, one thousand million instead of one million million. However, in science, confusion is avoided by using SI prefixes. The prefix giga- always means $10^9$ and tera- always means $10^{12}$, so 2 gigajoules means $2 \times 10^9$ joules. For a table listing other SI prefixes see http://www.unc.edu/~rowlett/units/prefixes.html |

### Alternative approach

Begin by asking the students if $2^3$ is the same as $3^2$. Mini whiteboards could be used here. Examine the responses and elaborate if and where necessary. Continue with $3^4$ and $4^3$; then ask students to consider $2^4$ and $4^2$ – why is this a special case? Continue with encouraging students to use mini whiteboards when extending to generalisation of indices, asking both for simplification of expressions and also for possible questions resulting in a simplified term. Encourage students to work in pairs to investigate possible rules for multiplying with same-base powers.

### Checkpoint

| Write these as a term with one index number: | $3^6 \times 3^4$ | $(3^{10})$ |
|---|---|---|
| | $2^{10} \times 2^5$ | $(2^{15})$ |
| | $x^4 \times x$ | $(x^5)$ |

## Starter – Four in a line

Ask students to draw a 5 × 5 grid and enter the numbers 1 to 25 in any order. Give questions involving primes, factors and multiples. For example,

What is the highest common factor of 12 and 20?

An even prime number?

A prime number between 8 and 12?

The lowest common multiple of 6 and 8?

A prime factor of 27?

An odd factor of 34?

The winner is the first student to cross out four in a line.

## Teaching notes

Review the notation carefully to ensure students do not confuse, for example, $3^5$ with $3 \times 5$. Ask students to write out a small number of cases similar to the examples as this may help them to learn the structure quickly and then develop an understanding of the rule for multiplying as described in the fourth example.

## Plenary

Ask students to work in pairs to compare the values of $2x^2$ and $(2x)^2$ when $x = 5$ and to explain why they are different.

Algebraically, what would be equivalent to $(2x)^2$?

## Exercise commentary

**Question 1**– These should be done without a calculator.

**Question 2** – Addresses the misconception that squaring is the same as multiplying by two. This could form the basis of introductory class discussion.

**Questions 3** and **4** – No evaluation is necessary and ensure students write the expressions using a clear 'floating' index.

**Question 5** – Again, evaluation should not be carried out.

**Question 6** – This question will also provide a valuable opportunity for discussing possible misconceptions as a class.

**Question 7** – Students can use the rule, or they can write out each expression in full before re-combining.

**Question 8** – An extension question with three or more terms and/or different bases. Students could discuss this question in pairs.

## Answers

| | | | | | | | |
|---|---|---|---|---|---|---|---|
| **1** | **a** 9 | **b** 64 | **c** 32 | **d** 343 |
| | **e** 100 000 | **f** 625 | **g** 1024 | **h** 1 |

**2** Nick is right because $3^2 = 3 \times 3 = 9$.

| | | | | | | | |
|---|---|---|---|---|---|---|---|
| **3** | **a** $4^5$ | **b** $7^3$ | **c** $9^7$ | **d** $5^8$ |
| | **e** $6^4$ | **f** $12^2$ | | |

| | | | | | | | |
|---|---|---|---|---|---|---|---|
| **4** | **a** $a^3$ | **b** $q^5$ | **c** $r^7$ | **d** $z^2$ |
| | **e** $d^4$ | **f** $f^8$ | | |

| | | | | | | | |
|---|---|---|---|---|---|---|---|
| **5** | **a** $3^5$ | **b** $8^7$ | **c** $4^{10}$ | **d** $7^7$ |
| | **e** $5^7$ | **f** $12^4$ | | |

**6** No. He can't simplify in this way because $4 \neq 5$.

| | | | | | | | |
|---|---|---|---|---|---|---|---|
| **7** | **a** $a^7$ | **b** $f^7$ | **c** $d^5$ | **d** $g^5$ |
| | **e** $z^6$ | **f** $b^8$ | **g** $s^{10}$ | **h** $t^{12}$ |

| | | | | | | | |
|---|---|---|---|---|---|---|---|
| **8** | **a** $9^9$ | **b** $7^8$ | **c** $2^9$ | **d** $4^6$ |
| | **e** $x^{15}$ | **f** $y^{15}$ | **g** $z^6$ | **h** $3^6 \times p^5$ |

## Objectives

(L6)
(L6)
(L6)

- Extend knowledge of integer powers of 10
- Convert between ordinary and standard index form representations
- Express numbers in standard index form

| Key ideas | Resources |
|---|---|
| 1  Familiarity with the meaning of powers of 10 when expressing both large and small numbers<br>2  Ability to express values in both ordinary form and standard form | ⊞ Standard form large    (1051)<br>Mini-whiteboards |

| Simplification | Extension |
|---|---|
| It might be worth revising multiplying and dividing by 10, 100 and 1000 with the weaker students.<br><br>The students will often latch onto the use of standard form very quickly but make sure they check that their answers are of the right order of magnitude and that they are moving the digits not the decimal point. | The students could extend the work of question **6** to look at the population densities of these cities. They would need to look up the size of the cities, possibly on the internet. This would make a good computer-based homework task. |

| Literacy | Links |
|---|---|
| Students may be unfamiliar or unconfident with the term standard form, though many will have come across numbers expressed in this way in contexts across the curriculum. The convention will need to be explained.<br><br>Remind students of common prefixes: centi, milli, kilo and so on with their power equivalents. | Micrometres (μm or microns) are used to measure the thickness or diameter of microscopic objects. One micrometre is a thousandth of a millimetre or $1 \times 10^{-6}$ meters. Human hair is about 100 μm wide and red blood cells are 7 μm in diameter. There is a picture of human eye tissue in clusters of 50-200 μm at http://www.sciencedaily.com/releases/2007/06/070624 121236.htm |

### Alternative approach

It is appropriate here to deal with both large and small numbers together, though expecting less able pupils to concentrate of large numbers only. Begin by examining the power sequence of the base 10, similar to previous work relating to other base sequences. Students may remember some of the key prefixes linked with some of the powers such as kilo for $10^3$. Activities relating to contexts will help to establish the concepts. Liaise with other curricular areas to find examples where standard form is used.

### Checkpoint

| | |
|---|---|
| Write in standard form: 48,000,000 | $(4.8 \times 10^7)$ |
| Write as a normal number: $5.6 \times 10^5$ | (560,000) |
| Write in standard form: 0.00045 | $(4.5 \times 10^{-4})$ |
| Write as a normal number: $3.78 \times 10^{-3}$ | (0.00378) |

## Starter – Order!

Write the following list of fractions on the board. $\frac{13}{40}, \frac{1}{3}, \frac{7}{20}, \frac{5}{16}, \frac{3}{10}, \frac{3}{8}, \frac{17}{50}, \frac{8}{25}$

Ask students to put them in order from the lowest value to the highest value.

Correct order: $\frac{3}{10}, \frac{5}{16}, \frac{8}{25}, \frac{13}{40}, \frac{1}{3}, \frac{17}{50}, \frac{7}{20}, \frac{3}{8}$

This task can be differentiated by the choice of fractions.

## Teaching notes

Is there a quick way to write large number like 100 000 000 000 or 1000 000? How are they said in words? Why could this become confusing? Look at these large number as powers of 10. Consider introducing a few new terms like trillion ($10^{12}$) and quintillion ($10^{18}$). How can a large number that does not start with a one be written as two different numbers multiplied together? Consider different possibilities, involving a power of ten, for example, 3 000 000 equals $3 \times 1000 000$ or $30 \times 100 000$ or $300 \times 10 000$. Use index form for the powers of ten. One of these ways is the 'standard' way of writing large numbers around the world, known as 'standard form' or 'standard index form'. Ask students to suggest which they think it is and why. Establish that the first number must be between one and ten, not including ten. Look at a few examples of conversions in both directions. Does the power of ten give the number of zeros in the number? No, but this is a common misconception.

## Plenary

Ask students to find equivalent pairs in the following numbers.
$3.1 \times 10^3$, 30100, $3.1 \times 10^5$, 3.1, 310, $3.01 \times 10^4$, $3.01 \times 10^2$, 30.1, 3100, $3.01 \times 10^0$, 310000, 3.01, $3.1 \times 10^2$, $3.01 \times 10^1$

Ask students to complete the pairs for any not matched up. ($3.01 \times 10^2$ and 3.1)

## Exercise commentary

**Question 1**– This question can form the basis of class discussion about how standard form numbers should be written.

**Questions 2** to **5** – Routine practice questions at converting to and from standard form for both large and small numbers. Ensure students are moving the digits through the decimal point and carefully counting the steps that they move.

**Question 6** – Students will likely convert all the numbers to normal numbers before comparing.

## Answers

1 a  E is incorrect because it is not multiplied by number written as $10^x$.

  b  B is incorrect because it does not start with a number between 1 and 10.

| 2 | a | 64000 | b | 31 000 000 |
|---|---|---|---|---|
| | c | 520000 | d | 9600 |
| | e | 43900000 | f | 6 530 000 |
| | g | 153000 | h | 524 000 000 |
| | i | 4230 | j | 7 325 000 000 |

| 3 | a | $7.4 \times 10^5$ | b | $9.3 \times 10^3$ |
|---|---|---|---|---|
| | c | $1.9 \times 10^6$ | d | $4.93 \times 10^7$ |
| | e | $9.27 \times 10^3$ | f | $2.64 \times 10^8$ |
| | g | $6.83 \times 10^6$ | h | $7.8 \times 10^4$ |
| | i | $1.35 \times 10^5$ | j | $6.491 \times 10^{10}$ |

| 4 | a | 0.053 | b | 0.00031 |
|---|---|---|---|---|
| | c | 0.000024 | d | 0.00374 |
| | e | 0.000 000 953 | f | 0.000 007 48 |
| | g | 0.000 032 9 | h | 0.000 000 047 |
| | i | 0.000 000 003 65 | j | 0.001 584 |

| 5 | a | $4.6 \times 10^{-3}$ | b | $2.7 \times 10^{-6}$ |
|---|---|---|---|---|
| | c | $5 \times 10^{-2}$ | d | $5.28 \times 10^{-3}$ |
| | e | $3.4 \times 10^{-6}$ | f | $4.1 \times 10^{-7}$ |
| | g | $8.9 \times 10^{-6}$ | h | $6 \times 10^{-7}$ |
| | i | $1.67 \times 10^{-5}$ | j | $9.21 \times 10^{-7}$ |

6  St. Helier (Jersey), San José (Costa Rica), Oslo (Norway), Ottawa (Canada), London (England), Tokyo (Japan)

| Key outcomes | Quick check |
|---|---|
| Identify and understand square numbers. L5 | **a** Write down the square of 8. (64) <br> **b** Work out the square of 14. (196) |
| Calculate and estimate square roots. L5 | **a** Write down the square root of 121. (11) <br> **b** Work out the square root of 67. (8.2 (1 d.p.)) |
| Know the meaning of an index. L6 | Simplify $5 \times 5 \times 5 \times 5$. ($5^4 = 625$) |
| Simplify expressions using indices. L6 | Simplify <br> **a** $x^6 \times x^3$ ($x^9$) **b** $y^4 \times y$ ($y^5$) |
| Multiply and divide numbers by powers of 10. L6 | Work out <br> **a** $34.2 \times 100$ (3420) **b** $68.7 \div 1000$ (0.0687) |
| Write numbers in standard form. L6 | Write these numbers in standard form <br> **a** 67,000 ($6.7 \times 10^4$) **b** 432 ($4.32 \times 10^2$) |

## ⊕ MyMaths extra support

| Lesson/online homework | | | Description |
|---|---|---|---|
| Squares and triangles | 1054 | L4 | What are square numbers and triangle numbers? |
| Rules and formulae | 1158 | L5 | Using letters to represent unknown numbers in simple formulae |

# My Review

## Check out

**You should now be able to ...**

| | | |
|---|---|---|
| ✓ | Identify and understand square numbers. | 1, 2 |
| ✓ | Calculate and estimate square roots. | 1, 3, 4 |
| ✓ | Know the meaning of an index. | 5, 6, 7 |
| ✓ | Simplify expressions using indices. | 8, 9 |
| ✓ | Multiply and divide numbers by powers of 10. | 10 |
| ✓ | Write numbers in standard form. | 11 |

| Language | Meaning | Example |
|---|---|---|
| Index notation | Using powers to show how many times a number has been multiplied by itself. | $5 \times 5 \times 5 \times 5 = 5^4$ |
| Square number | A number which is equal to another number multiplied by itself. | 49 is a square number because $49 = 7 \times 7$. 7 squared is written as $7^2$ |
| Square root | The square root of a number is the number you multiply by itself to get the number. | The square root of 144 is written as $\sqrt{144}$. $\sqrt{144} = 12$ as $12 \times 12 = 144$ |
| Standard form | A way to write very large or very small numbers. A number in standard form starts with a number between 1 and 10 and is multiplied by a power of 10. | A large number in standard form looks like: $13\,400\,000\,000 = 1.34 \times 10^{10}$. A small number in standard form looks like: $0.00000056 = 5.6 \times 10^{-7}$ |

1 Without using a calculator, find
   a $3^2$   b $1^2$   c $10^2$
   d $\sqrt{36}$   e $\sqrt{81}$   f $\sqrt{64}$

2 Which of these are square numbers?
   1   2   4   6
   8   9   12   16

3 This square has an area of 49 cm².
   What is the length of each of its sides?

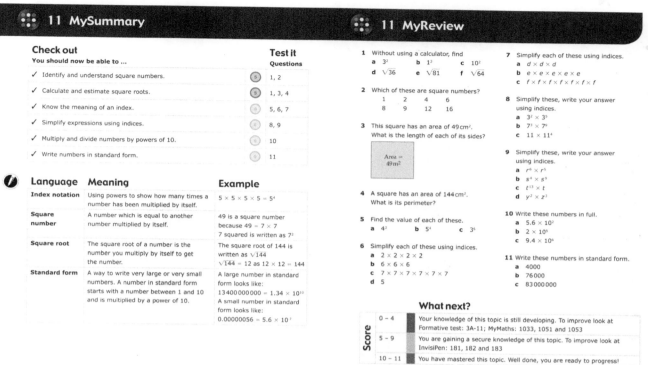

Area = 49 m²

4 A square has an area of 144 cm².
   What is its perimeter?

5 Find the value of each of these.
   a $4^3$   b $5^4$   c $3^6$

6 Simplify each of these using indices.
   a $2 \times 2 \times 2 \times 2$
   b $6 \times 6 \times 6$
   c $7 \times 7 \times 7 \times 7 \times 7 \times 7$
   d $5$

7 Simplify each of these using indices.
   a $d \times d \times d$
   b $e \times e \times e \times e \times e$
   c $f \times f \times f \times f \times f \times f \times f$

8 Simplify these, write your answer using indices.
   a $3^2 \times 3^5$
   b $7^3 \times 7^9$
   c $11 \times 11^4$

9 Simplify these, write your answer using indices.
   a $r^6 \times r^5$
   b $s^4 \times s^9$
   c $t^{13} \times t$
   d $y^2 \times z^3$

10 Write these numbers in full.
   a $5.6 \times 10^2$
   b $2 \times 10^5$
   c $9.4 \times 10^6$

11 Write these numbers in standard form.
   a 4000
   b 76000
   c 83000000

### What next?

| Score | | |
|---|---|---|
| 0 – 4 | Your knowledge of this topic is still developing. To improve look at Formative test: 3A-11; MyMaths: 1033, 1051 and 1053 |
| 5 – 9 | You are gaining a secure knowledge of this topic. To improve look at InvisiPen: 181, 182 and 183 |
| 10 – 11 | You have mastered this topic. Well done, you are ready to progress! |

## Question commentary

**Questions 1** to **4** – Students should solve these questions by fact recall.

**Question 5** – Where possible, students should avoid using a calculator for this question.

**Questions 6** to **8** – In each case, the answers should be written in simplest index form. Discourage the evaluation of numerical expressions.

**Questions 9** and **10** – Students should be reminded that it is the digits that move through the decimal point and that the number of places they move decides the power of 10.

## Answers

1 a 9   b 1   c 100   d 6
  e 9   f 8

2 1, 4, 9, 16

3 7 cm

4 48 cm

5 a 64   b 625   c 729

6 a $2^4$   b $6^3$   c $7^6$   d 5

7 a $d^3$   b $e^5$   c $f^7$

8 a $3^7$   b $7^{12}$   c $11^5$

9 a $r^{11}$   b $s^{13}$   c $t^{14}$   d $y^2z^3$

10 a 560   b 200000   c 9400000

11 a $4 \times 10^3$   b $7.6 \times 10^4$   c $9.3 \times 10^7$

# 11 MyPractice

**1** Copy and complete these statements about square numbers.

a $1^2 = 1 \times \square = 1$
b $10^2 = 10 \times \square = \square$
c $0^2 = \square \times \square = \square$
d $11^2 = \square \times \square = \square$
e $4^2 = 4 \times \square = \square$
f $12^2 = \square \times \square = \square$

**2** Copy and complete these statements about square roots.

a $\sqrt{16} = \square$
b $\sqrt{4} = \square$
c $\sqrt{1} = \square$
d $\sqrt{81} = \square$
e $\sqrt{49} = \square$
f $\sqrt{144} = \square$

**3** Without using a calculator, estimate the square roots of these numbers.

a $\sqrt{26}$
b $\sqrt{10}$
c $\sqrt{40}$
d $\sqrt{60}$
e $\sqrt{108}$
f $\sqrt{150}$
g $\sqrt{200}$
h $\sqrt{120}$
i $\sqrt{75}$

**4** Use your calculator to find the answers to these.

a $19^2$
b $23^2$
c $32^2$
d $5.4^2$
e $8.31^2$
f $14.1^2$
g $\sqrt{441}$
h $\sqrt{1296}$
i $\sqrt{1369}$
j $\sqrt{2.89}$
k $\sqrt{9.3025}$
l $\sqrt{44.3556}$

**5** Use your calculator to find the answer.
Round your answer to one decimal place.

a $3.77^2$
b $1.234^2$
c $0.999^2$
d $\sqrt{3}$
e $\sqrt{10}$
f $\sqrt{17}$
g $\sqrt{200}$
h $\sqrt{1000}$
i $\sqrt{1700}$

**6 a** Use a calculator to decide whether you can make a square from 625 square tiles.

**b** Explain how you know.

**7** A square garden with an area of 196 m² is to be fenced.

a What is the length of each side of the garden?

b The gardener has 50 m of fencing.
How many more metres of fencing will he need to put a fence all the way around the garden?

Area =
196 m²

**8** Rini wants to make the largest square possible from 500 square tiles.
How many tiles will she have left over?

---

**9** Find the values of each of these.

a $5^2$
b $3^3$
c $2^4$
d $4^3$
e $10^7$
f $5^5$
g $4^4$
h $2^9$
i $7^3$

**10** Simplify each of these by using indices. Do not work out the values.

a $7 \times 7 \times 7 \times 7$
b $10 \times 10 \times 10 \times 10 \times 10$
c $3 \times 3 \times 3 \times 3 \times 3$
d $4 \times 4 \times 4 \times 4 \times 4 \times 4 \times 4 \times 4$
e $2 \times 2 \times 2 \times 2 \times 2 \times 2 \times 2$
f $3$
g $6 \times 6 \times 6 \times 6 \times 6 \times 6$
h $12 \times 12 \times 12 \times 12 \times 12 \times 12 \times 12$

**11** Simplify each of these by using indices.

a $y \times y \times y \times y \times y \times y$
b $z \times z \times z \times z \times z$
c $t \times t \times t \times t \times t \times t$
d $g \times g \times g$
e $p \times p \times p \times p \times p \times p \times p \times p$
f $q$
g $r \times r \times r \times r$

**12** Simplify each of these using indices.

a $4^3 \times 4^5$
b $5^4 \times 5^5$
c $7^5 \times 7^6$
d $9^7 \times 9$
e $6^3 \times 6^7$
f $12^2 \times 12^4$

**13** Write these numbers in full.

a $3.1 \times 10^3$
b $1.8 \times 10^5$
c $7.83 \times 10^7$
d $1.29 \times 10^5$
e $2.89 \times 10^6$
f $8.39 \times 10^8$
g $1.002 \times 10^3$
h $7.62 \times 10^6$
i $8.804 \times 10^5$

**14** Write these numbers in standard form.

a $9300000$
b $46000$
c $940000$
d $4700000$
e $86900$
f $63800000$
g $300400$
h $627000$
i $909900000$

**15** Write these numbers in full.

a $4.7 \times 10^{-4}$
b $2.8 \times 10^{-3}$
c $3.45 \times 10^{-6}$
d $8.13 \times 10^{-5}$
e $5.49 \times 10^{-6}$
f $9.1 \times 10^{-7}$
g $1.234 \times 10^{-6}$
h $7.007 \times 10^{-3}$
i $9.631 \times 10^{-1}$

**16** Write these numbers in standard form.

a $0.055$
b $0.00038$
c $0.0092$
d $0.000023$
e $0.0000000445$
f $0.000000962$
g $0.1667$
h $0.000102$
i $0.0000007$

# Question commentary

**Questions 1** to **5** – A combination of fact recall, estimation and effective calculator skills should mean that these questions are reasonably straightforward.

**Questions 6** to **8** – Where possible discourage the use of calculators. Students need to remember to interpret their answers in context.

**Question 9** – Where possible, discourage the use of calculators, but they will almost certainly be needed for parts **e** to **i**.

**Questions 10** to **12** – These are simplification questions, not evaluation questions, so ensure students are giving their answers in simple index form.

**Questions 13** to **16** – Remind students that it is the digits that move through the decimal point and that the number of places they move left or right dictates the power of 10.

# Answers

1  **a** 1  **b** 10, 100
   **c** 0, 0, 0  **d** 11, 11, 121
   **e** 4, 16  **f** 12, 12, 144

2  **a** 4  **b** 2  **c** 1  **d** 9
   **e** 7  **f** 12

3  **a** 5.1  **b** 3.1-3.2  **c** 6.3  **d** 7.7-7.8
   **e** 10.4  **f** 12.2-12.3  **g** 14.1  **h** 10.9
   **i** 8.7

4  **a** 361  **b** 529  **c** 1024  **d** 29.16
   **e** 69.06  **f** 198.81  **g** 21  **h** 36
   **i** 37  **j** 1.7  **k** 3.05  **l** 6.66

5  **a** 14.2  **b** 1.5  **c** 1  **d** 1.7
   **e** 3.2  **f** 4.1  **g** 14.1  **h** 31.6
   **i** 41.2

6  **a** You can make a square.
   **b** $\sqrt{625} = 25$

7  **a** 14  **b** 6 m

8  16 tiles

9  **a** 25  **b** 27  **c** 16  **d** 64
   **e** 10000000  **f** 3125  **g** 256  **h** 512
   **i** 343

10 **a** $7^4$  **b** $10^5$  **c** $3^5$  **d** $4^8$
   **e** $2^7$  **f** 3  **g** $6^6$  **h** $12^8$

11 **a** $y^5$  **b** $z^4$  **c** $t^7$  **d** $g^3$
   **e** $p^9$  **f** $q$  **g** $r^4$

12 **a** $4^8$  **b** $5^9$  **c** $7^{11}$  **d** $9^8$
   **e** $6^{10}$  **f** $12^6$

13 **a** 3100  **b** 180 000
   **c** 78 300 000  **d** 129 000
   **e** 2 890 000  **f** 839 000 000
   **g** 1 002  **h** 7 620 000
   **i** 880 400

14 **a** $9.3 \times 10^6$  **b** $4.6 \times 10^4$
   **c** $9.4 \times 10^5$  **d** $4.7 \times 10^6$
   **e** $8.69 \times 10^4$  **f** $6.38 \times 10^7$
   **g** $3.004 \times 10^5$  **h** $6.27 \times 10^5$
   **i** $9.099 \times 10^8$

15 **a** 0.00047  **b** 0.0028
   **c** 0.000 003 45  **d** 0.000 081 3
   **e** 0.000 005 49  **f** 0.000 000 91
   **g** 0.000 001 234  **h** 0.007 007
   **i** 0.9631

16 **a** $5.5 \times 10^{-2}$  **b** $3.8 \times 10^{-4}$
   **c** $9.2 \times 10^{-3}$  **d** $2.3 \times 10^{-5}$
   **e** $4.45 \times 10^{-8}$  **f** $9.62 \times 10^{-7}$
   **g** $1.667 \times 10^{-1}$  **h** $1.02 \times 10^{-4}$
   **i** $7.0 \times 10^{-7}$

**G3** Draw and measure line segments and angles in geometric figures, including interpreting scale drawings
(L5)

**G4** Derive and use the standard ruler and compass constructions (perpendicular bisector of a line segment, constructing a perpendicular to a given line from/at a given point, bisecting a given angle); recognise and use the perpendicular distance from a point to a line as the shortest distance to the line (L6)

**G9** Identify and construct congruent triangles, and construct similar shapes by enlargement, with and without coordinate grids (L5)

## Introduction

The chapter starts by looking at measuring and constructing angles using a ruler and protractor and constructing triangles using these tools. Perpendicular lines, perpendicular bisectors and angle bisectors are all covered before a section on constructing triangles with either a ruler and protractor or a ruler and pair of compasses. The final section covers bearings.

The introduction discusses the Great Pyramid of Giza which was completed in 2560 BC. The height of the pyramid is 146.5 metres and its base is 230.4 metres along each side. The amount of blocks used has been estimated at two million and each block is thought to weigh about 2 tonnes. This makes the total weight of the pyramid 4 million tonnes. Its volume is over 2.5 million cubic metres and while there are large parts of the inside that are empty space, we could still estimate the density of the stones at approximately 1.6-1.7 tonnes per cubic metre.

The pyramid was constructed using right-angled corners and these were measured using a knotted rope arranged into a triangle of dimensions 3 cubits, 4 cubits and 5 cubits. This is the first recorded *use* of Pythagoras' Theorem and predates Pythagoras himself by over 2000 years!

## Prior knowledge

Students should already know how to…

- Draw and measure line segments
- Identify types of triangle

## Starter problem

The starter problem demonstrates to the students that in an equilateral triangle the perpendicular bisectors of each side meet at the centre of the triangle and go through the vertices. By finding the point where all of these bisectors meet, a circle can be drawn which fits exactly through the vertices of the triangle (the circumcircle, drawn using the circumcentre as the fixed point). Students are invited to try the technique on a range of different triangles. In general, the bisectors of the sides will all meet at a common point (the circumcentre) and a circle can be drawn through the vertices (the circumcircle) but the bisectors will *not* go through the vertices themselves.

The idea of triangle 'centres' has fascinated mathematicians right back to the days of classical geometry in Ancient Greece. There are several different centres, all of which can be constructed using simple techniques.

The incentre is the meeting point of the angle bisectors of the triangle and a circle drawn using this centre as its fixed point will fit exactly inside the triangle (the incircle).

If each vertex of the triangle is joined to the midpoint of the opposite side you get what is called the centroid of the triangle, or the barycentre. This is the centre of mass of the triangle and if it was to be suspended from any point on its edge, the direct line to the ground would pass through this point.

## Resources

**MyMaths**

| | | | | | |
|---|---|---|---|---|---|
| Measuring angles | 1081 | Bearings | 1086 | Constructing shapes | 1089 |
| Constructing triangles | 1090 | | | | |

**Online assessment**

| | |
|---|---|
| Chapter test | 3A–12 |
| Formative test | 3A–12 |
| Summative test | 3A–12 |

**InvisiPen solutions**

| | | | |
|---|---|---|---|
| Constructing a triangle | 371 | Constructing bisectors | 373 |
| Bearings | 374 | | |

# Topic scheme

Teaching time = 6 lessons/2 weeks

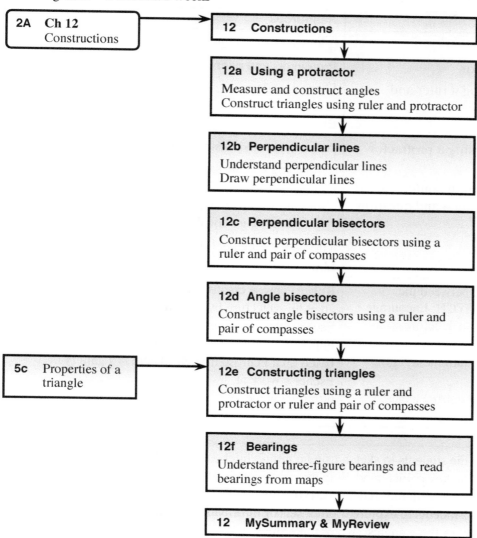

**2A   Ch 12**
Constructions

**12   Constructions**

**12a   Using a protractor**
Measure and construct angles
Construct triangles using ruler and protractor

**12b   Perpendicular lines**
Understand perpendicular lines
Draw perpendicular lines

**12c   Perpendicular bisectors**
Construct perpendicular bisectors using a ruler and pair of compasses

**12d   Angle bisectors**
Construct angle bisectors using a ruler and pair of compasses

**5c   Properties of a triangle**

**12e   Constructing triangles**
Construct triangles using a ruler and protractor or ruler and pair of compasses

**12f   Bearings**
Understand three-figure bearings and read bearings from maps

**12   MySummary & MyReview**

# Differentiation

**Student book 3A        214 – 231**

Constructing perpendicular lines, bisectors and angle bisectors
Constructing triangles
Bearings

**Student book 3B        212 – 227**

Constructing triangles using a ruler and protractor or ruler and pair of compasses.
Constructing perpendiculars, bisectors and simple loci
Understand and use Pythagoras' Theorem

**Student book 3C        210 – 223**

Understand and use Pythagoras' Theorem
Constructing triangles
Loci

## Objectives

- Construct a triangle, given two angles and the included side (ASA)  (L5)

| Key ideas | Resources |
|---|---|
| 1  Use a protractor correctly | ⊕  Measuring angles  (1081) |
| 2  Draw angles using a protractor | Protractors and rulers |
| 3  Construct ASA triangles using a ruler and protractor | Sharp pencils |

| Simplification | Extension |
|---|---|
| Some students may need help using a protractor correctly. Predrawn lines of the correct length could be used to help students complete question **4** and question **5** could be omitted completely. | Ask students to construct a triangle where, one angle is the same as the sum of the other two angles. all the angles are equal. two angles are equal. This task is suitable for paired work. |

| Literacy | Links |
|---|---|
| Remind students of the difference between the instruction CONSTRUCT and SKETCH. Encourage students to sketch as a preliminary task before constructing. Draw attention to the 'included' requirement, in the short form ASA. Involve the term congruent when requiring exact copies to be constructed. | Roger Penrose created the Penrose triangle after attending a lecture by the Dutch artist M C Escher. Escher went on to produce many works of art based on impossible figures including Waterfall (1961), which is based on a Penrose triangle. There is a gallery of Escher's work at http://www.mcescher.com |

## Alternative approach

For a given set of information, ask the students to sketch using a mini-whiteboard then discuss in pairs how they would construct accurately. Share the key points, modelling the construction using a geometry software package such as Geogebra or Autograph. Follow with the students carrying out the construction, measuring, sharing and comparing the missing details. Ask students to explore if other sets of information would be sufficient to draw specific traingles, such as one angles or three angles; two or three sides, and so on.

## Checkpoint

Construct a triangle with base 6cm and base angles 32° and 68°. (Answers can be checked by students comparing work, by a template, or by measuring the lengths of the other two sides or the third angle (80°))

## Starter – Four in a line

Ask students to draw a 5 × 5 grid and enter the numbers 1 to 25 in any order. Ask questions, for example,

> A polygon has an angle sum of 720°. How many sides does it have? (6)
>
> How many lines of symmetry does an isosceles triangle have? (1)
>
> How many sides altogether in two squares, three kites and one pentagon? (25)

The winner is the first student to cross out four in a line.

## Teaching notes

Before starting, make sure that all students have a ruler and protractor and a sharp pencil.

Practice drawing and measuring angles as a class, either using prepared diagrams or a protractor tool on an interactive whiteboard.

Draw a line (as a base for a triangle) and discuss with students what other information would be needed to draw a unique triangle. Highlight the ASA cases, and discuss whether where you draw the angle(s) makes a difference to the triangle produced.

Review how to use the protractor correctly, and the benefit of being able to estimate angles reasonably well by eye. Using the wrong scale on the protractor should be avoided if students consider whether their answer makes sense, or whether the triangle they draw looks right.

To encourage accurate constructions a points system could be used awarding 10 points for an unknown angle/side accurate to ±1°/±1 mm or 5 points for accuracies of ±3°/±2 mm.

## Plenary

Ask students how many different triangles they can construct which have an angle of 30°, an angle of 60° and a side 6 cm. (there are three: One where the 6 cm side is the hypotenuse of the right-angled triangle, one where it is the shortest side and one where it is the middle side length).

## Exercise commentary

**Question 1** – Students have to read and classify the angles. Make sure they are reading from the correct scale on the protractors.

**Questions 2 and 3** – Check students are using the correct scale on their protractors and that all the angles are correctly acute or obtuse.

**Question 4** – Students construct from the sketches. Encourage them to measure unknown sides and angles and compare with others.

**Question 5** – Both triangles in each case are ASA constructions so encourage students to orient their page appropriately before proceeding.

---

## Answers

1  a  60°, acute       **b**  120°, obtuse
   c  40°, acute       **d**  150°, obtuse

2,3,4,5                Check student constructions

## Objectives

- Use straight edge protractor to construct the perpendicular to a line. (L5)

| Key ideas | Resources |
|---|---|
| 1  Understand to term 'perpendicular<br><br>2  Construct a perpendicular line | Constructing shapes                              (1089)<br>Rulers, protractors and sharp pencils<br>Set squares if available<br>Geometry software such as Geogebra or Autograph |

| Simplification | Extension |
|---|---|
| Students may need help using their protractors correctly. Predrawn lines could also be used. | Students can use LOGO, or similar software, to generate shapes. This task is suitable for paired work. |

| Literacy | Links |
|---|---|
| Students will have met the terms here before, but it is unlikely that they will be familiar with them, let alone confident, so emphasise the correct definition of the term 'perpendicular' and the precise rules for construction. | Links can be made forwards to the idea of constructing a perpendicular bisector.<br><br>Alternatively emphasise the need to construct accurate perpendiculars when planning building designs (so the walls are straight and the rooms are 'square') and also the use of parallel and perpendicular lines in constructing things like railway tracks. |

## Alternative approach

Geometry software such as Geogebra, Autogarph, Geometer's Sketchpad or Cabri can be used to demonstrate the construction of a perpendicular line.

## Checkpoint

Ask students to construct another perpendicular line and get a partner to check it is accurate.

## Starter – Impossible triangles?

Ask students which of the following triangles cannot be constructed and why?

A triangle with sides 3 cm, 7 cm, 10 cm. (Impossible, flat)

A triangle containing angles of 43°, 111° and a side of 9.5 cm. (Possible)

A triangle containing angles of 103°, 89° and a side of 6 cm. (Impossible, 103 + 89 > 180)

## Teaching notes

The first part of the lesson is about recognising perpendicular lines and students should be given a clear definition of what it means to say something is perpendicular. Then walk them through the process of constructing a perpendicular line and allow them time to practice the skill.

## Plenary

Recap the learning and get students to write down, in as much detail as possible, the correct definition of perpendicular and the instructions for constructing a perpendicular line. They can compare answers with a partner.

## Exercise commentary

**Question 1** – Students should be able to recognise perpendicularity rather than needing to measure the angles.

**Question 2** – Here, students are expected to geometrical tools to find the perpendicular lines. Ask them to decide which they *think* are perpendicular before checking.

**Question 3** – Skills-testing questions.

**Question 4** – Students should pick their side lengths carefully so that the drawings fit on their page.

## Answers

| 1 | a | Yes | b | No | c | Yes | d | No |
|---|---|-----|---|----|---|-----|---|----|
|   | e | No  | f | No | g | No  | h | No |

2   c and f

3,4   Check students' constructions

## Objectives

- Use a ruler and compasses to construct the midpoint and perpendicular bisector of a line segment.                                                                 (L6)

| Key ideas | Resources |
|---|---|
| 1  To bisect is to cut into two halves.<br>2  A perpendicular bisector is a line that cuts another line in half at right angles to the line. | ⊕  Constructing shapes                    (1089)<br>Compasses, ruler, sharp pencil<br>Tracing paper<br>Geometry software<br>Mini whiteboards |

| Simplification | Extension |
|---|---|
| To use a pair of compasses accurately, students need a sharp pencil. They also need a good quality ruler and compasses that grip the pencil firmly. Some students may need help in adjusting the length of the pencil in the compasses. | Explain the process for constructing a perpendicular line through a given point. (The perpendicular line is not necessarily a bisector.) See how this construction links with the construction of a perpendicular bisector. |

| Literacy | Links |
|---|---|
| The words 'bisect', 'biannual', 'bicycle', 'biscuit' start with the prefix 'bi-' meaning 'two' in Latin (with 'biscuit' meaning 'twice-baked').<br>Words which include 'sect' such as 'bisect', 'disect', 'insect', 'section', all come from a Latin word meaning 'cut'. | Traditionally, bricklayers and carpenters used a plumb line to make sure that their construction was perpendicular to the horizontal plane. A plumb line is a weight, originally made from lead, suspended from a string. When allowed to hang freely, the weight points in the direction of gravity meaning that the string is vertical. The word 'plumb line' comes from the Latin word for lead, 'plumbum'. |

## Alternative approach

Draw a line on tracing paper. Fold the paper so that half the line lies on top of the other half. The crease is the perpendicular bisector. Check it with a ruler and protractor. Note that the crease passes through the midpoint of the line. Check this too.

## Checkpoint

The line AB is 6cm long. How far from A and B will the perpendicular bisector lie and at what angle to the line?

(3cm, at an angle of 90°)

## Starter – Quick fire

Recap work of previous chapters and this chapter so far. Particularly include mental and written computation. Ask rapid response questions with students responding on mini whiteboards. Discuss answers when there is a need.

## Teaching notes

Define the word 'perpendicular'. Explain that a 'perpendicular bisector' is a line which cuts another line exactly into two pieces and at right angles to it.

Construct a perpendicular bisector using the steps from the student's book. Students simultaneously construct one too.

Explain that, as only the crossing points of the pairs of arcs are needed, full circles do not need to be drawn.

## Plenary

Students describe, to the whole class in their own words, the steps required to construct a perpendicular bisector accurately. They mention the places where errors in the construction might occur.

## Exercise commentary

**Question 1** – This question is routine practice.

**Question 2** – This question is about constructing perpendicular bisectors of sloping lines.

**Question 3** – This question demonstrates an important geometrical rule, that the perpendicular bisector of a chord passes through the centre of the circle.

**Question 4** – Make the triangle large enough so the construction lines do not get confused.

The point where all of these bisectors meet is known as the circumcentre of the triangle. This question can be extended by asking students to draw the circumcircle – its centre is the circumcentre and it passes through all three corners of the triangle.

**Question 5** – Points W and X are found on the diagrams on the previous page in the student book. Check the rhombus by measuring its sides.

Students could be asked if they can construct different sized rhombuses using the same basic diagram. [Open their pair of compasses to different widths for each different sized rhombus.]

---

## Answers

1  Check students' constructions
2  Check students' constructions
3  Check students' constructions
   Yes, the bisector goes through O.
4  Check students' constructions
5  **a**  Check students' constructions
   **b**  Rhombus. All the sides are the same length because the compass was not adjusted.

## Objectives

- Use a ruler and compasses to construct the bisector of an angle. (L6)

| Key ideas | Resources |
|---|---|
| 1 To bisect is to cut into two halves.<br><br>2 An angle bisector is a line that cuts an angle in two halves. | Constructing shapes (1089)<br>Geometrical instruments<br>Tracing paper<br>Geometry software<br>Dictionaries<br>Mini whiteboards |

| Simplification | Extension |
|---|---|
| Students needs sharp pencils, good quality rulers and compasses. The basic construction should present no difficulty. | Students devise a way of constructing the angle bisector for a reflex angle. [They bisect the complementary angle and continue the line through the point of the angle.] |

| Literacy | Links |
|---|---|
| 'Bisect', 'trisect', 'quadrisect', 'disect' and 'transect' all mean to cut in a specific way. Taken in order, they mean to cut in two, in three and in four equal pieces; and then to cut into pieces as in biology and to cut crossways. | Bring in some dictionaries for the class to use. 'Bi-' is a Latin prefix meaning 'two'. How many words can the class find that begin with 'bi-'? What is the connection with the number two? |

## Alternative approach

Draw any angle on tracing paper. Fold the angle so one arm of it lies on top of the other arm. The crease is the angle bisector. Check with a protractor.

## Checkpoint

An angle of 124° is bisected. What is the angle between the bisector and each arm of the original angle? (62°)

## Starter – Quick fire

Recap work of previous chapters and this chapter so far. Particularly include mental and written computation. Ask rapid response questions with students responding on mini whiteboards. Discuss answers when there is a need.

## Teaching notes

State that the word 'bisect' means to cut into two equal pieces and that an 'angle bisector' cuts an angle into two equal angles. Using drawing equipment or geometry software, construct an angle bisector using the steps from the student's book. Students simultaneously construct one too.

Explain that, as only the crossing points of the pairs of arcs are needed, full circles do not need to be drawn.

## Plenary

Students describe, to the whole class in their own words, the steps required to construct an angle bisector accurately. They mention the places where errors in the construction might occur.

## Exercise commentary

**Questions 1** to **3** – These questions are routine practice. Students may need reminding how to use a protractor to draw an angle and, later, to measure an angle.

**Question 4** – Make the triangle large enough so the construction lines do not get confused.

The point where all of these bisectors meet is known as the incentre of the triangle.

**Question 5** – Students will need to use the skills learned in the previous section to complete the perpendicular bisector in part **a**.

## Answers

1 Check students' constructions
2 Check students' constructions
3 Check students' constructions
4 Check students' constructions
5 **a,b** Check students' constructions
   **c** 90°

## Objectives

- Construct a triangle given two sides and the included angle (SAS) or all three sides (SSS). (L6)

| Key ideas | Resources |
|---|---|
| 1 Unique triangles can be drawn if the right data is known about them.<br>2 Knowing either SAS or SSS is sufficient to draw a unique triangle. | ⊞ Constructing triangles (1090)<br>Geometrical instruments<br>A computer spreadsheet |

| Simplification | Extension |
|---|---|
| Draw triangles with angles that are simple to measure (30°, 60°, etc.) and sides with integer lengths. | Provide students with a triangle where two sides and an angle are given but where the angle is not *between* the two sides. Tell them it is possible to construct *two* different triangles and ask them to do so. |

| Literacy | Links |
|---|---|
| There are three ways that data about triangles is given so that they can be constructed without ambiguity.<br><br>Students learned about ASA triangles in Lesson **12a**. The order of the letters is important – two angles are given and the included side.<br><br>In this lesson they meet SAS triangles – two sides are given and the included angle.<br><br>They also meet the third way, known as SSS. No angles are needed, just the lengths of the three sides. | Roof trusses always employ one or more triangles in their construction to give them strength. Roof trusses are pre-built in a factory, usually from wood, and are lifted into place at the construction site. Each truss is designed to carry its own weight together with the extra weight of the roofing material. There are design drawings of roof trusses at www.raftertales.com/home-remodeling/roof-truss/ and www.troutcreektruss.com/Products/ |

## Alternative approach

Suggest that students draw a sketch first if one is not given. There is no real alternative to constructing SAS and SSS triangles.

## Checkpoint

Construct a triangle with side lengths 3cm, 4cm and 5cm. Measure and write down the angles. (90°, 37°, 53°)

## Starter – Quick fire

Recap work of previous chapters and this chapter so far. Particularly include mental and written computation. Ask rapid response questions with students responding on mini whiteboards. Discuss answers when there is a need.

## Teaching notes

The process of drawing accurate triangles involves accurate use of a ruler, protractor and, for SSS triangles, a pair of compasses.

Show the steps described in the student's book to construct an SAS triangle. Students work alongside the teacher in following the steps.

With different information (SSS), then another method of construction is needed. Work through this method with the students too.

Students can challenge each other to construct triangles from given information and can work collaboratively.

## Plenary

Students, in their own words to the whole class, describe the methods they have used to construct triangles. Emphasise the need for two different methods, depending on the information given to them.

## Exercise commentary

**Questions 1** to **3** – These questions provide routine practice. In question **3**, the triangles should be right-angled.

**Question 4** – Remind students that they can also construct ASA triangles. Take each way (ASA, SAS, SSS) in turn and discuss whether sufficient information is known to use each way.

## Answers

1　Check students' constructions
  - **a**　Right-angled
  - **b**　Isosceles
  - **c**　Equilateral
  - **d**　Scalene

2　Check students' constructions

3　**a**　$A = 53°$, $B = 90°$, $C = 37°$
　**b**　$X = 22°$, $Y = 90°$, $Z = 68°$

4　**a**　Equilateral triangle so either SAS, ASA or SSS methods
　**b**　Isosceles triangle so either SAS, ASA or SSS methods

## Objectives

- Use bearings to specify direction. (L6)

## Key ideas

1. A bearing gives the direction from a point.
2. A bearing is measured by the clockwise angle between north and the required direction.
3. A bearing is always written as a 3-digit angle.

## Resources

⊞ Bearings (1086)

Standard protractors and 360° protractors

Several (magnetic) compasses

Maps or diagrams showing places of interest

Large scale map on IWB

Mini whiteboards

## Simplification

Circular 360° protractors will help students with bearings greater than 180°.

## Extension

Give students information about landmarks and where they are located relative to a fixed point (that is, the bearing and distance from the fixed point). Ask them to draw, to a scale of their choice, a map based on this information and check their solutions with a partner.

## Literacy

Directions can still be given today using the major (or cardinal) points of the compass, north, south, east and west, rather than using a bearing given in degrees.

For example, due east is 090° as a bearing. Midway between north and east is north-east with a bearing of 045°.

A diagram which shows all the cardinal directions and their intermediate points is called a 'compass rose'. The rose can have 4, 8, 16 or 32 directions on it.

See them at http://en.wikipedia.org/wiki/Compass_rose

## Links

True north is the direction of the Geographic North Pole, where all lines of longitude meet. However, a compass points in the direction of the Magnetic North Pole. The angular difference between true north and magnetic north is called the 'magnetic declination'. It is often shown on maps. The Magnetic North Pole is currently moving northwest at a rate of around 40 km per year. Using a compass to find true north is explained at www.scoutingresources.org.uk/compass/compass_magvar.html

## Alternative approach

A class set of magnetic compasses, particularly those for orienteering and map-reading, can be used to measure bearings of places seen from the classroom or elsewhere in school. Students point the compass towards north. Keeping the needle and body of the compass in line, they turn the rotating part of the compass to point towards the required place. Then they read off the bearing from the rim of the compass. (See www.scoutingresources.org.uk/compass/compass_magvar.html for useful advice.)

## Checkpoint

The bearing of B from A is 132°. What is the bearing of A from B? (312°)

**Starter** – Angle estimation

Draw a mixture of acute, obtuse and reflex angles on the board. Ask students to estimate the size of each angle in degrees before measuring them.

Then, recap work of previous chapters and this chapter so far. Ask rapid response questions. Students reply by writing on their mini whiteboards. Discuss questions when their answers indicate a need.

## Teaching notes

Explain that 'bearings' are used for navigation. Define a bearing and emphasise the clockwise rotation from north.

Having a compass in hand, take the bearing of some local place through the classroom window. Explain that the bearing is a angle between 0 and 360° which is given using three digits, even if it is less than 100°. Explain how to measure bearings on a map with a protractor, when they are less than and greater than 180°.

Students practise measuring bearings using a map with places of interest marked. They challenge a partner to measure the bearing of a place of their choosing from a selected starting point.

## Plenary

Ask questions such as "What is the three-figure bearing of due west?", "And of south-east?", "Which compass direction is the bearing 045°?" and also questions about a map or chart for the whole class to refer to. Students reply using mini whiteboards and answers are discussed when necessary.

## Exercise commentary

**Question 1** – Explain that if a protractor is used accurately, the bearings of each place can be written down before looking to answer the questions. You should ensure that students are measuring bearings over 180° correctly.

**Question 2** – If the bearings have been written down in Question 1, this question becomes very straightforward.

**Question 3** – Ensure students understand the abbreviations in the compass rose before proceeding. Explain that we do not need to measure here, simply 'look' in that direction.

**Question 4** – This extends question 3 by putting actual bearings to the points of the compass rose.

**Question 5** – This question looks at the principle of a back-bearing. Students are guided to draw a sketch; they could try and generalise from their results.

## Answers

1  a  Old tree          b  Cave
   c  TV mast           d  Boat
   e  Windmill

2  a  135°      b  270°      c  085°      d  245°
   e  163°

3  a  Lighthouse        b  Water tower
   c  Boat              d  Windmill

4

| Direction | N | NE | E | SE |
|-----------|-----|------|------|------|
| Bearing | 000° | 045° | 090° | 135° |
| Direction | S | SW | W | NW |
| Bearing | 180° | 225° | 270° | 315° |

5  a  237°      b  110°

| Key outcomes | Quick check |
|---|---|
| Use a protractor to draw acute and obtuse angles. L5 | Draw the following angles:<br>**a** 62° **b** 125° (Check students' drawings) |
| Construct a triangle given two angles and the side between them (ASA). L5 | Construct a triangle with base 5cm and base angles 35° and 50°. (Check students' drawings – third angle should measure as 95°) |
| Use a ruler and compasses to construct the perpendicular bisector of a line. L6 | Draw the line AB = 8cm. Construct the perpendicular bisector of AB. Check by measuring the distance from each point to the bisector and by measuring the angles. |
| Use a ruler and compasses to bisect an angle. L6 | Draw an angle of 70°. Construct the angle bisector. Check by measuring each angle. |
| Construct a triangle given two sides and the angle between them (SAS). L5 | Construct a triangle ABC where AB = 5cm, BC = 6cm and angle ABC = 60°.<br>(Check students' drawings – third side should be 5.6cm) |
| Construct a triangle given three sides (SSS). L5 | Construct a triangle with side lengths 4.5cm, 6cm and 7.5cm.<br>(Check students' drawings – angles should measure 90°, 37° and 53°) |
| Use bearings to specify direction. L6 | The bearing of C from B is 072°. What is the bearing of B from C?<br>(252°) |

## ⊕ MyMaths extra support

| Lesson/online homework | | | Description |
|---|---|---|---|
| Map scales | 1103 | L5 | Use ratio notation for map scales |
| Scale drawing | 1117 | L5 | Draw scale plans and read measurements from scale plans |
| Measuring lengths | 1146 | L3 | Use this interactive ruler to test your measuring skills. Also, learn how to convert between cm and mm |

# My Review

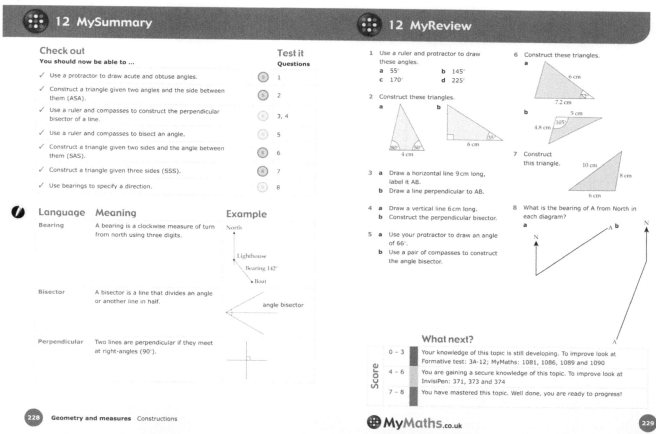

## Check out
**You should now be able to ...**

| | Test it |
|---|---|
| | Questions |
| ✓ Use a protractor to draw acute and obtuse angles. | (s) 1 |
| ✓ Construct a triangle given two angles and the side between them (ASA). | (s) 2 |
| ✓ Use a ruler and compasses to construct the perpendicular bisector of a line. | (R) 3, 4 |
| ✓ Use a ruler and compasses to bisect an angle. | (R) 5 |
| ✓ Construct a triangle given two sides and the angle between them (SAS). | (s) 6 |
| ✓ Construct a triangle given three sides (SSS). | (s) 7 |
| ✓ Use bearings to specify a direction. | (s) 8 |

| Language | Meaning | Example |
|---|---|---|
| Bearing | A bearing is a clockwise measure of turn from north using three digits. | North, Lighthouse, Bearing 142°, Boat |
| Bisector | A bisector is a line that divides an angle or another line in half. | angle bisector |
| Perpendicular | Two lines are perpendicular if they meet at right-angles (90°). | |

228  **Geometry and measures**  Constructions

1  Use a ruler and protractor to draw these angles.
 a  55°   b  145°
 c  170°   d  225°

2  Construct these triangles.
 a     b

3  a  Draw a horizontal line 9 cm long, label it AB.
 b  Draw a line perpendicular to AB.

4  a  Draw a vertical line 6 cm long.
 b  Construct the perpendicular bisector.

5  a  Use your protractor to draw an angle of 66°.
 b  Use a pair of compasses to construct the angle bisector.

6  Construct these triangles.
 a     b

7  Construct this triangle.

8  What is the bearing of A from North in each diagram?
 a     b

### What next?

| Score | |
|---|---|
| 0 – 3 | Your knowledge of this topic is still developing. To improve look at Formative test: 3A-12; MyMaths: 1081, 1086, 1089 and 1090 |
| 4 – 6 | You are gaining a secure knowledge of this topic. To improve look at InvisiPen: 371, 373 and 374 |
| 7 – 8 | You have mastered this topic. Well done, you are ready to progress! |

⊕ MyMaths.co.uk

229

## Question commentary

Ensure students have a protractor, a ruler, a pair of compasses and a sharp pencil that fits in them. Allow ±1° and ±1 mm on all constructions.

**Question 1** – Students should be able to draw simple acute and obtuse angles but may need assistance with the reflex angle in part **d**.

**Question 2** – These triangles are of the ASA form and can be done with simple (and accurate) angle measurement.

**Questions 3** to **5** – Basic constructions to test students' ability to recall the methods.

**Questions 6** and **7** – Accurate measurement is required in the constructions and students could be encouraged to measure the missing angles and side lengths and compare with others as a check.

**Question 8** – Ensure three-figure bearings are used and that students measure the reflex bearing correctly in part **b**.

## Answers

1  a  angle 55°   b  angle 145°
  c  angle 170°   d  angle 225°

2  a  check ASA: 80°, 4 cm, 50°
  b  check ASA: 90°, 6 cm, 35°

3  9 cm horizontal line with a perpendicular touching it at any point

4  6 cm line with a perpendicular bisector (3 cm along the line)

5  66° angle bisected to two 33° angles

6  a  check SAS: 7.2 cm, 52°, 6 cm
  b  check SAS: 4.8 cm, 105°, 5 cm

7  check SSS: 6 cm, 8 cm, 10 cm

8  a  055°   b  200°

# 12 MyPractice

1 Measure each angle and say whether it is acute or obtuse.

a        b

2 Draw these angles accurately.

   a 70°    b 140°    c 25°    d 108°

3 Construct these triangles accurately using a ruler and protractor.

a      5.5 cm   35°   70°

b      76°   38°   6.2 cm

4 Draw a horizontal line 6 cm long.
Draw a line perpendicular to your line.

6 cm

5 Draw a vertical line 7 cm long.
Draw a line perpendicular to your line.

7 cm

6 a Draw line RS.

R   7.5 cm   S

   b Using a pair of compasses, draw a
perpendicular bisector for line RS.

7 a Draw angle EFG.
   b Using a pair of compasses,
bisect angle EFG.

E   70°   F   G

8 Using a ruler, compasses and protractor, construct these triangles (SAS).

a   6 cm   80°   9 cm

b   5 cm   40°   8 cm

9 Using a ruler, compasses and protractor, construct these triangles (SSS).

a   5 cm   6 cm   8 cm

b   7.5 cm   10 cm   6.5 cm

10 Measure each bearing,
clockwise from north.
Give each answer as a
three-figure bearing.

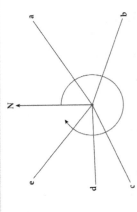

231

## Question commentary

**Questions 1, 2** and **3** – Careful measurement is required but these questions are basic practice at accurately using a protractor.

**Questions 4** to **7** – These constructions are basic practice of applying the methods taught.

**Questions 8** and **9** – Encourage students to measure the missing sides and angles and check with a partner that they agree.

**Question 10** – Check that three-figure bearings are being used and that reflex bearings are recorded correctly.

## Answers

1   **a**   125°, obtuse        **b**   75°, acute
2-9   Check students' constructions
10 **a**  056°   **b**  109°   **c**  245°   **d**  268°
    **e**  308°

| Related lessons | | Resources | |
|---|---|---|---|
| Rounding | 1b | 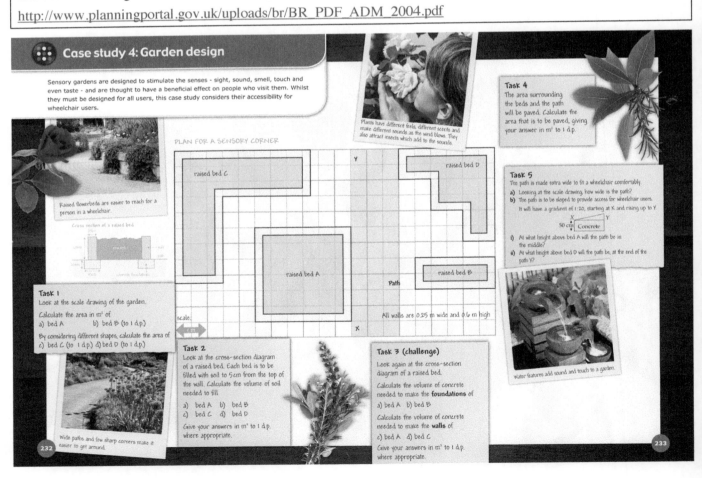 Decimal places | (1001) |
| Area | 2c | Area of a parallelogram | (1108) |
| Circumference of a circle | 2f | Area of a trapezium | (1128) |
| Using a calculator | 7f | Circumference of a circle | (1088) |
| Scale drawings | 9g | Area of circles | (1083) |
| Volume of a cuboid | 14d | Scale drawing | (1117) |
| | | Volume of cuboids | (1137) |
| | | Books and catalogues with information about plants | |

| Simplification | Extension |
|---|---|
| Encourage students to focus on a single task. Task 4, only requires areas to be calculated; suggest finding the total area of the garden then the areas of shapes A, B, D and then C. Ensure students are reading the correct dimensions from the plan. Working in pairs may help them to clarify their ideas. | Students could design their own sensory garden, working out quantities of materials needed for any hard landscaping included. They could research plants to use to give different sensory experiences throughout the year and maybe work out an approximate cost for the whole project, finding the cost of building materials and plants from catalogues and the internet. |

## Links

There are a number of websites that discuss the design of sensory gardens; see, for example

http://www.schoolplaygrounddesigners.co.uk/Sensory-Gardens.html

The UK requirements for disabled access are contained in: The Building Regulations 2010, Part M, Access to and use of buildings. Section 1 covers ramped access, p.21, with the constraints on gradients in 1.26

http://www.planningportal.gov.uk/uploads/br/BR_PDF_ADM_2004.pdf

### Case study 4: Garden design

Sensory gardens are designed to stimulate the senses - sight, sound, smell, touch and even taste - and are thought to have a beneficial effect on people who visit them. Whilst they must be designed for all users, this case study considers their accessibility for wheelchair users.

PLAN FOR A SENSORY CORNER

raised bed C

raised bed D

raised bed A

raised bed B

Path

Raised flowerbeds are easier to reach for a person in a wheelchair.

Cross section of a raised bed

Plants have different feels, different scents and make different sounds as the wind blows. They also attract insects which add to the sounds.

Wide paths and few sharp corners make it easier to get around.

All walls are 0.25 m wide and 0.6 m high

Water features add sound and touch to a garden.

**Task 1**
Look at the scale drawing of the garden.
Calculate the area in m² of
a) bed A    b) bed B (to 1 d.p.)
By considering different shapes, calculate the area of
c) bed C (to 1 d.p.) d) bed D (to 1 d.p.)

scale:

**Task 2**
Look at the cross-section diagram of a raised bed. Each bed is to be filled with soil to 5cm from the top of the wall. Calculate the volume of soil needed to fill
a) bed A    b) bed B
c) bed C    d) bed D
Give your answers in m³ to 1 d.p. where appropriate.

**Task 3 (challenge)**
Look again at the cross-section diagram of a raised bed.
Calculate the volume of concrete needed to make the **foundations** of
a) bed A    b) bed B
Calculate the volume of concrete needed to make the **walls** of
c) bed A    d) bed C
Give your answers in m³ to 1 d.p. where appropriate.

**Task 4**
The area surrounding the beds and the path will be paved. Calculate the area that is to be paved, giving your answer in m² to 1 d.p.

**Task 5**
The path is made extra wide to fit a wheelchair comfortably.
a) Looking at the scale drawing, how wide is the path?
b) The path is to be sloped to provide access for wheelchair users. It will have a gradient of 1:20, starting at X and rising up to Y

50 cm  Concrete

i) At what height above bed A will the path be in the middle?
ii) At what height above bed D will the path be, at the end of the path Y?

# Teaching notes

Look at the case study and discuss the purpose of a sensory area in a public garden. Talk about some of the features that such an area could have, using the information around the outside of the plan. Then look at the plan itself, noting that it is drawn to scale. Ask a few questions about the sizes of the flowerbeds to check that the students are using the scale correctly.

## Tasks 1, 2 and 3

Look at the information about the dimensions of the raised flowerbeds. Ask, how deep is the soil in the flowerbeds? How would you work out the volume of soil needed for flowerbed A?

Hear ideas and establish that the soil is 55 cm deep and that, to find the volume needed, you would first need to find the dimensions of the inner shaded part of the flowerbed and then work out the volume from those and the depth. As it is a cuboid (assuming level soil), multiplying the dimensions will give the volume needed. Then look at flowerbed B and ask, how would you work out the volume of soil needed for this flowerbed? Discuss how, if you can find the surface area of the soil, multiplying that by the depth of soil will give you the volume needed.

Then discuss how you could find the surface areas for the other two flowerbeds which are more complex shapes. Talk about methods such as splitting the shape into smaller parts, which might be a good way of tackling flowerbed D, and the idea of finding the area of a shape and taking away the bits that aren't there, which might be a better method for flowerbed C where the soil area could be found by removing a quarter of a circle from a square. Give the students time to tackle the questions about the volume of soil.

Ask, how will you find the volume of concrete needed for the foundations? Discuss how they will need to determine the dimensions of the foundations from the dimensions of the walls, noting that the foundations extend by equal amounts either side of the wall. Also discuss how, to get the surface area of the foundations. For flowerbed A you could break the shape into four rectangles and find the areas of those, but for flowerbed B that will not be possible. Ask, how could you find the surface area of the foundations for flowerbed B? Discuss ideas and establish that you can find the area of the outer and inner circles (foundations, not walls) and then subtract the inner from the outer. Mention that this might also be a quicker way of find the surface area of the foundations for flowerbed A. Give students time to tackle these questions.

## Task 4

Discuss how the work that students have already tackled might contain useful information that will help them with this and give them some time to work out the area. When they have, discuss the methods they used, which are likely to include finding the overall area and taking away the parts that do not need to be paved.

## Task 5

Look at the information about gradients of paths. Ask, What is meant by a gradient of 1 : 20? Establish that it means that there is a vertical rise of 1 unit for every 20 units of horizontal distance.

If the ground that the slope is built on is flat, what shape will the slope be and how will you find the volume of concrete needed for it? Hear the students' thoughts and discuss how to find the volume of a triangular prism. Give the students time to answer all the questions relating to the slope and then discuss their solutions.

---

## Answers

| | | | |
|---|---|---|---|
| 1 | A $1 \text{ m}^2$ | B | $4.5 \text{ m}^2$ |
| | C $5.8 \text{ m}^2$ | D | $3.5 \text{ m}^2$ |
| 2 | A $0.55 \text{ m}^3$ | B | $2.5 \text{ m}^3$ |
| | C $3.2 \text{ m}^3$ | D | $1.9 \text{ m}^3$ |
| 3 | a $0.5 \text{ m}^3$ | b | $0.8 \text{ m}^3$ |
| | c $4.5 \text{ m}^3$ | d | $1.3 \text{ m}^3$ |
| 4 | $29.0 \text{ m}^2$ | | |
| 5 | a $1.5 \text{ m}$ | | |
| | b i $0$ | ii | $20 \text{ cm}$ |
| | c $5.9 \text{ m}^3$ | | |

## MyAssessment 3

These questions will test you on your knowledge of the topics in chapters 9 to 12.
They give you practice in the types of questions that you may see in your GCSE exams.
There are 85 marks in total.

1 Copy this diagram onto square grid paper.

   a Reflect the shape in the x-axis which
     acts as a mirror line. (2 marks)
   b Rotate this shape through 180° clockwise
     about the point X. (2 marks)
   c Translate this shape 4 units up. (1 mark)
   d What do you notice about the original
     shape and this translated shape? (2 marks)

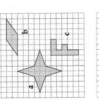

2 Copy these shapes onto square grid paper.

   i Draw any lines of symmetry on each shape. (3 marks)
   ii State the order of rotational symmetry in
      each case. (3 marks)

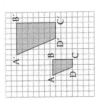

3 The quadrilateral ABCD is enlarged to give the
  quadrilateral A'B'C'D'.
  Copy the diagram onto square grid paper.

   a By drawing lines find the point of intersection.
     Mark this point O. (4 marks)
   b Measure the lines OA and OA' and OB, OB'
     to determine the scale factor. (3 marks)

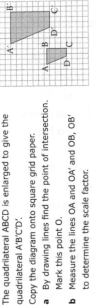

4 Are these equations true or false?
   a $13 \times 7 > 14 \times 6$ (1 mark)    b $48 \div 6 < 49 \div 7$ (1 mark)
   c $92 \times 3 = 4 \times 69$ (1 mark)    d $625 < 24 \times 26$ (1 mark)

5 Solve these equations.
   a $d - 15 = 6$ (1 mark)    b $\frac{e}{7} = 3$ (1 mark)
   c $7f + 12 = 33$ (2 marks)    d $5g - 4 = 46$ (2 marks)

6 Solve these equations.
   a $12a + 4 = 8a + 16$ (2 marks)    b $2v + 7 = v + 10$ (2 marks)
   c $5t + 3 = 7t - 15$ (2 marks)    d $7u + 2 = 13u - 4$ (2 marks)

**MyAssessment 3**

7 I collect 2 boxes (b) of apples together with 5 loose apples.
  I have 53 apples altogether. Write an equation for this problem
  and solve it to find the number of apples in a box. (2 marks)

8 a Draw an x-axis from 0 to 10 and a y-axis from 0 to 100 on
     square grid paper. (2 marks)
   b On your graph plot the square numbers from 1 up to 10. (3 marks)
   c Join up the points with a smooth curve. (2 marks)
   d Use your graph to estimate
     i $\sqrt{20}$ (1 mark) ii $8.5^2$ (1 mark) iii $\sqrt{72}$ (1 mark) iv $2.8^2$ (1 mark)

9 a A hectare of land covers an area of 10000 square metres.
     If this land area was square, how long would each side be? (2 marks)
   b An acre of land covers an area of 4046 square metres.
     If this land area was square, how long would each side be? (2 marks)
   c By what size factor (to 2 dp) is a hectare bigger than an acre? (2 marks)

10 Write these expressions in index notation.
   a $b \times b \times b \times b$ (1 mark)    b $4 \times y \times y \times y \times y$ (1 mark)
   c $3 \times g^2 \times 2 \times g^4$ (1 mark)

11 Draw a horizontal line 10cm long. Construct the perpendicular bisector
   of this line. Leave on your construction arcs. (3 marks)

12 i Copy these angles accurately
     onto plain paper using a ruler
     and a protractor. (4 marks)
   ii Using a pair of compasses
      bisect each angle. Leave on
      your construction arcs. (4 marks)

13 a Draw this triangle using a ruler and protractor. (3 marks)
   b Bisect each angle accurately to find the
     middle of the triangle. (4 marks)
   c Measure one of the centre angles. (2 marks)

14 A short sailing course starts at a point S.
   The boats sail on a bearing of 140° for 300m before rounding a buoy at A to sail
   on a new bearing of 045°. They continue on this bearing for 800m before
   reaching a second buoy B. From here they head straight for home at S.
   a Draw an accurate diagram of the course using a scale of 1cm = 50m. (3 marks)
   b Determine the bearing of S from B. (2 marks)

**⬢ MyMaths**.co.uk

# Mark scheme

## Question 1 – 7 marks

**a** 2 Shape correctly reflected in *x*-axis

**b** 2 correct rotation of 180°; correct point used

**c** 1 correct translation

**d** 2 translated shape is reflection of original shape; in *y*-axis

## Question 2 – 6 marks

**a i** 1 4 lines of symmetry

**ii** 1 no lines of symmetry

**iii** 1 no lines of symmetry

**b i** 1 order 4 about centre

**ii** 1 order 1 about centre

**iii** 1 order 1 about centre

## Question 3 – 7 marks

**a** 4 Correct drawing; lines from corners drawn; point of intersection identified; marked as O (7 left, 3 down from C)

**b** 3 OA = 3.8 cm; OA' = 7.6 cm

OB = 4.8 cm; OB' = 9.6 cm

scale factor = × 2

## Question 4 – 4 marks

**a** 1 T

**b** 1 F

**c** 1 T

**d** 1 F

## Question 5 – 6 marks

**a** 1 $d = 21$ **b** 1 $e = 21$

**c** 2 $f = 3$ **d** 2 $g = 10$

## Question 6 – 8 marks

**a** 2 $a = 3$ **b** 2 $v = 3$

**c** 2 $t = 9$ **d** 2 $u = 1$

## Question 7 – 2 marks

2 $2b + 5 = 53$; $b = 24$

## Question 8 – 11 marks

**a** 2 Correct axes drawn and labeled

**b** 3 All square numbers are plotted correctly

**c** 2 A smooth curve is drawn

**d i** 1 4.5; allow sensible amount of variation

**ii** 1 72.3; allow sensible amount of variation

**iii** 1 8.5; allow sensible amount of variation

**iv** 1 7.8; allow sensible amount of variation

## Question 9 – 6 marks

**a** 2 100 m × 100 m

**b** 2 63.6 m × 63.6 m

**c** 2 2.47; 10000/4046 for 1 mark

## Question 10 – 3 marks

**a** 1 $b^4$

**b** 1 $4y^4$

**c** 1 $6g^6$

## Question 11 – 3 marks

3 Correct length of line ±1mm; Correct construction of bisector

## Question 12 – 8 marks

**a i** 2 Correct lengths and angle

**ii** 2 Correct lengths and angle

**b i** 2 Correct bisected angle; arcs visible

**ii** 2 Correct bisected angle; arcs visible

## Question 13 – 9 marks

**a** 3 Correct length; and correct two angles

**b** 4 Correct bisector of three angles; lines meet at a point

**c** 2 123° or 111° or 126°; accept ±1°

## Question 14 – 5 marks

**a** 3 Correct diagram showing correct positions of buoys A and B

**b** 2 254°; 1 mark for 16° seen

## Learning outcomes

| | |
|---|---|
| **A14** Generate terms of a sequence from either a term-to-term or a position-to-term rule | (L6) |
| **A15** Recognise arithmetic sequences and find the $n$th term | (L6) |
| **A16** Recognise geometric sequences and appreciate other sequences that arise | (L6) |

## Introduction

The chapter starts by looking at term-to-term rules for number sequences and then position-to-term rules. Finding the general, or $n$th term rule of a sequence is covered in the third section. The final section looks at recursive sequences of the form $T(n + 1) = f(T(n))$.

The introduction discusses the famous puzzle of rice on a chessboard. The pattern looks simple enough to continue since on the first square is one grain, the second square two grains, the third square four grains, etc. The pattern is obviously doubling each time so the sequence will continue:

$1, 2, 4, 8, 16, 32, 64, 128, \ldots$

The formula for the number of grains on each square is two to the power of one less than the number of the square (or $2^{n-1}$) so on the $64^{\text{th}}$ square there will be $2^{63}$ grains of rice.

Abstracting from the practicalities of this, or the value of the rice, we can still look at the magnitude of such a number: $2^{63}$ is a number in excess of 9 quintillion (9 followed by 18 zeros!)

It is fair to say that the king has probably made a mistake agreeing to this prize!

## Prior knowledge

Students should already know how to…

- Perform simple arithmetic
- Substitute numbers into formulae
- Write down multiples of small numbers

## Starter problem

The starter problem considers how a specific sequence in context grows. The girl is asking for just 50 pence in the first week but then 20 pence more each week thereafter. At first it seems like she is taking a significant cut in pocket money but if you watch the sequence grow, you can see how long it takes her to get more than the original £3:

50p, 70p, 90p, £1.10, £1.30, £1.50, £1.70, £1.90, £2.10, £2.30, £2.50, £2.70, £2.90, £3.10

After 14 weeks, she gets more than the original, but remember that this will keep growing by 20 pence per week thereafter.

The father is clearly getting a good deal at the start, but it will not take him long after this period of time to be 'out of pocket'. Questions could be posed to the students such as:

How much does the girl lose out on in the first 13 weeks?

How long will it take her after her pocket money exceeds £3 to get this back?

How much pocket money would she get in one year?

How much *more* pocket money would she get in one year?

## Resources

**MyMaths**

| | | | |
|---|---|---|---|
| *nth* term | 1165 | Sequences | 1173 |

**Online assessment**

| | |
|---|---|
| Chapter test | 3A–13 |
| Formative test | 3A–13 |
| Summative test | 3A–13 |

**InvisiPen solutions**

| | | | |
|---|---|---|---|
| Next terms in a sequence | 281 | Term-to-term rules | 282 |
| Position-to-term rules | 283 | | |

## Topic scheme

Teaching time = 4 lessons/2 weeks

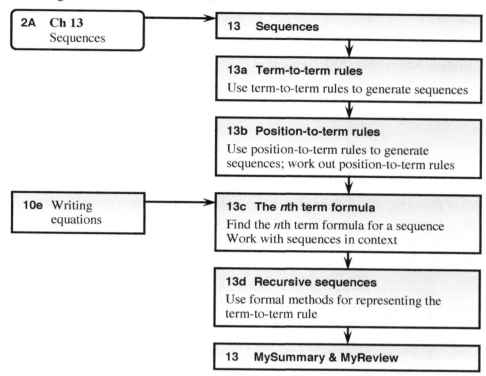

| 2A   Ch 13 |
| Sequences |

| 13   Sequences |

| **13a   Term-to-term rules** |
| Use term-to-term rules to generate sequences |

| **13b   Position-to-term rules** |
| Use position-to-term rules to generate sequences; work out position-to-term rules |

| 10e   Writing equations |

| **13c   The *n*th term formula** |
| Find the *n*th term formula for a sequence |
| Work with sequences in context |

| **13d   Recursive sequences** |
| Use formal methods for representing the term-to-term rule |

| **13   MySummary & MyReview** |

## Differentiation

| **Student book 3A**       236 – 249 |
|---|
| Term-to-term rules and position-to-term rules for generating sequences |
| Finding the general term of a sequence |
| Recursive sequences |

| **Student book 3B**       232 – 247 |
|---|
| Term-to-term rules and position-to-term rules for generating sequences |
| Finding the general term of a sequence |
| Understanding sequences in context |
| Recursive sequences |

| **Student book 3C**       228 – 241 |
|---|
| Position-to-term rules for generating sequences |
| Patterns and sequences |
| Quadratic sequences |
| General behaviour of a sequence |

## Objectives

- Generate terms of a sequence using term-to-term rules. (L6)
- Find term-to-term rules. (L6)

| Key ideas | Resources |
|---|---|
| **1** A sequence is an ordered set of numbers which follow a pattern. <br> **2** One number can be found from the previous one by using the term-to-term rule. <br> **3** A flow diagram is a useful way of defining a sequence. | Sequences (1173) <br> Computer spreadsheet <br> Mini whiteboards |

| Simplification | Extension |
|---|---|
| Provide students with more examples of flow charts where the rules are based on addition and subtraction rather than multiplication or division. From the exercise, concentrate on Questions **1a** and **c**, **2a-d** and **3**. | Give students examples of flow charts which have two or three steps and ask them to generate the sequence of terms. Ask them to design their own similar flow charts and test them on a partner. |

| Literacy | Links |
|---|---|
| *Flow charts* were invented by the American Frank Gilbreth in 1921. They can be used in this lesson to give a step-by-step list of directions that need to be followed to create a sequence. Such a list of directions is called an 'algorithm' (a word from the Arabic surname 'al-Khwarizmi' of the Islamic mathematician whose work dating from about 800AD introduced mathematics to Europe). | Sequences are often found in puzzle books and online quizzes. There is an example of a sequence quiz at www.funtrivia.com/quizzes/general/thematic_fun/sequences.html |

## Alternative approach

A sequence can be generated on a computer spreadsheet. Put the first term of the sequence into cell A1. Create a formula for cell A2 such as A2 = A1 + 4. Drag the formula down the sheet. A sequence is created with the term-to-term rule 'add 4'. By changing the formula, different sequences can be created.

## Checkpoint

For each sequence, write down the term-to-term rule and find the next two terms:

**a** $5, 7, 9, 11, \ldots$ (add 2; 13, 15)

**b** $1, 3, 9, 27, \ldots$ (multiply by 3; 81, 243)

## Starter – Quick fire

Recap work of previous chapters and especially work with number. Ask rapid response questions with students responding on mini whiteboards. Discuss answers when there is a need.

## Teaching notes

Give an example of a linear sequence such as $3, 7, 11, 15, \ldots$. Students describe the pattern in the sequence and how to get from one term to the next. Mention that there is a common difference between adjacent terms.

Introduce the flow chart as a list of instructions which are carried out in a specific order. The flow chart can be used to 'generate' sequences of numbers. Show how using the rule +4 in the flow chart will generate a sequence when you input the first term.

Give an example of a sequence with decreasing terms, such as $11, 8, 5, 2, \ldots$. Ask students to identify the rule that generates this sequence.

Give an example of a geometric sequence on the board, say $1, 2, 4, 8, 16, \ldots$, and ask students to identify the term-to-term rule.

Students devise their own flow charts and, working with a partner, generate the sequences given by their flow charts.

## Plenary

Give examples sequences using different term-to-term rules including positive and negative differences and sequences involving with multiplication or division. Students draw the flow charts to generate the sequences on their mini whiteboards.

## Exercise commentary

**Questions 1** and **2** – Students can refer to the worked examples on the previous page of the student book.

**Questions 3** to **5** – Real-life examples of sequences. Students could work in pairs for mutual support.

## Answers

1. a i  2, 4, 6            ii  + 2
   b i  8, 5, 2            ii  − 3
   c i  3, 7, 11           ii  + 4
   d i  1, 2, 4, 8         ii  × 2

2. a i  + 5               ii  26, 31, 36
   b i  + 9               ii  43, 52, 61
   c i  − 4               ii  9, 5, 1
   d i  + 8               ii  45, 53, 61
   e i  × 2               ii  48, 96, 192
   f i  ÷ 2               ii  60, 30, 15

3. a  4, 8, 12, 16, 20, 24        b  + 4

4. a  64, 32, 16, 8, 4            b  ÷ 2

5. a  1, 4, 9, 16                 b  3, 5, 7        c  25

## Objectives

- Generate terms of a sequence using position-to-term rules. (L6)
- Find position-to-term rules. (L6)

| Key ideas | Resources |
|---|---|
| 1 Each term of a sequence can be defined by its position in the sequence.<br>2 The rule is called a position-to-term rule. | Sequences (1173)<br>Flow chart templates |

| Simplification | Extension |
|---|---|
| Provide students with examples of position-to-term rules which are simply, for example, 'multiply by 3'. Initially avoid rules which involve a subsequent addition or subtraction adjustment. | Include examples in which the position-to-term rule involves 'squaring' the position number before using a second operation. |

| Literacy | Links |
|---|---|
| Contrast the two expressions 'term-to-term' and 'position-to-term'. Visually, a term-to-term rule runs along the length of the sequence, connecting each term with the next. Whereas, a position-to-term rule requires the terms to be numbered (1st, 2nd, 3rd, …) and the connection is then perpendicular to the length of the sequence from the positon number to the term. | Plant growth can be recorded using time-lapse photography. A photograph is taken from the same viewpoint at regular intervals and the resulting images edited together to form a video. There is an example of time-lapse photography of a plant growing at http://www.teachertube.com/video/plant-growth-31473 |

## Alternative approach

As in the previous lesson, a sequence can be created on a spreadsheet. It is rather more complicated as, in addition to the terms of the sequence, there also needs to be a row numbering the position of each term. For example, label cell A1 with 'Position' and cell A2 with 'Term'. Fill the A column with the positions 1, 2, 3, … . Then create a formula linking cell B1 (containing the number 1) with cell B2 to create the first term; for example, B2 = 3*B1 − 1. Drag cell B2 down the B column to create the sequence.

## Checkpoint

Write down the position-to-term rule and the next two terms for each of these sequences:

a 4, 7, 10, 13,…                        (multiply by 3 and add 1; 16, 19)

b 4, 9, 14, 19,…                        (multiply by 5 and subtract 1; 24, 29)

Write sequences on the board and ask students to find the missing terms; for example:

5, 8, □, 14, 17, □, □     [11, 20, 23]

47, 43, □, 35, 31, □, □     [39, 27, 23]

A, C, E, □, □     [G, I]

## Teaching notes

Give an example of a linear sequence. Discuss the term-to-term rule and illustrate the common difference using arrows. Above each term, write the position of the term: 1, 2, 3, 4, … .

Explain that what we are looking for is a way to describe the sequence so that we can work out, say, the 100th term without having to find all the previous 99 terms. The 100th term would be in the 100th position in the sequence and so there is a need for a position-to-term rule instead of the term-to-term rule of the previous lesson.

Using the idea of a flow chart (a blank, two-stage template could be used), students create a times table by multiplying the position by the common difference and then add or subtract as necessary to get the sequence. In tabular form, it would be:

| Position | Times table | Sequence |
|---|---|---|
| 1 | | |
| 2 | | |
| 3 | | |

At this point, you could fill in the two boxes for the flow chart.

Students generate their own linear sequences and, working with a partner, exchange them for their partner to fill in the steps in the flow chart.

## Plenary

Students show examples of their own sequences to the whole class and get others to explain the position-to-term rule.

Give an example of a flow chart and get the class to generate the sequence.

## Exercise commentary

**Question 1** – Explore the mapping diagram; ensure that students see that it is simply two columns giving the position and term. It might help to use the notation of arrows, as on the previous page of the student book, to 'see' the common difference.

**Question 2** – Have students copy the sequence and add the arrows giving the common difference. The tabular form from the **Teaching notes** can then lead to the completed flow chart.

**Question 3** – The row 'Day' is equivalent to 'position' and the row 'Height (cm)' is equivalent to 'term'.

## Answers

1   a   6

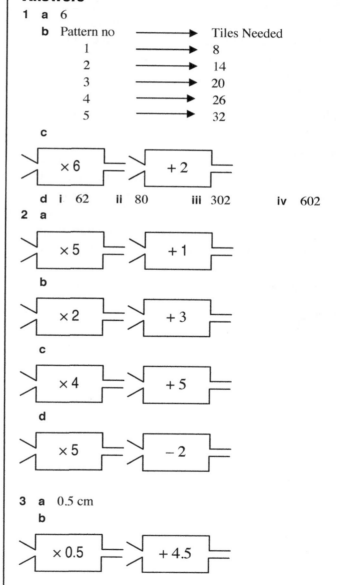

    b   Pattern no  ⟶  Tiles Needed

         1  ⟶  8

         2  ⟶  14

         3  ⟶  20

         4  ⟶  26

         5  ⟶  32

    c    [ × 6 ] [ + 2 ]

    d   i   62    ii   80    iii   302    iv   602

2   a   [ × 5 ] [ + 1 ]

    b   [ × 2 ] [ + 3 ]

    c   [ × 4 ] [ + 5 ]

    d   [ × 5 ] [ − 2 ]

3   a   0.5 cm

    b   [ × 0.5 ] [ + 4.5 ]

## Objectives

- Write and justify an expression to describe the nth term of an arithmetic sequence                    (L6)

| Key ideas | Resources |
|---|---|
| 1  Finding and using expressions for the $n$th term<br>2  Confidently using algebra in order to express properties of a sequence | ⊕  $n$th Term                    (1165)<br>Mini-whiteboards |

| Simplification | Extension |
|---|---|
| Introduce the general term for position-to-term rules requiring only a single multiplication. Students will find it straightforward to generalise the $n$th term, for example, for the sequence 4, 8, 12, 16,… The progression would then be to 5, 9, 13, 17,... where an extra 1 is also added to the $n$th term. | Working in pairs, students can write down a general term $T(n)$ and ask their partner to decide if the sequence will be linear or not and to explain their choice by generating and discussing the first six terms of the sequence. |

| Literacy | Links |
|---|---|
| Continue to refresh correct use of sequence vocabulary. Encourage students to use the correct terms in any responses and verbal descriptions.<br><br>In recording position and term, use both vertical tables as well as horizontal versions.<br><br>The notation for nth term, $T(n)$, will need to be included. | Time-lapse photography uses a sequence of photographs taken from the same view point at regular intervals. The resulting images are edited together to form a video. Examples of time-lapse videos can be seen on natural world programmes and in other contexts. Students could be asked to find some examples on the internet. |

### Alternative approach

Follow and extend the comparative work on term-to term rules with position-to-term rules encouraging students to use algebra to simplify the recording of these rules, evolving expressions to writing a formula for the $n$th term of a sequence. Students could record their versions of expressions using mini-whiteboards. Students will need to discuss those sequences that involve regular subtraction in order to increase confidence fully. Further consolidation work can involve students writing their own sequences and asking another student to give an expression for its $n$th term and vice versa.

### Checkpoint

Find the $n$th term formulae for each of these sequences:   7, 12, 17, 22, 27,...                    $(T(n) = 5n + 2)$

10, 4, -2, -8, -14,...                    $(T(n) = 16 - 6n)$

## Starter – Missing values

Write sequences on the board and ask students to fill in the gaps, for example,

    107, 99,  , 83, 75,  ,      (91, 67, 59)
    31, 28, 31, 30,  ,  ,     (31, 30, 31)
    (number of days in months in non-leap year)

## Teaching notes

Review basic work on the algebra of substituting values into linear expressions, using different variables. Students are likely to be familiar with the use of $x$ and $y$ but perhaps less so with other letters such as $n$.

The use of standard notation, such as $n$ rather than $1n$ and the meaning of $2n$ (and not $n2$) etc. is an important tool in this section and may need review.

## Plenary

Students work in pairs, one thinking of an expression for the $n$th term and using it to generate the start of a sequence, while the other student tries to find the formula for the $n$th term.

## Exercise commentary

**Question 1** – Students convert the function machines into $n$th term rules. While the use of T($n$) is not insisted upon, it might be worth introducing at this stage.

**Question 2** – Sequences are given now rather than function machines. Encourage students to model the method used in the examples.

**Questions 3** and **4** – These questions are set in practical situations.

**Question 5** – A classic investigation into 'T' totals. This can be extended as far as necessary to provide opportunities for challenge.

---

## Answers

1   **a**   $3n + 2$    **b**   $5n - 1$    **c**   $2n - 5$    **d**   $4n + 3$
   **e**   $3n$       **f**   $10n - 4$

2   **a**   $2n + 1$    **b**   $3n + 2$    **c**   $2n - 5$    **d**   $4n - 1$
   **e**   $5n - 3$    **f**   $10n + 1$    **g**   $7n + 2$    **h**   $6n$
   **i**   $-4n + 44$

3   $2n - 1$

4   **a**   $2n + 6$    **b**   36      **c**   186

5   $5n + 35$

## Objectives

- Understand that a linear sequence always has a constant difference between successive terms     (L6)
- Geometric sequences have a common multiplier     (L6)

| Key ideas | Resources |
|---|---|
| **1** Algebraic representations of term-to-term rules<br>**2** Applying term-to-term rules in context | Calculators |

| Simplification | Extension |
|---|---|
| More examples of simple linear sequences can be given such as those in question **2**.<br><br>Students may need guidance on how to write the recursive formulae for question **4**, particularly when there are gaps in the sequences. | Students can investigate other types of sequence such as the Fibonacci sequence. How can this sequence be written in recursive form?<br><br>What about if we allow our recursive formulae to involve squaring or cubing? For example $T(n + 1) = [T(n)]^2$ with $T(1) = 2$ gives $2, 4, 16, 256, \ldots$<br><br>What is we start with $T(1) = 1$? Or $T(1) = 0.5$? |

| Literacy | Links |
|---|---|
| Linear sequence<br>Geometric sequence<br>Recursion/recursive formula | Recursive sequences occur in many areas of real-life whenever there is a clear progression of a sequence of numbers over time. The exercise illustrates three examples such as bank account interest, population growth and 'viral' hits on the Internet. Students could investigate other real-life sequences that exhibit patterns such as exponential growth and/or decay in biology or physics. |

### Alternative approach

Students could be provided with two sets of cards (or two jumbled lists), one set with recursive formulae on and one set with the terms of sequences on. They can then try and work out, in pairs or threes, how the two sets link together and match them. This will encourage discussion about the structure of the algebraic formulae and how they link to the generation of recursive sequences.

### Checkpoint

Write the first five terms of this sequence: $T(n + 1) = 3T(n), T(1) = 1$     $(1, 3, 9, 27, 81)$

Describe this sequence using a recursive formula: $4, 9, 14, 19, 24, \ldots$     $(T(n + 1) = T(n) + 5, T(1) = 4)$

**Starter** – Number Jumble

These numbers belong to two different arithmetic sequences but have been jumbled up. Sort them into two sets and write down the two sequences:

1, 17, 4, 13, 7, 10, 8, 11, 5, 14, 16, 2

(1, 4, 7, 10, 13, 16 and 2, 5, 8, 11, 14, 17)

## Teaching notes

Since the recursive formula is basically a formal algebraic way of writing the term-to-term rule, students could be asked to look back at **13a** where term-to-term sequences are introduced first of all. Can they think of a way of writing the 'wordy' rule using symbols? Describe the structure of the algebraic statements and show, using a few simple examples, the way that a recursive formula works. Show the difference between a linear sequence and a geometric sequence. Students can then complete selected questions from the exercise and work through the practical problems in questions **4** to **7**. There is scope for students to 'invent' their own sequences and challenge a partner to find the recursive formula, or to generate terms with their own formula.

## Plenary

Are the following sequences (a) linear, (b) geometric, or (c) neither?

$T(n + 1) = T(n) + 4, T(1) = 7$     (linear)

$T(n + 1) = 3T(n) - 1, T(1) = 1$     (neither)

$T(n + 1) = 4T(n), T(1) = 4$     (geometric)

$T(n + 1) = -T(n), T(1) = 5$     (geometric)

$T(n + 1) = T(n) - \frac{1}{2}, T(1) = 7$     (linear)

## Exercise commentary

**Question 1** – Basic practice at identifying terms in a linear sequence.

**Question 2** – Basic practice at writing out linear sequences using the recursive formulae.

**Questions 3** and **4** – Writing the recursive formulae correctly may be a challenge for some students so check their notation early on. Where there are gaps in the sequences in question **4**, encourage them to fill these in before proceeding to write the recursive formulae.

**Questions 5** to **7** – Real-life problems which illustrate that sequences may occur in many different contexts. Encourage students to write out the terms of the sequences and look for patterns.

---

## Answers

**1 a** 5      **b** 10      **c** 25      **d** 33
  **e** -1      **f** -26

**2 a** 2, 3, 4, 5, 6      **b** 0, 2, 4, 6, 8
  **c** 1, 5, 9, 13, 17      **d** -1, -2, -3, -4, -5
  **e** 1, -1, -3, -5, -7      **f** -5, -8, -11, -14, -17

**3 a** $T(n + 1) = T(n) + 2, T(1) = 2$
  **b** $T(n + 1) = T(n) + 4, T(1) = 3$
  **c** $T(n + 1) = T(n) + 6, T(1) = -2$
  **d** $T(n + 1) = T(n) - 3, T(1) = 4$
  **e** $T(n + 1) = T(n) - 4, T(1) = -5$
  **f** $T(n + 1) = T(n) + 2, T(1) = 0.5$

**4 a** $T(n + 1) = T(n) + 3, T(1) = 5$
  **b** $T(n + 1) = T(n) + 2, T(1) = 13$
  **c** $T(n + 1) = T(n) + 6, T(1) = 9$
  **d** $T(n + 1) = T(n) + 14, T(1) = 13$
  **e** $T(n + 1) = T(n) + 6, T(1) = 4$
  **f** $T(n + 1) = T(n) - 7, T(1) = 38$

**5 a** $T(n + 1) = T(n) + 5, T(1) = 300$
  **b** 353, 356, 359, 362, 365
  **c** Zadie has £ 422 and Zach has £ 420, so Zadie has more money.
  **d** 25 months

**6 a i** 40 hits      **ii** 5120 hits
  **b** 12 weeks

**7** This will never happen.

| Key outcomes | Quick check |
|---|---|
| Identify and use term-to-term rules. <br> L6 | Write down the term-to-term rule and the next two terms for this sequence: 4, 12, 36, 108,... (multiply by 3; 324, 972) |
| Generate sequences using term-to-term rules. <br> L6 | A sequence starts with 2 and each term is found by adding 4 to the previous term. Write down the first five terms of the sequence. (2, 6, 10, 14, 18) |
| Find and use position-to-term rules. <br> L6 | Find the position-to-term rule for this sequence: <br> 5, 9, 13, 17,... (multiply by 4 and add 1) <br> Find the $10^{th}$ term of the sequence. (41) |
| Find and use the nth term. <br> L6 | Find the $n$th term formula for these sequences and write down the $50^{th}$ term: <br> **a** 2, 3, 4, 5,... ($n + 1$, 51) **b** 5, 8, 11, 14,... ($3n + 2$, 152) |

## ⊞ MyMaths extra support

| Lesson/online homework | Description |
|---|---|
| Squares and triangles  1154  L4 | Square numbers and triangle numbers explained and represented graphically |

# My Review

### Check out
**You should now be able to ...**

Test it ➡
Questions

| | | |
|---|---|---|
| ✓ | Identify and use term-to-term rules. | 1 |
| ✓ | Generate sequences using term-to-term rules. | 2 |
| ✓ | Find and use position-to-term rules. | 3 – 5 |
| ✓ | Find and use the *n*th term. | 6, 7 |

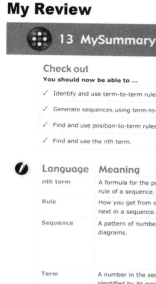

| Language | Meaning | Example |
|---|---|---|
| *n*th term | A formula for the position-to-term rule of a sequence. | The *n*th term for the sequence 3, 8, 13, 18, 23, ... is $5n - 2$ |
| Rule | How you get from one term to the next in a sequence. | The rule for the sequence 3, 8, 13, 18, 23, ... is 'add 5'. |
| Sequence | A pattern of numbers or diagrams. | 3, 8, 13, 18, 23, ... |
| Term | A number in the sequence, identified by its position. | For the sequence 3, 8, 13, 18, 23, ..., the first term is 3, the second term is 8, etc. |
| Flow Chart | A flow chart is a diagram that describes a sequence of operations. | Means 'multiply by two' then 'add six' |

246   Algebra   Sequences

## 13 MyReview

1 For each sequence, find the term-to-term rule and write the next two terms of the sequence.
 a 9 16 23 30
 b 35 32 29 26
 c 1 3 9 27

2 Write the first five terms of the sequences with these rules.
 a *Start with 6 and add 2*
 b *Start with 90 and subtract 8*
 c *Start with 5 and double*
 d *Start with 3, double and subtract 1*

3 This sequence of diagrams is formed by adding squares.

Position  1  2  3

 a Draw the diagram for position 4.
 b How many squares are added to the previous pattern to make the next pattern?
 c State the rule that connects the pattern number and the number of tiles needed.
 d Find how many squares are in the 15th term of the sequence.

4 Find the position-to-term-rule for each of these sequences.
 a 7 9 11 13 15
 b 4 9 14 19 24

5 Find the 12th term of the sequences with these position-to-term rules.
 a multiply the position by 4 then subtract 9
 b $2n + 11$
 c $8n - 20$
 d $4n - 4$

6 Write the *n*th term for these rules.
 a  ×4 +5
 b ×11 −2
 c ×3 −6

7 Find the *n*th term rule for each of these sequences.
 a 14 24 34 44 54
 b 5 13 21 29 37
 c 7 8 9 10 11
 d 150 250 350 450 550

### What next?

| Score | | |
|---|---|---|
| 0 – 3 | Your knowledge of this topic is still developing. To improve look at Formative test: 3A-13; MyMaths: 1173 and 1165 |
| 4 – 6 | You are gaining a secure knowledge of this topic. To improve look at InvisiPen: 281, 282 and 283 |
| 7 | You have mastered this topic. Well done, you are ready to progress! |

⊕ MyMaths.co.uk

247

---

## Question commentary

**Question 1** – Part **c** is most tricky. You could give students a hint by telling them to try multiplying rather than adding.

**Question 2** – Students convert the word rules into number sequences. Check in part **d** that they are correctly applying the rule step-by-step.

**Question 3** – A 'real-life' sequence which could lead to further investigation. For example what happens if I change the pattern to grow in three directions?

**Questions 4** and **5** – Students first write down the position-to-term rules and then work out the terms given the rule. These questions should provide basic practice.

**Question 6** – Conversion of the function machine to algebra. Check students use the correct notation.

**Question 7** – Students will need to identify the common difference. A tabular approach may be useful for some.

## Answers

1 a $+7, 37, 44$     b $-3, 23, 20$
  c $\times 3, 81, 243$

2 a $6, 8, 10, 12, 14$     b $90, 82, 74, 66, 58$
  c $5, 10, 20, 40, 80$     d $3, 5, 9, 17, 33$

3 a 

  b 2 squares     c $2n - 1$     d 29

4 a $2n + 5$   b $5n - 1$

5 a 39   b 35   c 76   d 44

6 a $4n + 5$   b $11n - 2$   c $3n - 6$

7 a $10n + 4$     b $8n - 3$
  c $n + 6$     d $100n + 50$

# 13 MyPractice

**13a**

1  **a**  Write the number sequence for this bead pattern.

   **b**  What is the term-to-term rule for the sequence?

2  For each of these sequences
   **i**  write the term-to-term rule
   **ii**  add three more terms.
   **a**  4, 11, 18, 25, ...
   **b**  12, 17, 22, 27, ...
   **c**  56, 48, 40, 32, ...
   **d**  2, 4, 8, 16, ...
   **e**  480, 240, 120, 60, ...
   **f**  -2, 4, 10, 16, ...

**13b**

3  Here is a mapping for the sequence 5, 9, 13, 17, ... .

| Position | Term value |
| --- | --- |
| 1 | 5 $\big)$ +4 |
| 2 | 9 $\big)$ +4 |
| 3 | 13 |
| 4 | 17 |

   **a**  State the rule that connects the position number and the value of the term.
   **b**  Use your rule to calculate the value of these terms.
   **i**  ninth term   **ii**  fifteenth term   **iii**  fiftieth term   **vi**  hundredth term

**13c**

4  This is the function for a mapping.

   Input → ×6 → −3 → Output

   **a**  Copy and complete this mapping of the function.

| Input | Output |
| --- | --- |
| 1 | 3 |
| 2 | [ ] |
| 3 | [ ] |
| 4 | [ ] |
| 5 | [ ] |

   **b**  What is the value of the $n$th term?

---

**13c**

5  Jane boils water in her science lesson.
At the beginning of her experiment the temperature is 20°C.
She checks the temperature of the water every minute.
The temperature rises by 3°C every minute.

   **a**  Copy and complete this mapping for the first six minutes.

| Time (minutes) | Temperature (°C) |
| --- | --- |
| 1 | 23 |
| 2 | [ ] |
| 3 | [ ] |
| 4 | [ ] |
| 5 | [ ] |
| 6 | [ ] |

   **b**  Find the $n$th term.

6  For each of these sequences
   **i**  find the $n$th term
   **ii**  and write down the thirtieth term.
   **a**  5, 7, 9, 11, 13, ...
   **b**  4, 11, 18, 25, 32, ...
   **c**  4, 9, 14, 19, 24, ...
   **d**  1, 5, 9, 13, 17, ...
   **e**  7, 17, 27, 37, 47, ...
   **f**  8, 11, 14, 17, 20, ...

**13d**

7  Write the first five terms of each of these sequences.
   **a**  $T(n + 1) = T(n) + 3$, $T(1) = 4$
   **b**  $T(n + 1) = T(n) + 5$, $T(1) = -1$
   **c**  $T(n + 1) = T(n) - 2$, $T(1) = 25$
   **d**  $T(n + 1) = T(n) - 0.5$, $T(1) = 9.5$

8  Describe each of these sequences using a recursive formula.
   **a**  3, 6, 9, 12, 15 ...
   **b**  22, 19, 16, 13, 10 ...
   **c**  3.5, 5, 6.5, 8, 9.5 ...
   **d**  13, 8, 3, -2, -7 ...
   **e**  -10, -6, -2, 2, 6, ...
   **f**  $\frac{1}{4}, \frac{3}{4}, 1\frac{1}{4}, 1\frac{3}{4}, 2\frac{1}{4}$ ...

9  Viv won a fortune on the lottery but her motto is 'spend, spend, spend'. At the start of January she has three million pounds but each month she spends £75000.
   **a**  If $T(n)$ represents the money Viv has at the start of the $n$th month
   **i**  write a recursive formula for $T(n + 1)$
   **ii**  write an $n$th term formula for $T(n)$.
   **b**  How much money does Viv have after  **i**  one year   **ii**  two years?
   **c**  When will Viv have spent all her money?

**MyMaths.co.uk**

## Question commentary

**Questions 1** and **2** – Check that students are correctly identifying the additive and multiplicative sequences.

**Question 3** – This question demonstrates the link between the sequence, the tabular form and the function machine.

**Questions 4, 5** and **6** – The approach adopted in questions **4** and **5** can similarly be employed in question **6** or students could tabulate the sequences.

**Questions 7, 8** and **9** – Link the work on recursive formulae back to the term-to-term rule if students struggle with the notation. Check they are using the correct structure in their formulae for questions **8** and **9** and that they are defining T(1).

## Answers

**1** a  3, 8, 13, 18          b  +5

**2** a  +7; 4, 11, 18, 25, 32, 39, 46

   b  +5; 12, 17, 22, 27, 32, 37, 42
   c  -8; 56, 48, 40, 32, 24, 16, 8
   d  ×2; 2, 4, 8, 16, 32, 64, 128
   e  ÷2; 480, 240, 120, 60, 30, 15, 7.5
   f  +6; -2, 4, 10, 16, 22, 28, 34

**3** a

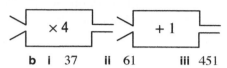

   b  i  37          ii  61          iii  451          iv  901

**4** a

| Input | Output |
|-------|--------|
| 1 | 3 |
| 2 | 9 |
| 3 | 15 |
| 4 | 21 |
| 5 | 27 |

   b  $6n - 3$

**5** a

| Input | Output |
|-------|--------|
| 1 | 23 |
| 2 | 26 |
| 3 | 29 |
| 4 | 32 |
| 5 | 35 |
| 6 | 38 |

   b  $3n + 20$

**6** a  i  $2n + 3$          ii  63
   b  i  $7n - 3$          ii  207
   c  i  $5n - 1$          ii  149
   d  i  $4n - 3$          ii  117
   e  i  $10n - 3$          ii  297
   f  i  $3n + 5$          ii  95

**7** a  4, 7, 10, 13, 16          b  -1, 4, 9, 14, 19
   c  25, 23, 21, 19, 17          d  9.5, 9, 8.5, 8, 7.5

**8** a  $T(n + 1) = T(n) + 3, T(1) = 3$
   b  $T(n + 1) = T(n) - 3, T(1) = 22$
   c  $T(n + 1) = T(n) + 1.5, T(1) = 3.5$
   d  $T(n + 1) = T(n) - 5, T(1) = 13$
   e  $T(n + 1) = T(n) + 4, T(1) = -10$
   f  $T(n + 1) = T(n) + 1/2, T(1) = ¼$

**9** a  i  $T(n + 1) = T(n) - 75\,000, T(1) = 3\,000\,000$
     ii  $-75\,000n + 3\,000\,000$
   b  i  £2 100 000          ii  £1 200 000
   c  40 months

| Introduction | Prior knowledge |
|---|---|
| The chapter starts by reviewing a range of facts about 3D shapes such as naming and describing them. Nets and plans and elevations are covered in the next two sections. The chapter finishes with work on the volume of a cuboid, shapes made from cuboids and the surface area of a cuboid. | Students should already know how to… <br> • Calculate the area of simple 2D shapes <br> • Carry out simple arithmetical calculations |

| | Starter problem |
|---|---|
| The introduction discusses the relative masses and surface areas of meerkats and humans in relation to how much they eat. Since the meerkat has the larger surface area relative to body mass, the more heat is lost through the skin and the more the meerkat must eat to replace this, relative to its mass. | The starter problem is a cube animal. The students are asked to work out the surface area and volume of the animal before considering the same facts about an enlarged version. Cubes could be used to physically build the animal to enable easier counting, but otherwise the students should be able to 'see' that the volume is 16 cubes and the surface area is 64 squares. |
| It is interesting to consider other mammals and birds in this context. Mice, for example, weight between 20 and 35 grams and eat on average 4 to 5 grams of food per day. This is means that they would eat their own body weight in food in 5 to 7 days, very similar to the meerkat. | If the shape is enlarged by scale factor two, each original cube is now made up of eight cubes and each original square is now made up of four squares. |
| | Hence the volume of the enlarged animal is 128 cubes and the surface area is 256 squares. |
| Birds typically eat between one half and one quarter of their body weight per day while bats eat the equivalent amount of insects in a single night as a person eating 20 pizzas! | Students could be asked to consider alternative scale factors of enlargement such as three or one half. |

## Resources

### ⊞ MyMaths

| | | | | | |
|---|---|---|---|---|---|
| 3D shapes | 1078 | Plans elevations | 1098 | Nets of 3D shapes | 1106 |
| Nets, surface area | 1107 | Volume of cuboids | 1137 | | |

| **Online assessment** | | **InvisiPen solutions** | | | |
|---|---|---|---|---|---|
| Chapter test | 3A–14 | Properties of 3D shapes | 321 | Surface area of cuboid | 322 |
| Formative test | 3A–14 | Volume of shapes made from cuboids | | | 323 |
| Summative test | 3A–14 | Isometric grids | 324 | Nets of simple 3D shapes | 325 |

# Topic scheme

Teaching time = 6 lessons/2 weeks

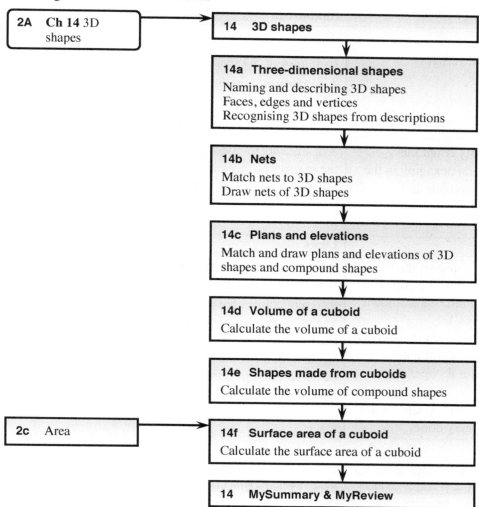

**2A    Ch 14** 3D shapes

**14    3D shapes**

**14a  Three-dimensional shapes**
Naming and describing 3D shapes
Faces, edges and vertices
Recognising 3D shapes from descriptions

**14b  Nets**
Match nets to 3D shapes
Draw nets of 3D shapes

**14c  Plans and elevations**
Match and draw plans and elevations of 3D shapes and compound shapes

**14d  Volume of a cuboid**
Calculate the volume of a cuboid

**14e  Shapes made from cuboids**
Calculate the volume of compound shapes

**2c    Area**

**14f  Surface area of a cuboid**
Calculate the surface area of a cuboid

**14    MySummary & MyReview**

# Differentiation

**Student book 3A        250 – 267**

Properties of 3D shapes
Nets
Plans and elevations
Volume of a cuboid and shapes made from cuboids
Surface area of a cuboid

**Student book 3B        248 – 263**

Properties of 3D shapes including faces, edges and vertices
Isometric drawing, plans and elevations
Planes of symmetry and nets of 3D shapes
Surface area and volume of a cuboid and other prisms

**Student book 3C        242 – 257**

3D shapes and 3D geometry
Introduction to trigonometry
Bearings

## Objectives

- Describe and visualise 3D shapes and their properties.                    (L5)

| Key ideas | Resources |
|---|---|
| 1 3D shapes can be solid or hollow.<br>2 3D shapes have faces, edges and vertices. | ⊕ 3D shapes                    (1078)<br>Examples of 3D shapes<br>A worksheet showing 3D shapes<br>Mini whiteboards |

| Simplification | Extension |
|---|---|
| Students handle solids and physically count the number of faces, vertices and edges. Packaging in the shape of cylinders, tubes, triangular prisms and cuboids can be used. | Ask students to investigate the relationship between the number of faces, edges and vertices (Euler's formula is $F + V - E = 2$). They can then look up Euler's formula on the Internet and also research his life. |

| Literacy | Links |
|---|---|
| Note the links between common 3D shapes: the cylinder, cube and cuboid are all prisms; the cone is a pyramid. The triangular-based pyramid is also known as a tetrahedron (meaning 'four faces').<br><br>Make the distinction between edge (for 3D shapes) and side (for 2D shapes). The word 'vertex' (plural: 'vertices') contrasts with 'apex' (plural: 'apexes' or 'apices').<br><br>When asked to draw a shape, the word 'sketch' means that the drawing need not be accurately done. | Triangular prisms are used in science to study light. When white light is passed through a prism, the different colours are refracted (or bent) at different angles to create a rainbow effect. Sir Isaac Newton was the first person to realise that the prism separates the white light into its constituent colours. There is a demonstration of refraction by a prism at http://mistupid.com/science/prism.htm |

## Alternative approach

Once 3D shapes have been seen, handled and discussed, other experiences are available at www.mymaths.co.uk/tasks/library/loadLesson.asp?title=shape/3dShape&taskID=1078

## Checkpoint

How many faces, edges and vertices are there on a tetrahedron (triangle-based pyramid)?                    (4, 6, 4)

## Starter – Reflect

Give students coordinates of points and ask them to give the transformed coordinates after reflection. For example:

$(4, 7)$ reflected in the line $x$-axis    $(4, -7)$
$(3, 2)$ reflected in the $y$-axis    $(-3, 2)$
$(4, 6)$ reflected in the line $y = 1$    $(4, -4)$

Recap work of previous chapters and especially number work. Ask rapid response questions. Students reply by writing on their mini whiteboards. Discuss questions when their answers indicate a need.

## Teaching notes

The students handle and name examples of 3D shapes.

Students, working in pairs, describe each shape in terms of the number of 'faces', 'edges' and 'vertices'. Students refer to actual solids and record their results on a worksheet.

Agree the information as a whole class.

## Plenary

Students compile a glossary of key names and properties.

They have a question-and-answer session, identifying features of various 3D shapes. Mini whiteboards can be used for quick assessment.

## Exercise commentary

**Questions 1 to 3** – These questions cover the basic vocabulary of 3D shapes. In Question **2e**, students could names the parallel lines.

**Question 4** – Students can refer back to the previous page in the student book.

**Question 5** – Explain to students that they do not need to use all of the pieces and they can mix and match the different shapes.

---

## Answers

1   **a**   12 edges   **b**   6 faces    **c**   8 vertices
    **d**   BF, CG or DH       **e**   A square

2   **a**   9 edges   **b**   5 faces    **c**   6 vertices
    **d**   EF       **e**   2

3   **a**   8 edges   **b**   5 faces    **c**   5 vertices
    **d**   A square   **e**   4 triangles

4   **a**   Sphere    **b**   Square based pyramid
    **c**   Cone      **d**   Triangular based pyramid
    **e**   Cube

5   Square based pyramid, triangular based pyramid, triangular prism, cuboid

## Objectives

- Construct and visualise 3D shapes from their nets. (L6)

| Key ideas | Resources |
|---|---|
| 1  A net is a 2D plan of a 3D shape.<br>2  A 3D shape can have several different nets. | ⊞  Nets of 3D shapes (1106)<br>A selection of empty boxes and cartons<br>Pre-cut nets of cubes and cuboids<br>Commercial construction kits<br>Squared paper and card<br>Scissors<br>Glue or sticky tape<br>Mini whiteboards |

| Simplification | Extension |
|---|---|
| Give initial priority to students disassembling packaging and then folding large-size nets already cut out for them. They use commercial construction kits to make 3D shapes.<br>Leave designing nets until later. | Students use nets for more complicated 3D shapes. Examples could include an octahedron or a dodecahedron.<br>Students could design their own net for a more complicated 3D shape. |

| Literacy | Links |
|---|---|
| The word 'net' is taken from fishing where a net is laid out flat on land and then closes up when catching fish.<br>Some 3D shapes have fascinating names with very complicated nets; for example, icosahedron, rhombicuboctahedron, truncated dodecahedron, rhombicosidodecahedron.<br>See the book 'Mathematical Models' by Cundy and Rollett. | Atoms are arranged in molecules to form characteristic shapes. Buckminsterfullerene contains molecules made up of 60 carbon atoms arranged in a shape similar to a soccer ball with hexagonal and pentagonal faces. The correct name for the shape is a truncated icosahedron but it has been nicknamed a 'buckyball'. There is a net for a buckyball at www.korthalsaltes.com/pdf/truncated_icosahedron.pdf and at http://mathforum.org/alejandre/workshops/ bucky.net.html |

## Alternative approach

There is no real alternative to disassembling packaging and assembling pre-cut nets. However, there are various commercial construction kits of plastic 2D shapes that clip together easily to make 3D shapes.

## Checkpoint

A triangular prism has length 7cm and the triangular face is isosceles with base 10cm, height 12cm and slant length 13cm. Write down the dimensions of the five 2D shapes that will make up the net of the triangular prism.

(2 triangles with base 10cm and height 12cm, two rectangles 13cm by 7cm and one rectangle 10cm by 7cm)

**Starter** – Name the shape

Students look at the shapes on page 252 of the student's book. Say "I am thinking of a shape. It has six vertices.". Continue with further clues such as "It has five faces…", "… and nine edges." until students guess the shape. [Triangular prism]

## Teaching notes

Explain to students that a 'net' is a plan of a 3D shape drawn on paper or card which is then cut out and folded in order to construct the 3D shape. Give the students a prepared net of a cube or cuboid. (There are many examples on the Internet which can be printed directly onto card.) Explain that the lines inside the net are the fold lines. Explain that the tabs are for sticking the shape together at the end.

Students cut out, fold and stick their net together. Give students further nets for them to construct other 3D shapes. Practise recognising 3D shapes from their nets.

## Plenary

Show the students a number of nets and ask them to write down (on mini whiteboards to aid assessment) the names of the 3D shapes that would be constructed by folding the nets.

## Exercise commentary

**Question 1** – Students can refer to the previous page of the student book to help with this question. Note that the net of the cone is not shown there, however students could be given a net of a cone to fold to make the 3D shape.

**Question 2** – Students should ensure that they count the number of faces carefully to ensure that their nets are complete.

**Question 3** – A practical construction. The students could be given a printed copy of the net (on card).

**Question 4** – This compound shape will challenge many. Ensure they count the number of faces required carefully before proceeding to design the net.

## Answers

1.
   a   Triangular based pyramid          b   Cuboid
   c   Cone                              d   Triangular prism
   e   Cylinder                          f   Cube

2.   a,b,c          Check students' constructions

3.   Check completed task

4.   Check students' constructions

## Objectives

- Draw and use simple plans and elevations.

(L6)

| Key ideas | Resources |
|---|---|
| 1 A plan of an object is the bird's-eye view seen from above.<br><br>2 A elevation of an object is a side view. | ⊞ Plans and elevations (1098)<br><br>A variety of 3D solids<br><br>Examples of technical drawings<br><br>Multi-link cubes and squared paper<br><br>Construction kits<br><br>Mini whiteboards |

| Simplification | Extension |
|---|---|
| In the first instance, students draw the plans and elevations of simple 3D shapes, using the actual solid shape to handle. They need to be secure in the use of correct terminology. | Students create their own solid from a number of multi-link cubes and then challenge a partner to draw the plan, side elevation and front elevation of the solid. Students working in pairs can challenge each other. |

| Literacy | Links |
|---|---|
| A plan is an overhead view looking down on a 3D object, like a bird's-eye view.<br><br>An elevation is a side view of a 3D object when viewed from the front, left or right, or back (and referred to as a front elevation, a side elevation, or a rear elevation).<br><br>Plans and elevations are used in architectural drawings and technical drawings. | The cyanotype process (*cyan* is a greenish blue colour) is a low-cost method for copying drawings and was widely used from the mid-nineteenth to mid-twentieth century. The resulting copies were composed of either white lines on a blue background or blue lines on a white background and so were called 'blueprints'. The term 'blueprint' later came to mean any technical drawing or design plan. There are examples of architectural drawings and engineering blueprints at www.armchairgeneral.com/rkkaww2/galleries/T-26/T-26M31_bp.htm |

### Alternative approach

Use clear plastic rectangular or square pieces from a construction kit to make a cuboid (or box) into which the chosen 3D shape will fit. Label three of the faces of the cuboid with the words *plan*, *front elevation* and *side elevation*.

Look through the three clear labelled faces of the cuboid and sketch with felt pen what is seen. Open out the cuboid and place the labelled pieces flat.

### Checkpoint

Describe the shapes of the plan, front and side elevation of a cylinder with diameter 4cm and height 6cm.

(Plan: a circle, diameter 4cm; front elevation: a rectangle 4cm by 6cm; side elevation: a rectangle 4cm by 6cm)

## Starter – Dice nets

Students are given three different nets of a cube. They number the faces 1 to 6, so that when each net is folded to make a dice, the numbers on opposite faces add up to 7.

## Teaching notes

A 'plan view' is what is seen when looking down on an object. If possible, show the students an example of an architectural plan. An 'elevation' is the view seen when an object is looked at from the front, back or side.

Students construct a simple 3D shape out of multi-link cubes. They draw (on squared paper) the plan view of the shape and label it. Ask them to clearly label it as 'plan view' and then draw and label the front elevation and side elevation of the shape. Ask students to check with a partner that they agree with their answers.

Students can now challenge each other to draw the plan view and elevations of further shapes constructed out of multi-link cubes.

## Plenary

Show the students examples of 3D shapes. Ask them to sketch a plan and then an elevation on their mini whiteboards. Discuss their results.

## Exercise commentary

**Question 1** – A matching exercise to encourage students to visualise the 3D shapes.

**Question 2** – Give students cubes to work with if available.

**Question 3** – Students could construct the shape using a net (see **14b**) and then draw the elevations and plan view.

---

## Answers

1  a – iv, b – v, c – ii, d – vi, e – i, f – iii
2  Check students' drawings

3
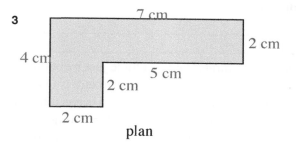

plan

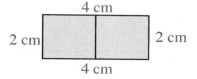

side elevation

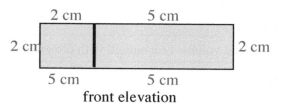

front elevation

## Objectives

- Know and use the formula for the volume of a cuboid. (L6)

| Key ideas | Resources |
|---|---|
| 1 Understand the reasoning behind the formula for the volume of a cuboid.<br><br>2 The units of volume are 'length cubed', such as $cm^3$ and $m^3$. | ⊞ Volumes of cuboids (1137)<br>Multi-link cubes<br>Various cuboid containers<br>Water and a measuring jug<br>Mini whiteboards |

| Simplification | Extension |
|---|---|
| Students use plastic cubes to make cuboids, layer by layer. They count the cubes to find the volume of the cuboid that they have made. They check their answer by using the formula. | Students calculate a more complicated volume comprising several sections, each of which is a cuboid. They suggest how to find the volume of a right-angled triangular prism – and then a triangular prism which is *not* right-angled. |

| Literacy | Links |
|---|---|
| A length can be turned into a volume just by putting the word "cubic" in front of it. A decimetre is one-tenth of a metre, and a cubic decimetre is equal to one litre. Can students imagine what a cubic kilometre might look like? It's called a teralitre, where the prefix tera indicates $1 \times 10^9$ | Swimming pools used for Olympic events must conform to the rules of FINA, the governing body of world swimming. An Olympic-sized pool is 50 metres long and 25 metres wide, with a minimum depth of 2 metres throughout the entire length. The pool contains 8 lanes which are 2.5 metres wide with a space on either side. What is the minimum volume of the pool? [$2\,500\ m^3$] There is a diagram of an Olympic-sized pool at http://en.wikipedia.org/wiki/File:Swimming_pool_50m_2008.svg |

## Alternative approach

The approach used in Question **1** is worth spending time on, as it provides the underlying reason for the formula for the volume of a cuboid. The first layer of cuboids has a rectangular 'footprint' of area $l \times w$ $cm^2$, so the layer contains $l \times w$ cubes and has a volume of $l \times w$ $cm^3$. Each layer thereafter also has a volume $l \times w$ $cm^3$, so if there are $h$ layers, the total volume is $l \times w \times h$ $cm^3$.

This notion of building up layers to find a volume works with any shape of 'footprint' and, although beyond the scope of this book, it can be used for any prism to give the formula $V = A \times h$.

## Checkpoint

Work out the volume of a cuboid with dimensions 5cm, 8cm and 4cm. ($160cm^3$)

Students draw a $3 \times 3$ grid and enter nine numbers between 10 and 30. Ask questions such as:

The base of a triangle is 4 cm and the perpendicular height is 8 cm. What is the area? [16 cm$^2$]

What is the area of a rectangle with a length of 10 cm and a width of 2.9 cm? [29 cm$^2$]

The winner is the first to cross out their nine numbers.

## Teaching notes

Students build various cuboids using multi-link cubes. They count the number of cubes used to build each cuboid to find the volume of the cuboid. They discover that the volume can be found by multiplying the length by the width by the depth (or height) of the cuboid.

Students then find volumes where counting cubes is not possible. For example, they could find the capacity of an empty carton of orange juice. They find other capacities and volumes of containers and solids used for commercial packaging – and check those labels which give the capacity.

All answers need units which are units of length cubed; for example, cm³ or m³.

## Plenary

Questions on finding volumes of cuboids can be presented orally or using diagrams. Some questions can be set in context. Students find the volumes and give the correct units on their mini whiteboards.

## Exercise commentary

**Question 1** – This question gives the conceptual basis for the formula for the volume of a cuboid. The first layer stands on a rectangular base of area $l \times w$. There are $h$ layers (where $h$ is the height) so the total volume is 'the volume of one layer $\times h$', giving $l \times w \times h$.

**Question 2** – Basic practice at applying the formula.

**Questions 3** and **4** – These are simple applications in context. In Question **4** note that the total volume of ten blocks (not just one) is wanted.

**Question 5** – Sketch diagrams may help here.

## Answers

1  a  8 cm³    b  16 cm³    c  24 cm³

2  a  45 cm³    b  30 cm³    c  32 cm³    d  48 cm³
   e  45 cm³    f  112 cm³

3  60 m³

4  1200 cm³

5  a  100 cm³    b  30 m³    c  60 cm³    d  110 cm³
   e  27 m³

## Objectives

- Use geometric properties of cuboids and shapes made from cuboids.          (L6)
- Know and use the formula for the volume of a cuboid.          (L6)
- Calculate volumes of 3D shapes made from cuboids.          (L6)

| Key ideas | Resources |
|---|---|
| 1  3D shapes can be made by combining cuboids.<br>2  The volumes of such shapes are found from the constituent cuboids. | Volume of cuboids          (1137)<br>Multi-link cubes<br>Isometric paper and squared paper<br>Shapes made from card<br>Sand or small polystyrene pieces<br>Mini whiteboards |

| Simplification | Extension |
|---|---|
| Students build simple compound shapes made from two cuboids. They split the compound shape into its two constituent cuboids and find the volume of each separately. They then find the total volume of the original shape. | Students use multi-link cubes to create a solid made from cuboids. They draw a diagram of the solid on isometric paper and a plan view of the solid on squared paper. They calculate the volume of the solid. |

| Literacy | Links |
|---|---|
| Note that for area the units use a $^2$, whereas for volume the units use a $^3$ (as in cm$^2$ and cm$^3$). This notation can be remembered by thinking of area as a measure in two dimensions, hence using $^2$ (spoken as 'squared'). Whereas volume is a measure in three dimensions, hence using $^3$ (spoken as 'cubed'). | Manufacturers use eye-catching designs for packaging to help sell their goods. There are designs and nets for unusual packaging designs based on cuboids at www.dtonline.org/apps/object/app?1&2&1&1&0&1&0 |

### Alternative approach

Compound shapes, made by the teacher from card, are designed to be containers with one open end. The capacity of such a container is found by (a) imagining the container split into cuboids (most likely two cuboids), measuring the dimensions, using the formula for each cuboid and so finding the total capacity, (b) filling the container with sand or small polystyrene packing pieces and measuring the amount using a measuring jar. Compare the results.

### Checkpoint

A tower is made by placing a cube of edge length 5cm on top of a cuboid measuring 6cm by 8cm by 10cm. What is the volume of the tower?          (605cm$^3$)

## Starter – 3D

Draw a 2D shape on the board representing elevation of a 3D shape and ask students to guess the 3D shape. For example,

Circle     [sphere, cone or cylinder]

Triangle   [triangular prism, square-based
                pyramid or triangular-based pyramid]

Then draw a plan and students narrow down their choice. Encourage students to think of the different possibilities for each plan or elevation, remembering that the shape can be orientated in different ways!

## Teaching notes

Explain that, if two or more cubes or cuboids are joined together, you get a compound shape. Use multi-link cubes to demonstrate this to students with prepared models or projected images.

To find the volume of these compound shapes, students split them up into the constituent parts. Again, this can be demonstrated using multi-link cubes.

Ask students to find the volume of each part and, hence, of the whole shape.

Students construct their own compound shapes out of multi-link cubes, exchange with a partner, and each then finds the volume of their partner's shape. The answer can then be checked by counting the cubes used in the model.

## Plenary

Show diagrams of compound shapes. Give a number of quick fire questions which involve finding the volume of these compound shapes. Students can give answers on mini whiteboards to enable easy assessment.

## Exercise commentary

**Question 1** – This question recaps volume of a cuboid.

**Question 2** – Students should treat the parts of the question as linked, each part building on the previous part.

**Question 3** – Students could sketch the constituent parts and work out their dimensions. There are two possible ways to divide each of the shapes.

**Question 4** – Part **a** is similar to Question **3** except the shape must be divided into three pieces. Part **b** can be drawn as a freehand sketch or on isometric paper. Students can be given cubes to work with.

---

## Answers

1  **a**  60 cm³   **b**  120 cm³  **c**  42 cm³   **d**  2

2  **a**  8 cm³    **b**  14 cm³   **c**  18 cm³  **d**  20 cm³

3  **a**  213 cm³  **b**  392 cm³

4  **a**  108 cm³  **b**  Check sketch and calculations

## Objectives

- Calculate surface areas of cuboids. (L6)

| Key ideas | Resources |
|---|---|
| 1  The surface area of a cuboid is the total of the areas of its six faces.<br>2  The surface area of a cuboid is the same as the area of its net. | ⊞  Nets, surface area (1107)<br>Squared paper<br>Mini whiteboards |

| Simplification | Extension |
|---|---|
| Students draw the six faces of a given cuboid separately on squared paper. To find the surface area of the cuboid, they simply add the areas of the six rectangular or square faces. | Students decide how to find the surface area of a triangular prism. They find the surface area for a particular triangular prism by taking measurements directly from the prism. |

| Literacy | Links |
|---|---|
| 3D shapes with curved surfaces also have surface area. It is important in chemistry where the more surface area, the faster the chemical reaction. For example, iron filings will burn easily, but a solid block of iron won't. It is also important in biology because a creature (such as a human baby) with a large surface area in relation to its size has greater difficulty keeping warm.<br><br>The underlying feature is the ratio of surface area to volume. | When wallpapering a room, the number of rolls of wallpaper required depends on the surface area of the walls to be covered. The surface area is calculated by measuring the width of the walls and their height, remembering that any areas with large windows and doors will not require paper. The larger the vertical 'repeat pattern' on the wallpaper, the more waste there will be as adjacent strips must match. |

## Alternative approach

Distinguish the three pairs of opposite faces of a cuboid by colouring the pairs in different colours. If a commercial construction kit is used, this can be easily achieved. Then ask for the areas of the six rectangular faces, but ask for them in pairs, colour by colour.

## Checkpoint

Calculate the surface area of cuboid with dimensions 4cm, 5cm and 8cm. (184cm$^2$)

## Starter – How many cuboids

Ask students to find cuboids with integer edges having a volume of 36 cm$^3$. Discuss their methods. Then ask:

Which cuboid is closest to a cube?     [3 × 3 × 4 cm]

Which is least like a cube?     [1 × 1 × 36 cm]

It can be extended by allowing edges with decimal lengths.

## Teaching notes

Explain to students that the surface area of any 3D shape is the area of the paper that would be needed to 'paper' its total surface (like wall paper). For a 3D shape that can be made from a net, the surface area is the area of the net.

Students take a net of a cuboid with known dimensions and they find the area of each constituent rectangle. They then find the sum of these areas to get the total surface area of the resulting cuboid.

Students are given a cuboid. They draw a net for the cuboid either to scale on squared paper or as a sketch with dimensions marked. They work with a partner to find the area of the net and the total surface area of the cuboid.

## Plenary

Show students a diagram of a cuboid with dimensions on it. They calculate the total surface area of the cuboid (by adding the areas of the six faces), displaying their working and final answer on mini whiteboards. Discuss their answers.

Repeat for other cuboids.

## Exercise commentary

**Question 1** – Counting squares on the nets is sufficient.

**Question 2** – Students can (a) just write the addition of six areas in a list, (b) sketch the separate rectangles and then find their areas, (c) draw a net and find the areas from the net. The three methods are in order of increasing workload.

**Question 3** – Methods (a) or (b) from Question **2** are preferred over method (c).

**Question 4** – Let students find for themselves that it is the original surface area plus the two newly-created surfaces formed by the cut. What if the cuboid is cut in half a different way?

---

## Answers

1   a   24 cm$^2$    b   62 cm$^2$    c   80 cm$^2$

2   a   62 cm$^2$    b   80 cm$^2$    c   164 cm$^2$    d   118 cm$^2$

3   a   40 cm$^2$    b   54 cm$^2$    c   82 cm$^2$    d   98 cm$^2$
   e   700 cm$^2$

4   a   136cm$^2$
   b   Surface area of original cuboid + the area of the newly created faces (4cm × 2cm × 2)
     136 cm$^2$ + 16 cm$^2$ = 152 cm$^2$

| Key outcomes | Quick check |
|---|---|
| Describe properties of solid shapes. L6 | How many faces, edges and vertices does a cuboid have? (6, 12, 8) |
| Construct and use nets of solid shapes. L6 | Describe the net of a square-based pyramid. (A square surrounded by four congruent triangles) |
| Use plans and elevations. L6 | Choose an object in the classroom and have students draw the plan and elevations. |
| Find the volume of a cuboid. L6 | A cuboid has dimensions 5cm, 10cm and 12cm. Find its volume. ($600cm^3$) |
| Find volumes of shapes made from cuboids. L6 | A shape is made by placing one cuboid of dimensions 3cm by 2cm by 4cm on top of another cuboid of dimensions 8cm by 7cm by 10cm. What is the total volume of the shape? ($584cm^3$) |
| Find the surface area of a cuboid. L6 | A cuboid has dimensions 5cm, 10cm and 12cm. Find its surface area. ($460cm^2$) |

## MyMaths extra support

| Lesson/online homework | Description |
|---|---|
| Isometric paper 6001 L2 | A template for putting together cubes on isometric paper with a mirror. |

# My Review

## Check out

**You should now be able to ...**

| | Test it ➡ Questions |
|---|---|
| ✓ Describe properties of solid shapes. | 1, 2 |
| ✓ Construct and use nets of solid shapes. | 3 |
| ✓ Use plans and elevations. | 4 |
| ✓ Find the volume of a cuboid. | 5 |
| ✓ Find volumes of shapes made from cuboids. | 6 |
| ✓ Find the surface area of a cuboid. | 7 |

| Language | Meaning | Example |
|---|---|---|
| Apex | The highest point of the shape. | apex |
| Base | The lowest face of the shape. | base |
| Face | A flat surface of a solid. | Vertex |
| Edge | The line where two faces meet. | Edge |
| Vertex | A point where three or more edges meet. | face |
| Prism | A solid shape with the same cross-section throughout its length. | A triangular prism has the same cross-section throughout its length. |
| Net | A 2D shape which can be folded to make a 3D solid. | Folds to make a cube |
| Surface area | The total area of all the faces of a 3D solid. | The area of a net equals the surface area of the solid. |

264   Geometry and measures   3D shapes

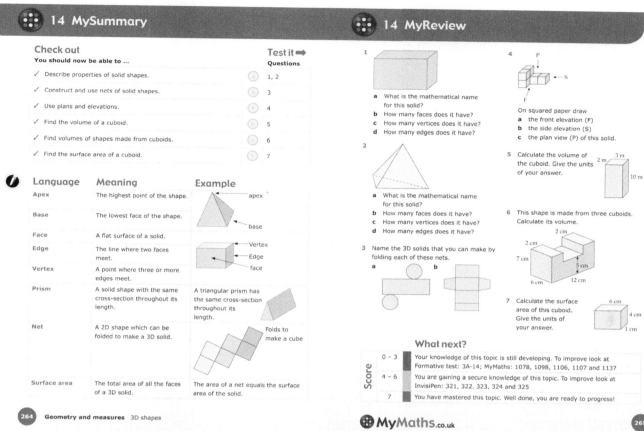

**1**
a What is the mathematical name for this solid?
b How many faces does it have?
c How many vertices does it have?
d How many edges does it have?

**2**
a What is the mathematical name for this solid?
b How many faces does it have?
c How many vertices does it have?
d How many edges does it have?

**3** Name the 3D solids that you can make by folding each of these nets.
a          b

**4**
On squared paper draw
a the front elevation (F)
b the side elevation (S)
c the plan view (P) of this solid.

**5** Calculate the volume of the cuboid. Give the units of your answer.  2 m  3 m  10 m

**6** This shape is made from three cuboids. Calculate its volume.
2 cm   2 cm   7 cm   5 cm   6 cm   12 cm

**7** Calculate the surface area of this cuboid. Give the units of your answer.  6 cm  4 cm  1 cm

### What next?

| Score | |
|---|---|
| 0 – 3 | Your knowledge of this topic is still developing. To improve look at Formative test: 3A-14; MyMaths: 1078, 1098, 1106, 1107 and 1137 |
| 4 – 6 | You are gaining a secure knowledge of this topic. To improve look at InvisiPen: 321, 322, 323, 324 and 325 |
| 7 | You have mastered this topic. Well done, you are ready to progress! |

⊞ MyMaths.co.uk

265

## Question commentary

**Questions 1 and 2** – Students should be able to count for each of these questions. Ensure they count 'hidden' faces, edges and vertices.

**Question 3** – Students should be able to visualise these shapes but if they struggle, nets could be provided for cutting out and assembling.

**Question 4** – Cubes could be provided to aid visualisation.

**Question 5** – A basic application of the formula.

**Question 6** – Emphasise that the compound shape can be broken up in several different ways. Students could try more than one way and check they give the same answer.

**Question 7** – Students may prefer to draw the net of the cuboid to help them visualise the surface area as the sum of the six rectangles.

## Answers

**1** a Cuboid
   b 6    c 8    d 12

**2** a Triangular-based pyramid
   b 4    c 4    d 6

**3** a Cylinder   b Trapezium prism

**4** a      b      c

**5** 60 m$^2$

**6** 408 cm$^3$

**7** 68 cm$^2$

# 14 MyPractice

**1** Name these 3D shapes.

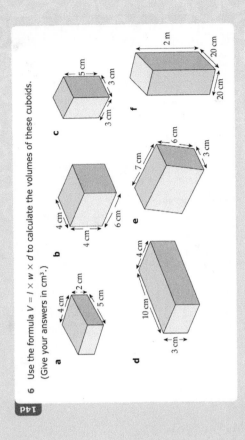

a   b   c   d   e

**2** Draw a net for this hexagonal pyramid.

6 cm
4 cm

**3** What is the volume of the cuboid made from this net?

2 cm
6 cm
4 cm
2 cm
4 cm

**4** This shape is made from two cuboids.
  **a** Draw an accurate plan view of the object.
  **b** Draw the front elevation.
  **c** Draw the side elevation.

plan
5 cm
3 cm
4 cm
5 cm
3 cm
side elevation
6 cm
5 cm
front elevation

**5** A shape is made from cubes. Sketch the shape given its plan, front elevation and side elevation.

Plan   Front elevation   Side elevation

---

**6** Use the formula $V = l \times w \times d$ to calculate the volumes of these cuboids.
(Give your answers in cm³.)

a   4 cm, 2 cm, 5 cm
b   4 cm, 4 cm, 6 cm
c   5 cm, 3 cm, 3 cm
d   10 cm, 4 cm, 3 cm
e   7 cm, 6 cm, 3 cm
f   2 m, 20 cm, 20 cm

**7** Find the total volume of the shape in question **4**.

**8 a** Draw an accurate net of this cuboid.
  **b** What is the volume of the cuboid?
  **c** What is its surface area?

5 cm, 4 cm, 3 cm

**9** Here is a net and the cuboid that it makes.

2 cm, 5 cm, 4 cm   A  B  C
C  B  A  D  E  F

  **a** Which is the opposite face to C?
  **b** Which is the opposite face to B?
  **c** Which is the opposite face to F?
  **d** What is the surface area of the cuboid?
  **e** What is its volume?

## Question commentary

**Question 1** – Students should recognise these simple solids by now.

**Questions 2** and **3** – The net in question **2** can just be a sketch, or it could be drawn accurately. For question **3**, ensure students can visualise the dimensions of the completed cuboid.

**Questions 4** and **5** – For question **5**, students could be given cubes to experiment with.

**Question 6** – Basic applications of the formula.

**Question 7** – How the shape breaks down should be obvious to the students. Could they do it a *different* way?

**Question 8** and **9** – Links to the net and the surface area and the volume can all be developed here. Students may use a variety of strategies.

## Answers

1  **a**  squared based pyramid   **b**   cylinder
   **c**  triangular prism   **d**   cuboid
   **e**  cone

2  Check students' constructions

3  48 cm$^3$

4  **a,b,c**   Check students' constructions

5  Check students' constructions

6  **a**  40 cm$^3$  **b**  96 cm$^3$  **c**  45 cm$^3$  **d**  120 cm$^3$
   **e**  126 cm$^3$  **f**  800 cm$^3$

7  186 cm$^3$

8  **a**  check construction  **b**  60 cm$^3$  **c**  94 cm$^2$

9  **a**  F   **b**  E   **c**  C   **d**  76 cm$^2$
   **e**  40 cm$^3$

| Related lessons | | Resources | |
|---|---|---|---|
| Rounding | 1b | Decimal places | (1001) |
| Area | 2c | Order of operations | (1167) |
| Using a calculator | 7f | Ratio dividing | (1039) |
| Position-to-term rules | 13b | Map scales | (1103) |
| Recursive sequences | 13d | Credit cards or business cards to measure | |
| Ratio | 15a | | |
| Dividing in a given ratio | 15b | | |

## Simplification

Students may need reminding what it means to say that shapes are mathematically 'similar'.

Students occasionally struggle with the accurate construction of geometric shapes. Hence task **3** part **bi** and task **5** could be omitted.

Calculators will help students to work out the required ratios quickly throughout.

## Extension

Students could use algebra to find the value of the golden ratio.

According to its definition the golden ratio is $\dfrac{x+1}{x} = \dfrac{x}{1}$ and so $\varphi = x$.

Solving the equation for the positive value of $x$ gives the value for $\varphi$.

## Links

The golden 'number' Phi has its own website which contains lots of useful information and articles:

www.goldennumber.net

Another good website for students to explore is http://www.mathsisfun.com/numbers/golden-ratio.html

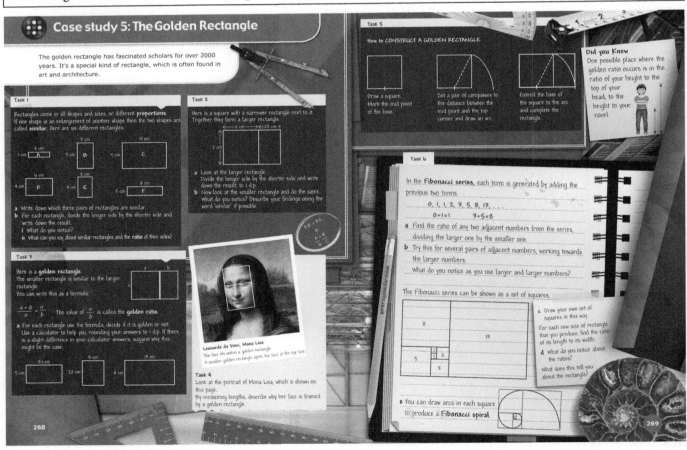

## Teaching notes

Phi (φ) is an irrational number defined by the geometric relationship: 'when line A is split at a particular point, the ratio of the whole line A to the larger segment B is the same as the ratio of the larger segment B to the smaller segment C or A : B = B : C'. This happens only when the line is split in one particular ratio now known as the golden ratio and gives a value for phi of approximately 1.618.

Explain that the golden rectangle is widely believed to have a balance and proportion that is pleasing to the eye, as are things that are divided into sections according to the golden ratio. Because of this, it is often suggested that the golden ratio has been used in art and architecture.

Look at the examples shown and claim that both the ancient Greeks and, later, Renaissance artists knew about φ. Discuss the possibility that, as the ratio is pleasing to the eye, artists and architects could produce work with features close to the ratio simply because they want their work to have pleasing visual balance.

### Task 5

Using the instructions at the top of the right hand page, give students a few minutes to construct a golden rectangle, suggesting that different groups use different sizes for the initial square. Once completed, remind students that the golden ratio is the ratio of the longer side to the shorter side. Ask them how they could find its value without actually measuring the rectangle. Establish that you need to know the size of the original square; ask them to assume that it is 2. Give them a few minutes to work with a partner and then hear their ideas. Elicit that you can use Pythagoras' theorem to find the radius of the arc (assuming a square of side 2, this will be $\sqrt{5}$ ) and, knowing that, you can find the length of the longer side $\left(1 + \sqrt{5}\right)$. Once they have the longer side, the golden ratio can be found by diving this by the length of the shorter side (2). Students could then measure their rectangles divide the longer side by the shorter side to see if they give approximately the same ratio, regardless of the original size of their square.

### Task 6

Look at the section on the Fibonacci series. Ask them to copy the series and continue it until they reach a number greater than 300. Then ask them to find the ratios of adjacent numbers, starting with the smaller ones and working towards the larger ones. Ask, what do you notice about the ratios of the numbers? Establish that, as the numbers get larger, the ratio settles around φ. You could ask students to set up a spreadsheet to explore this.

Now look at the diagram showing how the Fibonacci series can be represented as a set of squares, explaining that the diagram has been built up in a clockwise spiral starting with a square of side 1 and then adding another square of side 1 and then squares of sides 2, 3, 5, etc. Note how each time a square is added it results in a larger rectangle than before. Give the students

some time to draw their own set of squares in this way. Each time they add a new square, they should note down the ratio of the longer side to the shorter side of the rectangle created. Ask, what do you notice? What happens with the ratios of the sides? What does this tell you about the rectangle that you are creating?

Establish that the sides of the rectangles are always adjacent terms from the Fibonacci series, so the ratios of these numbers will get closer to the golden ratio as the numbers used become larger, in just the same way as the terms of the Fibonacci series did before. So, having started as a square, the rectangle must be becoming closer to a golden rectangle.

---

### Answers

1  a   A & F, B & C, D & E

   b   i 4, 1.67, 1.67, 1.5, 1.5, 4

   ii   Ratios are the same

2  a   1.6               b   1.6

   The two rectangles are similar

3  a   Yes, no, yes

   b   i 4.9 cm         ii   Check constructions

   c   1.6

4   The ratio of side lengths is approximately 1.6

5  a   Students' constructions

   b   $\varphi = \frac{\text{longer side}}{\text{shorter side}} = \frac{1+\sqrt{5}}{2} \approx 1.618...$

6  a   1, 2, 1.5, 1.6, 1.625, 1.615, 1.619, 1.618, 1.618,...

   b   The ratio tends to the golden ratio

   c   Students' constructions

   d   Length of rectangle = preceding rectangle's width, give the Fibonacci numbers: 1, 1, 2, 3, 5, 8, 13, 21, 34, 55, 89, 144, 233, 277,... so that the ratio tends to the golden ratio. The rectangle is a golden rectangle.

   e   Students' own drawings

## Learning outcomes

**SP2** Develop their use of formal mathematical knowledge to interpret and solve problems, including in financial
mathematics (L5)

**R3** Express one quantity as a fraction of another, where the fraction is less than 1 and greater than 1 (L6)

**R4** Use ratio notation, including reduction to simplest form (L5)

**R5** Divide a given quantity in two parts in a given part : part or part : whole ratio; express the
division of a quantity into two parts as a ratio (L6)

**R7** Understand that a multiplicative relationship between two quantities can be expressed as a ratio
or a fraction (L6)

**R8** Solve problems involving percentage change, including: percentage increase, decrease and
original value problems and simple interest in financial mathematics (L6)

## Introduction

The chapter starts by looking at ratio, simplifying and dividing into ratios. An introduction to proportion and the links to percentages are covered before a section on proportional reasoning using the unitary method. The final section looks at financial mathematics from the point of view of budgeting.

The introduction discusses the relationship between the amount of exercise we do and the amount of kilocalories we 'burn off'. The amount of kilocalories burnt off is directly proportional to both doing more exercise and the rate at which we do it. An example is given in the starter activity of 243 kilocalories burnt off walking three miles. Some other examples that you might give the students are:

- 30 minutes of jogging will burn on average 300 kilocalories;
- 8 hours sleep will burn off approximately 720 kilocalories;
- Watching TV for an hour will burn off 100 kilocalories;
- Sitting quietly and still for an hour will burn off approximately 80 kilocalories.

## Prior knowledge

Students should already know how to...

- Simplify fractions and work with equivalent fractions
- Carry out simple arithmetic

## Starter problem

The starter problem looks at how much exercise you would need to do to burn off the kilocalories in what you eat. At 243 kilocalories for a three mile walk, we can divide the amount of kilocalories in our food by this to find the equivalences.

Students could be asked to investigate the amount of kilocalories in the food they typically eat. The examples given are a chocolate bar and 'lunch'. All chocolate will vary in calorific value and it entirely depends what you have for lunch, but websites such as this one will give some guidelines:

http://www.nutracheck.co.uk/calories/calories_in_snacks_and_confectionary/calories_in_chocolate.html

Students could be asked to keep a diary of what they eat and the kilocalories contained within for a day or a week so that they can perform the kind of analysis suggested in the starter problem.

## Resources

# Topic scheme

Teaching time = 6 lessons/2 weeks

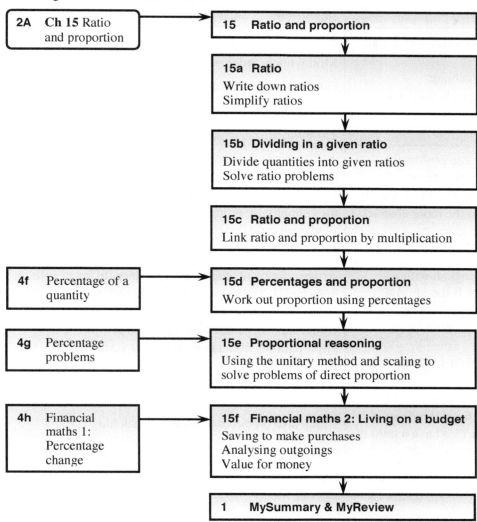

**2A  Ch 15** Ratio and proportion

**15  Ratio and proportion**

**15a  Ratio**
Write down ratios
Simplify ratios

**15b  Dividing in a given ratio**
Divide quantities into given ratios
Solve ratio problems

**15c  Ratio and proportion**
Link ratio and proportion by multiplication

**4f**  Percentage of a quantity

**15d  Percentages and proportion**
Work out proportion using percentages

**4g**  Percentage problems

**15e  Proportional reasoning**
Using the unitary method and scaling to solve problems of direct proportion

**4h**  Financial maths 1: Percentage change

**15f  Financial maths 2: Living on a budget**
Saving to make purchases
Analysing outgoings
Value for money

**1  MySummary & MyReview**

# Differentiation

**Student book 3A**  270 – 287
Ratio, dividing into a given ratio
Ratio and proportion
Percentages and proportion
Proportional reasoning
Financial mathematics: budgeting

**Student book 3B**  266 – 285
Direct proportion
Comparing proportions
Ratio
Using ratio and proportion to solve problems
Financial mathematics: budgeting

**Student book 3C**  260 – 277
Fractions and proportion
Ratio and proportion
Proportionality, scale and proportional reasoning
Financial mathematics: budgeting

## Objectives

- Use the notation of ratios and simplify ratios. (L5)

| Key ideas | Resources |
|---|---|
| 1  A ratio is often written using a colon, for example 1 : 2.<br>2  A ratio can be simplified by division or multiplication without changing its value, in a similar way to fractions. | ⊕  Ratio introduction (1052)<br>Mini whiteboards<br>Coloured beads or equivalent |

| Simplification | Extension |
|---|---|
| Students have counters which they can physically divide up according to the various ratios being described. Provide more visual examples like those in Questions **1** and **2** before moving to the more abstract concepts in Question **3**. | Ask students to simplify the ratios in Question **5** into the form 1 : *n* where *n* could be a decimal value. For some of these ratios, they could use a calculator but they should use written methods wherever possible. Find such ratios on charts and maps. |

| Literacy | Links |
|---|---|
| The word 'ratio' was first used in English with its mathematical meaning in the 1650s. It has several meanings connected with reckoning and reason, as in the words 'a rational explanation' meaning 'an explanation based on reason'.<br><br>A ratio is written using the colon, as in 1 : 2, but it can be written as '1 to 2'.<br><br>Ratios are used in everyday life. For example, older television screens have a 'width to height' ratio of 4 : 3, whereas modern widescreeen TVs have a ratio of 16 : 9. | Artists mix paints together to produce different colours and shades. The colour produced depends on the ratio of the component colours used in the mixture. Online colour mixing palettes can be found at http://painting.about.com/library/blpaint/blcolormixingpalette1.htm and at http://colorblender.com/ which also produces a palette of matching colours. |

## Alternative approach

There are a variety of activities at www.mymaths.co.uk/indexLog.asp?h=43927

Some of these activities make rapid progress and need to be used to match students' abilities.

## Checkpoint

Simplify these ratios:

**a** 16: 20 (4: 5)

**b** 80: 5 (16: 1)

## Starter – Four in a line

Students draw a $5 \times 5$ grid and enter the numbers 1 to 25 in any order. These numbers are percentages. Give fractions or decimals; for example,

$\frac{13}{100}$    0.17    $\frac{1}{4}$    $\frac{1}{100}$    0.2

Students cross out the equivalent percentage in their grid. The winner is the first student to cross out four percentages in a line.

## Teaching notes

Give an example where you have a number of coloured beads, say, two white and three red, and explain that the ratio of white to red is written as 2 : 3.

Students write other sets of coloured beads as ratios. Explain what is meant by an 'equivalent ratio' using an example with, say, four white beads and six red beads. Demonstrate by grouping them into two sets, each with two white and three red beads, that the ratios 2 : 3 and 4 : 6 are equivalent.

Explain that ratios such as 4 : 6 can be simplified by dividing both numbers by the 'common factor' (in this case, the number 2). Give students further examples of this type. Note that this process is very similar to simplifying fractions.

## Plenary

Show groups of red and white beads. Students write the ratio of red to white and, if possible, simplify the ratio. Answers are written on mini whiteboards and discussed.

Show ratios such as 25 : 30. Students find equivalent ratios. Again, answers are written on mini whiteboards and discussed.

## Exercise commentary

**Questions 1** and **2** – Basic practice at writing ratios from the given patterns.

**Questions 3** and **4** – These ratios could be set in various contexts such as mixing paint or diluting cordials. Use the term 'common factor'.

**Question 5** – Have students write the given ratio as well as the equivalent ratio; for example, 5 : 20 = 1 : 4.

**Question 6** – Find equivalent ratios for each of the three alternatives.

## Answers

| | | | | | | | | |
|---|---|---|---|---|---|---|---|---|
| **1** | a | 1 : 5 | b | 3 : 2 | c | 2 : 1 | d | 3 : 5 |
| **2** | a | 2 | b | 3 | c | 4 | d | 5 |
| **3** | a | 3 | b | 4 | c | 4 | | |
| **4** | a | 1 | b | 5 | c | 4 | | |
| **5** | a | 1 : 4 | b | 2 : 1 | c | 1 : 3 | d | 1 : 3 |
| | e | 3 : 2 | f | 3 : 2 | g | 4 : 3 | h | 4 : 5 |
| | i | 3 : 4 | j | 6 : 1 | k | 1 : 3 | l | 1 : 3 |
| **6** | a, c | | | | | | | |

## Objectives

- Divide a quantity into two (or more) parts in a given ratio.                    (L5)

| Key ideas | Resources |
|---|---|
| 1 Add the parts of the ratio to find the total number of parts. | ● Ratio dividing 1                    (1038) |
| 2 Find the value of one part by dividing the amount by the total number of parts in the ratio. | Mini whiteboards |
| 3 Multiply each of the numbers in the ratio by the value of one part to find the final answer. | Coloured beads or equivalent |

| Simplification | Extension |
|---|---|
| Students use real objects such as beads before moving to more abstract situations. Use more diagramatical questions or questions which involve solving the problems by drawing as in Question 1 before moving to Question 2. | Students make up their own question such as the baking problem in Question 9 and give it to a partner to solve. Emphasis should be placed on communicating the correct method and on showing the stages in the working out. |

| Literacy | Links |
|---|---|
| The words ration and rational both have ratio as their stem. A ration is particularly memorable to anyone who has fought in a war, as it means the amount that each soldier is allotted and also the notion that amounts of food and supplies are being restricted. Rational means being level-headed, agreeable to reason, using sound judgement, and also numbers that can be expressed as an integer numerator over an integer denominator. Very agreeable indeed! | Scale is usually shown on a map both as a ratio and as a graphic (or bar) scale. A graphic scale is a bar drawn on the map showing the actual corresponding distance on the ground.<br>If the map is copied and reduced or enlarged, the scale will change and therefore the given ratio will be inaccurate. However, the bar scale will also have been reduced or enlarged and so will remain accurate. There are instructions for using a graphic scale at www.map-reading.com/ch5-2.php |

## Alternative approach

Quantities can be divided into more than two parts in a given ratio. For example, when Mr Rich died, he left his savings of £18 000 to his four children Amy, Ben, Ceri and Donna in the ratio $4 : 3 : 3 : 2$. How much did each inherit?

The total of the parts is $4 + 3 + 3 + 2 = 12$.

Divide using short division. Each part is worth £18 000 ÷ 12 = £1500

$$\frac{1\ 500}{12\ )\ 18^{6}000}$$

Multiply by each number in the ratio to get the amount for each child.

Amy gets 4 × £1500 = £6000

Ben and Ceri each get 3 × £1500 = £4500

For Donna, use one of two methods:

She gets half as much as Amy £6000 ÷ 2 = £3000

Or she gets 2 × £1500 = £3000

## Checkpoint

Divide £72 into the ratio 5: 7.                    (£30: £42)

## Starter – Ratio bingo

Students draw a 3 × 3 grid and enter nine numbers between 1 and 24 inclusive.
Give ratios for example,

2 : 36   8 : 6   20 : 45   9 : 60   50 : 160   etc.
Students simplify each ratio and, in their grid, cross out one of the numbers corresponding to the left or right side of the simplified ratio. For example, for the given ratio 9 : 60, a student crosses out 3 or 20 if they have either 3 or 20 in their grid.

The winner is the first to cross out all of their nine numbers.

## Teaching notes

Remind students that a ratio is simply how a number of things are divided up. Using an example with, say, 20 beads, ask students to divide them up in the ratio 3 : 2. Since 3 + 2 = 5, they group the 20 beads into 5 groups of 4 beads each. Then gather 3 of these 5 groups into one pile and gather the other 2 groups in another pile. They now have a pile of 12 beads and another pile of 8 beads.

Give other examples and students divide the amounts into the given ratios. They can show their results on mini whiteboards and discuss them as a whole class.

Students can challenge a partner to divide a set of things into a given ratio. Examples could be set in context; for example, the contents of their pencil case, sets of counters, books on the shelf. This approach should encourage students to talk about their methods.

## Plenary

Give students examples of sets of things that have to be divided into a given ratio. Students write their working and answers on mini whiteboards to enable quick feedback from the whole class.

Some students could be asked to explain their thinking to the class.

## Exercise commentary

**Question 1** – Use either (or both) of the methods set out in the example on the previous page of the student book.

**Questions 2 to 6 and 9** – In all cases, the first question to ask is "How many parts in total?"

**Questions 7 and 8** – Students may need help finding the ratios from the stories. Question **8** actually involves finding an equivalent ratio rather than dividing in a given ratio.

## Answers

1  **a**  5 : 10     **b**  12 : 3     **c**  6 : 9

2  **a**  4 : 12     **b**  15 : 3     **c**  15 : 1 0     **d**  9 : 15
   **e**  16 : 12

3  Joubin gets £8. Alex gets £24.

4  Ashida gets £36. Her brother gets £24.

5  No. 25 is not divisible by 4.

6  12 litres of red paint and 16 litres of green paint

7  **a**  4 : 1     **b**  Sarah collects 24 and Martin collects 6.

8  £9 : £15

9  Fat 100 g, Flour 250 g

| Objectives | |
|---|---|
| • Apply understanding of proportional relationships and the use of ratio. | (L6) |

| Key ideas | Resources | |
|---|---|---|
| **1** To find an equivalent ratio, multiply (or divide) both parts of the ratio by the same number. | ⊕ Ratio dividing 2<br>Mini whiteboards<br>Sets of radio cards | (1039) |

| Simplification | Extension |
|---|---|
| Students work with unitary ratios in the form $1 : n$ in contexts which require mutiplication, before moving to the questions in the exercise. They acquire a full understanding that the 'multiplier' must be the same on both sides. | Students are given ratios such as $4 : 9$ and are asked to express it in a different form, such as $3 : x$, where the multipliers are not integers. They find answers using unitary ratios $1 : n$. |

| Literacy | Links |
|---|---|
| Ratio and proportion are different. Ratios compare different quantities within a batch, such as 2 red : 3 blue within a pile of beads. Whereas a proportion gives the fraction of one thing as part of the whole. So, the red beads make up of $\frac{2}{5}$ all the beads, which is the proportion of the red beads. | The time taken to download a file onto a computer is directly proportional to the size of the file but also depends on the speed of the modem. There is a conversion tool to estimate download speeds for different sized files at www.onlineconversion.com/downloadspeed.htm |

| Alternative approach |
|---|
| In worded problems set in a context, it is important to write the first sentence of the facts with what is required on the right-hand end of the sentence. Compare the biscuits in **Literacy** above. All subsequent calculation comes on the right. For example, Question **5** in Exercise **15c**, the first sentence could be "In 4 hours, Kia is paid £15" as it is £s that need to be found. In effect, the words here are an alternative to the almost word-free diagram in the students' book. |

| Checkpoint | |
|---|---|
| **a** The cost of a pencil is 15 pence. How much do 8 pencils cost? | (£1.20) |
| **b** Alex earns £52 for working a four hour shift. How much does he get paid per hour? | (£13) |

## Starter – How many?

Make the statement "The ratio of girls to boys in a class is 2 : 3". Ask questions such as:

If there are 10 girls, how many boys are there?  [15]

If there are 9 boys, how many girls are there?  [6]

What fraction of all the class is girls?  [$\frac{2}{5}$]

What percentage of the class are girls?  [40%]

What percentage of the class are boys?  [60%]

Students write answers on mini whiteboards. Discuss the responses as a whole class.

## Teaching notes

Explain that the term 'proportional' when used in 'proportional relationships' means 'always in the same ratio'. Use an example of a proportional relationship; for instance, a student who is paid £5 an hour will earn £10 in two hours, £15 in three hours, and so on. This proportional relationship could be written as the ratio 1 : 5 where the left-hand number is the number of hours worked and the right-hand number is the amount earned. Students write the equivalent ratios for four and five hours of work.

Explain what is meant by 'multiplier'. Students use a multiplier of 8 to find how much the person would be paid if they worked eight hours.

Give another example such as petrol costing £1.50 per litre and introduce the notion of a 'multiplier diagram'. Give examples which are not 1 : $n$ to reinforce the usefulness of the multiplier diagram.

## Plenary

Give cards displaying a ratio on each card. Students match cards in pairs of equivalent ratios. This could be in the form of 'Snap' with a partner. Students could call out the multiplier instead of saying the word 'snap' when they spot a match.

## Exercise commentary

**Questions 1** and **2** – These questions provide routine practice.

**Questions 3** to **5** – These questions are set in context but, as the diagrams are provided, they have a natural continuity from questions **1** and **2**. They could be supplemented by other questions where the diagrams are not provided and students have to construct their own.

**Question 5** – Students may need a calculator for this question.

## Answers

| 1 | a | 21 | b | 66 | c | 27 | d | 63 |
|---|---|----|---|----|---|----|---|----|
| 2 | a | 4, 4, 12 | b | 2, 2, 40 | c | 3, 3, 15 | d | 3, 3, 18 |

3  400 m

4  492 kg

| 5 | a | £90 | b | i | £7.50 | | ii | £3.75 |
|---|---|-----|---|---|-------|---|----|-------|

## Objectives

- Identify equivalent fractions and the equivalence between percentage and fraction.   (L4)
- Express one number as a percentage of another.   (L5)

| Key ideas | Resources | |
|---|---|---|
| 1  Interpret a percentage as a fraction given in hundredths.<br>2  Express fractions as percentages. | ⊕  Proportion<br>Fraction/Percentage cards<br>Food packaging<br>Calculators<br>Mini whiteboards | (1037) |

| Simplification | Extension |
|---|---|
| Use a 10 × 10 square to show the equivalence between the fractions 'out of one hundred' and the percentages. Concentrate on solving problems involving hundredths and tenths before moving to those which involve more complicated fractions. Encourage students to learn simple equivalents by heart. | Students explore fractions with denominators other than those which are factors of 100. For example, what is three-eighths as a percentage? They use written methods for division and check their answers with a calculator. |

| Literacy | Links |
|---|---|
| The word 'percent' means 'out of a hundred'. Make the link between percentages and fractions with a denominator of 100. As with fractions, if red beads make up 40% of all the beads, this is the proportion of the red beads. | Students read the information on food packaging. In addition to the nutrition information, there may be a panel showing the Reference Intakes (previously Guideline Daily Amounts or GDAs). The panel gives the calorie, fat, sugars and salt content of a typical serving, expressed as a percentage of the Reference Intake for an average adult. This information helps consumers make informed choices about their diet. There is more information about Reference Intakes labelling at www.gdalabel.org.uk/gda/reference-intakes.aspx |

### Alternative approach

Converting fractions to percentages presents a choice of methods.

- Mental methods using equivalent fractions apply when denominators are factors of 100; for example, $\frac{23}{50} = \frac{47}{100} = 47\%$. This is the method presented in the student's book.

- Short or long division applies when the denominator is not a factor of 100;
  for example, $\frac{3}{8} = $  $8\overline{)3.0^60^40}$  $\begin{array}{r} 0.375 \end{array}$

then multiplying by 100 gives 37.5%.

- Using the ÷ key on a calculator always works; for example, $\frac{3}{8}$ requires the keys 3 ÷ 8 = which gives 0.375, then multiplying by 100 gives 37.5%. Some decimal answers will need rounding.

### Checkpoint

Write these fractions as percentages:

a  $\frac{71}{100}$   (71%)

b  $\frac{13}{50}$   (26%)

c  $\frac{3}{100}$   (3%)

## Starter – Quick fire

Recap work of previous chapters and this chapter so far. Include questions on fraction and percentages and converting from one to the other. Ask rapid response questions with students responding on mini whiteboards. Discuss answers when there is a need.

## Teaching notes

Review the fact that a percentage can be written as a fraction with a denominator of 100.

One method to change a fraction to a percentage uses 'equivalent fractions' for any fraction which is not written in hundredths. The denominator must be scaled up by multiplication. For example, $\frac{23}{50}$ is scaled up by 2 to become $\frac{46}{100}$ which is 46%. Use further examples as necessary.

Students, in pairs, create their own examples and discuss them with the whole class.

## Plenary

Students give quick fire conversions of decimals and fractions into percentages and respond using mini whiteboards. Discuss responses as necessary.

A matching exercise can also be used where students use cards to match fractions with the equivalent percentages.

## Exercise commentary

Discuss and use the term 'multiplier' or even 'scale factor'.

**Question 1** – Basic practice.

**Question 2** – With a total distance of 100 metres, the shaded sections of the scale are tenths or 10%.

**Question 3** – A basic problem in context.

**Question 4** – An exercise in finding equivalent fractions. The focus is on the word 'multiplier'.

**Question 5** – This question follows on naturally from question 4. Students convert from 50ths to 100ths.

**Question 6** – A comparison is not possible until all the scores are written as fractions with the same denominator or as percentages. Ask which was Kieran's most successful subject.

## Answers

1.  a  77%  b  33%  c  25%  d  30%
    e  60%  f  15%  g  10%  h  9%
    i  5%   j  1%   k  54%  l  63%

2.  a  0%, 17%, 32%, 48%, 73%, 99%
    b  $0, \frac{17}{100}, \frac{8}{25}, \frac{12}{25}, \frac{73}{100}, \frac{99}{100}$

3.  a  $\frac{89}{100}$  b  89%

4.  a  10, $\frac{10}{100}$  b  20, $\frac{40}{100}$  c  5, $\frac{15}{100}$  d  25, $\frac{25}{100}$
    e  4, $\frac{48}{100}$  f  5, $\frac{45}{100}$  g  2, $\frac{46}{100}$  h  25, $\frac{75}{100}$

5.  a  $\frac{47}{50}$  b  $\frac{94}{100}$  c  i  94%  ii  6%

6.  a,b,c   Maths $\frac{35}{50} = \frac{70}{100} = 70\%$

    English $\frac{14}{20} = \frac{70}{100} = 70\%$

    Science $\frac{23}{25} = \frac{92}{100} = 92\%$

    PE $\frac{3}{5} = \frac{60}{100} = 60\%$

    Citizenship $\frac{9}{10} = \frac{90}{100} = 90\%$

    d  PE, English, Maths, Citizenship, Science

## Objectives

- Use the equivalence of fractions, decimals and percentages to compare proportions. (L6)
- Use the unitary method to solve simple problems involving ratio and direct proportion. (L6)

## Key ideas

1 A proportion is usually given as a fraction or as a percentage.
2 Direct proportion occurs when two variables increase at the same rate.

## Resources

⊞ Proportion unitary method (1036)

Mini whiteboards

Calculators

## Simplification

Remind students that fractions with denominators that are factors of 100 can be easily changed to percentages.

The scaling method (and unitary methods) for direct proportion should be linked to the use of a mental method for calculating percentages by finding multiples of 1% and 10%.

## Extension

Students could create conversion tables for different measures such as inches and centimetres.

They could investigate the prices of items bought at a supermarket to see if the prices of multiple purchases are in direct proportion to the number of items bought.

## Literacy

Direct proportion occurs when one variable increases at the same rate as another variable which is also increasing. For example, the cost of chocolate bars is directly proportional to the number of bars bought.

The graph of direct proportion is a straight line graph. For example, the number and cost of chocolate bars vary as in this table:

| Number | 1 | 2 | 3 | 4 |
|--------|-----|-----|-----|-----|
| Cost, p | 80 | 160 | 240 | 320 |

and when graphed give a straight line.

## Links

Wedding cake recipes often give scaling information for cakes of different sizes and shapes. The quantity of the mixture required depends on the volume of the tin, not its diameter. There is an example of a recipe at www.deliaonline.com/cookery-school/scaling-up-cake-recipes,1002,AR.html

## Alternative approach

A unitary ratio is always of the form 1 : $n$ and is useful in problems where a direct one-stage multiplication is awkard. For example, find the weight of 6 biscuits if 7 biscuits weigh 224 grams.

$$1 \text{ biscuit weighs } 224 \div 7 = 32 \text{ grams}$$
$$6 \text{ biscuits weight } 6 \times 32 = 192 \text{ grams.}$$

A one-stage multiplier from 7 to 6 is not as easy as a two-stage process via '1 biscuit'. This extra step via 1 gives its name to 'the unitary method'. Setting the working out as here is equivalent to the arrowed diagrams in the student's book.

## Checkpoint

**a** 8 apples cost 72 pence. What would 3 apples cost? (27 pence)

**b** 300g of butter costs £1.05. What would 500g of butter cost? (£1.75)

## Starter – Percentage pairs

Ask students to find pairs with the same value from the following calculations.

£20 increased by 10%,    £70 decreased by 40%,
£24 increased by 50%,    £90 decreased by 50%,
£35 increased by 20%,    £44 decreased by 50%,
£50 decreased by 10%,    £30 increased by 20%

[£20 increased by 10% = £44 decreased by 50% = £22
£70 decreased by 40% = £35 increased by 20% = £42
£24 increased by 50% = £30 increased by 20% £36
£90 decreased by 50% = £50 decreased by 10% = £45]

Discuss the results.

## Teaching notes

Remind students how to find one quantity as a percentage of another. For example, "What is my percentage profit, if I made £12 profit when I sold something that cost me £60?" Express 12 as a fraction of 60 and convert to a percentage by finding equivalent fractions.

Explain that, if a student has two test scores marked out of different total marks, the performances can be compared by converting both marks to percentages. Provide examples where the denominators are not factors of 100, such as a mathematics score of $\frac{31}{40}$ and an English score of $\frac{17}{24}$, and show how to convert them to percentages using division and rounding if necessary [77.5% and 70.8%].

Students practise making other comparisons using percentages.

Explain to students that two quantities are directly proportional if both increase at the same rate. For instance, one doubles in value as the other doubles in value. Both quantities can be multiplied by the same multiplier. Give examples of things that are directly proportional such as the price of petrol and the number of litres bought or the number of US dollars you get for UK pounds that you exchange.

## Plenary

Using mini whiteboards, ask students to calculate mentally and write the answers to quick fire questions on direct proportion. For example: if four apples cost 20 pence, what is the cost of one apple, ten apples, forty apples?

## Exercise commentary

**Question 1** – Parts **a** and **b** can be done mentally. Short division can be used to find the equivalent percentage in part **c**.

**Question 2** – This question follows on naturally from question **1**. Calculators will be needed.

**Questions 3** and **4** – Applications of the unitary method.

**Question 5** – This is a good question for paired work and discussion. Students explain any different strategies they use to work out the answers; that is, when they used a scaling method and when the unitary method. Link the arithmetic of the table with the drawing of a conversion graph; that is, every 10 miles on $x$-axis moves you 16 km up the $y$-axis.

**Question 6** – Students will need to refresh their memory of the details of question **3** and work backwards to find the initial investment.

## Answers

1   a   $\frac{3}{10} = 30\%$      b   $\frac{3}{4} = 75\%$
    c   $\frac{5}{8} = 62.5\%$

2   a   German
    b   Brian, 52%, Dean, 56.3%. Dean scores a higher proportion of the time
    c   Debbie

3   £180

4   a   £21     b   £12     c   600ml
    d   i   £13.50       ii   £1.35

5   a

| Miles | Kilometres |
|-------|------------|
| 1 | 1.6 |
| 5 | 8 |
| 10 | 16 |
| 18.75 | 30 |
| 30 | 48 |
| 62.5 | 100 |

    b   Straight line through the origin, gradient 1.6

6   £250

| Objectives | |
|---|---|
| • Interpret and solve problems in financial mathematics | (L5) |

| Key ideas | Resources | |
|---|---|---|
| 1  Solve problems involving budgeting<br>2  Solve problems involving value for money | Budgeting<br><br>Calculators | (1245) |

| Simplification | Extension |
|---|---|
| The amount of different types of expenditure can be reduced in order to simplify the calculations required of the students.<br><br>Value for money problems can be simplified to just be about comparisons, rather than adding in complexity to do with special offers and 'buy 1 get 1 free' deals. | Students could be asked to look at how prices change over time due to inflation. The consumer price index is made up of a 'basket of goods' (and services). The cost of these goods and services changes each month and it is this that dictates the rate of inflation. Internet research can be carried out to see what is in the 'basket', how this itself changes over time, and how the prices fluctuate on a monthly or yearly basis. |

| Literacy | Links |
|---|---|
| Budget<br>Salary<br>Inflation<br>Value for money<br>Financial literacy | The work in this section links into two key areas: the idea of running household accounts and the concept of value for money. Understanding both of these areas is an important 'life skill'. Encourage students to think about their own circumstances such as how they save and spend their pocket money, or whether they take advantage of special offers and bulk purchases in supermarkets and other shops.<br><br>An investigation into 'real-life' offers and deals in supermarkets can be carried out using information from websites such as www.tesco.com, www.sainsburys.com.uk and www.waitrose.com. |

| Alternative approach |
|---|
| There are lots of different ways of introducing the concept of value for money to students. Real-life examples of offers from the supermarket could be used – perhaps photos taken of price labels during the weekly shop can be used to provide specific and real examples. Comparisons of prices in different supermarkets could also be used to stimulate discussion. Are the claims of supermarkets really true when they say things like '35% cheaper than supermarket A!'? |

| Checkpoint |
|---|
| Joseph earns £1300 per month and spends £600 on rent. He spends a further £120 on food, £85 on bills and £60 on transport. How much does Joseph have left over?  (£435) |
| Two jars on jam are available: 180 grams for £1.50 or 250 grams for £2.20. Which represents the best value for money?  (The smaller jar) |

## Starter – Speed division

Divide these amounts up into the given number of equal parts as quickly as possible:

320 into 8 parts (40)

120 into 5 parts (24)

650 into 13 parts (50)

440 into 11 parts (40)

7.2 into 2 parts (3.6)

6.9 into 3 parts (2.3)

4.84 into 4 parts (1.21)

6.45 into 3 parts (2.15)

## Teaching notes

The first two ideas are about budgeting to save and budgeting to live. The first two examples cover these ideas and students could be asked to work through them to check they understand the principles involved. Guide students to read the scenarios carefully and extract the useful information from the text. Questions 1 and 2 can then be attempted.

The focus then changes to 'value for money' and some simple examples of direct comparisons can be given before turning to the example in the book where special offers are built into the problem. Students will need to be careful to take the special offers into account before drawing a conclusion.

## Plenary

Which is better value?

a)  A 300 gram packet of sweets with 20% extra free for £1.50, or

b)  A 500 gram packet of sweets with 15% extra free for £2.35?

(a: 2.4 grams per penny, b: 2.44 grams per penny, so b)

## Exercise commentary

**Question 1** – Each of these questions can be worked out by dividing the cost of the item by the monthly amount (and carefully rounding *up*).

**Question 2** – Part **a** requires simple subtraction before linking into previous work on fractions and percentages in part **b**.

**Questions 3** and **4** – Ensure students take account of the special offers before trying to compare the value for money.

**Question 5** – This question can be used to stimulate discussion about price changes due to inflation, the more general concept of budgeting when salaries, costs and prices are changing and about prioritising spending.

## Answers

1   a   7 months          b   8 months

    c   6 months          d   16 months

2   a   £300

    b   Accommodation: 5/12
        food: 1/6
        house: 1/24
        transport: 1/20
        other: 3/40

    c   Any suitable suggestions

3   Mountain Brands: £2.40 for 200g
    Club Coffee: £3.99 for 300g
        Recommend Mountain Brands

4   X: 75p for 200g
    Y: £1.50 for 300g
    Recommend X

5   Must cut down spending in other areas by £40 a month
    Any suitable suggestions, e.g. walking more and taking less public transport, etc.

| Key outcomes | | Quick check |
|---|---|---|
| Simplify equivalent ratio. | L5 | Simplify these ratios:<br>**a** 3: 15 (1: 5) **b** 20: 16 (5: 4) |
| Divide amounts into a given ratio. | L6 | Divide<br>**a** £64 in the ratio 5: 3 (£40: £24) **b** 720 litres in the ratio 5: 1 (600: 120) |
| Use multipliers to solve ratio and proportion problems. | L6 | **a** Phil gets paid £7.50 per hour. If he works for 5 hours, how much will he get paid? (£37.50)<br>**b** 8 oranges cost 96 pence. What is the cost of one orange? (12 pence) |
| Express an amount as a percentage of another amount. | L6 | **a** What is 12 as a percentage of 60? (20%)<br>**b** What is £30 as a percentage of £120? (25%) |
| Compare simple proportions by converting to percentages. | L6 | David scores 13 out of 25 in his maths test and 27 out of 50 in his physics test. Which test did he do better in? (maths: 52%, physics: 54%) |
| Solve problems involving direct proportion. | L6 | Wendy buys 5 boxes of vegetables for £8.70. How much would she pay for 8 boxes? (£13.92) |
| Make financial decisions. | L6 | Which of these jars of jam is the better value for money? (Brand B)<br>Brand A: 200g for £1.20<br>Brand B: 250g for £1.45 |

## ⊕ MyMaths extra support

| Lesson/online homework | | | Description |
|---|---|---|---|
| Fractions of amounts | 1018 | L5 | Shading in rectangles as fractions; finding fractions of whole numbers |
| Percentages of amounts 2 | 1031 | L5 | Finding harder percentages such as 72% of 150 and simple percentage discounts |
| Best Buys | 1243 | L5 | How to make sure you are getting the best buy and real value for money |
| Budgeting | 1245 | L7 | Learning to manage your money based on good budgeting will help you make better use of your earnings |

# My Review

## Check out

**You should now be able to ...**

**Test it ➡**
Questions

| | | |
|---|---|---|
| ✓ Simplify equivalent ratios. | | 1 – 3 |
| ✓ Divide an amount in a given ratio. | | 4, 5 |
| ✓ Use multipliers to solve ratio and proportion problems. | | 6 |
| ✓ Express an amount as a percentage of another amount. | | 7 |
| ✓ Compare simple proportions by converting to percentages. | | 8 |
| ✓ Solve problems involving direct proportion. | | 9 |
| ✓ Make financial decisions. | | 10 |

| Language | Meaning | Example |
|---|---|---|
| Ratio | Ratio compares the size of one part with the size of another part. | 2 : 3 means for every two red beads there are three green beads. |
| Equivalent | Two things are equivalent if they have the same value. | $\frac{2}{5}$ and $\frac{12}{20}$ are equivalent fractions. 2 : 7 and 10 : 35 are equivalent ratios. |
| Proportional | Proportional relationships always keep to the same ratio. | Donna gets paid £9 per hour. The ratio of time worked to the amount earned is always 1 : 9, regardless of how many hours are worked. |
| Simplify | Means to write as simply as possible by dividing the numbers in a ratio by the highest common factor. | 42 : 54 simplifies to 7 : 9. The highest common factor of 42 and 54 is 6, so divide them both by 6. |
| Unitary method | A method in which you find the value of one unit of a quantity to solve direct proportion problems. | The cost of 12 packets of crisps is £2.04. The cost of 1 packet = £2.04 ÷ 12 = £0.17 = 17p. You can now use the cost of one packet to find the cost of any number of packets of crisps. |

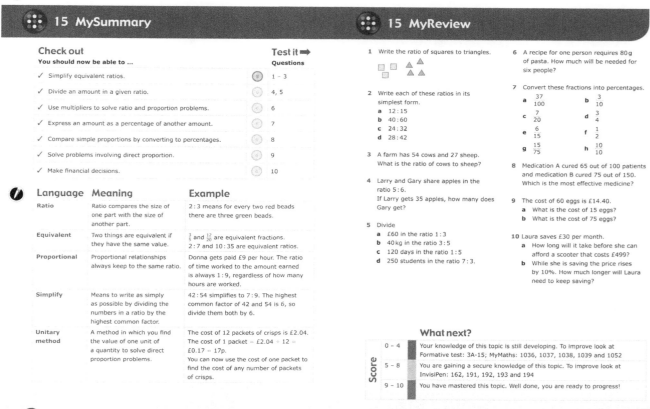

1   Write the ratio of squares to triangles.

2   Write each of these ratios in its simplest form.
   **a**   12 : 15
   **b**   40 : 60
   **c**   24 : 32
   **d**   28 : 42

3   A farm has 54 cows and 27 sheep. What is the ratio of cows to sheep?

4   Larry and Gary share apples in the ratio 5 : 6.
   If Larry gets 35 apples, how many does Gary get?

5   Divide
   **a**   £60 in the ratio 1 : 3
   **b**   40 kg in the ratio 3 : 5
   **c**   120 days in the ratio 1 : 5
   **d**   250 students in the ratio 7 : 3.

6   A recipe for one person requires 80 g of pasta. How much will be needed for six people?

7   Convert these fractions into percentages.
   **a**   $\frac{37}{100}$   **b**   $\frac{3}{10}$
   **c**   $\frac{7}{20}$   **d**   $\frac{3}{4}$
   **e**   $\frac{6}{15}$   **f**   $\frac{1}{2}$
   **g**   $\frac{15}{75}$   **h**   $\frac{10}{10}$

8   Medication A cured 65 out of 100 patients and medication B cured 75 out of 150. Which is the most effective medicine?

9   The cost of 60 eggs is £14.40.
   **a**   What is the cost of 15 eggs?
   **b**   What is the cost of 75 eggs?

10  Laura saves £30 per month.
   **a**   How long will it take before she can afford a scooter that costs £499?
   **b**   While she is saving the price rises by 10%. How much longer will Laura need to keep saving?

## What next?

| Score | | |
|---|---|---|
| 0 – 4 | | Your knowledge of this topic is still developing. To improve look at Formative test: 3A-15; MyMaths: 1036, 1037, 1038, 1039 and 1052 |
| 5 – 8 | | You are gaining a secure knowledge of this topic. To improve look at InvisiPen: 162, 191, 192, 193 and 194 |
| 9 – 10 | | You have mastered this topic. Well done, you are ready to progress! |

**⊕ MyMaths**.co.uk

## Question commentary

**Questions 1 to 3** – Simple practice questions including one application which should be simplified as far as possible.

**Question 4** – Check that students understand that the 35 only refers to Larry's 5 parts of the whole.

**Question 5** – This question should not require the use of a calculator.

**Question 6** – Simple proportional reasoning. Again, calculators should not be needed.

**Question 7** – Some of the fractions will need simplifying first before converting to 100ths.

**Question 8** – Students will need to convert both sets of results into a comparable form (either fractions with the same denominator or percentages).

**Question 9** – The unitary method can be employed here of students could modify it to suit the question. For example, dividing directly by 4 for part **a**.

**Question 10** – An applied question which looks at the effect of price changes on savings decisions.

## Answers

1   3 : 4

2   **a**   4 : 5   **b**   2 : 3   **c**   3 : 4   **d**   2 : 3

3   2 : 1

4   42

5   **a**   15 : 45   **b**   15 : 25   **c**   20 : 100   **d**   175 : 75

6   480 g

7   **a**   37%   **b**   30%   **c**   35%   **d**   75%
   **e**   40%   **f**   50%   **g**   20%   **h**   100%

8   A

9   **a**   £ 3.60   **b**   £ 18

10 **a**   17 months   **b**   2 months

# 15 MyPractice

**1** Write the ratio of green to yellow beads in each of these patterns.

a

b

c

d

**2** Use the factors to simplify each of these ratios.

a
$\div 3 \big( 12 : 9 \big) \div 3$
$4 : \square$

b
$\div 4 \big( 16 : 4 \big) \div 4$
$4 : \square$

c
$\div 3 \big( 27 : 6 \big) \div 3$
$\square : 2$

d
$\div 3 \big( 15 : 24 \big) \div 3$
$5 : \square$

**3** Use jottings to divide these amounts in the given ratios.

a Divide £18 in the ratio 1 : 2.

Remember 1 : 2 → 3 parts

b Divide 20 g in the ratio 4 : 1.

Remember 4 : 1 → 5 parts

c Divide 25 sweets in the ratio 3 : 2.

Remember 3 : 2 → 5 parts

d Divide 30 m in the ratio 2 : 3.

Remember 2 : 3 → 5 parts

e Divide $35 in the ratio 2 : 5.

Remember 2 : 5 → 7 parts

f Divide 28 litres in the ratio 9 : 5.

Remember 9 : 5 → 14 parts

**4** Copy and complete these diagrams.

a
$\times 3 \big( 6 : 7 \big) \times 3$
$18 : \square$

b
$\times \square \big( 4 : 9 \big) \times \square$
$\square : 63$

c
$\times \square \big( 3 : 8 \big) \times \square$
$12 : \square$

d
$\times \square \big( 5 : 12 \big) \times \square$
$\square : 72$

**5** Change each of these fractions to an equivalent fraction.

a $\dfrac{4}{5} = \dfrac{\square}{100}$
b $\dfrac{3}{10} = \dfrac{\square}{100}$
c $\dfrac{7}{10} = \dfrac{\square}{100}$

d $\dfrac{23}{50} = \dfrac{\square}{100}$
e $\dfrac{19}{25} = \dfrac{\square}{100}$
f $\dfrac{7}{20} = \dfrac{\square}{100}$

g $\dfrac{4}{25} = \dfrac{\square}{100}$
h $\dfrac{13}{20} = \dfrac{\square}{100}$
i $\dfrac{17}{20} = \dfrac{\square}{100}$

**6** Change each fraction in question **5** to a percentage.

**7** Change each of these fractions to percentages.

a $\dfrac{3}{4}$
b $\dfrac{3}{5}$
c $\dfrac{9}{10}$
d $\dfrac{41}{50}$
e $\dfrac{13}{25}$
f $\dfrac{11}{20}$

g $\dfrac{24}{25}$
h $\dfrac{19}{20}$
i $\dfrac{11}{25}$
j $\dfrac{8}{40}$
k $\dfrac{8}{50}$

**8** a Betty took two tests.
   In history she scored 24 out of 40.
   In geography she scored 42 out of 60.
   In which test did she do better?

   b Rufus put £200 into a savings account.
   After one year the interest was £8.
   Christabel put £160 into a savings account.
   After one year the interest was £7.
   Who had the better rate of interest?

**9** Solve each of these problems using direct proportion.

   a 10 pizzas cost £25. How much will 15 pizzas cost?

   b 3 kg of pears cost £6. How much will 14 kg of pears cost?

   c A recipe for four people uses 200 g flour.
   How much flour is needed for the same recipe for seven people?

**10** Geoff's earns £325 per week. His rent is £530 per month.
   His monthly travel pass costs £75. He spends £60 a week on food. Other expenses
   are £85 per month.

   a How much money does Geoff have left over each month?

   b What proportion of Geoff's expenses is spent on travel?

   c Geoff's food costs rise by 10% how much money does he now have left over a
   month?

**11** Ed has to decide between two brands of rice.
   Brand A: £4.75 for 1 kg
   Brand C: £3.00 for 450 g + buy one bag get second bag half price
   Which brand should Ed buy? Give your reasons.

**MyMaths.co.uk**

## Question commentary

**Questions 1** and **2** – Simple starter questions on basic ratio.

**Question 3** – The hints should make these questions very straightforward for the students.

**Question 4** – Simple applications of the multiplier principle.

**Questions 5** to **7** – Question **5** provides the scaffolding for questions **6** and **7**. In part b of question **7**, students will need to simplify the fraction first.

**Questions 8** and **9** – Applications of proportional reasoning. Some students may need help extracting the information from the word problems.

**Questions 10** and **11** – Problems with a financial 'slant'. Again, some students may need help extracting the information from the word problems.

## Answers

**1 a** $1:2$  **b** $3:2$  **c** $2:1$  **d** $3:1$

**2 a** $3$  **b** $1$  **c** $9$  **d** $8$

**3 a** $6:12$  **b** $16:4$  **c** $15:10$  **d** $12:18$
  **e** $10:25$  **f** $18:10$

**4 a** $21$  **b** $7,28,7$  **c** $4,32,4$  **d** $6,30,6$

**5,6 a** $\frac{80}{100}=80\%$  **b** $\frac{30}{100}=30\%$
  **c** $\frac{70}{100}=70\%$  **d** $\frac{46}{100}=46\%$
  **e** $\frac{76}{100}=76\%$  **f** $35/100=35\%$
  **g** $\frac{16}{100}=16\%$  **h** $\frac{65}{100}=65\%$
  **i** $85/100=85\%$

**7 a** $75\%$  **b** $60\%$  **c** $90\%$  **d** $82\%$
  **e** $52\%$  **f** $55\%$  **g** $96\%$  **h** $95\%$
  **i** $44\%$  **j** $20\%$  **k** $16\%$  **l** $32\%$

**8 a** Geography  **b** Christabel

**9 a** £ 37.50  **b** £ 28  **c** 350 g

**10 a** 550  **b** $75/1300$  **c** 544

**11** A: £4.75 for 1kg
  C: £3 for 900g
  Recommend C

## Learning outcomes

**P1** Record, describe and analyse the frequency of outcomes of simple probability experiments involving randomness, fairness, equally and unequally likely outcomes, using appropriate language and the 0-1 probability scale (L5)

**P2** Understand that the probabilities of all possible outcomes sum to 1 (L5)

**P3** Enumerate sets and unions/intersections of sets systematically, using tables, grids and Venn diagrams (L6)

**P4** Generate theoretical sample spaces for single and combined events with equally likely, mutually exclusive outcomes and use these to calculate theoretical probabilities (L5/6)

## Introduction

The chapter starts by reviewing the language of probability and chance. Mutually exclusive events are looked at along with calculating probabilities from single events. Counting outcomes and the probability from two trials are then covered along with a section on experimental probability. The final section looks at Venn diagrams, sets and probability using Venn diagrams.

The introduction discusses how manufacturers test products in order to find out the probability of them breaking, etc. The focus is on cars but nearly all consumer products are tested in a similar way using small samples across the production range. Manufacturers will set limits as to the acceptable failure rate (2%, or 5% for example) before a batch is thrown out or tested more extensively. This kind of probability analysis is covered in much more detail at A level but there is enough scope to discuss the general strategies with Key Stage 3 students.

It might also be interesting to discuss the ethical implications of allowing faulty goods to make it into the market place, linking to cross-curricular issues with, for example, Religious Studies.

## Prior knowledge

Students should already know how to…

- Draw a probability scale and use the language of probability
- Calculate simple probabilities for single events

## Starter problem

The starter problem looks at the probability of getting a five when you roll a number of dice. The first situation, a single dice, has simple probability equal to 1/6. How does this change when you roll two dice?

You could now get a five on *either* dice (or both) and we will have to look in more detail at the possible outcomes – here a sample space diagram might be useful. It turns out that there are 11 ways of rolling the two dice so that at least one of them shows a five, giving the overall probability of rolling a five as 11/36 (just under 1/3).

The simple answer to the question posed at the end of the starter problem is 'yes'. To analyse this further, and work out *how* it changes would require students to list large numbers of outcomes (216 for 3 dice) or draw (construct?) 3D sample spaces. The discussion might instead be focussed on trying to find a logical argument for working out the number of ways it can be done on 3 dice.

## Resources

**MyMaths**

| | | | | | |
|---|---|---|---|---|---|
| Listing outcomes | 1199 | Probability intro | 1209 | Simple probability | 1210 |
| Relative frequency | 1211 | The OR rule | 1262 | Probability revision | 1263 |

**Online assessment**

| | |
|---|---|
| Chapter test | 3A–16 |
| Formative test | 3A–16 |
| Summative test | 3A–16 |

**InvisiPen solutions**

| | | | |
|---|---|---|---|
| Probability scale | 451 | Finding probabilities | 452 |
| Probability rules | 453 | Mutually exclusive events | 454 |
| Experimental and theoretical probability | | | 461 |
| Outcomes | 462 | | |

# Topic scheme

Teaching time = 7 lessons/3 weeks

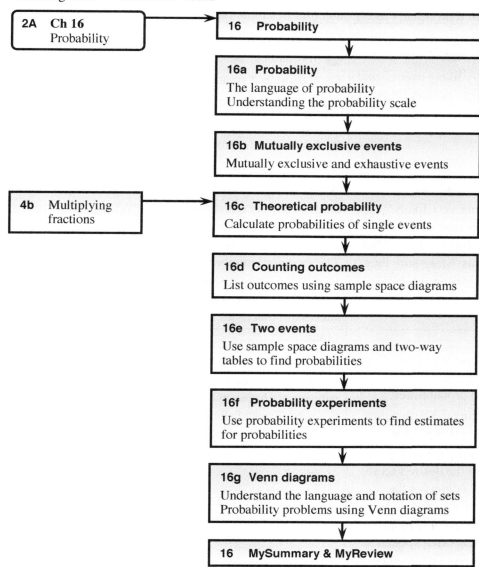

**2A   Ch 16**
Probability

**16   Probability**

**16a   Probability**

The language of probability
Understanding the probability scale

**16b   Mutually exclusive events**

Mutually exclusive and exhaustive events

**4b   Multiplying fractions**

**16c   Theoretical probability**

Calculate probabilities of single events

**16d   Counting outcomes**

List outcomes using sample space diagrams

**16e   Two events**

Use sample space diagrams and two-way
tables to find probabilities

**16f   Probability experiments**

Use probability experiments to find estimates
for probabilities

**16g   Venn diagrams**

Understand the language and notation of sets
Probability problems using Venn diagrams

**16   MySummary & MyReview**

# Differentiation

**Student book 3A        288 – 307**

The language of probability
Mutually exclusive events
Calculating probabilities from
single events and two events;
counting outcomes
Experimental probability
Venn diagrams and sets

**Student book 3B        286 – 305**

The language of probability
Mutually exclusive events
Calculating probabilities from
single events and two events
Experimental probability and its
comparison to theoretical
outcomes
Venn diagrams, sets and set
notation

**Student book 3C        278 – 297**

The language of probability
Independent events
Tree diagrams and the probability
of combined events
Experimental probability
Simulation
Venn diagrams and sets

## Objectives

- Interpret the results of an experiment using the language of probability. (L5)
- Find and justify probabilities based on equally likely outcomes in simple contexts. (L5)

| Key ideas | Resources |
|---|---|
| **1** Describing a probablity in words and as a fraction. <br><br> **2** Knowing the meaning of 'equally likely events' and how they are necessary to calculate probabilities. | ⊕ Probability intro (1209) <br> Dice, coins and spinners <br> Coloured balls in bags <br> Packs of playing cards <br> Probability scales from 0 to 1 |

| Simplification | Extension |
|---|---|
| Give students more practice using words such as 'impossible', 'highly likely', and 'not very likely' before moving to working with fractions. Allow students to give probabilities in the form '1 in …', but ask them to re-state them as fractions. Make sure they understand the concept of outcomes being 'equally likely'. | When asking students to work with a pack of playing cards to answer questions such as "What is the probability of choosing a red card", be aware that knowledge of cards is culturally dependent. <br> The increased number of possible outcomes when selecting a card provides the extension and makes students think about a situation in which counting the successful outcomes is more difficult. |

| Literacy | Links |
|---|---|
| 'Odds' (in expressions such as 'the odds against it raining tomorrow are pretty high') are not probabilities, but they are related to probabilities. <br><br> For example, the probability of rolling a 3 with a dice is one-sixth ($\frac{1}{6}$). The 'odds against' rolling a 3 with a dice are 5 : 1 (spoken as '5 to 1 against'). The 5 gives the number of ways of *failing* to get the desired score and the 1 gives the number ways of *achieving* the desired score. <br><br> The phrase 'odds on' means that the event is more likely to happen than not happen. It is often spoken as '2 to 1 on', which means that the desired event is twice as likely to happen as not happen. | Predicting the future by the use of supernatural means is called 'divination', one of Harry Potter's curriculum subjects at Hogwarts. There is a list of words used to describe forms of divination at www.dailywritingtips.com/words-for-telling-the-future/ |

## Alternative approach

Extend the range of vocabulary to describe probabilities. Students place these words on the probability scale from 0 to 1 in the most appropriate order:

*Quite likely, Almost impossible, Evens, Very unlikely, Almost certain, Quite unlikely, Very likely.*

## Checkpoint

Twelve cards are numbered from 1 to 12. What is the probability of getting

**a** an even number? ($\frac{1}{2}$)

**b** a factor of 12? ($\frac{1}{2}$)

## Starter – Four in a line

Ask students to draw a 5 × 5 grid and enter numbers between 2 and 12 inclusive. The same number can be used once, twice or three times. Throw two dice and add the scores. Students cross out one occurrence of the total from their grid. The winner is the first student to cross out four in a line.

Ask which numbers are the 'best' to enter on the grid.

## Teaching notes

Explain that 'probability' is a measure of the likelihood of an event happening. Give the students a number of statements such as 'the probability of winning the national lottery', 'the probability of it raining tomorrow' and ask them to say how likely they think these events are, using appropriate vocabulary.

Explain that the probability of events happening can be expressed as a number between 0 and 1, where 0 is the probability of an impossible event and 1 is that of a certain event.

Students draw a probability scale and mark on it their estimates of the probabilities of different scenarios.

Give the students a number of further events such as selecting a ball in a bag, throwing dice, twirling spinners and tossing coins. Explain the notions of 'equally likely events' and 'choosing at random'. Define probability as the proportion (fraction) of desirable events out of all possible events.

## Plenary

Pairs of students are given a list of events and a probability scale. They agree where each event goes on the scale and place them in the correct order. The outcomes are discussed as a whole class.

## Exercise commentary

**Question 1** – The same word may apply to more than one event.

**Question 2** – This question assumes that the events for each part of equally likely. For example, in part **b**, the probability of picking any one of the balls is $\frac{1}{7}$. Ask students how the events can be structured to ensure they are equally likely, such as choosing items randomly using a blindfold.

**Question 3** – Students will need to copy the scale and mark their fractions carefully. Check they are ordered correctly.

**Question 4** – Students may simplify fractions where possible.

## Answers

1  a  Likely                 b  Impossible
   c  Unlikely             d  Unlikely
   e  Likely                 f  Even chance

2  a  $\frac{1}{4}$      b  $\frac{5}{7}$      c  $\frac{1}{9}$      d  $\frac{5}{8}$
   e  $\frac{4}{9}$      f  $\frac{2}{9}$

3

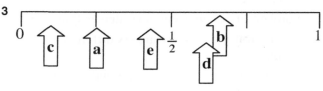

4  a  $\frac{2}{5}$      b  $\frac{1}{2}$      c  $\frac{1}{10}$      d  $\frac{3}{5}$
   e  $\frac{1}{5}$      f  $\frac{3}{10}$

## Objectives

- Find and justify probabilities based on equally likely outcomes in simple contexts. (L5)
- Identify all the possible mutually exclusive outcomes of an event. (L5)
- Know that the sum of probabilities of all mutually exclusive outcomes is 1 and use this when solving problems. (L6)

| Key ideas | Resources |
|---|---|
| **1** Mutually exclusive events cannot happen together at the same time. <br> **2** The total of the probabilities of all mutually exclusive outcomes of an event is 1. | The OR Rule (1262) <br> Coins, dice, spinners, packs of cards <br> Mini whiteboards |

| Simplification | Extension |
|---|---|
| Give students examples in which there are only two possible mutually exclusive events and have them count the number of desirable and undesirable outcomes in each case. Keep reiterating that the two events can never occur at the same time and that their probabilities will always add to 1. | Give students problems where there are more than three possible outcomes, such as a bag of balls in which there are several different colours. Ask them for the probability that they get, for example, a red *or* a green ball. Ask them for the probability that they will get a colour *not* in the bag. |

| Literacy | Links |
|---|---|
| 'Mutually exclusive events' are events that cannot occur at the same time. For example, when tossing a coin, 'getting a head' and 'getting a tail' are mutually exclusive events. <br><br> The probability of an event is written as P(an event). <br><br> When you roll a dice, there are six different 'outcomes'. <br><br> So, P(a desirable outcome) + P(all undesirable outcomes) = 1 when 'desirable outcomes' and 'undesirable outcomes' are mutually exclusive and also cover all possibilities. <br><br> For example, P(a 1 on a dice) + P(not a 1) = $\frac{1}{6} + \frac{5}{6} = 1$. | Probability theory originated in 1654 after the French mathematician, Blaise Pascal, was asked some questions about betting by the gambler, Chevalier de Mere. Pascal corresponded with his friend Pierre de Fermat and eventually the two mathematicians agreed on a general theory about probability. There are translations of Fermat and Pascal's letters at www.york.ac.uk/depts/maths/histstat/pascal.pdf |

## Alternative approach

Different approaches, including investigative approaches, are available at the following two websites:

www.mymaths.co.uk/indexLog.asp?h=40156

and

http://nrich.maths.org/8494

## Checkpoint

There are five green balls, two yellow balls and seven blue balls in a bag. One ball is chosen at random. What is the probability that it is green? ($\frac{5}{14}$)

What is the probability that it is *not* yellow? ($\frac{6}{7}$)

## Starter – Make one

Students are given decimals between 0 and 1. Ask students to find the decimal that would add to make exactly 1. For example,

    0.3    0.65    0.07                [0.7, 0.35, 0.93]

This task can be extended by

- giving a fraction and asking for the second fraction needed to make exactly 1, or
- giving two decimals and asking for the third decimal to make exactly 1.

## Teaching notes

Explain that events which are 'mutually exclusive' cannot happen at the same time. Give a number of examples such as rolling a 6 on a single dice. Use the term 'outcomes' to describe the various possibilities in a scenario. Explain that the total probability of all possible outcomes when added together will always be 1 if the outcomes are mutually exclusive and exhaustive. Introduce the notation P(an event).

Clearly, 'an event happening' and 'the event *not* happening' are mutually exclusive. So we can write

P(an event) + P(not the event) = 1.

Give examples of finding the probability of the event *not* happening using this fact.
For example, P(scoring a 3 on a dice) = $\frac{1}{6}$,
so P(not scoring a 3) = $1 - \frac{1}{6} = \frac{5}{6}$.

## Plenary

Give the students a number of scenarios and ask them to record various probabilities on their mini whiteboards. Discuss their responses and make an assessment of their understanding.

## Exercise commentary

**Question 1** – Students should know what a 'favourable' outcome is for each spinner.

**Question 2** – Students need to take each fraction away from one whole.

**Questions 3** and **4** – Practical contexts for probability problems are given here.

**Question 5** – This question lends itself to discussion between students. Can they think of a set of probabilities which *are* mutually exclusive?

---

## Answers

1  a  i  $\frac{3}{7}$     ii  $\frac{4}{7}$        b  i  $\frac{2}{5}$     ii  $\frac{3}{5}$

   c  i  $\frac{2}{3}$     ii  $\frac{1}{3}$        d  i  $\frac{1}{2}$     ii  $\frac{1}{2}$

2  a  $\frac{4}{7}$        b  $\frac{5}{9}$        c  $\frac{1}{3}$        d  $\frac{7}{8}$

3  a  $\frac{1}{5}$        b  $\frac{1}{2}$        c  $\frac{7}{10}$       d  $\frac{3}{10}$

4  a  $\frac{1}{6}$        b  $\frac{1}{2}$        c  $\frac{2}{3}$        d  $\frac{1}{3}$

5  a  No        b  Yes

## Objectives

- Find and justify probabilities based on equally likely outcomes in simple contexts.   (L5)

| Key ideas | Resources |
|---|---|
| 1  Theoretical probabilities are based on events being equally likely. <br> 2  Theoretical probabilities can be found using a simple formula. | ⊞  Simple probability   (1210) <br> Coins, dice, spinners, bags of beads <br> Mini whiteboards |

| Simplification | Extension |
|---|---|
| Work with simple examples where there are only two possible outcomes and keep the numbers small; for example, work with spinners with two or four divisions only. Students look at the *size* of each sector before deciding on whether the outcomes are equally likely. | Students work with spinners which have several different-sized sectors where they will need to measure the angle of each sector in order to work out whether the probability of getting the various colours are equally likely. |

| Literacy | Links |
|---|---|
| Because certain objects have the same shape and size (such as beads in a bag) or because an object has a certain symmetry (such as a dice), it is resonable to suppose that certain outcomes of an action (selecting a bead or rolling a dice) are 'equally likely' to happen. This notion of 'equal likeliness' allows us to assume the turn of events without having to do any experiment to see if the events truly are equally likely to happen. | Roulette is a game of chance which originated in France in the 18th century. Players decide on where they think a ball will come to rest when it is spun inside a numbered horizontal wheel. They can bet on either individual numbers or groups of numbers. The amount won depends on the probability of the ball landing on that particular choice. However, the odds are always in favour of the bank. There are pictures of roulette wheels at http://en.wikipedia.org/wiki/Roulette |

## Alternative approach

Is a dice or a coin fair? Students can test either a dice or a coin by comparing results based on theoretical probability with the results of a practical experiment. For example, if a dice is fair (that is, all its scores are equally likely), then P(a 3 on a dice) = $\frac{1}{6}$ and , in 60 rolls of the dice, the score of 3 is likely, in theory, to occur 10 times – and 'not a 3' to occur 50 times.

Each student rolls their dice 60 times and records their results in a table:

| Score | 3 | Not 3 | |
|---|---|---|---|
| Tally | | | Totals |
| Observed frequency | | | |
| Expected frequency | 10 | 50 | 60 |

Ask "Is it reasonable to expect *exactly* 10 scores of 3?", "Are your results near enough to 10 to be satisfied that the dice is fair and that its scores are equally likely?"

## Checkpoint

What is the probability of rolling a prime number on a fair six-sided dice?   ($\frac{1}{2}$)

What is the probability of rolling a factor of 6?   ($\frac{2}{3}$)

## Starter – Quick fire

Recap work of previous chapters and this chapter so far. Ask rapid response questions with students responding on mini whiteboards. Discuss answers when there is a need.

## Teaching notes

Explain to students that there are situations in which outcomes are equally likely and situations where the outcomes are *not* equally likely. Give examples, using spinners, coins and dice, in which both situations occur. Explain that if outcomes are equally likely, the 'theoretical probability' can be worked out using a simple formula.

Explain that theoretical probabilities are found by dividing the number of favourable outcomes by the total number of outcomes. The answer is given as a fraction.

Discuss various scenarios and find theoretical probabilities.

## Plenary

Provide students with a number of situations in which outcomes are equally likely and ask them to write probabilities on their mini whiteboards. As a simple example, "I have a bag containing 6 blue beads and 4 red beads. I select a bead without looking. Find the probability (in its lowest terms) of it being blue." Another example is to write the probability of rolling either an even score *or* a 5 on a dice – this means that an even score or a 5 are both acceptable as a favourable outcomes.

## Exercise commentary

**Question 1** – Note the total area for each colour, taking account of the size of each sector.

**Question 2** – Simple examples of applying the formula given.

**Questions 3** and **4** – The colour of the card is irrelevant.

**Question 5** – Students should include the notation P(event) as part of their answers.

## Answers

1  **a** and **d**

2  **a** $\frac{1}{4}$     **b** $\frac{1}{2}$     **c** $\frac{4}{9}$     **d** 0
   **e** $\frac{1}{3}$     **f** 1

3  **a** $\frac{3}{5}$     **b** $\frac{1}{5}$

4  **a** $\frac{2}{7}$     **b** $\frac{3}{7}$

5  **a** $\frac{1}{2}$     **b** $\frac{2}{5}$     **c** $\frac{1}{3}$     **d** $\frac{9}{14}$

## Objectives

- Generate theoretical sample spaces for single and combined events with equally likely and mutually exclusive outcomes
(L5)

| Key ideas | Resources |
|---|---|
| 1 Using sample space diagrams to produce lists and tables of possible outcomes. | ⊞ Listing outcomes (1199)<br>Prepared sample space tables |

| Simplification | Extension |
|---|---|
| Students could do further work on listing outcomes for single events such as dice and spinners.<br><br>Prepared sample space tables could also be used to avoid the time wasted copying tables out. | Students could start to work out the probabilities associated with the sample spaces. For example, in question **1**, what is the probability of tossing one head and one tail? In question **2**, what is the probability of Mr Ross wearing *some* blue?<br><br>The sample space associated with the dice in question **4** could be modified to be the difference between the numbers or the product. |

| Literacy | Links |
|---|---|
| Sample space<br><br>Event<br><br>Combination<br><br>Generally, emphasise the importance of using the correct terminology when working with probability. | When writing out sample spaces, we are generally considering choice. How many choices does Mr Ross have when picking something to wear? How many choices do the students in Year 9 at Henry Compton School have?<br><br>Students could investigate further the idea of choice and combinations. For example, in a sports day race with six competitors, how many options are there for first, second and third? Mathematics of this type is known as *combinatorics* and students could investigate further by doing some internet research. |

### Alternative approach

Students could be provided with props, for example a stack of (clean!) socks and asked to write down the possible combinations of 'pairs' of socks that could be made from the socks in the stack. Questions could be asked such as how many unique pairings are there or how many pairs are there that match?

### Checkpoint

A six-sided dice and a three-sided spinner are spun. If the spinner is numbered from 1 to 3, how many options are there for the total score? (9: The numbers from 2 to 9)

## Starter – The school fete

A stall at the school fete offers people a chance to win a prize if they pick a numbered ball from a bag which shows a prime number. The student running the stall says that there are twelve balls in the bag and that people have an equal chance of winning or losing. Is he right? (No: there are only 5 prime numbers between 1 and 12)

Follow-up question: Give an example of a set of numbered balls from 1 to *n* which *does* give an equal chance of winning (1-2, 1-4, 1-6, 1-8)

## Teaching notes

Once the students understand the nature of the two-way sample space tables, they should have little problem filling in the entries. However, if time is an issue and the students tend to work slowly, pre-drawn sample space tables could be issued. Ensure students are listing outcomes systematically where required.

## Plenary

Take the table from question **3** and ask questions such as:

How many options would a student have if they wanted to take History or Art in option A? (10)

How many options would a student have if they didn't want to do Food Tech or Photography in option B? (9)

## Exercise commentary

**Question 1** – This question can be used to start to develop the idea that HH, TT and TH are *not* equally likely, something students often forget.

**Questions 2** and **3** – Questions which model the example and students have to complete the sample space diagrams. These could be used for later work on probabilities in **16e**.

**Question 4** – This question may be modelled as an example for the next section (and links to question **4** on page 299).

---

## Answers

**1 a**

|  | Heads | Tails |
|---|---|---|
| Heads | Heads Heads | Tails Heads |
| Tails | Heads Tails | Tails Tails |

**b** 4

**2 a**

|  | Stripe | Yellow | Blue | White |
|---|---|---|---|---|
| Red | Stripe Red | Yellow Red | Blue Red | White Red |
| Blue Stripe | Stripe Blue Stripe | Yellow Blue Stripe | Blue Blue Stripe | White Blue Stripe |

**b** 8

**3 a** 5 columns    **b** 3 rows

**c**

|  | ICT | Food | Geog | Latin | Photo |
|---|---|---|---|---|---|
| French | ICT French | Food French | Geog French | Latin French | Photo French |
| Art | ICT Art | Food Art | Geog Art | Latin Art | Photo Art |
| History | ICT History | Food History | Geog History | Latin History | Photo History |

**d** 15

**4**

| + | 1 | 2 | 3 | 4 | 5 | 6 |
|---|---|---|---|---|---|---|
| 1 | 2 | 3 | 4 | 5 | 6 | 7 |
| 2 | 3 | 4 | 5 | 6 | 7 | 8 |
| 3 | 4 | 5 | 6 | 7 | 8 | 9 |
| 4 | 5 | 6 | 7 | 8 | 9 | 10 |
| 5 | 6 | 7 | 8 | 9 | 10 | 11 |
| 6 | 7 | 8 | 9 | 10 | 11 | 12 |

## Objectives

- Use tables to record in a systematic way all possible mutually exclusive outcomes for two successive events.

(L6)

| Key ideas | Resources |
|---|---|
| 1  A two-way table can be used to list all possible outcomes for two successive events. | ⊞ Listing outcomes  (1199) <br> Mini whiteboards |

| Simplification | Extension |
|---|---|
| For simple cases, students list the various possible outcomes rather using a sample-space diagram. Examples could include two coins, two spinners or sets of two or three cards. They count the number of items in their list to find simple probabilities such as P(two heads). | Students work with alternative 'dice-based' sample spaces such as 'the product of the scores when two dice are rolled' or 'the difference of the scores when two dice are rolled'. Students challenge a partner to find the probability of a particular outcome in these cases. |

| Literacy | Links |
|---|---|
| A 'sample space' is a list of all the possible outcomes of an event. When the event is actually two successive events, then the sample space is found systematically using either a two-way table or a tree diagram. Only the two-way table is considered in the student's book. A two-way table has the outcomes of each event listed like labels on two axes across and down the edges of the grid. The cells of the grid contain all possible outcomes of the two events – and all these outcomes are called the 'sample space'. | From 1711 until 1960, decks of playing cards printed and sold in the UK were subject to tax and were sealed with a special wrapper. Until 1862, the ace of spades was used to show that the tax had been paid. An official version of the card was printed with an ornate design bearing the maker's name. Even today the ace of spades is usually very ornate and shows the name of the manufacturer. There is more about the history of playing cards at www.wopc.co.uk/cards/collecting.html |

## Alternative approach

A tree diagram is an alternative way of listing the members of a sample space.

For example, when two coins are tossed, the tree diagram looks like this. The sample space appears as a list running down the ends of the branches of the tree. In this case, the sample space is HH, HT, TH, TT.

The advantage of the tree diagram over the two-way table is that, when there are *three* successive events (such as the outcomes of tossing three coins), the tree diagram simply sprouts extra branches. The two-way table would have to move into three dimensions with a third axis – not a practical solution.

| 1st coin | 2nd coin | Outcome |
|---|---|---|
| H | H | HH |
|  | T | HT |
| T | H | TH |
|  | T | TT |

## Checkpoint

A fair spinner has three equal sectors numbered 1, 2 and 3. It is spun twice.

What is the probability of the total score being 2?  $\left(\frac{1}{9}\right)$

What is the probability of the total score being even?  $\left(\frac{5}{9}\right)$

**Starter** – Dice bingo

Ask students to draw a 3 × 3 grid and enter nine numbers from the following: 1, 2, 3, 4, 5, 6, 8, 9, 10, 12, 15, 16, 18, 20, 24, 25, 30, 36.

Roll two dice. Students cross out the product of the scores if it is in their grid. The winner is the first to cross out all of their nine numbers.

Then recap work of previous chapters. Ask rapid response questions. Students reply by writing on their mini whiteboards. Discuss questions when their answers indicate a need.

## Teaching notes

Explain that, in situations where there are two successive events, a systematic way of recording the possibilities is useful to make sure all the possibilities are included. A two-way table creates a sample-space diagram of all possible outcomes. As an example, students use such a table to list all the possible outcomes when a die is rolled and a coin is tossed.

Another example for students to list is two spinners each with four equal sectors marked 1, 2, 3 and 4. Students draw the sample-space diagram.

Students create the sample-space diagram for the sum of the scores when two dice are rolled. They consider the probabilities of scoring a total of 7 or 11.

## Plenary

Students complete the sample-space diagram for other two-event scenarios with coins being tossed, dice rolled or spinners spun. Then they find the probability of certain outcomes which can be displayed on mini whiteboards and discussed.

## Exercise commentary

**Question 1** – Students should write the different combinations in the spaces in the diagram.

**Question 2** – The rules of the game need careful reading. Note that Wheel 2 gives a multiplier of the score from Wheel 1, rather than just another possible score.

**Question 3** – Students should again write the different combinations in the spaces in the diagram and then read off the ones which give at least one red.

**Question 4** – As an extension, it is useful to see the pattern produced when this table is completed:

| Total score | 2 | 3 | 4 | 5 | 6 | ... | 12 |
|---|---|---|---|---|---|---|---|
| Frequency | | | | | | | |

## Answers

**1  a**

| | Blue | Green | Pink | Yellow |
|---|---|---|---|---|
| Dotty | Blue Dotty | Green Dotty | Pink Dotty | Yellow Dotty |
| Striped | Blue Striped | Green Striped | Pink Striped | Yellow Striped |

   **b**  8

**2  a**

| | 1 | 2 | 4 | 5 |
|---|---|---|---|---|
| ×1 | 1 | 2 | 4 | 5 |
| ×2 | 2 | 4 | 8 | 10 |
| ×4 | 4 | 8 | 16 | 20 |

   **b** 12    **c**  20    **d**  $\frac{1}{6}$    **e**  $\frac{1}{4}$

**3  a**  12    **b**  $\frac{1}{2}$

**4  a**  11
   **b**  Count how many different values appear in the table
   **c**  7    **d**  1/6    **e**  no    **f**  4 and 10

## Objectives

- Estimate probabilities by collecting data from a simple experiment and recording it in a frequency table. (L5)
- Compare estimated experimental probabilities with theoretical probabilities. (L6)

| Key ideas | Resources |
|---|---|
| 1   When events are not equally likely, probabilities can be estimated from experimental data.<br><br>2   Outcomes from experiment and theory can be compared as a test for bias. | Relative frequency (1211)<br>Polyhedral dice<br>Coins and irregular spinners<br>Packs of cards<br>Mini whiteboards |

| Simplification | Extension |
|---|---|
| For a practical approach, keep the number of possibilities small (coins, three-sector spinners or dice). Although dice have more possibilities than coins or spinners, they are easier to handle in class. | Students, in pairs, devise their own experiment. They write a plan of how they will carry out the experiment, how many trials they will do, etc. They should be realistic about what can be done in the classroom. |

| Literacy | Links |
|---|---|
| Experimental probability is sometimes called relative frequency. An experimental probability is found by experiment involving many trials, where a trial is one repetition of the same event. The more trials there are, the more accurate the experimental probability will be.<br><br>When there is a suspicion that events that were expected to be equally likely may not to be, then the results may be biased. Bias is a systematic (rather than a random) deviation from the true value. For example, when the weight of a dice is not uniformly distributed, it is a biased dice. | Gregor Mendel (1822–1884) was the first person to apply probability to the field of genetics. Mendel was an Austrian monk and studied peas growing in the monastery garden. He experimented by breeding different pea plants together and investigated how features were passed on from one generation to the next. His work was largely ignored until several years after his death. There is more about Mendel and his experiments at www.biotechlearn.org.nz/themes/mendel_and_inheritance/mendel_s_principles_of_inheritance |

## Alternative approach

This investigation compares experimental results with theoretical probabilities.

A pack of cards has a *success* when it is cut at a diamond. Cut the pack ten times, record the number of successes and write the experimental probability of cutting a diamond as a decimal. Repeat a further 10 times making a total of 20 cuts and, again, write the experimental probability as a decimal. Repeat for 50 cuts, 100 cuts, 200 cuts (by combining the results of students across the class).

Enter all the results into a table where the three rows of the table are labelled: 'Number of times cut', 'Number of diamonds cut' and 'Experimental probability of cutting a diamond'. Analyse the results. Do the values of the experimental probability seem to be settling down as the number of cuts increases? What value does the probability seem to be settling down to?

What value would a theoretical approach give if all fours suits of the pack are assumed to be equally likely to be cut? Do theory and experiment agree?

How would you introduce bias into this experiment? [Do not have equal numbers of each suit.]

## Checkpoint

A basketball player shoots 20 free throws. He scores baskets with 12 of them. Estimate the probability that he scores with each throw. ($\frac{3}{5}$)

How many baskets would you expect him to score if he had 50 free throws? (30)

## Starter – Money, money!

Show students a four-sided spinner labeled 2p, 5p, 10p and 20p. Spin it twice. Ask questions, for example,

What is the probability of the total amount being:

an odd number of pence?                  [ $\frac{3}{8}$ ]

greater than 20p?                            [ $\frac{7}{16}$ ]

a prime number?                              [ $\frac{1}{8}$ ]

## Teaching notes

Suggest a situation where the theoretical probability cannot be worked out, such as 'toast landing butter-side down', because the outcomes are not thought to be equally likely. Explain that, in order to get an estimate of probabilities of such events, an experiment is needed.

The number of trials carried out in the experiment is important: the more trials that are done, the better the estimate will be. The experimental probability is then calculated by dividing the number of successful trials by the total number of trials.

Students can generate their own experimental probabilities using dice, coins or spinners. Explain that you suspect the dice or coins to be biased or, with spinners made from thick card, the edges are clearly of different lengths so scores are not equally likely.

Students use the dice, coins or spinners (and polyhedral dice make an interesting change) and generate a frequency table of results with the experimental probabilities listed in another row of the table. They draw a conclusion about whether they think the dice or coins are indeed biased and whether the spinner's results are what might have been expected from the irregular shape of the spinner.

## Plenary

Provide students with tables of experimental outcomes of various experiments. They write experimental probabilities on their mini whiteboards as rounded decimals (using their calculators). Discuss their results as necessary.

## Exercise commentary

**Question 1** – Students could check that the sum of the frequencies is 100.

**Question 2** – In part **b**, students have to work out the expected frequency. They may need help seeing that they can calculate this by multiplying the experimental probability by the number of trials.

**Question 3** – Students should make a tally of the results. They should check that the sum of the frequencies is 50. They could actually carry out this experiment themselves.

## Answers

1   a   No – B and E seem to have a lot more marbles than the other trays.
    b   A=1/10, B=1/4, C=3/25, D=3/20, E=27/100, F=11/100
    c   B or E
    d   There are two 'routes' into trays B and E, while there is only one route to each of the other trays.

2   a   $\frac{1}{4}$            b   25

3   a   $\frac{10}{50} = \frac{1}{5}$            b   Right hand

## Objectives

- Enumerate sets and unions/intersections of sets systematically using Venn diagrams (L6)

| Key ideas | Resources |
|---|---|
| 1 Understand sets<br>2 Use Venn diagrams to work out probabilities | Mini whiteboards |

| Simplification | Extension |
|---|---|
| Problems involving algebra such as question **4** can be avoided.<br><br>The notation associated with the Venn diagrams could be explained in words rather than symbols to help the students 'visualise' the regions of the Venn diagram they are to consider. | Students could be encouraged to explore the idea of conditional probability. Using the example in question **2**, what is the probability that a member chosen at random does kickboxing *given that* they do aerobics? (10/18 or 0.556).<br><br>Similar problems to this could be given to the students and they could also be asked to try and develop an understanding of independence of events and formalise more of the algebra of probability.<br><br>Three (and four?) region Venn diagrams can also be explored. |

| Literacy | Links |
|---|---|
| The language of sets, for example 'universal set', and 'element'.<br>The mathematical notation associated with sets. | This is a nice topic to link to aspects of the history of mathematics. John Venn, the inventor of Venn diagrams, was born in 1834 and was a contemporary of another famous mathematician called Charles Dodgson. Dodgson also went on to develop techniques for analyzing probability using diagrams. His diagrams are called Carroll diagrams since Charles Dodgson is better known as Lewis Carroll, the author of the Alice in Wonderland books!<br>http://lewiscarrollsociety.org.uk/index.html |

## Alternative approach

Students could be given a set of probabilties and the associated Venn diagram and asked to work out what the question was. For example, in a Venn diagram with numbers 3, 5 and 2 across the three regions in the circles and 2 outside, the probability $\frac{3}{12}$ represents the probability of A and not B.

## Checkpoint

A set P comprises the first 15 whole numbers. A set Q contains the factors of 60.
Which elements are common to both sets? $(1, 2, 3, 4, 5, 6, 10, 12, 15)$

## Starter – Factors Game

Ask students to choose three two digit numbers (e.g. 12, 15 and 17). 'Randomly' generate one and two digit numbers and ask students to tick off each time they get a factor of one of their three numbers (each generated number can be used for more than one of theirs). The winner is the person who collects all their factors first.

## Teaching notes

The concept of sets and elements is covered first of all. Students need to be able to define the universal set, the intersection, the union and the complement. You can check understanding of these concepts by providing examples such as those given in the exercise.

Work on Venn diagrams follows and the main thing to think about is how can probabilities be worked out from the Venn diagram? Students may have trouble visualizing the regions indicated by the notation so further practice on this could be provided, or word descriptions given instead of notation.

## Plenary

Identify the region. By taking a standard '2-circle' Venn diagram, ask students to write down, either using notation or in words, the regions indicated by, for example, the 'moon-shaped' section of B plus the 'moon-shaped' section of A (A or B but not both). This can be tailored for ability and regions combined as appropriate.

## Exercise commentary

**Question 1** – Students may need reminding of the terminology used in this question. Answers should be in the form of lists of numbers.

**Question 2** – Students may need help identifying the correct region(s) for parts **c** to **f**. Word descriptions could be used to simplify this.

**Question 3** – This is an example of working in reverse from the probabilities to the numbers in the Venn diagram. For part **a**, check that the total of the numbers is 19.

**Question 4** – By introducing an unknown into the problem, students will have to think more carefully about what each region in the Venn diagram represents

**Question 5** – This question is particularly suitable for discussion in pairs and/or as a whole class.

## Answers

1  a  i  3, 6, 9, 12
      ii  1, 2, 4, 5, 7, 8, 10, 11
      iii  2, 4, 6, 8, 10, 12
      iv  1, 3, 5, 7, 9, 11
      v  2, 3, 4, 6, 8, 9, 10, 12
      vi  6, 12
   b  i  1, 2, 3, 5, 8, 13
      ii  21, 34, 55
      iii  1, 2, 3, 8
      iv  5, 13, 21, 34, 55
      v  1, 2, 3, 5, 8, 13
      vi  1, 2, 3, 8
   c  i  1, 3, 5, 7, 9, 11, 13, 15
      ii  2, 4, 6, 8, 10, 12, 14, 16
      iii  2, 3, 5, 7, 11, 13
      iv  1, 4, 6, 8, 9, 10, 12, 14, 15, 16
      v  1, 2, 3, 5, 7, 9, 11, 13, 15
      vi  1, 3, 5, 7, 11, 13

2  a  $\frac{3}{5}$  b  $\frac{1}{2}$  c  $\frac{2}{5}$  d  $\frac{1}{2}$
   e  $\frac{1}{3}$  f  $\frac{23}{30}$

3  a  Going from left to right: 6, 4, 7, 2
   b  We do not know how many objects there were in the set, so a Venn diagram with values that are multiples of Jaime's is an alternative.

4  a  $11 - x + x + 9 - x + 5 + x = 25$
   b  i  $\frac{11}{25}$  ii  $\frac{16}{25}$  iii  $\frac{18}{25}$  iv  $\frac{2}{25}$
   c  $x = 5$

5  Check students' answers.

| Key outcomes | Quick check |
|---|---|
| Understand and use the probability scale from 0 to 1.     L5 | List the following in ascending order of likelihood: (a) it raining somewhere in the world today, (b) winning the national lottery, and (c) a fair coin landing heads. (b, c, a) |
| Find probabilities for mutually exclusive events.     L5 | A fair spinner has seven equally sizes sectors numbered from 1 to 7. What is the probability that it spins a one or a two? ($\frac{2}{7}$) |
| Find probabilities based on equally likely outcomes.     L5 | The same spinner is spun. What is the probability that it spins a prime number? ($\frac{4}{7}$) |
| Use a sample-space diagram to show the possible outcomes of two events.     L6 | Draw a sample space diagram showing the total score on a dice and a three-sided fair spinner numbered 1 to 3.<br>(6 by 3 table with numbers ranging from 2 to 9 – check students' diagrams) |
| Find and interpret probabilities based on experimental data.     L5 | A golfer find he hits the green with probabilty $\frac{4}{5}$. If he plays 80 shots into the green in a week, how many would he expect to hit? (64) |
| Use Venn diagrams to find probability.     L6 | 30 students are asked if they like football or rugby. 7 students said they like both, 18 students said they liked football and 15 said they liked rugby. What is the probability that a student chosen at random likes *neither*? (Venn diagram with 11, 7 and 8 across the middle, leaving 4 outside: P(neither) = $\frac{4}{30}$ or $\frac{2}{15}$) |

# My Review

## Check out

**You should now be able to ...**

Test it ➡
Questions

| ✓ | Understand and use the probability scale from 0 to 1. | ⑤ | 1 |
| ✓ | Find probabilities for mutually exclusive events. | ⑤ | 2 |
| ✓ | Find probabilities based on equally likely outcomes. | ⑤ | 3, 5 |
| ✓ | Use a sample-space diagram to show the possible outcomes of two events. | ⑤ | 4, 5 |
| ✓ | Find and interpret probabilities based on experimental data. | ⑤ | 6, 7 |
| ✓ | Use Venn diagrams to find probability. | ⑤ | 8 |

| Language | Meaning | Example |
|---|---|---|
| Outcome | The result of an activity. | For a regular dice the outcomes are 1, 2, 3, 4, 5, and 6. |
| Event | A group of one or more possible outcomes. | The event 'odd number' consists of the outcomes 1, 3 or 5. |
| Trial | A single occurrence of an activity whose outcome is random. | Tossing a coin once is a trial. Tossing a coin 100 times is an experiment. |
| Experiment | A collection of repeated trials. | |
| Mutually exclusive | Events that cannot both happen at the same time. | Rolling an even number and an odd number on a regular dice. |
| Experimental probability | The number of favourable outcomes divided by the total number of outcomes in an experiment. | If a coin is tossed 50 times and comes up heads 23 times, then the experimental probability of heads is $\frac{23}{50}$. |
| Theoretical probability | Assuming all outcomes are equally likely, the number of favourable outcomes divided by the total number of outcomes. | For a regular dice, the theoretical probability of obtaining a factor of 6 (that is a 1, 2, 3 or 6) is $\frac{4}{6} = \frac{2}{3}$. |

1 A bag contains 2 white and 7 red counters. What is the probability that a randomly chosen counter will be
   a red
   b green?

2 The probability that Jeremy wins his game of chess is 0.6. What is the probability he doesn't win?

3 Mandy has a pack of 76 cards. Twenty of the cards have pictures on them. Find the probability of Mandy selecting a picture card at random. Give your answer as a fraction in its lowest terms.

4 Ashleigh can choose white, brown or seeded bread for her sandwiches. As a filling she could have cheese, ham or egg.
   a Draw a sample-space diagram to show all the possible outcomes.
   b How many different combinations can she choose from?

5 A game involves flipping a coin and rolling a dice.
   a Copy and complete the sample space diagram to show all the possible outcomes.

| Dice | | 1 | 2 | 3 | 4 | 5 | 6 |
|---|---|---|---|---|---|---|---|
| Coin | H | H1 | | | | | |
| | T | | | | | | |

5 b How many possible outcomes are there?
   c What is the probability of getting a head and a 5?
   d What is the probability of getting an odd number and a tail?

6 The test results of 15 students are as follows:

   | 12 | 10 | 13 | 10 | 16 |
   | 18 | 15 | 13 | 9 | 7 |
   | 10 | 12 | 14 | 15 | 17 |

A mark of 12 or more was needed to pass.
Estimate the probability that a student chosen at random would have passed the test.

7 Zak plays a game 40 times and wins 16 times.
   a Estimate the probability he will win the next time he plays.
   b If Zak plays the game 30 more times, how many times would you expect him to win?

8 Construct a Venn diagram from this information.
$\Omega = \{$whole numbers 1–40$\}$
$P(A) = \frac{1}{2}$, $P(A \cap B) = \frac{1}{8}$, $P(A \cup B)' = \frac{1}{4}$

### What next?

| Score | | |
|---|---|---|
| 0 – 3 | | Your knowledge of this topic is still developing. To improve look at Formative test: 3A-16; MyMaths: 1199, 1209, 1210, 1211, 1262 and 1263 |
| 4 – 6 | | You are gaining a secure knowledge of this topic. To improve look at InvisiPen: 451, 452, 453, 454, 461 and 462 |
| 7 – 8 | | You have mastered this topic. Well done, you are ready to progress! |

◉ **MyMaths**.co.uk

## Question commentary

In general, theoretical probabilities are given as fractions and experimental probabilities are given as decimals. Fractions need not always be fully simplified.

**Questions 1 to 3** – Contextualised single event probability questions which should be fairly straightforward.

**Questions 4 and 5** – Check the sample space diagrams are correct before answering follow-up questions if possible.

**Question 6** – A counting exercise which should lead directly to the solution.

**Question 7** – Part **b** is a relative frequency question.

**Question 8** – Students should be encouraged to fill in the Venn diagram bit by bit from the information given. (Simple) fraction calculations will be required.

## Answers

1 a $\frac{7}{9}$     b $\frac{0}{9} = 0$

2 $1 - 0.6 = 0.4$

3 $\frac{20}{76} = \frac{5}{19}$

4 a

| | | Bread | | |
|---|---|---|---|---|
| | | White | Brown | Seeded |
| Filling | Cheese | (C, W) | (C, B) | (C, S) |
| | Ham | (H, W) | (H, B) | (H, S) |
| | Egg | (E, W) | (E, B) | (E, S) |

 b $3 \times 3 = 9$

5 a

| | 1 | 2 | 3 | 4 | 5 | 6 |
|---|---|---|---|---|---|---|
| H | H1 | H2 | H3 | H4 | H5 | H6 |
| T | T1 | T2 | T3 | T4 | T5 | T6 |

 b $2 \times 6 = 12$     b $\frac{1}{12}$     c $\frac{3}{12} = \frac{1}{4}$

6 $\frac{10}{15} = \frac{2}{3} = 0.67$ (2 dp)

7 a $\frac{16}{40} = \frac{2}{5} = 0.4$     b $0.4 \times 30 = 12$

8

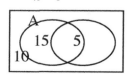

# 16 MyPractice

**1** Twelve cards numbered from 1 to 12 are shuffled and placed face down.

| 1 | 2 | 3 | 4 | 5 | 6 | 7 | 8 | 9 | 10 | 11 | 12 |

As a fraction, what is the probability of picking a card which is

**a** a number greater than 8    **b** an odd number

**c** a multiple of 5    **d** an orange card

**e** a prime number    **f** a green card

**g** a multiple of 3?

**2** This is a **fair** spinner.

**a** What is the probability of the arrow pointing to 5?

**b** What is the probability of the arrow pointing to a pink sector?

**c** What is the probability of the arrow pointing to a number less than 4 **or** a green sector?

**3** When choosing a ball at random from the bag there are three possible outcomes.

First outcome → P(red) – the probability of choosing a red ball.

Second outcome → P(green) – the probability of choosing a green ball.

Third outcome → P(blue) – the probability of choosing a blue ball.

**a** As a fraction, what is the probability of choosing red?   P(red) = ☐

**b** As a fraction, what is the probability of choosing green?   P(green) = ☐

**c** As a fraction, what is the probability of choosing blue?   P(blue) = ☐

**d** Add the outcomes: P(red) + P(green) + P(blue) = ☐ What is the total?

**4** Ellen throws 12 darts at a target.

**a** Give an estimate of the probability that her next throw will hit red.

**b** Give an estimate of the probability that her next throw will hit blue.

**c** Give an estimate of the probability that her next throw will miss the target.

**d** Give an estimate of the probability that Ellen's next throw will hit red or blue.

**5** **a** Copy and complete the table to list all of the possible combinations of flipping a coin and rolling a dice.

| Coin | Dice | | |
|---|---|---|---|
| | 1 | 2 | 3 |
| H | | | |
| T | | | |

**b** How many combinations are there altogether?

**6** Stefan buys a bag of mixed flower bulbs. There are

8 snowdrop bulbs    6 daffodil bulbs

10 crocus bulbs    12 iris bulbs.

If Stefan takes a bulb at random from the bag, what is the probability that it will be

**a** a daffodil bulb    **b** an iris bulb?

Stefan takes two bulbs at random and plants them in a flowerpot.

**c** Draw a sample-space diagram to show the possible combinations of flowers that might grow.

**7** Sandra has sowed tomato seeds in trays. Each tray holds 12 seeds. Sandra records how many seeds have grown and how many have failed in the first 10 trays.

| Tray | 1 | 2 | 3 | 4 | 5 | 6 | 7 | 8 | 9 | 10 | Totals |
|---|---|---|---|---|---|---|---|---|---|---|---|
| **Seeds grown** | 8 | 10 | 12 | 10 | 8 | 11 | 10 | 9 | 12 | 10 | = 100 |
| **Seeds failed** | 4 | 2 | 0 | 2 | 4 | 1 | 2 | 3 | 0 | 2 | = 20 |

**a** Give an estimate of the probability that the eleventh tray will have 12 seeds growing successfully.

**b** Give an estimate of the probability that the eleventh tray will have less than 12 seeds growing successfully.

**c** What is the **mean** average number of seeds grown successfully in each tray?

**8** Two hundred students were sorted into the sets
B = {has a brother} and S = {has a sister}.
The results are shown in the Venn diagram.
A teacher picks one student at random.

Find the probability of these events.
Give your answer as a fraction in its simplest form.

**a** P(B)    **b** P(S)    **c** P(B′)

**d** P(S′)    **e** P(B ∩ S)    **f** P(B ∪ S)

**MyMaths**.co.uk

## Question commentary

**Questions 1** and **2** – Simple probability questions which lend themselves to counting outcomes.

**Question 3** – A fairly elaborate set-up for a simple enough problem if students count carefully.

**Question 4** – The probabilities will be based on the actual outcomes from the first 12 throws.

**Question 5** – Students will need to extend the table from the partial one given in the question.

**Question 6** – In part **b** the amount of each bulb he has is irrelevant.

**Question 7** – Students will need to realise that the total amount of seeds grown is irrelevant for parts **a** and **b** while part **c** links to work on mean average (**8f**).

**Question 8** – Students should take care to select the correct regions from the Venn diagram for their numerator and denominator. Fractions can be simplified where appropriate.

## Answers

**1** a $\frac{1}{3}$  b $\frac{1}{2}$  c $\frac{1}{6}$  d $\frac{3}{4}$
e $\frac{5}{12}$  f $\frac{1}{4}$  g $\frac{1}{3}$

**2** a $\frac{1}{8}$  b $\frac{1}{8}$  c $\frac{1}{2}$

**3** a $\frac{1}{2}$  b $\frac{1}{5}$  c $\frac{3}{10}$  d 1

**4** a $\frac{1}{6}$  b $\frac{1}{3}$  c $\frac{1}{2}$  d $\frac{1}{2}$

**5** a

|   | 1 | 2 | 3 | 4 | 5 | 6 |
|---|---|---|---|---|---|---|
| H | H1 | H2 | H3 | H4 | H5 | H6 |
| T | T1 | T2 | T3 | T4 | T5 | T6 |

b 12

**6** a $\frac{1}{6}$  b $\frac{1}{3}$

c

|          | Snowdrop           | Daffodil           | Crocus           | Iris           |
|----------|--------------------|--------------------|------------------|----------------|
| Snowdrop | Snowdrop           | Daffodil Snowdrop  | Crocus Snowdrop  | Iris Snowdrop  |
| Daffodil | Snowdrop Daffodil  | Daffodil Daffodil  | Crocus Daffodil  | Iris Daffodil  |
| Crocus   | Snowdrop Crocus    | Daffodil Crocus    | Crocus Crocus    | Iris Crocus    |
| Iris     | Snowdrop Iris      | Daffodil Iris      | Crocus Iris      | Iris Iris      |

**7** a $\frac{1}{5}$  b $\frac{4}{5}$  c 10

**8** a $\frac{11}{25}$  b $\frac{3}{5}$  c $\frac{14}{25}$  d $\frac{2}{5}$
e $\frac{11}{50}$  f $\frac{41}{50}$

| Related lessons | | Resources | |
|---|---|---|---|
| Formulae | 3c | Conversion graphs | (1059) |
| Interpreting real life graphs | 6f | Distance time graphs | (1132) |
| Time series graphs | 6g | Scatter graphs | (1213) |
| Solving equations | 10b | Trial and improvement | (1057) |
| Writing equations | 10e | Standard form large/small | (1051, 1049) |
| Standard form | 11d | Soft pencils, clear sticky tape | |
| | | Magnifying glasses | |

## Simplification

Students could think about the scenario in task **1** with fewer windows to begin with to try to build up a pattern of how the combinations work.

In task **2**, students could be given guidance that the solution lies between 14 and 15 before narrowing the solution down to one decimal place.

Students may need help graphing the data in task **4**. Prepared axes with scales marked will help to ensure they have enough room to extend their graph to answer part **g**.

## Extension

Braking efficiency has not been included in the tyre marks equation; the equation that is given assumes 100% efficiency. Discuss how that might not be the case in reality and show a revised equation that takes into account efficiency: $s = \sqrt{90 \times L \times F \times E}$, where $E =$ braking efficiency. Students could research information on braking efficiency, maybe including the minimum braking efficiency required by the MoT test and find the effect that different efficiencies would have on the results.

## Links

An interesting website on DNA matching can be found at:

http://science.howstuffworks.com/life/genetic/dna-evidence4.htm

How to remember stopping distances in your driver theory test:

http://tips.drivingtestsuccess.com/learner-car/stopping-distances-theory-test-uk/

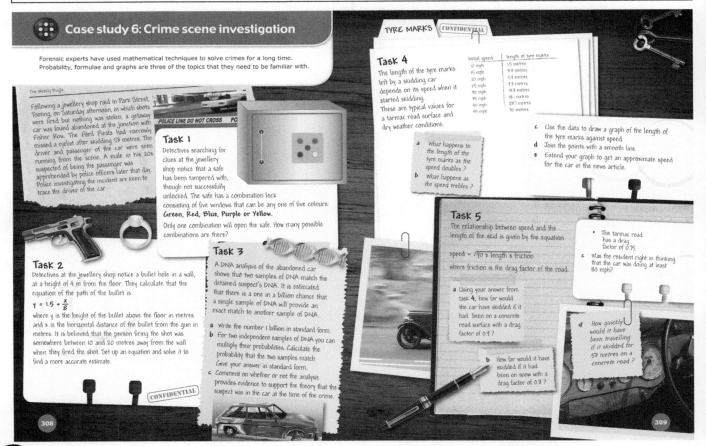

### Case study 6: Crime scene investigation

Forensic experts have used mathematical techniques to solve crimes for a long time. Probability, formulae and graphs are three of the topics that they need to be familiar with.

*The Weekly Bugle*

Following a jewellery shop raid in Park Street, Tooting, on Saturday afternoon, in which shots were fired but nothing was stolen, a getaway car was found abandoned at the junction with Fisher Row. The Ford Fiesta had narrowly missed a cyclist after skidding 53 metres. The driver and passenger of the car were seen running from the scene. A male in his 20s suspected of being the passenger was apprehended by police officers later that day. Police investigating the incident are keen to trace the driver of the car.

**Task 1**

Detectives searching for clues at the jewellery shop notice that a safe has been tampered with, though not successfully unlocked. The safe has a combination lock consisting of five windows that can be any one of five colours: Green, Red, Blue, Purple or Yellow.

Only one combination will open the safe. How many possible combinations are there?

**Task 2**

Detectives at the jewellery shop notice a bullet hole in a wall, at a height of 4 m from the floor. They calculate that the equation of the path of the bullet is

$y = 1.5 + \frac{x}{8}$

where y is the height of the bullet above the floor in metres and x is the horizontal distance of the bullet from the gun in metres. It is believed that the person firing the shot was somewhere between 10 and 20 metres away from the wall when they fired the shot. Set up an equation and solve it to find a more accurate estimate.

**Task 3**

A DNA analysis of the abandoned car shows that two samples of DNA match the detained suspect's DNA. It is estimated that there is a one in a billion chance that a single sample of DNA will provide an exact match to another sample of DNA.

a Write the number 1 billion in standard form.
b For two independent samples of DNA you can multiply their probabilities. Calculate the probability that the two samples match. Give your answer in standard form.
c Comment on whether or not the analysis provides evidence to support the theory that the suspect was in the car at the time of the crime.

TYRE MARKS   CONFIDENTIAL

**Task 4**

The length of the tyre marks left by a skidding car depends on its speed when it started skidding. These are typical values for a tarmac road surface and dry weather conditions.

| Initial speed | length of tyre marks |
|---|---|
| 10 mph | 1.5 metres |
| 15 mph | 3.9 metres |
| 20 mph | 5.4 metres |
| 25 mph | 9.3 metres |
| 30 mph | 13.9 metres |
| 35 mph | 18.1 metres |
| 40 mph | 23.7 metres |
| 45 mph | 30 metres |

a What happens to the length of the tyre marks as the speed doubles?
b What happens as the speed trebles?
c Use the data to draw a graph of the length of the tyre marks against speed.
d Join the points with a smooth line.
e Extend your graph to get an approximate speed for the car in the news article.

**Task 5**

The relationship between speed and the length of the skid is given by the equation

$speed = \sqrt{90 \times length \times friction}$

where friction is the drag factor of the road.

a Using your answer from task 4, how far would the car have skidded if it had been on a concrete road surface with a drag factor of 0.9?
b How far would it have skidded if it had been on snow with a drag factor of 0.3?

• The tarmac road has a drag factor of 0.75

c Was the resident right in thinking that the car was doing at least 80 mph?
d How quickly would it have been travelling if it skidded for 53 metres on a concrete road?

## Teaching notes

Read The weekly Bugle article together and ask students to identify all the actual information that it contains and any speculation, such as the speed that the car was travelling at.

Ask, how might the police be able to identify the driver and passenger?

They could get descriptions from any witnesses and they could take fingerprints from the car.

### Task 1

Initially it might seem like there will be many, many combinations, but only 3125 different combinations doesn't seem enough, or does it? What would the number of combinations jump to if numbers 0 to 9 were used instead of colours? Is a safe's combination any more or less secure using colours than numbers? Do the students think that a colour-coded combination would be easier to remember than a number-coded one? Ask students to write down as many phone numbers for people that they know. It is likely that this number will be very small, given that we all programme numbers into our phones and then don't need to memorise them. Not so with passwords. How many passwords do students use for all the websites and services that they use? Is it safe to make them all the same password?

### Task 2

Students could be asked to graph the equation on paper, or by using a digital geometry software package. How would such a graph help them with this problem? (Plot the graphs of $y = x - \frac{1}{20}x^2$ and $y = 4$)

### Task 4

For the second part of the case study, look together at the table of speeds and lengths of tyre marks. Give students a few minutes to consider the questions on the grey notes before discussing their ideas.

Ask, does the length of the skid double when the speed doubles? How did you find out?

Hear their thoughts and elicit that the length does not double but that it is approximately quadrupled. Discuss how you can find out by comparing the lengths for any two speeds where one speed was double the other. As the lengths in the table are rounded to 1 decimal place, rounding errors will be magnified when the smaller length is multiplied by 4.

Then discuss what happens if the speed is trebled before asking, what do you think will happen if the speed is quadrupled? Hear ideas and establish that the length will be 16 times longer. Check that this is about right by looking at the data for 10 mph and 40 mph.

Discuss how rounding errors have been magnified even more this time.

### Task 5

Finally, look at the equation that relates length of skid to speed. Discuss how the friction of the road surface needs to be included as a car will stop more quickly on a dry road than on a wet or icy road.

Using the information by the equation, give the students a few minutes to find out what speed the car in the article was travelling at. Check that students can use the equation (the speed is 59.8 mph) and then give them time to try the questions on the notes. They could work in groups to set up two spreadsheets: one that finds skid lengths from given speeds and drag factors and the other that finds initial speeds from given skid lengths and drag factors.

---

### Answers

1  $5^5 = 3125$

2  14 gives 4.2, 15 gives 3.75. 14.4 gives 4.032, 14.5 gives 3.9875. To one decimal place, $x = 14.5$ m

3  a  $1 \times 10^9$          b  $1 \times 10^{18}$

   c  It is extremely strong evidence

4  a  4 times as long

   b  9 times as long

   c  non-linear

   d  Students' graphs

   e  Quadratic relationship

   f  60 mph

5  a  44.4 m          b  133.3 m

   c  Wrong, the formula gives 59.8 mph

   d  65.5 mph

# MyAssessment 4

These questions will test you on your knowledge of the topics in chapters 13 to 16.
They give you practice in the types of questions that you may see in your GCSE exams.
There are 90 marks in total.

1 Write the first five terms of these sequences.
  a *Start with 25 subtract 3* (2 marks)
  b *Start with 4, double and subtract 3.* (3 marks)
  c The $n$th terms is $2n - 7$ (2 marks)

2 For each of these sequences
  i find the term-to-term rule (3 marks)
  ii write the next two terms in each sequence. (3 marks)
  a 9, 14, 19, 24, ...  b 25, 16, 7, -2, ...  c 2, 10, 26, 58, ...

3 For each of these sequences
  i find the term-to-term rule (3 marks)
  ii use this to find the position-to-term rule (3 marks)
  iii write each position-to-term rule as an equation in terms of $n$
    where $n$ is the $n$th term (3 marks)
  iv use this $n$th term formula to find the 20th term of each sequence. (3 marks)
  a 3, 10, 17, 24, ...  b 12, 8, 4, 0, ...  c 21, 28, 35, 42, ...

4 Describe these shapes in terms of the number of
  i edges  (2 marks)  ii faces  (2 marks)  iii vertices. (2 marks)
  a
  b

5 For the two shapes in question 4
  a name the particular shapes shown (2 marks)
  b on centimetre squared grid paper draw the nets of these two shapes. (4 marks)

6 Here is a six-cube shape.
  On squared paper draw
  a the plan view (P) (2 marks)
  b front elevation (F) (2 marks)
  c side elevation (S). (2 marks)

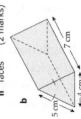

7 An earth trench is being dug to take concrete as a foundation for brickwork.
The trench is 25cm wide, 40cm deep and 4m long. What volume of concrete is needed to fill the trench? (3 marks)

8 For the two cuboids shown
  i calculate the surface area  (8 marks)  ii calculate the volume. (6 marks)
  a
  b

9 a In a school there are 396 students with a ratio of boys to girls of 10 : 8.
    How many boys and girls are there in the school? (3 marks)
  b £1350 was left between two children in the ratio of 7 : 2.
    How much does each child receive? (3 marks)

10 a The hourly rate for a part-time job is £6.50 per hour.
    Lara works a shift of seven hours. How much does she receive? (2 marks)
  b Lara spends £4.55 on travel. What is this as a percentage of Lara's wages? (1 mark)

11 Solve these problems by direct proportion.
  a In a recent set of exams Sophie scored 43/60 in Maths and 29/40 in Biology.
    In which exam did she do better? Show your working to support your answer. (3 marks)
  b Adam scored 14 goals in 11 games and Tom scored 16 goals in 13 games.
    Who is the better goal scorer? (3 marks)

12 There are 12 marbles in a bag: 5 red marbles, 4 blue marbles and 3 green marbles.
A marble is chosen at random from the bag.
  a Find the probability that the marble is
    i green  ii blue  iii either red, or blue or green. (3 marks)
  b Are the events red and green mutually exclusive? Explain your answer. (1 mark)

13 A four sided dice is thrown at the same time as a coin is tossed.
  a Draw a sample space diagram to show all the possible outcomes. (3 marks)
  b What is the probability of getting a tail and a 3. (1 mark)

14 a Draw a Venn diagram to show these sets A = {2, 3, 5, 6, 8}
    B {3, 5, 7, 10} and $\Omega$ = {1-10} (4 marks)
  b Calculate  i $P(A \cap B)$  ii $P(A \cup B)$  iii $P(A')$ (3 marks)

**MyMaths.co.uk**

# Mark scheme

**Question 1** – 7 marks

a   2    25, 22, 19, 16, 13

b   3    4, 5, 7, 11, 19

c   2    -5, -3, -1, 1, 3

**Question 2** – 6 marks

a   i    1    start at 9 and + 5

   ii    1    start at 25 and – 9

   iii   1    start at 2, double it and + 6

b   i    1    29, 34

   ii    1    -11, -20

   iii   1    122, 250

**Question 3** – 12 marks

a   i    1    start at 3 and +7

   ii    1    multiply by 7 and - 4

   iii   1    $7n - 4$

   iv   1    136

b   i    1    start at 12 and -4

   ii    1    multiply by -4 and + 16

   iii   1    $-4n + 16$

   iv   1    -64

c   i    1    start at 21 and +7

   ii    1    ×7, +14

   iii   1    $7n + 14$

   iv   1    c154

**Question 4** – 6 marks

a   i   1   8 edges      ii   1   9 edges

b   i   1   5 faces      ii   1   5 faces

c   i   1   5 vertices    ii   1   6 vertices

**Question 5** – 6 marks

a   i    1    square-based pyramid

   ii    1    triangular prism

b   i    2    correct net drawn

   ii    2    correct net drawn

**Question 6** – 6 marks

a   2    correct plan view; 4 faces shown

b   2    correct front elevation; 4 faces shown

c   2    correct side elevation; 5 faces shown

**Question 7** – 3 marks

3    0.4 m$^3$ or 400 000 cm$^3$; 0.25 × 0.4 × 4 seen for 1 mark or 25 × 40 × 400;

**Question 8** – 14 marks

a   i    4    188 cm$^2$; attempt made to evaluate areas of faces

   ii    3    120 cm$^3$; attempt made to split volume up into two sections

b   i    4    184 cm$^2$; attempt made to evaluate areas of faces

   ii    3    88 cm$^3$; attempt made to split volume up into three sections

**Question 9** – 6 marks

a   3    220 boys, 176 girls   b   3   £1050, £300

**Question 10** – 3 marks

a   2    £45.50      b   1    10%

**Question 11** – 6 marks

a   3    Biology; 71.7% Maths, 72.5% Biology

b   3    Adam; 14/11 = 1.27; Tom 16/13 = 1.23

**Question 12** – 4 marks

a   1    3/12 or ¼    b   1    4/12 or 1/3

c   1    12/12 = 1

d   1    Yes, they cannot happen at the same time

**Question 13** – 4 marks

a   3    all correct 12 outcomes are shown tabulated

b   1    1/12 or 8.3%

**Question 14** – 7 marks

a   4    Correct Venn diagram drawn

bi   1    3 and 5

bii   1    2, 3, 5, 6, 8, 7, 10

biii   1    1, 4, 7, 9, 10

## Learning outcomes

**DF2** Select and use appropriate calculation strategies to solve increasingly complex problems (L6)

**DF3** Use algebra to generalise the structure of arithmetic, including to formulate mathematical relationships (L6)

**DF5** Move freely between different numerical, algebraic, graphical and diagrammatic representations [for example, equivalent fractions, fractions and decimals, and equations and graphs] (L6)

**DF7** Use language and properties precisely to analyse numbers, algebraic expressions, 2-D and 3-D shapes, probability and statistics (L6)

**RM2** Extend and formalise their knowledge of ratio and proportion in working with measures and geometry, and in formulating proportional relations algebraically (L6)

**RM6** Interpret when the structure of a numerical problem requires additive, multiplicative or proportional reasoning (L6)

**RM7** Explore what can and cannot be inferred in statistical and probabilistic settings, and begin to express their arguments formally (L6)

**SP1** Develop their mathematical knowledge, in part through solving problems and evaluating the outcomes, including multi-step problems (L6)

**SP2** Develop their use of formal mathematical knowledge to interpret and solve problems, including in financial mathematics (L6)

**SP4** Select appropriate concepts, methods and techniques to apply to unfamiliar and non-routine problems (L6)

| Introduction | Prior knowledge |
|---|---|
| The chapter consists of a sequence of five spreads based on the theme of a group of six British students travelling to Africa to help rebuild a school. This allows questions to cover a wide range of topics taken from algebra, statistics, geometry and number. The questions are word-based and often do not directly indicate what type of mathematics is involved. Therefore students will need to work to identify the relevant mathematics and in several instances which of a variety of methods to apply before commencing. This approach is rather different from the previous topic based spreads and students may require additional support in this aspect of functional maths. | The chapter covers many topics; lessons which contain directly related material include<br>• 2a, b, c, f<br>• 7c<br>• 8d, e, f<br>• 9g<br>• 10b, e<br>• 12f<br>• 14d<br>• 15a, b, c, e<br>• 16c |

### Using mathematics

The student book start of chapter suggests three areas of everyday life where aspects of the ability to apply mathematical ideas prove highly valuable.

**Fluency**: Scale drawings based on careful measurements and 3D reasoning are used throughout building and engineering to plan projects. many of the same ideas are used to produce graphics in computer games.

**Mathematical reasoning**: In the information age we are bombarded with statistics. Making sense of them requires understanding of the mathematics and the ability to reflect on what the statements might mean. Perhaps you will be asked to produce a report explaining some statistics

**Problem solving**: Scientists use mathematics to describe and reason about the world around us. By understanding how forces change on a scale model engineers can investigate the drag on a real car and using their real and mathematical models design it to be more fuel efficient.

# Topic scheme

Teaching time = 5 lessons/2 weeks

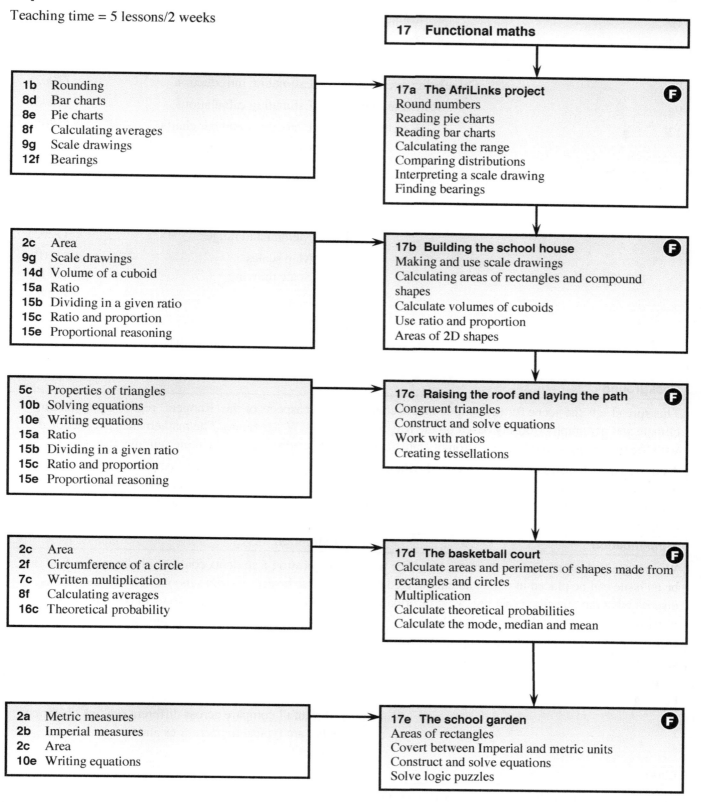

**17  Functional maths**

| 1b | Rounding |
| 8d | Bar charts |
| 8e | Pie charts |
| 8f | Calculating averages |
| 9g | Scale drawings |
| 12f | Bearings |

**17a  The AfriLinks project**  **F**
Round numbers
Reading pie charts
Reading bar charts
Calculating the range
Comparing distributions
Interpreting a scale drawing
Finding bearings

| 2c | Area |
| 9g | Scale drawings |
| 14d | Volume of a cuboid |
| 15a | Ratio |
| 15b | Dividing in a given ratio |
| 15c | Ratio and proportion |
| 15e | Proportional reasoning |

**17b  Building the school house**  **F**
Making and use scale drawings
Calculating areas of rectangles and compound shapes
Calculate volumes of cuboids
Use ratio and proportion
Areas of 2D shapes

| 5c | Properties of triangles |
| 10b | Solving equations |
| 10e | Writing equations |
| 15a | Ratio |
| 15b | Dividing in a given ratio |
| 15c | Ratio and proportion |
| 15e | Proportional reasoning |

**17c  Raising the roof and laying the path**  **F**
Congruent triangles
Construct and solve equations
Work with ratios
Creating tessellations

| 2c | Area |
| 2f | Circumference of a circle |
| 7c | Written multiplication |
| 8f | Calculating averages |
| 16c | Theoretical probability |

**17d  The basketball court**  **F**
Calculate areas and perimeters of shapes made from rectangles and circles
Multiplication
Calculate theoretical probabilities
Calculate the mode, median and mean

| 2a | Metric measures |
| 2b | Imperial measures |
| 2c | Area |
| 10e | Writing equations |

**17e  The school garden**  **F**
Areas of rectangles
Covert between Imperial and metric units
Construct and solve equations
Solve logic puzzles

| Related lessons | | Resources | |
|---|---|---|---|
| 1b | Rounding | ⊕ Rounding to 10, 100 | (1003) |
| 8d | Bar charts | Rounding decimals | (1004) |
| 8e | Pie charts | Real life graphs | (1184) |
| 8f | Calculating averages | Estimating introduction | (1002) |
| 9g | Scale drawings | Estimating calculations | (1043) |
| 12f | Bearings | Pictograms and bar charts | (1205) |
| | | Reading pie charts | (1206) |
| | | Drawing pie charts | (1207) |
| | | All averages | (1192) |
| | | Mean and mode | (1200) |
| | | Median and range | (1203) |
| | | Map scales | (1103) |
| | | Scale drawing | (1117) |
| | | Bearings | (1086) |
| | | Spare protractors and rulers | |
| | | Examples of statistical graphs | |
| | | Local area map(s) | |

## Background

This spread sets the scene for the chapter and is concerned with aspects of the 'Kangera' region's population, climate and geography (loosely based on the Kagera region of NW Tanzania). The mathematics is concerned with the presentation and interpretation of statistical data and accurate geometrical measurement.

As this chapter focuses on skills associated with using and applying mathematics and employs a different style of question it may be useful to reorganise the class and to establish how the students should approach the work. For example, as individuals, pairs or small groups, *etc.*, should they work at their own pace, should they start right away or will an introduction be given, *etc.*

## Simplification

Weaker students or those for whom the language may be an issue can be placed in pairs and encouraged to discuss what the question is asking, what information it provides and what calculation needs to be done.

Have available a number of lines and angles for students to measure before progreessing to converting these with a scale or quoting them as a three-figure bearing.

## Extension

In question **5** students could be challenged to find the reverse bearings, from school to the various homes. This can be done by measurement or by reasoning about parallel lines, as in spread **5a**. Reflex and non-reflex angles should be treated as separate cases.

Africa contains many climatic regions and there is great scope for carrying out comparative investigations. For example, how do the yearly patterns of rainfall compare across different regions of Africa, what are typical temperatures and temperatures ranges?

## Links

Links can be made with geography in particular through this spread. Analysing climate, climate change and the effects of climate change link particularly well into questions **3** and **4**. Maps, map reading and bearings likewise link well into question **5**.

# Teaching notes

To set the context, put students into small groups and ask them to discuss how life might be different if they lived in equatorial Africa. What would the climate be like? How many young people versus old people would there be? How would they get to school? What would they eat and where would they get their food? Take feedback and explain how this spread provides them with some of the information they need to answer these questions.

To help with interpreting graphs show a number of examples of different types and ask students to read off values, calculate simple statistics and provide interpretations. Place an emphasis on describing and interpreting the data, helping students to articulate their ideas in complete sentences.

To make bearings and interpreting scales more real, have available a large map of your school and local area, perhaps projected on an IWB. Ask students to measure distances on the map and convert them into real-life distances. Ask if the answers match with their expectation based on experience of the real distance. Review and revise their calculations as necessary.

Pick a point on the map and ask students to describe the journey to school in terms of approximate distances and directions, first using compass points and then using three-figure bearings. Check that students measure clockwise from North and quote three digits, adding leading zeros as required. Include examples where a protractor will need to be correctly used to measure the acute/obtuse/reflex angles.

## Exercise commentary

**Question 1** – A gentle start; discuss how this is done in preparation for question **2c**.

**Question 2** – For parts **a** and **b**, do you need to look at the numbers or can they be done 'by eye'? The angles in the graph are calculated from the rounded numbers. Students could be asked about the sizes of the angles: 41-60, is a quarter of the population or 90°; 60+ is a tenth of the population, 1000 people, or 36°.

**Question 3** – Before starting ensure students are clear on how to interpret the composite bar chart. Students could be asked for other statistics, for example, what is the modal temperature? (22°) or the median rainfall? $(148+122) \div 2 = 135$ mm)

**Question 4** – Allow students to give their own explanations before suggesting drawing a graph with both this years and the average rainfall on it. Encourage students to try to quantify their statements. Ask, how much more rainfall fell in April or in the rainy season than on average?

**Question 5** – Distance should be measured to ±1 mm and angles to ±1°. Not all distances are 'nice numbers'; ask students what distance 1 mm corresponds to in real life? It will be easiest to measure the bearings in the order given in the table. For Michael, ask: why are bearings quoted using three digits? For Mary and Frieda, does subtracting the non-reflex angle from 360° give the same result as adding the acute/obtuse angle onto 180°? A 360° degree protractor will help here.

## Answers

1  10 000

2  **a**  0 – 20       **b**  60+
   **c**  **i**  3500       **ii**  3000
        **iii**  2500      **iv**  1000

3  **a**  March       **b**  $26 - 21 = 5°C$
   **c**  279 mm       **d**  July
   **e**  July and August

4  **a**  January had below average rainfall but March, April and May had significantly higher rainfall that the 30 year average.
   **b**  A lot of rain would saturate the ground causing it to become soft and unable to absorb more water. Further rain would then wash over the ground, possibly washing it away.

5

| Name | Distance (km) | Bearing in ° |
|---|---|---|
| Albert | 4.5 | 150° |
| Constance | 7.5 | 106° |
| Michael | 3.7 | 020° |
| Mary | 5.6 | 321° |
| Frieda | 6.4 | 235° |

| Related lessons | | Resources | |
|---|---|---|---|
| 2c | Area | ⊞ Area of rectangles | (1084) |
| 9g | Scale drawings | Map scales | (1103) |
| 14d | Volume of a cuboid | Scale drawing | (1117) |
| 15a | Ratio | Volume of cuboids | (1137) |
| 15b | Dividing in a given ratio | Ratio introduction | (1052) |
| 15c | Ratio and proportion | Ratio dividing 1 | (1038) |
| 15e | Proportional reasoning | Ratio dividing 2 | (1039) |
| | | Proportion unitary method | (1036) |
| | | Mini whiteboards | |
| | | Squared paper | |

## Background

This spread takes up the theme of rebuilding the school house. The mathematics involves drawing and interpreting scale drawings, calculating areas and volumes and working with ratios.

It is possible that some students might have direct knowledge of aspects of building work, and their knowledge can be used to enliven discussion and provide alternative real life scenarios to discuss.

## Simplification

Several of these questions are multifaceted and it may be appropriate to focus attention on fewer aspects. For example, in question **2** only part **a**, in questions **3** only part **a** and in question **4** only parts **a** and **b**. Once these parts are succesfully done students can go back to complete the remaining parts.

Pairing students will allow them to discuss approaches and clarify what needs to be calculated.

## Extension

Question **6** can be further extended by asking students to calculate how much paint would be need for all the outside walls of the school. This will require the numbers and areas of doors and windows to be taken into account. The number of tins of paint, cost and time taken, given a number of painters and their rate of work, could also be investigated. Pairing students will allow the calculations to be agreed and the workload shared.

## Links

This spread requires students to employ skills in visualization. It links well to Design and Technology among other subjects where working with scales is important in producing accurate drawings and models before producing full-sized products.

Students could also investigate the various techniques that architects and builders use to accurately estimate the amount of materials they will need for constructing their buildings.

## Teaching notes

One of the themes of this spread is areas and volumes. To test understanding, provide students with an L-shaped hexagon and ask them to calculate its area.

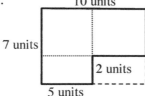

10 units

7 units

2 units

5 units

Ask students to explain how they did the calculations and what alternative methods were used. Which missing sides need calculating? Is it better to divide the shape into two sub-areas or three? Are the two sub-areas unique? Can the calculation be done using a subtraction?

Discuss which methods the students found 'best': which is easier to remember? Which is less likely to result in an error?

If the L-shape were the plan of a building 4 units high what would be its volume? Check that appropriate units are given.

Question **5** revolves around ratios. Test understanding using mini whiteboards. Ask students to simplify some simple ratios, 8 : 4 (= 2 : 1), 2 : 8 (= 1 : 4), 9 : 12 (=3 : 4) *etc*. Pose the questions like the following, if $a : 3 = 2 : 1$ what is $a$? (6) If $2 : b = 4 : 6$ what is $b$? (3) If $a : b = 1 : 2$ and $a + b = 9$ what are $a$ and $b$? (3, 6). When each new type of question is introduced discuss with the students their strategies for finding the answers. As a class, agree which methods give the right answer and which are the best ones to use.

## Exercise commentary

**Question 1** – Using squared paper will help with accuracy. Ask students how big the scale drawing will be before starting (14 cm × 7 cm).

**Question 2** – In part **a** encourage students to draw each room and mark on their dimensions before finding the area. Agree that the corridor lies between rooms 3 and 4. In part **b**, the obvious method is to add up the component areas. can any students explain why these expressions also give the total area: $14 \times 28 - 6 \times 12$ or

$8 \times 28 + 6 \times 8 + 6 \times 8$ or

$8 \times 14 + 12 \times 8 + 8 \times 14$. (1.4, 1.5)

**Question 3** – Make sure that students understand the difference between rounding the numbers to make an estimate of the answers and rounding the answer.

**Question 4** – Part **c** can be done in two ways: either divide the volume of the cube by that of one breeze block or see how many breeze blocks are needed to make up each side, $2 \times 10 \times 5$.

**Question 5** – This exercises various aspects of ratio and proportion. In part **aiii** beware the reversed order of sand and cement.

**Question 6** – For part **a**, ask students how do find the area of a triangle? and, if necessary, can you see a triangle in the gable wall? For part **b**, students should be careful to include two factors of two. You could extend the questions by giving a size and price per tin and asking for the cost; students will need to round up

the number of tins. What if they had to pay someone to do the painting?

## Answers

1 Check students' drawings

2 **a,b**

| Room | Area (m²) |
|---|---|
| 1 | $8 \times 8 = 64$ |
| 2 | $8 \times 6 = 48$ |
| 3 | $8 \times 6 = 48$ |
| 4 | $8 \times 7 = 56$ |
| Hall | $12 \times 8 = 96$ |
| Corridor | $8 \times 1 = 8$ |
| Total | 320 m² |

3 **a** $4480 \approx \$ 4500$     **b** $980 \approx \$ 1000$

4 **a** 10 000 cm³     **b** A cube

  **c** 100

5 **a i** Strong     **ii** Weak

    **iii** Medium

  **b** 6 parts

  **c** 600 kg of sand and 200 kg of sand

6 **a** 24 m²     **b** 9.6 litres

7 $72

8 **a** 7 hours   **b** $54

| Related lessons | | Resources | |
|---|---|---|---|
| 5c | Properties of triangles |  Angle reasoning | (1080) |
| 10b | Solving equations | Ratio introduction | (1052) |
| 10e | Writing equations | Ratio dividing 1 | (1038) |
| 15a | Ratio | Ratio dividing 2 | (1039) |
| 15b | Dividing in a given ratio | Proportion unitary method | (1036) |
| 15c | Ratio and proportion | Interior exterior angles | (1100) |
| 15e | Proportional reasoning | Simple equations | (1154) |
| | | Rules and formulae | (1158) |
| | | mm squared paper | |

## Background

This spread continues the building theme with an investigation of some of the issues associated with laying paving. The mathematics involved covers congruence, ratio and proportion, simple formulae and lowest common multiples.

It is possible that your school grounds might provide examples of tiling patterns the details of which could be substituted for those in the spread to make the questions seem more real.

## Simplification

For questions **2** and **3** the benefits and meaning of the formulae can be drawn out by repeating several similar calculations all based on the same basic calculation.

Question **4** can be approached using an accurate scale drawing, say on mm squared paper, and actually counting the numbers of blocks and slabs drawn. Students could then be encouraged to find the same answers by calculation.

Pairing students will allow them to discuss approaches and clarify what needs to be calculated.

## Extension

The patterns of tiles used in the paths are essentially linear. Students could be asked to investigate tiling an area. Start with symmetric patterns based on two colours of square tiles. Can they identify all the symmetries? Are there formulae for the numbers of coloured tiles need to cover a rectangular area given its dimensions. What would happen if one type of tile was rectangular, say 2 × 1?

## Links

Practical applications of planning designs and calculating areas occur in both Art and Design. Students could be asked to investigate 'famous' tiling patterns such as those that occur in the Alhambra Palace in Spain. The website for the palace can be found at http://www.alhambradegranada.org/en/

## Teaching notes

The questions in this spread all provide realistic scenarios where the need for basic mathematics arises naturally. Use this as an opportunity to discuss other everyday situations where mathematics is used. Examples can be taken from this chapter, the students' own lives, the work that their parents/guardians do, *etc*. Try to impress upon them the idea that mathematics is all around and not just confined to the classroom.

Question **1** is the first time congruence is encountered. Ask students to explain when they would say two shapes are the same, that is, can be placed exactly on top of one another. Agree that for general shapes all the corresponding lengths and angles must be equal. Ask if all these checks are necessary for triangles? What information do students need in order to be able to construct a (unique) triangle? What would they need to do to show that two triangles are not congruent? Only one pair of corresponding lengths needs to be shown to be unequal.

Questions **2** and **3** both involve deriving a linear function. It is worth spending some time to show how the use of variables can capture the essence of a repetitive calculation. Once a putative formula has been written down, stress the importance of checking it. At this point ensure that students understand about 'hidden' multiplication signs and the correct order of precedence (BIDMAS) when substituting numbers into a formula. If merited, the formula can be used to generate coordinate pairs and the connection made between the formula and its corresponding straight line graph.

## Exercise commentary

**Question 1** – The meaning of the word congruent will have to be established. The difference is small and so accurate measurement of corresponding lengths is essential. Discourage measuring angles, as though valid, higher accuracy is needed to see a difference.

**Question 2** – In part **a**, insist that the students write out their calculation in the form $3 \times 25 + 15$ to draw out the connection with the formula required in part **b**. As necessary, repeat part **a** with different distances to establish the pattern. The answers to part **d** can be used to produce a graph of cost versus distance which could be used to quickly find the cost of further deliveries.

**Question 3** – In part **a**, make sure the students include the red tiles at the top and bottom of the yellow tiles. After part b, ask students how they will test their function machine? In part **c**, place an emphasis on a clear written explanation of why the two ratios are equal.

**Question 4** – Part **a** can be done using an accurate drawing or by calculating the lowest common multiple of 20 and 50. In part **b**, what would happen in practice if the path weren't a multiple of 100 cm in length? In part **ci**, check that the four rows of blocks are all included in the calculation. Part **d** could be elaborated to finding a formula for the cost of the path in terms of the numbers of blocks and slabs.

## Answers

**1** B is not congruent.

**2** **a** $90          **b** $C = 15 + 3d$
    **c** $C = 15 + 3 \times 10 = 15 + 30 = 45$
    **d** **i** $75    **ii** $165    **iii** $51      **iv** $46.5

**3** **a** 6 : 1     **b** $\times 6$     **c**

$$\div 2 \underset{1:20}{\overset{2:40}{\huge(}} \div 2$$

**4** **a** 2
    **b** 9 times
    **c** 180 blocks and 18 slabs
    **d** $ 414

| Related lessons | | Resources | |
|---|---|---|---|
| 2c | Area | Area of rectangles | (1084) |
| 2f | Circumference of a circle | Circumference of a circle | (1088) |
| 7c | Written multiplication | All averages | (1192) |
| 8f | Calculating averages | Mean and mode | (1200) |
| 16c | Calculating probabilities | Median and range | (1203) |
| | | Simple probability | (1210) |
| | | Football results | |

## Background

This spread has a loose focus around a game of basketball. The mathematics covered includes perimeters and the formula for the circumference of a circle, estimating probabilities, calculating the mean and interpreting mathematical data.

For added realism the school grounds may provide examples of sports pitches marked out in a similar fashion to the basketball court in question **1**. It may also be possible to use actual results for question **4** and **5**.

## Simplification

For questions **1** to **3** provide versions with simpler numbers so that students can focus their attention on the essential mathematics rather than the arithmetic. Once students understand what they are supposed to do, then the more realistic numbers can be used.

Pair students for questions **4** and **5** to reduce their workload and allow discussion of what to do and what any results mean.

## Extension

Invite students to find statistics on, for example, the number of goals scored by various football teams during a season. Using this data calculate the mode, median and mean number of goals scored by each team. Ask which average is most representative. How would you rank the teams based on the averages? Do the averages reflect the positions that the teams finished in their league? If not what other factors do they think might be important?

## Links

There are some clear links in this spread to sports pitches and court dimensions. Students could investigate whether there are fixed dimensions for various pitches, e.g. a football pitch (no, but there are limits between what the length and width must be, and the internal markings are all standard) or a hockey pitch (yes).

http://en.wikipedia.org/wiki/Association_football_pitch

http://www.realbuzz.com/articles/hockey-pitch-dimensions

# Teaching notes

Students will need to be familiar with the formula for the circumference of a circle and confident in applying it. Recap what the terms in the formula $C = \pi d$ mean and what value should be used for $\pi$. Practice finding the circumference given the diameter before asking for the diameter given the radius. Agree that the multiplication by $\pi$ is undone by doing a division by $\pi$ and that the answer can be checked by going back to the original formula. If students are allowed to use calculators make sure that they know how to use the $\pi$ key as well as typing in 3.14. It will also be useful to look at the arc lengths of semicircles and quadrants.

Questions 4 involves estimating a probability based on a number of successful trials. Ensure that students know what is meant by a probability; that it is a number between 0 and 1 expressed as a decimal, a percentage or a fraction. Do not permit alternative expressions of probability.

## Exercise commentary

**Question 1** – In part **a**, make sure students understand the relationship between radius and diameter. In part b, check that the 4 cm overlap has been included.

**Question 2** – Suggest that students first calculate the perimeter of the basketball court and then look to see which expression corresponds to their calculation. In part **c**, emphasize that the semicircular arc has half the circumference as a whole circle and that two straights must be added in.

**Question 3** – Reversing formula $C = \pi d$ will give the diameter; check that students give the radius. Students could be asked how they would mark out the whole basketball court using a rope, sticks and tape measure. Remind students that a taut rope provides a straightedge and if one end is fixed a pair of compasses.

**Question 4** – Students will need to add the number of times one of the player scores (success) to the number of times they miss to obtain the 'number of trials' and hence estimated probabilities. Could the best shot taker be identified without doing a written calculation?

**Question 5** – Remind students that the mean is the total number of baskets scored over the total number of games played. In part **b**, it is clear from both sets of data that Wah Wah is best player but how would students rank all players? For example, who is better Imran or Maxine? How to combine the two sets of results could form the topic of a discussion.

## Answers

**1 a** 148      cm      **b** 2 cm

**2 a** C
  **b** 82.5 m
  **c** 20.84 m

**3** 103 cm

**4 a i** $\frac{2}{5}$    **ii** $\frac{1}{2}$    **iii** $\frac{3}{5}$    **iv** $\frac{1}{3}$
     **v** $\frac{1}{4}$    **vi** $\frac{4}{5}$

  **b** Wah Wah, she has the highest probability of success when shooting.

  **c** 63

**5 a** Greg – 6, Ella – 5, Imran – 7, Maxine – 7, Josh - $5\frac{1}{2}$ Wah Wah - 8

  **b** Wah Wah, she both averages more scores per game and is the most successful shot taker.

  **c** Greg, Josh, Imran

| Related lessons | | Resources | |
|---|---|---|---|
| 2a | Metric measures | ⊞ Metric Conversion | (1061) |
| 2b | Imperial measures | Converting measures | (1091) |
| 2c | Area | Area of rectangles | (1084) |
| 10e | Writing equations | Rules and formulae | (1158) |
| | | Mini whiteboards | |
| | | Squared paper | |
| | | Scissors | |

## Background

This spread uses activities associated with gardening to allow a variety of mathematics to be covered. This includes: finding areas, factors, metric–imperial conversions and using systematic approaches to problem solving.

## Simplification

Questions **2 – 4** are all on the theme of metric-imperial conversions. Using lengths given in both inches and centimetres students could be asked to convert from one to the other by first by doing a calculation. Then by accurately drawing a line in the initial units and then measuring it in the final units. Ensure that any discrepancies are reconciled and understood. Once students are confident in calculating length conversions move on to weight conversions avoiding a reliance on scales to check calculations.

In questions **1** and **5** encourage students to cut out shapes that they can use on a scale drwaing to see how they might fit together.

## Extension

Challenge pairs of students to come up with puzzles like that in question **1**. Once two pairs have their questions, and answers, they should swap and race each other to see who can solve the puzzle first.

## Links

Question **2** links well with Food Technology where there is an emphasis on mixing ingredients together in the correct ratios in order for recipes to be made (and so the food tastes good!) There are also links to gardening and practical outdoor mathematics. If your school is fortunate to have good outdoor facilities, these tasks can be linked to the projects run by the school to take advantage of the facilities (e.g. a kitchen garden, or an area for animals to live).

## Teaching notes

Students may need reminding why knowing about metric-imperial conversions is useful. Ask them for examples of when non-metric units are commonly encountered. For example, British roads use miles, people often quote heights in feet and inches and weights in stones and pounds, pints and gallons are still commonly encountered units of capacity, (for impact) newspapers often quote temperatures in Farenheit rather than centigrade, *etc*.

Discuss the basic conversions, as they appear on the yellow post it note, and in particular any strategies students have for remembering them. Then test their application with a few quick fire questions using mini whiteboards. Ensure that the numbers are quite straightforward so that errors in understanding rather than arithmetic are more easily made apparent.

As preparation for question **1**, ask students how many rectangles they can make given 16 or 24 small squares. Once students have their answers discuss their strategies for finding all the possibilities. Steer students towards the idea of finding all the factor pairs of 16 or 24.

### Exercise commentary

**Question 1** – Ask students what are the possible dimensions of the individual, rectangular vegetable plots? Prompt further by asking what are the factors of, say, 9? (Only integer lengths and widths need be considered.) So the tomato plot could be $3 \times 3$ or $1 \times 9$. However the later could not fit on the vegetable plot, thereby further restricting the options. The solution is not unique. Suppose the question said the tomatoes occupied 10 m² how would you know that there is no valid solution?
The total area of the plots = 46 m² > $5 \times 8 = 40$ m².

**Question 2** – Most of the parts require a division calculation. Ask students to think if they expect the conversion to make the answer numerically bigger or smaller in the new units; is this what they see?

**Questions 3** and **4** – Both sets of questions require multiplications

**Question 5** – Check that students remember the meaning of the words congruent and tessellate before leaving them to tackle the question in pairs. Only when the students have had plenty time to think and experiment should you consider dropping hints. How many squares will there be in each of the four congruent shapes? How could they be arranged? Once they realize it is three in an 'L' shape it may still take some experimentation to fit them into the field.

### Answers

1  Check students diagrams

2  **a**  $11\frac{1}{9}$  **b**  $4\frac{4}{9}$  **c**  $3\frac{1}{3}$
  **d**  3.5 litres = 3.5 ÷ 0.6 pints = $5\frac{5}{6}$
  **e**  Yes  **d**  24''

3  **a**  15 cm  **b**  10 cm  **c**  30 cm  **d**  22.5 cm
  **e**  7.5 cm

4  **a**  2.25 kg  **b**  120 g  **c**  3.825 kg  **d**  360 g

5  **a**

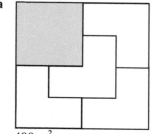

  **b**  400 m²
  **c**  300 m²